THE
Perfect Hostess Cook Book

DESIGN AND DECORATIONS BY

WARREN CHAPPELL AND FRITZ KREDEL

"*There is no sincerer love than the love of food.*"
　　　　　GEORGE BERNARD SHAW: *Man and Superman*

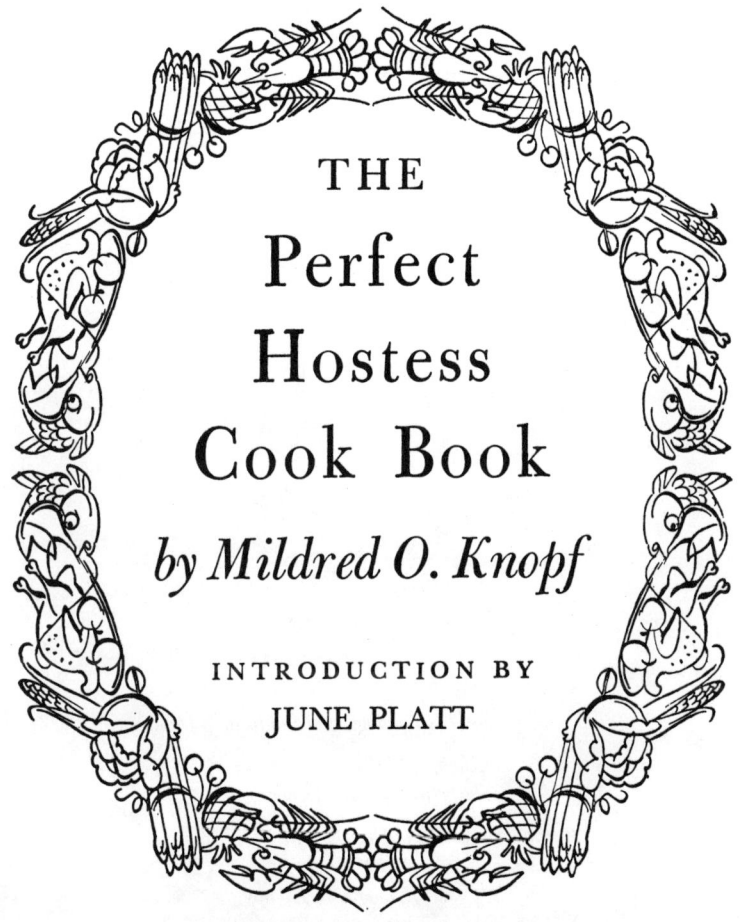

THE
Perfect Hostess Cook Book

by Mildred O. Knopf

INTRODUCTION BY
JUNE PLATT

NEW YORK
ATHENEUM
1985

Library of Congress Cataloging in Publication Data

*Knopf, Mildred O., ——
The perfect hostess cook book.*

*Reprint. Originally published: New York: Knopf,
© 1950.
1. Cookery, American. I. Title.*
TX715.K699   1985   641.5   85-47640
ISBN 0-689-70696-0 (pbk.)

*Copyright 1950 by Mildred O. Knopf
All rights reserved
Published simultaneously in Canada by Collier Macmillan Canada, Inc.
Manufactured by Fairfield Graphics, Fairfield, Pennsylvania
First Atheneum Edition*

To Edwin

WHO HAS ESTABLISHED THE STANDARD FOR THE UNCOMPROMISING GOURMET AND IS THEREFORE RESPONSIBLE FOR THIS BOOK

INTRODUCTION BY

June Platt

WHEN *Mildred Knopf asked me to write a foreword to her book,* THE PERFECT HOSTESS COOK BOOK, *I was first pleased and proud, then slightly panicky. Pleased and proud to have been chosen (considering her entourage of gourmet friends and relatives), panicky lest I be unable to express in a few words my very real appreciation of her talents both as cook and as hostess.*

I have known and admired Mildred Knopf for some ten years, having instantly sensed a kindred spirit the first time I met her. Quick as a flash we had found ourselves talking about enthusiasms we shared, good food, the joy of cooking, the love of flowers and gardening, the difficulties of trying to write and paint and entertain all at the same time, the soothing effect to be derived from doing needle-point, and the trials and tribulations as well as delights of bringing up children.

An invitation to lunch the next day and to see her house and garden and meet her children was accepted as promptly as it was offered. The children were lively and lovely, the garden was beautiful, the house radiated hospitality, and the lunch was divine, ending with Violet Sherbet decorated with real violets from the garden.

That Mildred Knopf is a perfect hostess as well as a perfect cook I can testify, for it so happens that during this delightfully feminine feast, I chanced to remark that I longed to know how to make a Cheese Cake that didn't sink miserably in the middle, and a Dobosch Tart that would look and taste like Rumpelmayers. Now, who but the most gracious and generous expert in the field of entertaining would have offered at this point to go straight back into her kitchen and make the two above-mentioned delicacies just to please a greedy guest, and to prove that all that is necessary is a good recipe?

The Cheese Cake and the Dobosch Tart were tossed together with the utmost grace and ease while I stood by, fascinated, and the fact that both were perfection when done proves that Mildred Knopf is a really talented cook and undeniably qualified, in my opinion, to tell us how to prepare and achieve this collection of delectable dishes.

When the eagerly awaited galleys of her book at last arrived, I literally devoured each recipe, noting to my personal delight, as I skipped merrily through the 653 recipes given in the sixteen chapters, that almost everything had been included for which I have been hunting reliable recipes for years. To name a few, Jellied Borsch, Cutlets Kiev, Apple Pancake, Spätzle, Bienenstick Cake; and there are dozens more.

Mildred Knopf firmly believes that if you love good food, you can cook good food, and in her book she stresses the fact that it is not difficult to cook good food provided you have simple, accurate directions to follow and have enthusiasm and confidence *in yourself and pride in what you serve. She has evolved a method that takes the novice by the hand, so to speak, and each recipe tried becomes a cooking lesson. The ingredients have been carefully listed, and if the simply stated directions are followed in the order given, one step at a time, I am sure the results will prove gratifying to even the most timid beginner.*

I have but one criticism of the book. I found no recipe for Locust Blossom Fritters, for which I have nostalgically yearned since convent days in Paris. It is a wonderful cook book, however, and, as one writer of cook books speaking of another's, I can think of no greater tribute to pay than to say I wish I had written it.

May 2, 1950

A DEDICATION TO

The Nostalgic Past

This book would scarcely be complete without special mention of my mother's fabulous cook, Marie Agress. Marie was in my mother's house for over twenty-five years. During that time, I can remember her taking only two days off. Once to go to a wedding, and once to a funeral—both of these events pertaining to the family life of her only close friend, my mother's cleaning-woman, Cristina Wogatsky. In order that you do not get the impression that my mother ruled her house like a tyrant, I hasten to explain that it was rather Marie who ruled my mother's kitchen with an iron hand, and with her own determination to live her own life in her own way.

Some years before she came to America, Marie worked as a young apprentice in Kaiser Franz Josef's palace kitchens at Schoenbrunn in Austria. It was there that she perfected the magnificent cooking of which we were all so proud, and it was there too that she fell in love with a young coachman. But this, the only romance of her life, was never to come to fruition, as the Kaiser's young coachman drowned one day when the ice pond looked frozen but was not.

After his death Marie left Austria, and it was at the Immigration Bureau at Ellis Island that my mother took the forlorn young woman home with her. There she stayed for twenty-five years, caring nothing for the world, caring only passionately for her cooking and for the kitchen realm over which she reigned supreme.

I am proud to present a number of her recipes to you in my book and wish only to add my deepest and most profound thanks to my sister, Margaret Niddrie, who before her marriage painstakingly spent hours in our family kitchen translating Marie's recipes into English as Marie dictated them to her in her soft Austrian German. Nor would it have been possible to have brought them to you had my sister not tested them out in her own apartment kitchen, to bring to practical interpretation Marie's bewildering instructions to "use enough eggs to thicken" or "enough flour to bind" or "enough sugar to sweeten." If you enjoy Marie's contributions to this book, you have Margaret Niddrie to thank.

Well begun is half done

HORACE: *Epistles* I, C. 5 B.C.

Foreword

IF YOU love good food, you can cook good food. If you love novel and interesting food, you can cook novel and interesting food.

The recipes in this book come from all over the world: from restaurants and hotels whose names are by-words throughout the epicurean world; from the files of hostesses, celebrated and obscure, who take pride in the reputations of their tables; from the penciled bits of paper found in the kitchens of private homes where cooks long ago, once upon a time, put their art above any other consideration; from the imaginings of friends; from my husband, whose talent for cooking still causes me to tremble when I remember what happened to my rationed butter in his eager hands throughout the unhappy years of the war; from my young daughter, whose gastronomic experiments reveal a very startling gift. In short, this is a collection of recipes from a group of remarkable gourmets compiled (and a number invented) by me for the timid gourmet who believes that only in expensive, high-toned restaurants, is fine food to be had.

If you love good food, you can cook good food. And it isn't

difficult—please remember that—because the recipes that follow are set forth in such a way that you have only to follow one direction at a time—just one at a time, and try not to look ahead. The list of ingredients at the top of each recipe is there only for the purpose of purchasing and assembling. After that, forget it. The ingredients and what to do with them and about them are repeated in each direction, "in the order of their appearance." It will no longer be necessary to read and to reread directions because you have lost your place. You need only follow each direction in turn and then go on to the next; you have only to remember the number of the direction next in line.

If you love good food, you can cook good food. There is no reason to fear any recipe, no matter how elaborate the finished product. For in *all* cooking there are just a certain number of things that you do—processes that are called by name: to stir, to beat, to fold, to baste, to fry, to broil, to sift, to measure, to blend, to simmer, to peel. The average amateur cook, even the "plain cook," has heard of these. It is the manner in which they are used that makes all the difference between fine food and dull, uninteresting food. Few foreign words are used; at least four young friends have begged me not to use directive foreign words such as: "sauté." Why be confusing? The entire purpose of this book is to clarify rather than to confuse. I like to believe that because of this clarification this book makes it possible to bring into the American home dishes of great foreign distinction. Clearly and without confusion it is now possible for anyone to present superlative cooking in the kitchen languages of many tongues.

If you love good food, you can cook good food. No one could possibly have been more overjoyed, more surprised than I when I discovered this for myself on a summer holiday in 1933, when we had just enough money to rent a farm in Maine but not a penny left over for help. Up to that time my complete culinary repertoire consisted of chocolate fudge, scrambled eggs with minced ham and tomato sauce, and one very fancy cake, which sometimes rose and sometimes didn't. The business of learning about steaks and chops came easily, but I don't believe that anything has ever terrified me half so much as finding myself face to face with chocolate eclairs! Why? Because I had a fixed, preconceived notion that chocolate eclairs were eaten only as I had eaten them as a child in Maillard's Tea Room in New York or at Rumpelmayer's exquisite patisserie in Paris. But to make them in my own kitchen? Those heavenly chocolate, cream-filled, glamorous pastries! Me? Yes me! And you! I shall take it upon myself to show you how.

I will lead you by the hand—and lead you gently, never rushing you. I have purposely not condensed these recipes, but have inserted as many details as seemed necessary to make things simple and to assure you of being unafraid of the world of sophisticated gourmets into which you have now entered. On your way then toward learning to be one of the world's outstanding gourmets! I give you my solemn promise that it will not be in the least difficult if in turn you will promise to remember to have four simple things:

FIRST: Enthusiasm.
SECOND: Pride in what you serve.
THIRD: Confidence in yourself.
FOURTH: Confidence once again.

And there you have the secret of the only four things you need to know to make it possible for you to set your feet on the pathway that leads directly to the pinnacle where dwell the kitchen giants!

Mildred O. Knopf

My wife has got ready a fine dinner—viz., a dish of marrow bones; a leg of mutton; a loin of veal; a dish of fowl; three pullets and two dozen larks all in one dish; a great tart, a neat's tongue, a dish of anchovies, a dish of prawns and cheese.
SAMUEL PEPYS: *Diary, November 9, 1665*

Contents

CHAPTER I	*Appetizers*	page 3
CHAPTER II	*Soups*	27
CHAPTER III	*Egg Dishes*	51
CHAPTER IV	*Seafood*	63
CHAPTER V	*Poultry*	87
CHAPTER VI	*Meats*	121

Chapter VII	*Starches* (Starches, Noodles, Rice etc.)	153
Chapter VIII	*Vegetables and Potatoes*	169
Chapter IX	*Sauces* (For use with meats, fish, poultry, vegetables and eggs)	201
Chapter X	*Salads* (Salad Dressings)	217
Chapter XI	*Cheese Dishes*	255
Chapter XII	*Desserts* (Dessert Sauces)	280
Chapter XIII	*"Baking and Caking"* (Icing and Frostings)	369
Chapter XIV	*Strawberries*	429
Chapter XV	*Fruits*	455
Chapter XVI	*Coffee Cakes, Hot Breads and Waffles*	477
WEIGHTS AND MEASURES		500
INDEX		follows page 500

APPETIZERS

HOT

Blankets, 3
Brazil Nuts Rolled in Bacon, 3
Cheese Biscuits, 4
Cheese Rolls, 4
Cheese Sticks, 5
Cocktail Cheese Puff, 5
Chicken Livers and Mushroom Caps, 6
Deviled Pecans, 6
Potato Peels, 6
Slices of Dill Pickle with Grated Cheese, 7
Swiss Pufflets, 7
Tiny Hamburgers (hot or cold), 8
Toasted Cheese Fingers, 8
Warm Cream Cheese on Rounds, 9

COLD

Anchovy Spread, 9
Bologna Pie with Chives, 10
Cauliflower Flowerlets, 10
Caviar Cream, 11
Cheese Spread Cornell, 11
Cheese Spreads, 12
Chipped-Beef Rolls, 12
Chopped Chicken Livers, 13
Cream-and-Cheese Dip, 13
Cream Cheese Porcupine, 14
Delectable Cheese Spread, 14
Filled Tiny Red Tomatoes, 15
Filled Yellow Tomatoes, 15
Fish-and-Tongue Spread, 15
Ham That Looks like Bacon, 16
Hawaiian Huacamole, 16
Italian Prosciutto, 17
Lilies of Salami, 17
Little Ham Tarts, 18
Lobster Rounds, 18
Mosaic Cocktail Sandwich, 19
Marinated Herring, 20
Red Caviar with Sour Cream on Rye, 20
Roquefort Spread, 20
Sardines on Fingers of Bread, 21
Scallops around Tartar Sauce, 21
Shrimp New Orleans, 22
Smoked Salmon Rolls, 22
Stuffed Cucumbers, 23
Stuffed Eggs Curried, 23
Stuffed French Endive, 24
Stuffed French Rolls, 24

SOUPS

COLD

Apple and Banana Soup with Curry, 27
Choldnik Soup, 27
Carrot Soup, 28
Curry Soup, 28
Iced Pea Soup, 29
Jellied Borsch, 30
Potage Louis, 30
Red Caviar Madrilène, 31
Senegalese Soup, 31
Sherried Consommé, 32
Summer Borsch, 32
Squash Soup, 33
Tomato Soup, 33
Vichyssoise, 34

HOT

Barnyard Soup with Matzo Balls, 34
Boothbay Broth, 35
Chicken-Liver Soup, 36
Consommé Garni, 36
Chowder
    Curry, 37
    Monterey Peninsula Abalone, 37
    Mussel, 38
    New England Clam, 39
Fancy Carcass Soup, 40
Mongol Soup, 40
Moules à la Marinière, 41
Mushroom Soup Edwin, 41
Mushroom Soup Wendy, 42

CONTENTS

Mushroom Broth with White Wine, 43
Noodleroom, 43
Pea Soup, dried, 44
Pea Soup, fresh, 45
Potage de Mardi, 45
Supa Shetgia, 46
Tomato Soup with Cheese, 46
Tomato-Surprise Soup, 47
Turtle and Mushroom Broth, 47

EGGS

COLD

Anchovy Eggs and Sour Cream, 51
Eggs in Aspic I, 51
Eggs in Aspic Tarragon II, 52
Egg Ring, 52
Swans on the Lake, 53

HOT

Baked Eggs in Spinach Boxes, 54
Creamed Poached Eggs à la Hash, 55
Curried Eggs Jane Cowl, 56
Eggs with Mushroom Stems, 56
French Soufflé Omelette, 57
Omelette Jurassienne, 58
Scrambled Eggs, Edwin, 58
Scrambled Eggs, Paysanne, 59
Swiss Eggs, 59
Swiss Scrambled Eggs, 60

SEAFOOD

SHELLFISH

Baked Scallops with Mushrooms in Cream, 63
Crab Mayonnaise, 63
Crab Pie, 64
Crab Wendy, 65
Crawfish, Shrimp, or Lobster Superb, 66
Deviled Clams, Grandmère, 67
Baked Lobster, 68
Broiled Live Lobster with Pink Lobster Butter, 68

Lobster Thermidor, 69
Fried Shrimp, 70
Shrimp Jambalaya, 70
Seafood Goulash, 71
Oyster Patties, 71
Scalloped Oysters Virginia, 72

FISH DISHES

Basted Tuna Squares, 73
Brook Trout in an Aspic Pond, 73
Eighteen Small Crêpes Filled, 75
Fillets of Sole Florentine, 75
Fillets of Sole Marguery, 76
Fillets of Sole in Parchment Paper Cases, 77
Fillets of Sole in Parmesan Cheese, 78
Fillets of Sole Queen Victoria, 78
Fillets of Sole with Ham, 79
Fillets of Sole with Rieseling, 80
Fillets of Sole with White Wine, 80
Salmon Mousse (hot), 81
Salmon Mousse Beauzon (cold), 82
Shad-Roe Ring, 82
Swedish Fish, 83
Whitebait Fried, 83

POULTRY

CHICKEN

A Bird in Tarragon Cream, 87
Baked Broilers in Cream, 88
Budapest Chicken Paprika, 88
Buttery Chickens, 89
Capon par Excellence, 90
Chicken à la King, Lily, 91
Chicken Blintzes, Sylvia, 92
Chicken Breasts on the Wing, 93
Chicken in Custard and Rice, 94
Chicken in Garlic Cream, 94
Chicken Georgia, 96
Chicken Malibu, 97
Chicken Mervyn, 98
Chicken Normande, 99
Chicken Romanoff, 99
Chicken Timbale, 100

Cutlets Kiev, 101
Danish Chicken, 102
Fricassee of Chicken, Espagnole, 102
Parisian Chicken Croquettes, 103
Poulet à l'Archiduc, 104
Two Chickens in White Wine, 104
Young Chicken in Burgundy, 105

CHICKEN LIVERS

Chicken Livers on Artichoke Hearts, 106
Chicken-Liver Pâté, Paul, 106
Chicken-Liver Ring, 107

DUCK

Duckling with Sour Red Cherries, 108
Duck Fredericka, 108
Duck Pickings San Vicente, 109
Duck Superb, 110

PHEASANT

Pheasant Knopf, 111
Pheasant Knopf in Gravy Aspic, 112
Pheasant in Sour Cream, 112
Young Pheasant with Raisin Purée, 113

SQUAB

Broiled Squab in Brandy, 114
Squabs in Marjoram, 115
Stuffed Squabs, 116
Wild-Rice Stuffing, 116

TURKEY

Turkey Cutlets Nela, 117
Turkey in Yellow Cream Sauce, 117
Turkey Stuffing Peter, 118

MEATS

BEEF

Beef Casserole, 121
Beef Stew Bourguignonne, 122
Beef Stew with Tomato Sauce, 122
Beef Stew in Six Minutes, 123
Beef Tongue with Raisins, Prunes and Almonds, 124
Bœuf à la Mode Margot, 125
Broiled Steak with Roquefort Cheese, 126
Economical Country Casserole, 127
Fillets of Beef Rapallo, 127
Frankfurters in Casserole, 128
Grenadine of Beef, 129
Meat Balls
  with Buttermilk, 129
  in Mushroom-Stems Sauce, 130
  Swedish, 131
Race-Horse Steaks, 131
Sirloin Strip the Magnificent, 132
Steaks Brizola, 133
Thin Tenderloin Steaks, 134

HAM

Baked Virginia Ham, 134
Ham Butt (with Sauerkraut and Salami), 135
Ham Decorated for a Buffet Table, 136
Ham Steak from Virginia, 136
Tenderized Ham with Apricots, 137

LAMB

Lamb Chops, Wendy, 137
Lamb Stew Dellarobbia, 138
Rack of Spring Lamb, 139
Stuffed Lamb Chops, 140

PORK

Chop Suey, 141
Polish Pâté, Rubinstein, 141
Pork Chops in Gravy, 142

VEAL

Calves' Brains au Beurre Noir, 143
Calves' Liver in Sour Cream, 144

Hungarian Stew, 144
Stuffed Breast of Veal, 145
Veal Casserole with Sour Cream, 146
Veal Chops in Tomato Sauce, 146
Veal Cutlets in Sherry, 147
Veal Cutlets Vienna (Wiener Schnitzel), 148
Veal Kidneys in Brandy Sauce, 149
Veal Kidneys in White Wine with Mushrooms, 149

STARCHES

(SPAGHETTI, NOODLES, RICE, ETC.)

ITALIAN DISHES

Gnocchi Gruyère with Sour Cream, 153
Gnocchi with Cream Sauce, 153
Gnocchi with Parmesan Cheese, 154
Italian Lasagne, 154
Risotto
  Mario's, 156
  with Sausages, 157
Spaghetti, 138
  al Dente with Spaghetti Sauce, Edwin, 159
  Green, 159
  Nests, 160

NOODLE DISHES

Noodle Ring, 161
Noodles with Cottage Cheese, 161
Skillet Noodles, 162

RICE DISHES

Fried Philippine Rice, 163
Spanish Rice, 163

ASSORTED STARCH DISHES

French Toast with French Bread, 164

Hominy, Tomato and Cheese Soufflé, 164
Macaroni Ring of Plenty, 165
Marie's Spätzle, 165
Schupfnudeln or Bubbenspritze, 166

VEGETABLES

The Preparation of Vegetables, 169

ARTICHOKES

Artichokes Filled with Mushrooms, 172
Artichoke Hearts, 173
Artichoke Hearts Parisian, 173

ASPARAGUS

Asparagus Almondine and Variations, 174
  Hollandaise, 175
  Mousseline, 175
  Parmesan, 175
Asparagus Soufflé, 175

Beans, Black, in Rum, 175

BEETS

Harvard Beets, 176
Polish Beets, 176

Cabbage, Red, 177

Carrots, Glazed, 177

Celery in Consommé, 178

CORN

Baked Corn, 178
Corn on the Cob Country Style, 179
Corn Ring, 180
Virginia Corn Fritters, 180

MUSHROOMS

Creamed Mushrooms, 181

CONTENTS

Mushrooms Edwine, 181
Mushrooms Marie, 182

Onions, French Fried, 183

Parsnips in Parmesan, 183

PEAS
French Peas in a Lettuce Bowl, 184
Peas in Sour Cream, 184

Sauerkrauts, Three, 185

SPINACH
Creamed Spinach, 186
Creamed Spinach, Baked, 187

SQUASH
Squash Purée, 187
Squash with Shredded Almonds, 188
Zucchini Shredded with Sour Cream, 188

STRING BEANS
Whole String Beans, with Crumbed Brown Butter and Variations, 189
  Hollandaise, 189
  Almondine, 189
  Chopped Pecans, 189

Tomatoes, Hot and Raw, 189

POTATOES
Baked Herb Potatoes, 190
Bird's Nest, 191
Creamed Potatoes, 191
Edwin's Potatoes au Gratin, 192
Filled Oranges, Sweet Southern Style, 192
Four Ways of Preparing Spring Potatoes, 193
  in Salted Jackets, 193
  with chopped chives, 193
  with Parmesan cheese, 194
  left-overs, 194

"Pertaters"!, 195
Potato Charlotte, 195
Potato Crumbles, 196
Potato Pancakes, 197

SAUCES

(FOR USE WITH MEAT, POULTRY, VEGETABLES AND EGGS)

Almondine Sauce, 201
Bahama Sauce for Fish, 201
Bread Sauce with Poultry or Game, 201
Cold Mustard Sauce, 202
Cream Sauces, 203
  Cream Sauce, 203
  Marie's Cream Sauce, 203
  Rich Cheese Sauce, 204
  Yellow Cream Sauce, 204
Cucumber Sauce, 205
Curry Sauce, 205
Glaze for Meats and Fowl, 206
Hollandaise I, 207
Hollandaise II (very rich), 208
Horseradish Mold, 209
Mushroom Stems in Sherry Sauce, 209
Mushroom Stems and Tomato Sauce, 210
Paprika Butter, 210
Pink Lobster Butter, 211
Raisin Sauce for Cold Fish, 211
Sauce Allemande, 212
Sauce for Meats, 212
Sauce Mousseline, 213
Sauce Tartar, 213
Steak Butter, 214

SALADS

Notes on Salad-Making, 217

SALADS USING VEGETABLES, TOMATOES, AND POTATOES

Celery Hearts in Tarragon Vinegar, 218

Celery Root Sticks in Mustard Marinade, 210
Celery Roots with Pears, 219
Cucumber Boats, 219
Cucumbers in Sour Cream or French Dressing, 220
Double Cole Slaw, 220
Hot Potato Salad, 221
Ice-Cold Cauliflower, 221
Large Beets Sliced with Spring Onions, 222
Russian Salad, 222
Spinach Salad, Dave Chasen, 223
String-Bean Salad, 223
Tomatoes en Marinade, 224
Tomato Towers, 224
Tomatoes Stuffed with Smoked Salmon, 225
Vegetable Salad Diddie, 226
Zucchini Canoes, 226

SALADS USING SEAFOOD

Green Goddess Salad, 227
Herring Salad, 228
Herring Salad with Fruits and Endive, 228
Sardine Salad, 229
Seafood Salad Knopf, 229
Shrimp, Crab, or Lobster Salad, 230

SALADS USING MEATS OR FOWL

Beef Salad, 231
Chicken Salad Diddie, 232
Endive with Breast of Turkey, 232
Salad Greens with Chicken Livers, 233
Sweetbread Salad, 233

SALADS USING FRUITS

Bunches of Grapes, 234
Cantaloupe Balls in a Nest, 234

SALAD RINGS

Beet Ring, 235
Borsch Ring, 235
Cucumber Ring, 236
Lime Ring, 236
Pineapple Ring, 237
Relish Ring, 237
Tomato-Aspic Ring, 238

SALADS USING GREENS

Chiffonade Salad, 238
Company Salad Josephine, 239
Field Salad, 239
French or Belgian Endive, 240
Garden Salad with Sour Cream, 240
Romaine Amsterdam, 241
Salade au Pernod, 241
Tossed Salad with Pecan Nut Balls, 242

GARNISHES FOR SALAD

Cream Cheese Balls and Variations, 242
  Rolled in Minced Ham, 243
  Rolled in Minced Tongue, 243
  Rolled in Shredded Swiss Cheese, 243
  Rolled in Caviar, 243
  Rolled in Chives, 243
  Rolled in Raw Chopped Onions, 243
Roquefort Cream Cheese Balls, 243

SALAD-DRESSINGS

Boiled Salad-Dressing, 247
French Dressing, 247
French Dressing George Fitzmaurice, 248
Mayonnaise Marguerite, 248
Mayonnaise with Horseradish, 249
Roquefort Dressing I, 249
Roquefort Dressing II, 249
Russian Dressing, 250
Thousand Island Dressing, 250
Vinaigrette, 251

CHEESE DISHES

SWISS TOASTS (CROUTES)

Croutes Emmental, 255
Croutes Vaudoises, 255
Croutes Oberland, 256
Croutes Bonne Femme, 257

FONDUES

Fondue Neuchâteloise, 257
Fontina, 258
Bouchées "Golden Buck," 259
Old French Fondue, 259

SOUFFLÉS

Chaeswaehe (Cheese Pie), 260
Cheese Charlotte, 261
Ramequin, 261
Swiss Soufflé, 262

MEATS

Ham Roulades with Swiss Mornay Sauce, 262–3
Piccata, 264
Stuffed Veal Cutlets, 264

VEGETABLES

Egg Plant au Gratin, 265
Cauliflower Bernese, 265
Stuffed Potatoes, 266
Stuffed Tomatoes, 266
Swiss-Chard Stalks, 267

SALADS

Salade Bonne Femme, 267
Salade Bruxelloise, 268
Salade au Tomates, 268
Tomatoes Fribourgeoises, 269

A VARIETY OF OTHER CHEESE RECIPES

Bologna Éclairs Jonathan, 269
Cheese Balls, 270

Cheese Casserole with Hard-Boiled Eggs and Tomato Sauce, 270
Crêpes Farcies, 271
Fried Camembert, 272
Gay Nineties Rarebit, 272
Hostess Tartlets, 273
Midnight Sandwiches, 273
Simple Cheese Tartlets, 274
Swiss Tartlets, 274
Truffes Vertes, 275
Waffle Sandwiches, 275

DESSERTS

Instructions on the Use of Gelatin, 280

CHEESE DESSERTS

Cheese Blintzes, 280
Cheese Cake Irene, 281
Cœur à la Crème, 283
Refrigerator Cheese Cake, 283
Rum Cheese Pie, 284
Top Secret, 285

CHOCOLATE DESSERTS

Black Chocolate Dessert Cake, 286
Chocolate Bavarian Cream, 287
Chocolate Date Cake with Whipped Cream, 288
Chocolate Icebox Cake, 289
Chocolate Roll I, 290
Chocolate Roll II, 291
Chocolate Soufflé (cold), 292
Chocolate Soufflé (hot), 293
Devil's Food Cake as a Box, 294
"Korsu Cake," 294
Molded Chocolate Hidden Away, 295
Molded Chocolate Pudding, Marie's, 296
Petits Pots au Chocolat, 297
Têtes de Nègres, 298

CUSTARDS

Crème Brûlée June Platt, 299

Custard White or Amber, 300
Indian Pudding Custard, 301

MOLDED DESSERTS

Cold Rice Pudding in a Mold, 302
English Gooseberry Fool, 303
Fruit Salad in Layer Cake, 304
Ginger Cream, 305
Macaroon Fluff, 305
Maple Mousse, 306
Molded Eggnog Pudding, 307
Orange Cream, 308
Peach Cream, 309
Peppermint-Stick Cream, 309
Punch Bavarian, 310
Rote Greutze, 311
Rum Bavarian, 311
Wine Jelly, 312

DESSERTS WITH ICE CREAM OR WHIPPED CREAM

Apricot Icebox Cake, 313
Cornucopias, 314
Cream Puffs and Éclairs, 315
Coconut Cream Torte Lashanska, 316
Icebox Pudding Parfait, 317
Mishmash Merinque, 318
Orange Cream with Cake, 319
Profiterolles, 320
Rien de Tout, 321
Sponge-Cake Ring, 321
Sponge-Cake Surprise, 322
Queen's Delight, 323

SIX HOT DESSERTS

Apple Charlotte, 324
Beignets Soufflés, 325
Boothbay Blueberry Betty, 326
Kaiserschmarren, 327
Sabayon, 328
Puff Omelette Edwin, 328

FRUIT TORTES

Applesauce Torte, 329

Black-Bread Cherry Torte, 330
Grandmother's Three Tortes, 331
 Lemon with Meringue, 331
 Strawberry with Cream Sauce, 332
 Huckleberry or Blueberry with Whipped Cream, 333

ICE CREAMS

Cranberry Cream, 333
Lemon Ice Cream in Lemon Shells, 334
Mousse au Chocolat, Lashanska, 334
Rummy Coffee Ice Cream, 335
Vanilla Ice Cream, 336
 New York's Best Vanilla Ice Cream, 336
 Old Vienna Vanilla Ice Cream, 337
 Vanilla Ice Cream with Anisette and Coconut, Dave Chasen, 338

NUT DESSERTS

Chestnut Desserts (Marrons), 338
 Marrons Purée (Chestnut Purée), 338
 Marrons Purée en Meringue (in Meringue), 339
 Marrons Purée sous Chocolat (under Chocolate), 340
 Marrons Purée with Marguerites, 340
Date-and-Walnut Torte, 341
Nut Torte, 341
Peanut-Brittle Dessert, 343

PANCAKES AND CRÊPES

Apple Pancake, 343
Crêpes au Kirsch, 344
Crêpes Suzette, 345
Little Jelly Pancakes, 347
Maple Pancake Dessert Elizabeth, 348

PUDDINGS

Cake Pudding, 349
Rice Pudding Norma, 349
Rice Pudding Round Table, 350
Ten Original Victorian Puddings, 352
    Chocolate Cream, 352
    Coffee, 353
    Fruit-Juice, 353
    Hazelnut Cream, 354
    Lemon (or Orange), 355
    Punch, 356
    Rum, 356
    Vanilla Cream, 357
    Wine, 358

DESSERT SAUCES

Apricot Sauce, 359
Caramel Sauce, 359
Chocolate Sauce I, 359
Chocolate Sauce II, 360
Crème d'Isigny, 360
Custard Cream Sauce, 361
Foamy Sauce, 361
Fruit Custard Sauce, 362
Hard Sauce, 362
Peach Sauce, 362
Pineapple Cream Sauce, 363
Vanilla Sauce I, 363
Vanilla Sauce II, with Rum, 363
Warm Wine Sauce, 364
Wine Froth Sauce, 364

"BAKING AND CAKING"

CAKES

Anna's 1-2-3-4 Cake, 369
Banana Cake, 369
Brown-and-White Cinnamon Cake, 370
Bienenstich Cake, 371
Butter-Lemon Sponge, 372
Chocolate Cake (Hungarian), 373
Chocolate Cake (Old Vienna), 374
Chocolate Cake Helene (Rich), 374
Chocolate Linzer Torte, 375
Devil's Food Cake Maria, 376
Family Birthday Cake, 376
Fruit Sponge Cake, 378
Good Plain Cake, 379
Lady Baltimore Cake, 379
Lemon-Curd Cake, 380
Mocha Torte, 381
Nut Cake with Coal-Black Chocolate Icing, 382
Old-Fashioned Coconut Layer Cake, 384
Orange Cake, 384
Orange-Nut Sponge Cake, 385
Orange Puff Cake, 386
Pound Cake, Chris, 387
Sand Torte, 388
Sponge Cake, 389
Trieste Tart (Old Vienna), 389
Watermelon Cake, 390

COOKIES

Apple Cookies, 391
Christmas Cookies, 391
Currant Cookies, 392
Favorite Cookies, Miggie, 393
Old-Fashioned Cookies, 393
Pretzel Cookies, 394

SMALL PASTRIES

Apricot Turnovers, 395
Butter Balls, 395
Canadian Coconut Squares, 396
Cherry Tartlets, 397
Cup Cakes, 398
Currant-Jelly Squares, 399
Fudge Squares, 399
Lemon-Curd Tartlets, 400
Lemon Tartlets with Meringue, 401
Macaroons with Almonds, 401
Macaroons with Cornflakes, 402
Madeleines, Sylvia, 402

Marvelous Brownies, Wendy, 403
Scotch Shortbread I, 404
Scotch Shortbread II, 404
Spice Squares, 405
Spoon Sponge Biscuits, 406
Vanilla Crescents, 406
Vienna Kipfel, 407

PASTRY CRUSTS FOR TARTS AND PIES

Cream-Cheese Crust, 408
Marie's Tart Crust, 408
Polish Tart Crust, 409
Puff Paste, 409
Swedish Tart Crust, 411

PIES AND TARTS

Apple Graham-Cracker Pie Wendy, 412
Apple Tart, 412
Apricot-Fluff Pie, 414
Cherry Tart, 414
Chess Pie, 415
Citrus-Grove Pie, 416
Lemon Chiffon Pie, 417
Lemon Fluff Pie, 417
Plum Strip, 418
Prune Tart, 419
Pumpkin Pie, Ruth, 420

ICINGS AND FROSTINGS

Black Chocolate Cup Cake Icing, 421
Boiled Icing, 421
Butter-Cream Icing, 422
Chocolate Filling, 422
Chocolate Icing, 422
Crumbly, Not Creamy, Fudge, 423
Emperor's Frosting, 424
Glazed Nuts and Fruits, 425
Old-Time Decorator's Icing, 425
Powdered-Sugar Icing, 426
Seven-Minute Frosting, 426
Thin Icing, 427

STRAWBERRIES

DESSERT AND CREAM RECIPES

Rhubarb Ring with Strawberries, 431
Strawberry Baked Alaska, 431
Strawberry Cream with Kirsch, 432
Strawberries Curaçao, 433
Strawberry Divine, 434
Strawberry Icebox Cake, 435
Strawberry Mousse, 435
Strawberries over Mock Cheese Cake, 436
Strawberry Parfait, 437
Strawberry Pink Rice Pudding, 437
Strawberry Romanoff, 438
Strawberry Torte, 439
Strawberries with Sherbet, 440
Winter Strawberry Ice Cream, 441

PIES

Glazed Strawberry Pie, 441
Strawberry Chiffon Pie, 442
Strawberry Pie with Wine, 443
Winter Strawberry Pie, 444

TARTS AND PASTRIES

Coconut Strawberry Cream Tarts, 445
Parisian Strawberry Tarts, 445
Strawberry-Preserve Turnovers, 447
Strawberry Tartlets, 448
Strawberry Tarts without Filling, 449

SAUCES AND PRESERVES

Strawberry Preserves, 449
Strawberry Sauce for Ice Cream, 450
Strawberry Sauce for Winter Use, 450

FRUITS

APPLES

Apples and Cheese Albert, 455
Apples Meringue in Casserole, 455
Apples under Blanket, 456
Butterscotch Apples in Rum, 456
Buttery Baked Apples, 457
Snow Apples, 458
Stewed Apples Dressed Up, 458

BANANAS

Baked Bananas, 459
Bananas from Brussels, 460

CHERRIES

Black Cherries in Brandy Sauce, 460
Cherries in Wine, 461
Cherry Cocktail, 461
Hot Rum Cherries, 461

MELONS

Iced Honeydew Melon with Lime, 462
Watermelon Basket, 462
Watermelon Surprise, 463

PEACHES

Baked Peaches, Cornell, 464
Peaches in Cups, 464
Peach Surprise, 465
Yellow Peaches with a Red Blanket, 465

PEARS

Baked Pears, 466
Blushing Pears, 466

PINEAPPLE

Pineapple Quarters with Crème de Menthe, 467
Meli Melo, 467
Pineapple Boat, 468

ASSORTED FRUITS

Apricots Joined Together, 468
Citrus-Fruit Ring, 469
Figs in Crème de Cacao and Sour Cream, 470
Frozen Fruit Salad, 470
Fruit Salad, 471
Fruit Salad Dressing, 472
Nectarines Evangeline, 472
Orange Slices in Chilled Red Wine, 473
Three Hot Fruits, 473

COFFEE CAKES, HOT BREADS, AND WAFFLES

Apple Coffee Cake, 477
Apple Muffins, 477
Bacon Popovers, 478
Blueberry Coffee or Tea Cake, 479
Bran Muffins, 479
Bundt Cake, 480
Coffee Kringel, 481
Corn Pouches, 481
Cream-Cheese Crescents, 482
Dimpas Dampas, Grandmère, 483
Garlic Loaf, 484
Gesundheits Kuchen (Health Cake), 484
Ginger Coffee Cake, 485
Hot Cross Buns, 485
Lebkuchen for Christmas, 486
Nut Bread, 487
Pecan Bread, 488
Sally Lunn, 488
Shortcake Smetana, 489
Six Yeast-Dough Coffee Cakes, 491
　Yeast Dough, 491
　Bundt Kuchen, 492
　Cinnamon Coffee Cake, 492
　Eisenkuchen, 492
　Filled Coffee Cake, 493
　Schnecken Noodle Strips, 494
　Superlative Schnecken, 494

Virginia Batter Bread, 495	Virginia Johnnycake, 497
Virginia Batter Cakes, 496	Pat's Waffles, 497
Virginia Corn Bread, 496	Wendy's Waffles, 498

Finis

Serenely full, the Epicure would say,
"Fate cannot harm me, I have dined today."

LADY HOLLAND: *1855*

Chapter I: *Appetizers*

Let the first satisfaction of appetite be always the measure to you of eating and drinking; and appetite itself the sauce and the pleasure.

EPICTETUS: *Encheiridion,* 110 A.D.

APPETIZERS

HOT

Blankets
Brazil Nuts Rolled in Bacon
Cheese Biscuits
Cheese Rolls
Cheese Sticks
Cocktail Cheese Puff
Chicken Livers and Mushroom Caps
Deviled Pecans
Potato Peels
Slices of Dill Pickle with Grated Cheese
Swiss Pufflets
Tiny Hamburgers (Hot or Cold)
Toasted Cheese Fingers
Warm Cream Cheese on Rounds

COLD

Anchovy Spread
Bologna Pie with Chives
Cauliflower Flowerlets
Caviar Cream
Cheese Spread Cornell
Cheese Spreads
Chipped Beef Rolls

Chopped Chicken Livers
Cream and Cheese Dip
Cream Cheese Porcupine
Delectable Cheese Spread
Filled Tiny Red Tomatoes
Filled Yellow Tomatoes
Fish and Tongue Spread
Ham That Looks Like Bacon
Hawaiian Huacamole
Italian Prosciutto
Lilies of Salami
Little Ham Tarts
Lobster Rounds
Mosaic Cocktail Sandwich
Marinated Herring
Red Caviar with Sour Cream on Rye
Roquefort Spread
Sardines on Fingers of Bread
Scallops Around Tartar Sauce
Shrimp New Orleans
Smoked Salmon Rolls
Stuffed Cucumbers
Stuffed Eggs Curried
Stuffed French Endive
Stuffed French Rolls

BLANKETS

2 cups flour
rounded ½ teaspoon salt
3 teaspoons baking powder

¼ pound butter *or*
½ cup vegetable shortening
¾ cup milk

FIRST Sift 2 cups flour. Measure and resift twice with rounded ½ teaspoon salt and 3 teaspoons baking powder.

SECOND Cut in ¼ pound butter or vegetable shortening with a pastry blender or 2 knives, until you have a crumbly-looking meal. Slowly add ¾ cup milk, beating to a smooth paste. Place in refrigerator for several hours.

[*Pre-heat oven to 450°*]

THIRD Roll out dough very thin—the thinner, the better. Cut into even squares, 3″ x 3″. Encase sardines (with a sprinkling of lemon juice over them), or lightly fried little pig sausages, or seasoned, cooked chicken livers, or tiny, cooked hamburgers, mixed with a little onion. Bake on a cookie sheet in a 450° oven till light brown. Remove and sprinkle with salt.

NOTE There are countless ways to use these "Blankets." My only suggestion is that they be reserved for encasing something with a piquant or well-seasoned flavor.

BRAZIL NUTS ROLLED IN BACON

[*Pre-heat broiler*]

12 Brazil nuts
1 tablespoon butter

salt
6 slices bacon

FIRST Fry 12 Brazil nuts in 1 tablespoon melted butter. Remove and salt.

SECOND Cut 6 slices raw bacon in half. Wrap each nut in a half slice of bacon. Broil in the oven, turning so that all sides of the bacon are evenly browned.

NOTE Brazil nuts must be fresh. Old ones are dry and tasteless.

CHEESE BISCUITS

[to serve with salad or soups]

2 cups sifted flour
¼ pound grated Swiss cheese
¼ pound butter

2 eggs
salt, pepper

FIRST Sift 2 cups flour. Measure and resift onto a pastry board, forming a ring, leaving an empty center.

SECOND In this center mix ¼ pound grated Swiss cheese, ¼ pound butter, 2 whole eggs, salt, and pepper. Work the flour gradually into the other ingredients in order to make a stiff dough. Let stand for several hours.

[Pre-heat oven to 400°]

THIRD Roll the dough out to a ¼-inch thickness. Cut it with cookie forms, placing the biscuits on a buttered cookie sheet. Bake golden brown in a 400° oven.

CHEESE ROLLS

½ pound grated Swiss cheese
½ pound soft butter
small amount cream
½ cup Swiss cheese cut into *tiny* cubes

¼ cup blanched pistachio nuts (chopped)
4 hard French rolls

FIRST Mix ½ pound grated Swiss cheese with ¼ pound soft butter. Add enough cream to make a paste of firm consistency.

SECOND With this mixture blend ½ cup Swiss cheese cut into *tiny* little cubes and ¼ cup chopped blanched pistachio nuts.

THIRD Cut the ends off 4 hard French rolls and hollow out the soft insides, leaving 4 empty shells. Stuff these shells with the cheese mixture and place in the refrigerator for several hours to harden. When ready to serve, cut crosswise, in thin slices, like a sausage.

NOTE Instead of pistachio nuts, any other preferred chopped nuts may be used. Or, instead of chopped nuts, chopped chives, chopped parsley, or chopped ham may be used.

CHEESE STICKS

1 cup pastry flour
¼ teaspoon salt
¼ pound butter

½ cup cold water
½ cup grated Parmesan cheese

FIRST Sift 1 cup flour. Measure and resift with ¼ teaspoon of salt.

SECOND Cut in ¼ pound of butter with a pastry blender or two knives, gradually adding ½ cup cold water. Work until you have a smooth dough. Place in the refrigerator for several hours.

[*Pre-heat oven to 350°*]

THIRD Sprinkle a lightly floured board with ¼ cup Parmesan cheese. Place the dough on top and roll out as thin as possible. Sprinkle with the remaining ¼ cup of Parmesan cheese. Cut into thin strips and bake until light brown in a 350° oven.

COCKTAIL CHEESE PUFF

[*Pre-heat broiler*]

1 egg
½ pound grated Cheddar cheese

Worcestershire sauce
salt and pepper

FIRST Beat 1 egg and add to ½ pound grated Cheddar cheese. Stir well. Add Worcestershire sauce, salt, and pepper to taste. Beat.

SECOND Spread on rounds of toast, arranging mixture higher in the center than on the sides. Place under broiler and cook rapidly for a minute or two.

NOTE Leave broiler door open and watch the rounds carefully.

CHICKEN LIVERS AND MUSHROOM CAPS

24 small mushroom caps
6 fresh chicken livers

2 ounces butter

FIRST Remove the stems from 24 small mushroom caps. Cut each of 6 fresh chicken livers into four even pieces.

SECOND Render 2 ounces of butter in a skillet. Lightly fry the mushroom caps and chicken liver pieces in the butter until tender, being careful not to overcook. The mushroom caps must retain their shape and not become shriveled and dry.

THIRD Place a toothpick through the outside top head of the mushroom cap and attach a piece of chicken liver on the inserted point of the pick. Serve immediately while still hot.

DEVILED PECANS
[Pre-heat oven to 400°]

2 ounces butter
2 tablespoons A-1 Sauce
1 cup pecan halves

salt
cayenne pepper

FIRST Melt 2 ounces butter in skillet. Add 2 tablespoons A-1 Sauce. Place 1 cup pecan halves in melted butter. Stir, salt well, and add a pinch of cayenne pepper.

SECOND Place skillet in 400° oven for 20 minutes.

THIRD Drain pecans and serve hot, using extra salt if desired.

POTATO PEELS
[Pre-heat oven to 450°]

4 *or* 5 large baked potatoes
butter

salt

FIRST Bake 4 or 5 large baking-potatoes without greasing skins.

APPETIZERS

Remove the insides of the potatoes and cut peels into medium strips. Butter and salt both sides of each strip.

SECOND Place strips on a cookie sheet in a 450° oven until well browned on both sides.

NOTE It is surprising how many of your guests will not recognize this dish. Be prepared for its being a great success! Of course you will reserve the insides of the potatoes for any number of dishes.

SLICES OF DILL PICKLE WITH GRATED CHEESE
[Pre-heat broiler]

rounds of toast
2 dill pickles

1 cup grated Cheddar *or* nippy New York cheese

FIRST Cut out rounds of white bread the approximate diameter of the dill pickles. Toast on a cookie sheet. Butter sparingly.

SECOND Cut 2 dill pickles into rounds about ⅛" thick. Place on toast rounds.

THIRD Grate 1 cup Cheddar cheese or nippy New York cheese. Mound generously on top of each slice of pickle. Place on cookie sheet and pop under the broiler. Leave broiler door open and watch cheese melt. If it runs over, so much the better. As soon as cheese is melted, remove from oven, place on a hot plate, and serve immediately.

WARNING Once you take these from the oven, handle them quickly. They get a little rubbery as they cool.

SWISS PUFFLETS

tiny cocktail puffs (page 315) (approximately 2 dozen)
½ pound grated Swiss cheese
¼ pound butter

small amount grated Sap Sago cheese *or* anchovy paste
cream

FIRST Make approximately two dozen *tiny* cocktail puffs (p. 315).

APPETIZERS

SECOND Mix ½ pound grated Swiss cheese with ¼ pound soft butter until well worked and smooth.

THIRD Add a small amount of Sap Sago cheese (or, if preferred, anchovy paste) and enough cream to make a paste of firm consistency. Fill the tiny puffs with this mixture. Serve them either cold or heated in a hot oven for five minutes.

TINY HAMBURGERS
[Pre-heat broiler]

½ pound freshly ground round steak
salt, pepper
ketchup
raw onion
Triscuits

FIRST The most important thing is to get your butcher to put your ½ pound round steak twice through the grinder, and *not* to give you some of the meat that has been ground for hours and left standing in the pan awaiting some disinterested customer. It *must* be freshly ground. Having that, season well with salt and pepper.

SECOND Spread the meat on Triscuits and pop them under the broiler until well browned. Garnish each with a tiny blob of ketchup. Serve with or without onion as preferred. Or the meat may simply be spread on the Triscuits, garnished with a small bit of raw onion, and served as is.

NOTE In either case these are guaranteed to disappear!

TOASTED CHEESE FINGERS
[Pre-heat broiler]

¼ cup grated Cheddar cheese
¼ cup Swiss cheese
1 beaten egg yolk
¼ teaspoon dry mustard
1 tablespoon grated onion
tiny pinch cayenne pepper
3 *or* 4 tablespoons cream
12 very thin slices white bread with crusts removed
paprika

FIRST Grate ¼ cup Cheddar cheese and ¼ cup Swiss cheese.

SECOND Stir in 1 beaten egg yolk. Season with ¼ teaspoon dry mustard, 1 tablespoon grated onion, and a tiny pinch cayenne pepper. Work with 3 or 4 tablespoons cream until soft enough to spread.

THIRD Spread mixture on 12 very thin slices white bread with crusts removed. Roll each slice, and press so that the rolls will stay rolled. Place in pre-heated broiler. Brown on top. Turn and brown on under side. Sprinkle with paprika and serve sizzling hot.

NOTE There is paprika and there is paprika. Taste it gingerly before using. It may be very potent, in which case you will be glad that you did not use it too lavishly.

WARM CREAM CHEESE ON ROUNDS
[Pre-heat broiler]

1 package cream cheese
sufficient cream to smooth
1 teaspoon horseradish

toasted rounds of white bread and
black bread (pumpernickel)

FIRST Soften 1 package cream cheese with sufficient cream to achieve a smooth paste. Stir in 1 teaspoon horseradish and spread on toasted rounds of white bread and black bread (pumpernickel).

SECOND Place the rounds under the broiler until slightly brown on top.

ANCHOVY SPREAD

½ small onion, minced
1 package cream cheese

anchovy paste to taste

FIRST Mince ½ small onion.

SECOND Mash 1 package cream cheese with anchovy paste to taste. Cream until blended. Add the minced onion. Spread on toast, crackers, or potato chips.

NOTE If you prefer this mixture somewhat creamier, add 1 tablespoon cream when blending the cheese and anchovy paste.

BOLOGNA PIE WITH CHIVES

2 packages cream cheese
cream to moisten
¼ cup chopped chives

1 pound sliced broad bologna
(not too thinly sliced)

THIS MAKES 2 PIES

FIRST Crush 2 packages cream cheese with fork. Moisten with sufficient cream to make a smooth paste. Fold in ¼ cup chives and mix until well distributed.

SECOND Remove all casings from bologna, being careful not to tear the meat. Place the first slice on a plate or board. Spread this thickly with the cream-cheese mixture. Place another slice on top. Spread this one in turn. Continue until six slices are used, leaving the top slice unspread.

THIRD Wrap "pie" in wax paper. Set in refrigerator on a plate until thoroughly cold.

FOURTH Slice into pie-shaped wedges with a sharp knife. Serve in its original shape in center of an hors-d'oeuvres platter, surrounded by other hors d'oeuvres.

CAULIFLOWER FLOWERLETS

¼ cup horseradish
¼ cup chili sauce
½ cup sour cream

1 package cream cheese
1 small head raw cauliflower

FIRST Mix ¼ cup horseradish, ¼ cup chili sauce, ½ cup sour cream, and 1 package cream cheese (mashed) until well blended. Set in refrigerator in serving-bowl.

SECOND When ready to serve, place sauce bowl in center of a round plate and surround with the separated flowerlets of one small head of raw cauliflower.

CAVIAR CREAM

2 ounces preserved caviar
2 tablespoons fresh cream
2 ounces soft sweet butter

3 tablespoons whipped cream
toasted rounds of white bread

FIRST Mash 2 ounces of preserved caviar. Little by little add 2 tablespoons fresh cream and 2 ounces soft sweet butter.

SECOND Rub through a fine sieve. Carefully fold in 3 tablespoons whipped cream. Set to cool in refrigerator. When ready to serve, spread on toasted rounds of white bread.

SMOKED SALMON CREAM

Substitute smoked salmon for caviar and proceed as for Caviar Cream.

CHEESE SPREAD CORNELL

1½ pounds Cheddar cheese
¼ teaspoon salt
¾ teaspoon dry mustard
¼ cup chopped parsley
¼ cup chopped onion

2 tablespoons soft butter
dash of Tabasco sauce
dash of Worcestershire sauce
¼ cup tomato ketchup
⅓ cup good sherry wine

FIRST Grate 1½ pounds Cheddar cheese. Add ¼ teaspoon salt, ¾ teaspoon dry mustard, ¼ cup chopped parsley, and ¼ cup chopped onion. Chop these as fine as possible.

SECOND Work in 2 tablespoons soft butter. Add a dash of Tabasco, a dash of Worcestershire sauce, ¼ cup tomato ketchup, and ⅓ cup good sherry wine. Work together until all the lumps are eliminated and the mixture is smooth and creamy. Set in any small serving-dish or bowl. An earthenware crock makes a very attractive receptacle for this spread.

NOTE This recipe was discovered many years ago by Dr. Cornell, father of the brilliant actress Katharine Cornell. Only recently Miss

Cornell rediscovered it, and has told me of the pleasure she has had in filling small earthenware bowls and crocks with this spread to give as gifts to her friends.

CHEESE SPREADS

[twelve varieties]

THE BASE

½ pound Swiss cheese   ¼ pound soft butter
small amount cream

FIRST Grate ½ pound Swiss cheese on finest grater.

SECOND Cream the grated cheese with ¼ pound soft butter until well blended. Add just enough cream to make a paste of firm consistency.

NOTE This base may be used for sandwiches or for cocktail appetizers. Odd and interesting effects may be obtained by adding different things to suit different tastes. Any one of the following ingredients is an excellent addition to the base:

chopped raw onion	chopped cooked mushrooms
minced chives	chopped nuts
minced parsley	anchovy paste
chopped celery	creamed liverwurst
chopped olives	chopped ham
chopped pimientos	

CHIPPED-BEEF ROLLS

½ pound chipped beef   small sweet pickles
2 packages cream cheese   horseradish to taste
sufficient cream to smooth

FIRST Lay out ½ pound chipped beef on a board, with pieces overlapping a little, until the whole measures about 12″ long and 5″ wide.

SECOND Crush 2 packages cream cheese with a fork. Add sufficient cream to achieve a smooth paste. Season to taste with horseradish. Spread beef generously and smoothly with this mixture.

THIRD Trim both rounded ends of small sweet pickles and place them end to end lengthwise 1″ inside left edge. Fold edge of beef over the pickles and roll tightly toward the far edge until roll is completed. Wrap in wax paper. Place in refrigerator for at least 2 hours before serving.

FOURTH When ready to serve, cut roll into ½″ thick slices with a very sharp knife.

NOTE It is not necessary to serve these slices on rounds of buttered toast, but if your guests have an aversion to licking their fingers at a formal party, they will appreciate having them served that way.

CHOPPED CHICKEN LIVERS

6 *fresh* chicken livers
2 tablespoons chicken fat *or* butter
1 medium-sized onion
2 hard-boiled eggs

pepper and salt
butter
finger-length strips rye toast

FIRST Carefully remove gall from 6 *fresh* chicken livers and lightly fry them in 2 tablespoons melted chicken fat or butter. Add 1 medium-sized onion coarsely chopped. Cook slowly over moderate heat until onion is golden.

SECOND Put mixture through meat-grinder with 2 hard-boiled eggs, or hand chop, if preferred. Add pepper, salt, and melted chicken fat or butter to make a smooth paste. Serve in bowl surrounded by strips of lightly buttered rye toast.

NOTE If a stronger onion flavor is preferred, put raw onion through the grinder with the cooked livers.

CREAM-AND-CHEESE DIP

1 clove garlic
1 package cream cheese
1 can razor clams, minced

½ cup heavy cream
clam juice

FIRST Rub mixing bowl with one cut clove of garlic. Mash

one package cream cheese into garlic-flavored bowl.

SECOND Whip ½ cup heavy cream. Use fork to blend with mashed cheese. Add one can razor clams (minced) and sufficient clam juice to thin the mixture a little. Serve with potato chips.

CREAM-CHEESE PORCUPINE

¼ cup minced chives *or* spring onion tops
½ pound double cream cheese *or* 3 packages cream cheese

sufficient cream to moisten to a smooth paste
pretzel sticks

FIRST Mix ¼ cup minced chives or spring onion tops with ½ pound double cream cheese or 3 packages cream cheese moistened to a thick paste with cream. Place in a small attractive serving-bowl.

SECOND Stick a generous number of pretzel sticks into the cream cheese. Arrange them upright to create the impression of porcupine quills.

NOTE The cream cheese is eaten by twirling a small mound at the end of each "porcupine quill." Do not permit the "quills" to stand too long in the cream cheese—they will soften.

DELECTABLE CHEESE SPREAD

3 packages cream cheese
1½ tablespoons bottled mushroom sauce

½ tablespoon minced chives *or* spring onion tops
½ tablespoon paprika

FIRST Mash 3 packages cream cheese. Add 1½ tablespoons bottled mushroom sauce. Cream together. Then add ½ tablespoon minced chives or spring onion tops and ½ tablespoon paprika.

SECOND Spread on toast, crackers, or potato chips, as preferred.

NOTE This cheese spread may be heaped in a bowl, and the process of spreading may be attended to by the individual guest.

FILLED TINY RED TOMATOES

1 can flaked tuna
2 tablespoons mayonnaise
1 tablespoon chopped parsley
pinch of cayenne pepper
½ pound *tiny* red tomatoes

FIRST Blend 1 can flaked tuna with 2 tablespoons mayonnaise. Add 1 tablespoon chopped parsley and a pinch of cayenne pepper.

SECOND Scoop the contents of ½ pound tiny red tomatoes, leaving each tomato a hollow shell. Fill each with the tuna mixture. Serve cold.

FILLED YELLOW TOMATOES

½ pound little yellow tomatoes
½ cup chopped mustard pickles
French Dressing

FIRST Scoop out the contents of ½ pound little yellow tomatoes, leaving each tomato a hollow shell.

SECOND Fill each hollow with an even distribution of ½ cup of chopped mustard pickles. Marinate for 1 hour in French Dressing (page 247). Drain and serve.

FISH-AND-TONGUE SPREAD

1 tin boneless and skinless sardines
¼ pound cooked tongue
5 *or* 6 small sweet pickles
Russian Dressing
slices of Russian rye bread cut in half

FIRST Grind contents 1 tin boneless and skinless sardines, ¼ pound cooked tongue, and 5 or 6 small sweet pickles together.

SECOND Add just enough Russian Dressing (page 250) to bind the mixture together. It must be moist but not fluid. Serve with pieces of buttered Russian rye bread cut in half.

HAM THAT LOOKS LIKE BACON *Marie's*

1 small loaf of sandwich bread, unsliced   ¼ pound *soft* sweet butter
12 slices of cold boiled ham

FIRST Trim all the crusts from a small loaf of sandwich bread. Cut the loaf lengthwise into 4 even slices.

SECOND Butter these slices generously with ¼ pound soft sweet butter as follows:

    slice #1 on one side   slice #3 on both sides
    slice #2 on both sides   slice #4 on one side

THIRD Remove fat from 12 slices of cold boiled ham. Place enough ham on bread slice #1 to cover. Top with bread slice #2. Cover with ham. Top with bread slice #3. Cover with ham. Top with bread slice #4 plain side up.

FOURTH Not only wrap, but bind tightly in wax paper. Press down with the hands until the loaf shrinks in size to about one-third its former size. Turn wax paper at ends to keep out air. Place in refrigerator the day before using.

FIFTH When ready to serve, remove from paper. Allow to stand about a half hour at room temperature. Then slice carefully about ⅛" thick.

NOTE When binding the loaf inside the wax paper don't be afraid to be a little tough. The entire purpose is to force the loaf to shrink in size. If the strips of the loaf should separate while slicing, it is because they are too cold.

HAWAIIAN HUACAMOLE

1 small tomato, skinned
3 stalks celery
1 ripe avocado

pepper and onion salt
1 cut clove of garlic

FIRST Chop 1 small skinned tomato and 3 stalks of celery into tiny pieces.

APPETIZERS 17

SECOND Skin 1 avocado, remove pit, and crush with a fork, working until it is almost a paste. Add the chopped celery and tomato. Season to taste with onion salt and pepper.

THIRD Rub a small serving-bowl with one cut clove of garlic. Put mixture in bowl and place in refrigerator until ready to serve. Serve with crackers or potato chips.

ITALIAN PROSCIUTTO

[Ham wrapped around fingers of ripe melon]

1 ripe cantaloupe *or* **Persian melon**   **1 pound thinly sliced prosciutto (Italian ham)**

FIRST Cut the ripe cantaloupe or Persian melon into long pieces about the thickness of your middle finger.

SECOND Cut off *some* of the fat from 1 pound thinly sliced prosciutto (Italian ham). Wrap the meat around the melon fingers. Place in refrigerator until ready to serve.

NOTE In wrapping the prosciutto around the melon it is fun to conceal the melon entirely. In this way the melon comes as a complete surprise.

LILIES OF SALAMI

little, finger-length sweet pickles   **very, very thinly sliced Italian salami (with casing removed)**

FIRST Cut little, finger-length sweet pickles into long, pointed pieces like the stamen of a lily.

SECOND Fold very, very thinly sliced Italian salami like a lily (folded together at the base, open at the top, cornucopia fashion). Push a sliver of pickle down inside the center. Run a toothpick through the salami and the pickle to fasten them together.

NOTE This makes an excellent effect if placed in a ring around a platter with other hors d'oeuvres in the center. The amounts for this recipe have not been given because it depends chiefly on how many lilies are to be made. One quarter pound very, very thinly sliced Italian salami in conjunction with other hors d'oeuvres should be sufficient to serve six. The most important part is to see that it is sliced to order, thin, thin, thin; and have the casing removed before slicing—afterward is too late, as the slices will tear.

LITTLE HAM TARTS
[*Pre-heat oven to moderate heat*]

Cream Cheese Crust (page 408)
½ cup cooked ham, chopped very fine
1 tablespoon prepared mustard
pinch of cayenne pepper
2 tiny white onions, minced
½ cup whipping-cream
paprika

FIRST Prepare small tarts (as small as possible) by covering the back of any small cupcake or muffin tin with Cream Cheese Crust (page 408). Bake to pale gold in a moderate oven.

SECOND Combine ½ cup cooked ham, chopping very fine in a chopping-bowl, with 1 tablespoon prepared mustard, a pinch of cayenne pepper, and 2 tiny white onions well minced.

THIRD Beat ½ cup whipping-cream until stiff. Fold into ham mixture. Fill tart shells with mixture. Sprinkle each with paprika and serve.

LOBSTER ROUNDS
[*Pre-heat oven to 400°*]

½ small onion, chopped
1 tablespoon chopped water cress
paprika
salt
saffron
1 tablespoon flour
1 cup minced lobster
½ cup cream
Buttered toast rounds

FIRST Combine ½ small onion chopped, 1 tablespoon chopped

water cress, a dash of paprika, salt, saffron, 1 tablespoon flour, and ½ cup cream. Cook, stirring constantly, until thick.

SECOND   Add 1 cup minced lobster (preferably fresh). Cook very briefly. Spread on buttered toast rounds. Set in 400° oven until slightly browned. Serve hot.

NOTE   The saffron adds to the flavor and to the color, but if it is difficult to procure, it may be omitted. This recipe is equally good with flaked crab (preferably fresh).

MOSAIC COCKTAIL SANDWICH   *Marie's*

3 soft, thin rolls about 4 inches long
¼ pound soft sweet butter
½ cup tiny cubes American *or* Swiss cheese
½ cup tiny cubes bologna sausage
½ cup tiny cubes sweet pickles

FIRST   Cut off the ends of 3 soft, thin rolls about 4 inches long. Scoop out the insides. Butter the hollow shells with ¼ pound soft, sweet butter, reserving a small amount.

SECOND   Combine ½ cup tiny cubes American or Swiss cheese, ½ cup tiny cubes bologna sausage, and ½ cup tiny cubes sweet pickles with whatever soft sweet butter is left. Stuff the rolls compactly.

THIRD   Wrap in a slightly damp cloth and set in refrigerator over night. When ready to serve, cut slices ⅛ to ¼" thick.

NOTE   In order to make the cubes, the cheese, sausage, and pickles must be sliced ¼" thick.

These were my mother's favorite bridge-party sandwiches. I well remember the child who had wearily been attending to homework in the nursery reaching with eager, ink-stained fingers for the platters of Mosaic Sandwiches as they were carried back past her to the pantry to be refilled.

MARINATED HERRING

1 cup sour cream
3 marinated herrings in sour-cream sauce with sliced, raw onions

slices of Russian rye bread
butter
paprika

FIRST Place 1 cup sour cream in a mixing-bowl. Into the cream, cut 3 marinated herrings in two-inch pieces. Also add any cream sauce and any sliced raw onions that may have come with the herring when it was purchased.

SECOND Place a piece of herring on a buttered piece of Russian rye bread, and garnish each piece with a piece of the onion and a generous covering of the cream sauce. Sprinkle with paprika.

RED CAVIAR WITH SOUR CREAM ON RYE

1 two-ounce jar red caviar
½ cup sour cream
rounds of toasted Russian rye bread

butter
paprika

FIRST Fold the contents of 1 two-ounce jar of red caviar into ½ cup sour cream, being careful not to break the eggs.

SECOND Cut out rounds from thinly sliced Russian rye bread and toast on a cookie sheet. Butter sparingly while warm. Place generous mounds of the sour cream and red caviar on each round. Sprinkle with paprika.

ROQUEFORT SPREAD

¼ pound Roquefort cheese
sufficient cream to soften
½ teaspoon Worcestershire sauce

1 drop Tabasco sauce *or tiny* pinch cayenne pepper

FIRST Mash ¼ pound Roquefort cheese with a fork. Soften with sufficient cream until smooth.

SECOND Add ½ teaspoon Worchestersire sauce and one drop Tabasco sauce or a *tiny* pinch cayenne pepper. Serve on crackers, toast rounds, or potato chips.

SARDINES ON FINGERS OF BREAD

4 thin slices white bread	lemon juice
2 tins skinless and boneless sardines	minced parsley

FIRST Remove the crusts from 4 thin slices white bread. Cut each slice into 3 long pieces. Toast. These are the "fingers."

SECOND Place the contents of two tins of skinless and boneless sardines (either whole or split lengthwise into halves), on the "fingers." Squeeze lemon juice sparingly on each, sprinkle with minced parsley, and serve.

NOTE Toast the "fingers" if you like. But the great pianist Artur Rubinstein (one of the most meticulous gourmets I know) swears that nothing is as good as sardines on plain untoasted "fingers" of bread, the sardine oil soaking into the soft white bread. Try it and see!

SCALLOPS AROUND TARTAR SAUCE

1 dozen scallops	parsley
crumbs	slices of lemon
butter	small bowl of tartar sauce

FIRST Drop 1 dozen scallops into rapidly boiling water. Boil for one minute, then drain on soft cloth.

SECOND Roll in fine crumbs and fry lightly in hot butter until golden brown.

THIRD Place a toothpick in each scallop to facilitate handling and serve on a bed of parsley with slices of lemon in a ring around a small bowl of tartar sauce.

SHRIMP NEW ORLEANS

3 dozen frozen shrimp
1 medium-sized onion, finely minced
1 clove of garlic, finely minced
½ cup French Dressing
¼ jar horseradish (approximately 1 ounce)
2 tablespoons Bahama mustard
pinch of thyme

(FOR 12)

FIRST Boil and shell 3 dozen frozen shrimp. Cool.

SECOND Make a marinade in which to soak the shrimp as follows: Mince 1 medium onion and 1 clove of garlic as finely as possible. Add ½ cup of French Dressing (page 247), ¼ jar (approximately 1 ounce) of horseradish, 2 tablespoons of Bahama mustard, and a pinch of thyme. Beat this together until well combined.

THIRD Place the shrimp in this mixture and cover them with the marinade by pouring the entire mixture, shrimp and all, from one bowl to another until completely blended. Place in the refrigerator overnight.

FOURTH Arrange on an attractive dish and serve very cold with toothpicks.

SMOKED SALMON ROLLS

½ pound of the best smoked salmon, cut as thin as possible
black pepper, freshly ground
capers

FIRST Buy ½ pound of the best smoked salmon you can procure. Taste it before you buy it. If it is more than slightly salty, leave it alone. "When it's good it's very, very good, and when it's bad it's horrid."

SECOND Cut the slices in half and roll them. They are oily and will stick together, but, just the same, spear them with a toothpick for the sake of your guests' fingertips.

THIRD Grate black peppercorns through a pepper mill over the salmon rolls. Also add a few capers. If the rolls must wait, place in the refrigerator, but *not for long*, as they dry out quickly.

NOTE Ordinary black pepper may be used instead of the peppercorns in the pepper mill, but we much prefer it through the mill!

STUFFED CUCUMBERS

1 cucumber
1 package cream cheese
1 rounded teaspoon mayonnaise
1 tablespoon ketchup
1 tablespoon chopped chives *or* parsley
round crackers, buttered

FIRST Pare one cucumber of the approximate diameter of round crackers. Cut off one end and core the cucumber with a flexible knife. Score the outside of the pared cucumber for its entire length with the prongs of a fork.

SECOND Mash 1 package cream cheese with 1 rounded teaspoon mayonnaise and 1 tablespoon ketchup. When soft and well blended, add 1 tablespoon chopped chives or parsley. Stuff the hollowed cucumber. Wrap and place in refrigerator.

THIRD When ready to serve, cut into $\frac{1}{4}''$ slices. Set each slice on buttered round crackers of the approximate diameter of the cucumber slice.

STUFFED EGGS CURRIED

6 hard-boiled eggs
2 tablespoons mayonnaise (not too sweet)
Salt and pepper
curry powder to taste
3 strips fried bacon, finely minced
chutney

FIRST Cut 6 hard-boiled eggs in half. Remove yolks and mash.

SECOND Blend yolks with 2 tablespoons mayonnaise, salt, pepper, and curry powder to taste. Add 3 strips fried bacon, finely minced.

THIRD Place in refrigerator. Just before serving, put a few dabs of chutney on top of each egg.

STUFFED FRENCH ENDIVE

3 stalks French endive
¼ pound creamy Blue cheese
sufficient cream to smooth
paprika

FIRST Carefully separate the leaves of three stalks of French endive.

SECOND Crush ¼ pound creamy Blue cheese with a fork and gradually add sufficient cream to make a smooth paste. Stuff endive leaves with cheese mixture. Dust with paprika and place in refrigerator. Serve very cold.

NOTE This recipe may be used with celery stalks instead—but only the white stalks. For an added effect, place cheese mixture in a decorator's bag and squeeze onto each leaf in a fancy pattern.

STUFFED FRENCH ROLLS *Marie's*

2 sour-dough French rolls
soft butter
smoked liverwurst *or* pâté de foie gras *or* smoked rainbow trout pâté
Chopped parsley *or* chopped chives

FIRST Cut off both ends of 2 sour-dough French rolls. With a sharp flexible knife, scoop out all the soft centers of the rolls. Butter the insides of the hollow rolls generously.

SECOND Mash the liverwurst or any preferred pâté and stuff the rolls. Flatten the top and bottom so that the stuffing does not overflow.

THIRD Wrap the rolls individually in wax paper and place in refrigerator until thoroughly cold. This is best done the day before.

FOURTH When ready to serve, slice the rolls very thin, sprinkling each slice with minced parsley or minced chives.

NOTE I find that a grapefruit knife makes an excellent instrument with which to remove the soft centers of the rolls.

Chapter II: *Soups*

Of soup and love, the first is best.

THOMAS FULLER: *Gnomologia*, 1732

COLD

Apple and Banana Soup with Curry
Choldnik Soup
Carrot Soup
Curry Soup
Iced Pea Soup
Jellied Borsch
Potage Louis
Red Caviar Madrilène
Senegalese Soup
Sherried Consommé
Squash Soup
Summer Borsch
Tomato Soup
Vichyssoise

HOT

Barnyard Soup with Matzo Balls
Boothbay Broth
Chicken Liver Soup
Consommé Garni
Chowder
Curry
Monterey Peninsula Abalone
Mussel
New England Clam
Fancy Carcass Soup
Mongol Soup
Moules à la Mariniére
Mushroom Soup, Edwin
Mushroom Soup, Wendy
Mushroom Broth with White Wine
Noodleroom
Pea Soup, dried
Pea Soup, fresh
Potage de Mardi
Supa Shetgia
Tomato Soup with Cheese
Tomato Surprise Soup
Turtle and Mushroom Broth

APPLE AND BANANA SOUP WITH CURRY

1 pint chicken stock *or* consommé
1 apple
1 banana
1 potato
1 onion
1 pint cream
1 tablespoon curry powder
chives

SERVES 6

FIRST Heat 1 pint chicken stock or consommé. Cut up 1 apple, 1 banana, 1 potato, and 1 onion, and cook in the broth until soft. Mash through a strainer.

SECOND Add 1 pint of cream and 1 tablespoon curry powder. Place in refrigerator until cold. Serve thoroughly chilled and sprinkled with minced chives.

CHOLDNIK SOUP

3½ pints sour cream
1 overflowing cup beet juice (pickled with onions and vinegar)
liquid from beet tops
3 beets, cooked
3 bunches beet tops, cooked and chopped
2 peeled dill pickles in cubes
2 fresh cucumbers, sliced thin
1 cup left-over veal roast, cubed
½ pound tiny shrimp, *or* ½ pound large shrimp, chopped
3 tablespoons dill
2 tablespoons green chives, chopped
salt and pepper to taste

SERVES 12

FIRST Gradually add 3½ pints of sour cream to 1 overflowing cup of pickled beet juice and the cooled liquid in which 3 bunches of beet tops have been cooked. Stir until blended.

SECOND Add the following ingredients, one at a time: 3 cooked beets forced through a sieve, 3 cooked and chopped bunches beet tops, 2 peeled dill pickles in cubes, 2 thinly sliced fresh cucumbers, 1 cup cubed left-over veal roast, ½ pound shrimp, 3 tablespoons dill, 2 tablespoons chopped green chives, salt and pepper to taste.

THIRD Place 4 or 5 ice cubes in a bowl with the soup and set in the refrigerator until thoroughly chilled. This soup must be served very, very cold.

CARROT SOUP

¼ pound butter
½ teaspoon sugar
½ teaspoon salt
2 pounds sliced carrots
1 quart chicken broth
1 cup cream

1 tablespoon chopped chives *or* chopped parsley
pepper
1 hard-boiled egg
additional chopped chives *or* chopped parsley

SERVES 6

FIRST Render ¼ pound butter in a saucepan. Add ½ teaspoon sugar and ½ teaspoon salt. Place 2 pounds sliced carrots in the butter and cook until soft (about 20 minutes). Keep flame low and watch carefully to see that carrots do not scorch.

SECOND Add 1 quart chicken broth and simmer for about an hour.

THIRD Drain carrots, rub through a sieve, taste for seasoning, cool. When cool, pour in 1 cup cream, 1 tablespoon chopped chives or parsley, and sprinkle with black pepper to taste. Place in refrigerator to chill.

FOURTH Chop 1 hard-boiled egg and place 1 teaspoon in each soup cup. Fill the cups with the soup, then sprinkle with chopped chives or parsley.

CURRY SOUP

1 can green pea soup (concentrated)
1 can bouillon *or* consommé (concentrated)
½ can tomato madrilène
1¼ cups cream

salt
coarse black pepper
juice of 3 lemons
1½ tablespoons curry powder
raw apple, grated

SERVES 6

FIRST Combine 1 can concentrated green pea soup, 1 can concentrated bouillon or consommé, ½ can tomato madrilène, and 1¼ cups cream. Heat and stir until well blended. Add salt and coarse black pepper to taste, the juice of 3 lemons, and 1½ tablespoons curry powder. Cool, then chill in the refrigerator.

SECOND Just before serving, divide evenly into six individual bouillon cups and grate a generous amount of raw apple into each cup. Serve immediately.

NOTE Additional curry powder may be used if you like things hot. The amount given is for a mild curry flavor. This soup may be made ahead of time, but the apple must not be added until the last minute. Your guests will have a difficult time recognizing the apple, which of course only adds to your prestige!

ICED PEA SOUP

2 cups fresh *or* frozen peas	4 level teaspoons potato flour
½ sliced onion	4 cups chicken broth
salt, pepper	½ cup thick cream
1 cup water	chopped fresh mint to taste

SERVES 8

FIRST Cook 2 cups peas, ½ sliced onion, salt, and pepper in 1 cup water over low flame until mushy. Remove from fire.

SECOND Stir in 4 level teaspoons potato flour. Add 4 cups chicken broth. Return to fire and stir until it comes to a boil. Simmer for 3 minutes and remove from fire again.

THIRD Rub through a strainer into a bowl. Pack bowl in a larger bowl filled with cracked ice. Stir occasionally while it chills.

FOURTH When chilled, add ½ cup thick cream and finely chopped fresh mint to taste.

NOTE This wonderful old recipe calls for potato flour, a thickening always used by our grandmothers. I am sentimental about these things and try as best I can to follow the old, original directions. I feel sure, however, you will be able to achieve the same success with ordinary flour which will give practically the same results.

JELLIED BORSCH

2 #2 cans beets
2 cabbage leaves
2 cans consommé
3 whole cloves
1½ tablespoons red wine vinegar
½ teaspoon salt

½ chopped onion
1 tablespoon gelatin
¼ cup cold water
sour cream
chopped chives *or* spring onions

SERVES 6

FIRST Boil 2 #2 cans beets together with beet juice, 2 cabbage leaves, 2 cans consommé, 3 whole cloves, 1½ tablespoons red wine vinegar, ½ teaspoon salt, and ½ chopped onion until vegetables are well cooked.

SECOND Strain through fine sieve. Add 1 tablespoon gelatin soaked 5 minutes in ¼ cup cold water, and dissolve in hot beet soup. Cool to room temperature. Set in bouillon cups or champagne glasses and place in refrigerator until thoroughly chilled.

THIRD Serve topped with a generous dab of sour cream and a sprinkling of chopped chives or chopped spring onions over the cream.

POTAGE LOUIS

4 egg yolks
1½ cups heavy cream
1 quart chicken broth
sorrel (approximately 1 dozen leaves)

salt, pepper
nutmeg
paprika

SERVES 6

FIRST Mix 4 egg yolks with 1½ cups of heavy cream.

SECOND Add 1 quart of boiling chicken broth and approximately 1 dozen coarsely chopped sorrel leaves. Season with salt, pepper, and nutmeg to taste. Bring to a boil—but do not under any circumstances boil.

THIRD Cool to room temperature. Then place in the refrigerator and chill thoroughly. Place in bouillon cups and sprinkle the top of each cup with a dash of paprika. Equally delicious served hot or cold.

RED CAVIAR MADRILÈNE

3½ pints of tomato madrilène
2 ounces red caviar

½ pint sour cream
¼ cup chopped chives

SERVES 6

FIRST Pour 3½ pints tomato madrilène into 6 individual bouillon cups. Stir a heaping teaspoon of red caviar into each cup. Place the cups in the refrigerator until set.

SECOND Just before serving, top each cup with a *heaping* tablespoon of sour cream and sprinkle with minced chives.

NOTE This soup is equally exciting if prepared in the same way with a clear chicken madrilène and black caviar.

SENEGALESE SOUP

FROM NEW YORK'S FAMED 21 CLUB

2 leeks
2 onions
1 bunch celery
¼ pound butter
1 tablespoon curry powder

3 tablespoons flour
2 quarts strong chicken broth
1 cup heavy cream
2 cooked breasts of chicken
curry powder

SERVES 12

FIRST Chop 2 leeks, 2 onions, and 1 bunch of celery. Brown lightly in a skillet in ¼ pound of rendered butter. Stir in 1 tablespoon curry powder (more if preferred) and 3 tablespoons flour.

SECOND Remove to a large saucepan and add 2 quarts strong chicken broth. Cook for half an hour, then strain and cool.

THIRD When the soup is cold add 1 cup of heavy cream. Serve the soup very cold in bouillon cups. Just before sending to the table, finely sliver 2 cooked breasts of chicken, divide them evenly in the cups, and add a pinch of curry powder to float atop each cup.

NOTE This soup is truly superb. Its quality depends chiefly on the richness of the chicken broth, the richness of the cream, and of course the quality of the curry powder.

SHERRIED CONSOMMÉ

1 quart cold consommé water cress
2 tablespoons best dry sherry

SERVES 6

FIRST Stir 1 quart cold consommé. Season to taste with 2 tablespoons best dry sherry.

SECOND Pour into individual bouillon cups and let stand in the refrigerator until thoroughly chilled. Top each cup with a sprig of water cress.

SUMMER BORSCH

2 medium white onions 2 hard-boiled eggs
2 cucumbers 1 quart buttermilk
1½ #2 cans beets 1 cup sour cream

SERVES 6

FIRST Chop the following vegetables first separately, then together: 2 medium white onions, 2 peeled cucumbers, and the contents of 1½ #2 cans of beets. Chop 2 hard-boiled eggs, but do *not* chop the eggs with the vegetables.

SECOND Add the chopped eggs and all the chopped vegetables to 1 quart of buttermilk. Some of the canned beet juice may be added to color the whole. Divide into equal portions in individual bouillon cups or soup plates. Place in the refrigerator until thoroughly cold. Serve with a side dish containing 1 cup of sour cream.

SQUASH SOUP

3 onions
1 rounded tablespoon butter
6 or 8 tender summer squash
2 cans chicken broth
pinch of nutmeg

pinch of sugar
1 pint heavy cream
salt
chopped chives or parsley

SERVES 6

FIRST Mince 3 onions and cook until just soft in rounded table spoon butter. Be careful not to burn.

SECOND Cut 6 or 8 tender summer squash into very small pieces. Add squash and the onions to the contents of 2 cans of chicken broth and cook until tender. Put through a sieve, add a pinch of nutmeg and a pinch of sugar. Cool to room temperature. When cool, add 1 pint heavy cream, salt to taste, and then place in refrigerator to chill. Serve very cold in bouillon cups with chopped chives or parsley.

NOTE The lowly squash turned glamorous! This is also good served hot, but be careful not to boil.

TOMATO SOUP

1 can cream of tomato soup
onion juice to taste
1 teaspoon chopped parsley
1 tablespoon chopped celery
1 teaspoon soy sauce

salt, pepper
1 cup cream
4 tablespoons lime juice
chopped chives or chopped
    blanched pistachio nuts

SERVES 4

FIRST To 1 can cream of tomato soup add onion juice to taste, 1 teaspoon chopped parsley, 1 tablespoon chopped celery, 1 teaspoon soy sauce, salt and pepper to taste, and 1 cup cream. Chill in refrigerator.

SECOND Strain and add 4 tablespoons lime juice. Serve in cold bouillon cups with chopped chives or chopped blanched pistachio nuts on top.

VICHYSSOISE

6 leeks
3 onions
¼ pound butter
2 quarts chicken broth
1 pound potatoes
salt, pepper

¼ pound sweet butter
1 pint heavy cream *or*
1 cup heavy cream and 1 cup sour cream
¼ cup chopped chives

SERVES 12

FIRST Chop 6 leeks and 3 onions very fine. Melt ¼ pound butter in large skillet. Cook leeks and onions in butter until soft but not colored. Add a few spoonfuls of water if necessary to keep from burning. Remove to soup pot, add 2 quarts chicken broth and 1 pound potatoes peeled and sliced very thin. Add salt and pepper to taste. Cook, and when potatoes are soft, strain and force vegetables through sieve.

SECOND Add ¼ pound sweet butter, stirring until melted. Add 1 pint of heavy cream, or 1 cup cream and 1 cup sour cream. Serve hot or ice cold in individual bouillon cups with chopped chives sprinkled on top.

BARNYARD SOUP WITH MATZO BALLS

1 quart chicken broth
salt, pepper
2 cooked chicken breasts
thin slices raw radishes

thin slices spring onion tops
1 recipe Matzo Balls
½ cup heavy cream (optional)

SERVES 6

FIRST Heat 1 quart chicken broth. Season to taste with salt and pepper.

SECOND Cut 2 cooked chicken breasts into long thin slivers. Drop them into chicken broth with thin slices of raw radishes and thin slices of spring onion tops. Serve with Matzo Balls, two for each serving.

NOTE If a cream soup is preferred, add ½ cup of heavy cream, in which case, however, omit the Matzo Balls.

MATZO BALLS FOR SOUP

2 eggs
2 tablespoons marrow fat *or* butter
¼ cup matzo meal
½ teaspoon baking powder

½ teaspoon salt
paprika
chopped chives, minced onions, *or* minced parsley (optional)

FIRST Beat 2 eggs and stir in 2 tablespoons marrow fat or butter. Add ¼ cup matzo meal mixed with ½ teaspoon baking powder. Add ½ teaspoon salt and a pinch of paprika. Chopped chives, minced onion, or minced parsley may be added if desired.

SECOND Roll a small amount into a ball the size of a small walnut. If it does not hold together, add a *little* more matzo meal. Now shape the rest of the mixture into balls by rolling them between your palms. Place in the refrigerator for several hours.

THIRD A short time before serving the soup, drop the matzo balls into the boiling soup. Allow them to boil for about 10 or 15 minutes. Turn them over occasionally.

WARNING Use as little matzo flour as possible. Too much has a tendency to make the balls heavy. You may chill before rolling.

BOOTHBAY BROTH

1 pint clear chicken broth
½ pint clam juice
½ cup light cream
croutons

paprika
minced clams (optional)
whipped cream (optional)

SERVES 6

FIRST Blend 1 pint clear chicken broth with ½ pint clam juice. Heat and add ½ cup light cream.

SECOND If you wish to keep this soup simple, just bounce a few croutons on top of each cup and sprinkle lightly with paprika. However, if you wish, you may add 1 tablespoon minced clams to each bouillon cup and 1 tablespoon whipped cream on top instead of the croutons.

NOTE Croutons are tiny squares, about ¼" thick, of white bread fried lightly in a skillet with melted butter until well browned on all sides.

CHICKEN-LIVER SOUP

3 hard-boiled eggs
6 chicken livers
2 tablespoons butter
1 medium onion
3 tablespoons butter
3 tablespoons flour

1 cup purée of spinach
1 pint chicken broth
1 cup light cream
pepper, salt, celery salt
1 tablespoon tarragon
chopped parsley

SERVES 6

FIRST Boil 3 eggs almost hard.

SECOND Lightly fry 6 chicken livers in 2 tablespoons butter.

THIRD Chop 1 medium onion together with the eggs and the chicken livers. Blend 3 tablespoons melted butter with 3 tablespoons flour. Add to one cup purée of spinach and combine with the chopped liver mixture. Place in a soup pot and add 1 pint chicken broth and 1 cup light cream. Season with pepper, salt, celery salt, and 1 tablespoon of tarragon. Heat well and serve in soup plates with a sprinkling of parsley on top of each.

CONSOMMÉ GARNI

2 cans consommé
green olives

cheddar cheese

SERVES 6

FIRST Heat 2 cans consommé according to the direction on the can.

SECOND Cut up a preferred amount of green olives into small bits and a preferred amount of cheddar cheese into tiny cubes. Put some olives and cheese into individual soup plates or consommé cups and pour the hot soup into each.

SOUPS

CURRY CHOWDER

¼ pound butter
⅓ stalk celery
2 onions
1 #2 can tomatoes
1 pound halibut
1 pound salmon
1 pint milk

1 pint light cream
pepper, salt
2 tablespoons curry powder
walnut sauce
½ pound picked crab
paprika

SERVES 12

FIRST Place ¼ pound of butter in a large skillet. When melted, cook ⅓ stalk chopped celery, and 2 chopped onions until gold. Pour in 1 # 2 can of tomatoes. Simmer.

SECOND Boil 1 pound halibut and 1 pound salmon. When done, put through food-grinder.

THIRD Strain tomato mixture over ground fish. Add 1 pint milk, 1 pint light cream, plenty of pepper and salt, 2 tablespoons curry powder, and a dash of bottled walnut sauce. Mix well. Place in refrigerator.

FOURTH Serve ice cold in bouillon cups with a few pieces of picked crab floating on top of each cup and a dash of paprika to decorate.

MONTEREY PENINSULA ABALONE CHOWDER

2 onions
2 leeks
3 sprigs celery
1 green pepper
¼ pound butter
1 tablespoon flour
3 abalones
salt

Worcestershire sauce
thyme
Tabasco sauce
2 quarts water
2 medium potatoes
1 pint light cream
1 teaspoon flour

SERVES 12

FIRST Chop 2 onions, 2 leeks, 3 sprigs of celery, and 1 green pepper. Simmer together in ¼ pound rendered butter. Rub in 1 tablespoon flour to thicken.

SECOND Grind 3 abalones through the meat-chopper and combine with the chopped vegetables and the butter. Add salt, Worcestershire sauce to taste, fresh or dried thyme, and a tiny dash of Tabasco sauce. Pour in 2 quarts of water and boil slowly for about an hour.

THIRD Dice 2 medium potatoes and boil in a separate pan until they have just begun to soften. Add to chowder and continue to cook until potatoes are soft but not mushy.

FOURTH Shortly before serving, pour in 1 pint of light cream and sprinkle in 1 teaspoon flour.

NOTES 1. This famous Western chowder may be served as above or with the cream and flour omitted, in which case use 1 cup chopped fresh tomatoes added to the vegetables. The potatoes are boiled separately before adding to the soup in order to prevent the potato starch from clouding the chowder.

2. This recipe calls for the use of thyme, either fresh or dried. The chances are that most of you will be using the preserved, therefore, I should like to say a word about the use of all dried herbs. Do not leave the little herb jars on your kitchen shelves for months and months at a time and expect them to be as potent as they were the day you first brought them home! Take a pinch between your fingers, put it in your mouth, and munch thoughtfully. Then, and then only, will you know how much the use of that particular herb will help in preparing the recipe of your choice.

MUSSEL CHOWDER

3 dozen mussels
1 large carrot
1 large onion
1 heaping tablespoon parsley
1 green pepper
1 tablespoon thyme
1 glass white wine
bay leaf
1 small piece garlic
salt, pepper

SERVES 4

FIRST Clean and scrub 3 dozen mussels. Place them in a pot and steam them open with a little water lightly salted.

SECOND In another pot, place 1 large carrot chopped, 1 large onion chopped, 1 heaping tablespoon chopped parsley, 1 chopped green pepper, 1 tablespoon thyme, 1 glass of white wine, and the water in which the mussels have been steamed. Tie 1 bay leaf and 1 small piece of garlic in a cheesecloth bag and add to pot. Cook over a slow fire for about half an hour.

THIRD Add the mussels and cook them slowly until well flavored, about an hour and a half. Add salt and pepper to taste and remove the bag of garlic and the bay leaf.

NOTE This is one of the superb offerings of France's culinary art. Lucky those residents of the United States who live where fresh mussels are obtainable. For those who are not so fortunate, canned mussels may be used, adding the juice from the cans together with a little water to the vegetables, and placing the mussels in the soup at the end. Of course, since they are already cooked, the mussels must not be heated for very long. This is offered as a substitute. I do not promise it to be the same.

NEW ENGLAND CLAM CHOWDER

¼ pound butter	2 quarts boiling water
2 medium onions	1 large potato
1 pint clams	1 pint light cream
1 cup clam juice	1 pint milk
1 tablespoon salt	paprika
1 teaspoon black pepper	

SERVES 12

FIRST Melt ¼ pound butter in skillet. Fry 2 chopped medium onions until a pale gold. Add 1 pint chopped clams. Simmer 5 minutes and remove to saucepan.

SECOND Add 1 cup clam juice, 1 tablespoon salt, and 1 teaspoon of black pepper (freshly ground preferred). Add 2 quarts boiling water, 1 large potato diced and cook for half an hour.

THIRD Add 1 pint light cream and 1 pint milk. Cook together but do not boil. Pour into individual soup plates and sprinkle each lightly with paprika.

FANCY CARCASS SOUP

carcass of turkey, 2 chickens *or* 2 ducks
2 large onions
2 large carrots
3 celery stalks
2 tablespoons parsley
2 bay leaves
salt, pepper
1½ pounds cooked asparagus
½ pound mushrooms
2 ounces butter
6 sprigs parsley
8 sprigs water cress
½ cup sherry

SERVES 8

FIRST Heat 3 quarts of water and simmer for about 2 hours the carcass of one turkey, or 2 ducks or 2 chickens with 2 large onions quartered, 2 large carrots cut into pieces, 3 cut stalks of celery, 2 tablespoons coarsely chopped parsley, 2 bay leaves, and salt and pepper to taste. Prepare this a day before soup is to be served. Strain into bowl. When at room temperature, place in refrigerator overnight.

SECOND Skim off fat and reheat soup. To reheated soup add: 1½ pounds cooked asparagus cut into small pieces, ½ pound mushrooms that have been simmered in 2 ounces of butter (include the butter), 6 sprigs parsley, 8 sprigs water cress cut with kitchen shears. Heat to boiling point. Just before serving, stir in ½ cup sherry.

NOTE This is a glamorous way in which to serve left-over carcasses of turkey, chicken, or duck. Asparagus is not necessarily the only vegetable that may be used. Fresh spring peas or finely cut string beans also make an attractive addition. The vegetables need not be freshly cooked. Any little dish of left-over vegetables may be successfully used.

MONGOL SOUP

1 recipe Curry Soup (page 28)
½ cup milk
1 can tomato paste
salt
1 can minced clams *or* abalone

SERVES 6

FIRST Heat 1 recipe Curry Soup (page 28) with ½ cup milk, 1 can tomato paste, and salt to taste. Blend well and heat thoroughly.

SECOND Add the contents of one can of minced clams or abalone. Stir and heat well.

MOULES À LA MARINIÉRE

1 cup water
salt, pepper
whole peppercorns
1 teaspoon thyme
2 bay leaves
1 clove garlic

¼ cup parsley
1 carrot
1 medium onion
1 cup white wine
1 quart mussels

SERVES 4

FIRST Place 1 cup of water into a pot. Add salt, pepper, a few bruised whole peppercorns, 1 teaspoon thyme, 2 bay leaves, 1 minced clove of garlic, ¼ cup of minced parsley, 1 carrot cut into small pieces and 1 medium-sized onion cut into small pieces. Bring to a boil. Simmer for 10 minutes.

SECOND Add 1 cup white wine and 1 quart of mussels. Place a cover on the pot and cook on a medium flame for approximately 10 minutes or until the mussel shells have opened.

THIRD Serve the mussels in their shells in a tureen swimming in their broth, or in individual deep soup plates with as much broth as the plates will hold.

NOTE This is a traditional dish of France. I only hope that you are among the more fortunate Americans who live where mussels are to be found in the market.

MUSHROOM SOUP EDWIN

½ pound fresh mushrooms
flour
2 ounces butter
1½ quarts chicken broth

½ cup heavy cream
chopped parsley
paprika

SERVES 8

FIRST Wash ½ pound fresh mushrooms. Remove the heads, slicing each head 3 times across. Set aside.

SECOND Wash the mushroom stems, chop fine, then mash a little. Set them in a skillet, sprinkle with flour, and pour over 2 ounces of melted butter. Simmer slightly.

THIRD Add the sliced mushroom heads to 1½ quarts chicken broth (homemade preferred). Bring to a slow boil and cook until soft. Add the cooked stems, butter and all. Add ½ cup of heavy cream. Heat thoroughly.

FOURTH When ready to serve, pour into hot bouillon cups or soup plates. Sprinkle each with chopped parsley and paprika and serve at once.

MUSHROOM SOUP WENDY

½ cup dried mushrooms
½ cup water
¼ pound butter
1 pound fresh mushrooms
2 tablespoons flour

1 pint heavy cream
1 pint milk
salt, pepper
¼ cup best sherry
parsley

SERVES 6

FIRST Before you do anything else, put ½ cup of dried mushrooms to soak in ½ cup of water for at least six hours.

SECOND Render ¼ pound of butter in a skillet. Chop the stems of 1 pound of fresh mushrooms and fry lightly in the butter until soft. Add the mushroom caps and cook them until they are tender, but not so soft as to have lost their shape. Rub in 2 tablespoons of flour, continuing to rub until well blended.

THIRD Lower the flame and gradually add 1 pint of heavy cream and 1 pint of milk, stirring constantly until thickened. Add salt and pepper to taste. Simmer gently.

FOURTH Remove the soaked dried mushrooms from the water. Chop them fine and reserve the water. Add both the water and the chopped dried mushrooms to the soup. Heat thoroughly. Just before serving, add ¼ cup of the best sherry. Sprinkle the individual soup plates with minced parsley.

MUSHROOM BROTH WITH WHITE WINE

2 ounces butter
1 small white onion
½ pound mushrooms
1 pint clear, rich chicken broth

salt, pepper
½ teaspoon dried tarragon
2 tablespoons parsley
½ cup dry white wine

SERVES 4

FIRST Render 2 ounces butter in a skillet. Chop 1 small white onion and glaze in the butter.

SECOND Remove the caps of ½ pound of mushrooms and set them aside. Chop the mushroom stems and add them to the onion in the skillet. When they have softened, add the mushroom caps and cook until tender, but not so soft as to have lost their shape.

THIRD Place 1 pint of clear rich chicken broth into a stew pan and scrape the contents of the skillet into the broth. Season with salt and pepper to taste and add ½ teaspoon of dried tarragon, 2 tablespoons of coarsely chopped parsley, and, just before serving, ½ cup of dry white wine.

NOODLEROOM

1 cup fine noodles
1 pound mushrooms
2 ounces butter
2 cups strong chicken broth
1 cup heavy cream

½ cup rich milk
salt, pepper
1 tablespoon dried tarragon
paprika

SERVES 6

FIRST Boil 1 cup of fine noodles in salted water until tender. Drain well and set aside.

SECOND Wash 1 pound of fresh mushrooms. Separate the stems from the caps and chop the stems. Fry lightly both caps and stems in 2 ounces of butter until lightly browned, but not so much as to have lost their shape.

THIRD Bring 2 cups of strong chicken broth to a boil. Add 1 cup of heavy cream and ½ cup of rich milk. Season with salt and pepper and sprinkle with 1 tablespoon of dried tarragon. Bring to a simmer.

FOURTH Add the mushrooms, the mushrooms stems, and any butter left in the skillet. Add the noodles and continue to simmer until everything is well heated, but not too long or the noodles will become mushy. Pour the soup into individual soup plates. Distribute the noodles and mushrooms evenly into each plate. Sprinkle with paprika and serve at once.

DRIED PEA SOUP

6 medium onions
1 small bunch celery
12 ounces dried green peas
1 package concentrated chicken soup (noodles, too)
salt, pepper
marjoram

2 bay leaves
9 quarts water
1 ham bone
3 short ribs of beef
½ pound cubed salt pork
6 frankfurters

SERVES 12

FIRST Cut 6 medium-sized onions into quarters and cut 1 small bunch of celery into inch pieces. Place these vegetables in a large pot with 12 ounces of dried green peas, 1 package of concentrated chicken soup, noodles and all. Season with salt, pepper, marjoram to taste, and 2 bay leaves. Simmer the whole in 9 quarts of water.

SECOND When the soup has started to simmer, add 1 ham bone, 3 short ribs of beef, and ½ pound cubed salt pork. Cook together very slowly for about 3 or 4 hours.

THIRD Strain the soup into a large bowl. Work as many of the vegetables as possible into the soup by forcing them through a substantial strainer. Allow the soup to stand for several hours—if possible, overnight. Remove almost all the excess fat, then serve very hot in individual plates with ½ sliced frankfurter floating in each soup plate.

NOTE Wonderful on wintry evenings! Try it with warm, crusty, sour-dough French bread.

FRESH PEA SOUP

4 cups fresh young peas
1 chopped onion
3 cups chicken broth
1 cup water
white pepper, salt
3 tablespoons butter

3 tablespoons flour
2 egg yolks
1 cup light cream
whipped cream
paprika

SERVES 6

FIRST Boil 4 cups fresh young peas and 1 chopped onion in 3 cups chicken broth and 1 cup water with salt and white pepper to taste. Boil until vegetables are soft. Rub through sieve. Cool the purée slightly.

SECOND Render 3 tablespoons butter. Rub in 3 tablespoons flour. Beat in 2 egg yolks and add 1 cup heavy cream. Stir this into the purée of peas. Gradually heat, being careful not to boil. Pour into hot soup plates, topping each with a tablespoon of whipped cream and a sprinkling of paprika.

NOTE This soup is equally good cold.

POTAGE DE MARDI

½ package frozen mixed vegetables
1 can chicken broth
1 can clam chowder

1 cup heavy cream
1 can mussels
salt, pepper
paprika

SERVES 6 GENEROUSLY

FIRST Cook ½ the contents of 1 package of frozen mixed vegetables. Drain thoroughly and set aside.

SECOND Place 1 can of chicken broth, 1 can of clam chowder, and 1 cup of heavy cream in a stew pot. Bring to a simmer.

THIRD Add 1 can of mussels (liquid as well as the mussels) and stir gently so as not to break up the mussels. Season with salt and pepper and add the pre-cooked mixed vegetables. Heat well, divide into equal portions, and sprinkle each with a light dusting of paprika.

SUPA SHETGIA
THE CHEESE SOUP OF THE ENGADIN

2 slices sour-dough French bread
4 tablespoons shredded Swiss cheese
1 cup milk
1 tablespoon butter
salt, pepper
nutmeg

SERVES 1

FIRST Place a slice of toasted, stale, sour-dough French bread in the bottom of a deep soup plate and cover with 4 tablespoons shredded Swiss cheese. Top the cheese with a second slice of the same bread and pour over it enough boiling milk (approximately 1 cup) to almost fill the dish. Cover the soup plate and allow to stand for 3 minutes.

SECOND Serve topped with 1 tablespoon brown, melted butter and season with salt, pepper, and nutmeg to taste.

NOTE This is the recipe for one serving in an individual soup plate. The recipe may be enlarged for as many as required.

TOMATO SOUP WITH CHEESE

2 ounces butter
3 leeks
2 stalks celery
½ pound mushrooms
1 can concentrated tomato soup
3 cups light cream
salt, pepper
thyme
6 small tomatoes
¼ pound diced Swiss cheese
parsley

SERVES 6

FIRST Render 2 ounces of butter in a skillet. Cut up the whites of three leeks and 2 stalks of celery and fry lightly in the butter. Slice ½ pound of mushrooms, stems as well as caps, add to the skillet, and continue to fry together until the mushrooms are soft.

SOUPS   47

SECOND Add 1 can concentrated tomato soup and 3 cups of light cream. Season with salt, pepper, and thyme to taste. Heat very gently.

THIRD Skin 6 small tomatoes (about two inches across the top) and simmer in the soup until soft. Remove the tomatoes and set one in each bouillon cup. Place 3 or 4 cubes of Swiss cheese inside each tomato. If there is any cheese left, add it to the soup. Then pour the hot soup over the tomatoes, sprinkle with chopped parsley, and serve immediately.

TOMATO-SURPRISE SOUP

1 onion	3 cups ripe tomatoes
4 tablespoons celery	soda
6 tablespoons butter	salt, pepper
5 tablespoons flour	flaked crab
1 quart milk	½ cup best sherry
1 pint light cream	

SERVES 8

FIRST Cut up 1 onion and 4 tablespoons celery. Cook until soft in 6 tablespoons butter. Remove from flame and rub in 5 tablespoons flour until smooth. (No lumps, please.)

SECOND Add 1 quart milk, a little at a time. Stir until it thickens. Add 1 pint light cream and stir again. Bring to a boil and boil 3 minutes, stirring constantly.

THIRD Cook 3 cups ripe skinned tomatoes until soft. Strain and rub through sieve into bowl. Add a pinch of soda. Combine with cream sauce. Season with salt and pepper to taste. Add as much fresh flaked crab as preferred, and just before serving, reheat with ½ cup best sherry stirred in.

TURTLE AND MUSHROOM BROTH

1 quart turtle soup (with turtle meat)	1 medium white onion
3 tablespoons chopped parsley	1 pound fresh mushrooms
2 ounces butter	best sherry

SERVES 6

FIRST Set 1 quart of turtle soup with turtle meat, into a stew pot over a very small flame. Add 3 tablespoons of chopped parsley.

SECOND Render 2 ounces of butter in a skillet. Chop one medium white onion. Fry lightly in the butter until the onion begins to glaze. Add the caps from 1 pound of fresh mushrooms, reserving the stems for another time. Move the onion and the mushrooms about in the butter with a spatula and allow the mushrooms to cook until tender, but not so soft as to have lost their shape.

THIRD Add the entire contents of the skillet to the broth. Stir until blended. Turn the flame up for a moment or two until the soup is thoroughly heated. Serve in individual soup plates or cups, dishing out an equal amount of mushrooms into each portion. Serve immediately with a bottle of the best sherry. Allow the guests to serve themselves to the sherry, pouring it according to individual preference into their soup.

Chapter III: *Egg Dishes*

A Priest's rule that is true:
Those eggs are best are long and white and new.

JOHN HARINGTON: *The Englishman's Doctor,* 1608

EGG DISHES

COLD

Anchovy Eggs and Sour Cream
Eggs in Aspic I
Eggs in Aspic Tarragon II
Egg Ring
Swans on the Lake

HOT

Baked Eggs in Spinach Boxes
Creamed Poached Eggs à la Hash
Curried Eggs, Jane Cowl
Eggs with Mushroom Stems
French Soufflé Omelette
Omelette Jurassienne
Scrambled Eggs, Edwin
Scrambled Eggs, Paysanne
Swiss Eggs
Swiss Scrambled Eggs

ANCHOVY EGGS AND SOUR CREAM

6 hard-boiled eggs
1 cup sour cream
1 teaspoon lemon juice

4 teaspoons anchovy paste
buttered toast
paprika

SERVES 6

FIRST Cut 6 hard-boiled eggs lengthwise. Remove yolks and mash with 2 tablespoons sour cream, 1 teaspoon lemon juice, and 4 teaspoons anchovy paste.

SECOND Fill whites with this mixture. Set eggs on thin, hot, buttered pieces of toast with crusts removed. Cover thickly with the remaining sour cream and sprinkle with paprika.

EGGS IN ASPIC I

6 eggs
1 tablespoon vinegar
½ cup milk
6 tablespoons paté de foie gras

paprika
1 envelope gelatin
2 cups clear chicken broth
6 slices truffles

SERVES 6

FIRST Gently poach 6 eggs in a skillet with 2 cups water, 1 tablespoon vinegar and ½ cup milk. When still soft, remove from water and drain on paper towels. Cool.

SECOND Place 1 tablespoon paté de foie gras in each of 6 individual ramekins or small bouillon cups. Cover with the cooled poached eggs. Sprinkle eggs lightly with paprika.

THIRD Soak 1 envelope gelatin in ¼ cup cold water for 5 minutes. Dissolve over hot water and add 2 cups clear chicken broth. Pour broth into ramekins to cover the eggs. Place in refrigerator. When nearly set, decorate the top of each with 1 slice truffle.

NOTE If truffles are not available, fresh tarragon leaves, slices of black olives, or a sliver of pimiento may be used.

EGGS IN ASPIC TARRAGON II

1 quart chicken broth
2 envelopes gelatin
8 poached eggs
8 fresh tarragon leaves *or* 1 tablespoon dried tarragon
paté de foie gras (preferably with truffles)
lettuce
mayonnaise
dry mustard

SERVES 8

FIRST Heat 1 quart chicken broth. Soak 2 envelopes gelatin in ½ cup warm water for 5 minutes. Then dissolve in hot broth and cool.

SECOND Poach 8 eggs and cool completely.

THIRD Pour enough aspic into small custard cups to cover the bottoms. Add 1 tarragon leaf (or, sprinkling dried tarragon).

FOURTH Mask each egg with paté de foie gras, smoothing it on with a knife, placing an egg in the center of each cup. Fill the cups with the remaining aspic and place in refrigerator until set. When ready to serve, invert cups on individual lettuce leaves and cover with a mayonnaise containing dry mustard to taste.

EGG RING

10 hard-boiled eggs
salt, pepper, dry mustard, chili sauce
2 tablespoons mayonnaise
2 heaping tablespoons gelatin
½ tablespoon vinegar
¾ cup cold water
1 cup heavy cream

FIRST Put 10 hard-boiled eggs through a potato ricer. Season with salt, pepper, dry mustard, and chili sauce to taste. Stir in 2 tablespoons mayonnaise.

SECOND Soak 2 heaping tablespoons of gelatin in ¾ cup cold water. Mix with ½ tablespoon of vinegar and soak together for 5 minutes. Dissolve over hot water. Add to the egg mixture and mix well.

EGG DISHES 53

THIRD Whip 1 cup of heavy cream until stiff. Fold into the egg mixture, blending well. Pour into a ring mold and place in the refrigerator until set.

NOTE Any tart green salad placed in the center of this ring is an appropriate addition to this recipe.

SWANS ON THE LAKE *Marie's*

2 envelopes gelatin
1 quart chicken broth
raw carrot, turnip, beet, and radish slices
water cress
12 hard-boiled eggs
fresh caviar *or* paté de foie gras

12 three-inch pieces uncooked spaghetti
paraffin
lemon wedges
toasted rye bread
truffles *or* black olives
mayonnaise

SERVES 12

FIRST Soak 2 envelopes gelatin in ½ cup cold water and dissolve over hot water. Stir into 1 quart chicken broth. Pour onto a round platter that has been decorated previously with "flowers" cut from slices of raw carrots, turnips, beets, and radishes, and the stems and leaves of water cress. Place the platter in the refrigerator until the aspic is set. *Be careful to arrange a place in the refrigerator beforehand, to accommodate the platter.*

SECOND Cut 12 hard-boiled eggs lengthwise, cutting away only enough of the white to permit the removal of the yolks. Fill the hollow white cases with fresh caviar or paté de foie gras.

THIRD Boil 12 three-inch spaghetti lengths only long enough to permit you to bend them without fear of breaking. Place them on a bread board and bend into the shape of swans' necks. Pin them in this fashion onto the board and add enough melted paraffin to cover. When the paraffin has hardened, the necks may be trimmed.

FOURTH While the "swans' necks" are cooling, place the filled egg whites carefully on top of the aspic. Replace all in the refrigerator. When ready to serve, put the necks in place and decorate the "lake" with pieces of canoe-shaped wedges of lemon. Serve with buttered, thin slices toasted rye bread.

NOTE "Wings" for the "swans" may be fashioned out of truffles if you are lucky enough to have some, or out of black olives. Paste on with a little mayonnaise. You can also give the "swans" eyes by painting the ends of the spaghetti. Other fillings may be used inside the egg-white cases.

BAKED EGGS IN SPINACH BOXES *Marie's*
[*Pre-heat oven to 400°*]

1 large loaf unsliced white sandwich bread
somewhat more than quarter pound soft butter
2 cups creamed spinach
1 cup minced creamed chicken or 1 cup finely cut creamed mushrooms
6 eggs
6 slices butter
salt, pepper, paprika

SERVES 6

FIRST Carefully remove all crusts from 1 large unsliced white sandwich bread. Cut entire loaf into six thick, *even* slices. With a sharp knife, scoop out the top and insides of each slice, leaving an even half-inch shell all around, so that each slice resembles an open box. Toast these "boxes" until brown. Cool.

SECOND Spread "boxes" thickly inside and out with somewhat more than a quarter pound soft butter. Then spread thickly with 2 cups creamed spinach (creamy enough to spread easily). Place "boxes" on a buttered cookie sheet. Fill "boxes" with 1 cup minced creamed chicken or finely cut creamed mushrooms.

THIRD Break an egg on top of each filling. Cap each egg with a slice of butter and salt, pepper, and paprika. Bake in 400° oven until egg whites are set. Serve quickly.

NOTE Nothing accompanies this dish so well as a tart salad. Serve no other bread.

CREAMED POACHED EGGS À LA HASH *Marie's*

2 tablespoons flour
½ cup grated cheese (optional)
½ pint cream
4 egg yolks
½ cup milk
salt, pepper
4 egg whites

2 tablespoons minced parsley
1 cup meat hash moistened with cream, soup, or gravy, or 1 cup creamed chicken
6 poached eggs
paprika

SERVES 6

SOUFFLÉ SAUCE

FIRST Beat together 2 tablespoons flour, ½ cup grated cheese (optional), and ½ pint of cream. Beat until free of all lumps. Add 4 beaten egg yolks and beat well.

SECOND Boil ½ cup milk and place in a double boiler. Stir the egg mixture into the milk. Continue to stir until it thickens and coats the spoon, as when making a custard sauce. Remove from the stove and stir until slightly cooled and very smooth and creamy. Add salt and pepper. Cool.

THIRD Add the stiffly beaten whites of 4 eggs and fold in 2 tablespoons of minced parsley.

[*Pre-heat oven to 375°*]

THE HASH AND THE EGGS

FIRST Put 1 cup hash, slightly moistened with cream, soup, or left-over gravy, into the bottom of a well-buttered baking-dish. Place 6 poached eggs on top of the hash and cover with the Soufflé Sauce. Place in a 375° oven for 25 minutes. Just before serving, sprinkle lightly with paprika.

NOTE Left-over lobster, crab, or shrimp may be used to good advantage in this recipe.

CURRIED EGGS JANE COWL

¼ pound butter
1 large onion, minced
1 heaping tablespoon curry powder
1 scant tablespoon flour

½ cup consommé
½ cup cream
12 hard-boiled eggs
cooked rice *or* toast

SERVES 6

FIRST Melt ¼ pound butter in skillet. In the butter brown 1 large, minced onion, stirring occasionally. Be careful not to allow onion to get too dark in color. Stir in 1 heaping tablespoon curry powder and 1 scant tablespoon flour. Rub in well, being careful not to permit any lumps to form. Continue to stir until smooth.

SECOND Blend in ½ cup consommé, a little at a time. Then add ½ cup cream, stirring until sauce thickens. When thick and smooth, add 12 hard-boiled eggs cut in half. Baste them with the sauce. Be careful not to crush the yolks.

THIRD Pour the eggs and sauce over a nest of rice or simply on rounds of toast.

NOTE Here is another way of preparing: Mash the hard-boiled yolks, add cream to soften, curry powder to taste, and a dash of salt. Fill the whites with this mixture. Stick the two halves together to give the appearance of whole eggs. Then cover with the curry sauce as given above.

EGGS WITH MUSHROOM STEMS

chopped stems from ½ pound fresh mushrooms
2 ounces butter
1 teaspoon flour
pepper, salt
2 egg yolks
½ cup light cream

2 tablespoons sherry *or* red wine
8 poached eggs
1 tablespoon vinegar
¼ cup milk
8 slices cooked ham
paprika

SERVES 8

FIRST Thoroughly chop the stems of ½ pound fresh mushrooms and fry lightly in 2 ounces melted butter until soft. Rub in 1 teaspoon

EGG DISHES 57

flour and add pepper and salt to taste. Beat 2 egg yolks with ½ cup light cream and 2 tablespoons sherry or red wine. Stir into the mushroom mixture until smooth and slightly thickened.

SECOND Poach 8 eggs very gently in simmering mixture of water, vinegar and milk in a large skillet. (1 tablespoon vinegar and ¼ cup milk to 2 cups water.) Remove and drain. Set on 8 individual slices of cooked ham on a hot platter. Pour sauce over the eggs and sprinkle with paprika. Serve hot.

FRENCH SOUFFLÉ OMELETTE Marie's
[*Pre-heat oven to 350°*]

6 egg whites
6 egg yolks
2 tablespoons cream
salt, pepper

1 tablespoon flour
chopped parsley
paprika

SERVES 4

Suggestions for filling: Creamed chicken, lobster Newburg, creamed peas, creamed asparagus.

FIRST Beat 6 egg whites until stiff. Add 6 egg yolks, one at a time. Beat together with a rotary beater until light and foamy.

SECOND Add 2 tablespoons cream, salt and pepper, 1 tablespoon flour, and some finely chopped parsley.

THIRD Bake in two 8-inch buttered pans in 350° oven just long enough to brown the omelet on the bottom and to have it retain its creaminess on top.

FOURTH When serving, place bottom of one layer on warm platter. Add filling (see above). Place second layer, creamy side against the filling. Sprinkle with chopped parsley and paprika. A small amount of the filling may be reserved to place on top of omelette for decoration, or a cross may be cut in the top of the omelette and the four corners at the center of the cross turned back to reveal the filling underneath.

NOTE This omelette should be light and airy and must be served immediately.

OMELETTE JURASSIENNE

1 tablespoon diced *or* shredded lean bacon	4 tablespoons grated Swiss cheese salt, pepper
1 shallot *or* 1 small onion	chopped chives *or* parsley
1 small boiled potato	3 eggs

SERVES 1

FIRST Lightly and slowly fry 1 tablespoon diced or shredded lean bacon. Add 1 chopped shallot or 1 small onion chopped fine and 1 small boiled potato diced.

SECOND When this is all lightly fried together, add 4 tablespoons grated Swiss cheese, salt and pepper to taste, and a generous sprinkling of chopped chives or parsley.

THIRD Beat three eggs and pour into the pan. Allow the omelette to set. While the top is still moist and somewhat creamy, fold the omelette with a spatula. Slide it from the frying-pan onto a warm plate and serve at once while still very warm.

SCRAMBLED EGGS, EDWIN

8 eggs	2 ounces butter
4 tablespoons sour cream	chopped chives (optional)
¼ teaspoon salt	

FIRST Beat 8 whole eggs with 4 tablespoons sour cream and ¼ teaspoon salt until well blended and light.

SECOND Melt 2 ounces butter in a double boiler. When rendered, pour in the eggs and allow them to set for 20 minutes, stirring occasionally. Chopped chives may be added if desired.

SCRAMBLED EGGS PAYSANNE

1 medium onion
2 cups canned tomato sauce
1 thick slice tenderized ham (about 1 pound)
pepper

12 eggs
salt, pepper
chives
2 ounces melted butter
paprika

SERVES 6

FIRST Chop 1 medium onion and cook with 2 cups canned tomato sauce in a pre-heated skillet. When the onion begins to soften, add 1 thick slice tenderized ham (about one pound) cut into cubes. Add a generous shake of black pepper and cook about 10 minutes.

SECOND Beat 12 eggs with salt, pepper, and chives to taste. Scramble them in 2 ounces melted butter, stirring constantly until set but not too dry. Arrange on a hot platter and surround with a wreath of the tomato-and-ham mixture. Sprinkle eggs with paprika.

NOTE A green salad and hot French bread go well with this.

SWISS EGGS

[*Pre-heat oven to 350°*]

6 thick slices Swiss cheese
6 eggs
2 tablespoons grated Swiss cheese

salt, pepper
½ cup milk

SERVES 6

FIRST Place 6 slices Swiss cheese in a flat, buttered baking-dish. Carefully break 1 egg on top of each slice of cheese. Sprinkle with 2 tablespoons grated Swiss cheese.

SECOND Sprinkle with salt and pepper. Add ½ cup warm milk and bake in 350° oven for 10 or 15 minutes.

SWISS SCRAMBLED EGGS

[*Pre-heat oven to 400°*]

3 tablespoons butter
8 eggs
½ cup milk *or* light cream
salt, pepper

thin slices Swiss cheese
1 tablespoon finely sifted bread crumbs

SERVES 4

FIRST Render 2 tablespoons of butter in a skillet. Beat 8 eggs with ½ cup of milk or light cream and pour into the skillet, stirring constantly with a fork until it begins to set. Salt and pepper to taste, then continue to stir until the eggs are set but still soft, and, *on no account, dry*. They are to be cooked more in the oven and must therefore *definitely be left soft.*

SECOND Pour them into a glass pie plate. Top with thin slices of Swiss cheese and dot with small portions of 1 tablespoon of butter.

THIRD Sprinkle with 1 tablespoon finely sifted bread crumbs and bake in a 400° oven until the top is lightly browned.

Chapter IV: *Seafood*

I wiped away the weeds and foam

I fetched my sea-born treasures home

RALPH WALDO EMERSON: (*1803–82*)

SHELLFISH

Baked Scallops with Mushrooms and Cream
Crab Mayonnaise
Crab Pie
Crab Wendy
Crawfish, Shrimp or Lobster Superb
Deviled Clams, Grandmère
Baked Lobster
Broiled Live Lobster with Pink Lobster Butter
Lobster Thermidor
Fried Shrimp
Shrimp Jambalaya
Seafood Goulash
Oyster Patties
Scalloped Oysters, Virginia

FISH DISHES

Basted Tuna Squares
Brook Trout in an Aspic Pond
Eighteen Small Crêpes Filled
Fillets of Sole Florentine
Fillets of Sole Marquery
Fillets of Sole in Parchment Paper Cases
Fillets of Sole in Parmesan Cheese
Fillets of Sole Queen Victoria
Fillets of Sole with Ham
Fillets of Sole with Rieseling
Fillets of Sole with White Wine
Salmon Mousse (hot)
Salmon Mousse Beauzon (cold)
Shad Roe Ring
Swedish Fish
Whitebait Fried

SEAFOOD

BAKED SCALLOPS WITH MUSHROOMS IN CREAM
[*Pre-heat oven to 400°*]

2 pounds scallops
salt and pepper
½ pound mushrooms
2 ounces butter

2 cups Marie's Cream Sauce (page 203)
½ cup grated cheese, either Swiss or American

SERVES 8

FIRST Butter a two-quart glass casserole. Place a layer of scallops in the bottom of the dish. Sprinkle with salt and pepper, cover with a layer of sliced mushrooms that have been lightly fried in 2 ounces of butter. Cover with 1 cup of Marie's Cream Sauce (page 203). Top this with a second layer of scallops, a second layer of mushrooms, and a second cup of Cream Sauce.

SECOND Sprinkle ½ cup of grated cheese (either Swiss or American) evenly on top of the casserole and place in a 400° oven for about 20 minutes.

CRAB MAYONNAISE

1 teaspoon gelatin
¼ cup cold water
1 cup mayonnaise (page 248)
1 quart picked crab meat
3 cups minced celery
2 tablespoons minced parsley
2 tablespoons minced chives (*or young onions*)

1 teaspoon chopped tarragon (fresh preferred)
6 olives
3 hard-boiled eggs
12 cold boiled shrimp
ketchup

SERVES 12

FIRST Soak 1 teaspoon gelatin in ¼ cup cold water for five minutes. Dissolve over hot water. Cool.

SECOND Stir the cooled gelatin into 1 cup mayonnaise (page 248). Fold the mayonnaise into 1 quart of picked crab meat.

THIRD Fold in 3 cups minced celery, being careful so as not to flake the crab meat into shreds. Add 2 tablespoons minced parsley,

2 tablespoons minced chives (or young onions), and 1 teaspoon chopped tarragon (fresh preferred).

FOURTH Put in a rinsed and chilled mold, and place in the refrigerator until set. When ready to serve, unmold onto a bed of shredded lettuce. Surround with olives, quartered hard-boiled eggs, and, if you like the idea, cold boiled shrimp, each shrimp dipped into ketchup.

NOTE Have you a mold shaped like a fish? Any attractive mold will do, but a fish shaped mold makes an extremely attractive picture.

CRAB PIE

Baked crust for 1 pie
¼ pound butter
3 cups picked crab
salt and pepper
pinch of sugar

5 egg yolks
1 cup heavy cream
¼ cup sherry
chopped chives *or* parsley

SERVES 6

FIRST Melt ¼ pound of butter in a deep skillet. Heat 3 cups of picked crab in the butter for several minutes. Season with salt, pepper, and a pinch of sugar.

SECOND Beat 5 egg yolks. Then beat 1 cup of heavy cream into the yolks. Pour over the crab and stir carefully without shredding the crab, stirring it over a medium flame until it is thick and smooth. Carefully and gradually add ¼ cup of sherry.

THIRD Pour this into a baked pie crust and sprinkle the crab with chopped chives or parsley. Serve immediately. Cut into wedges at the table, as for any pie.

WARNING The only thing to worry about are the egg yolks. Do not let them get too hot or they will curdle. Just stir and watch.

CRAB WENDY

2 ounces butter
½ cup flour
1 cup cream
1 cup milk
salt and pepper
2 beaten egg yolks
2 ounces butter
½ pound mushrooms

2 whole sliced shallots, *or* 1 small minced onion
1 dozen *tiny* white boiling onions
2 cups crab meat (fresh preferred)
½ cup sherry
Parmesan cheese
few thin slices of butter

SERVES 6

FIRST Melt 2 ounces of butter in a skillet. When melted, remove from the fire and rub in ½ cup of flour. Return to the fire and gradually stir in 1 cup of cream and 1 cup of milk. Season with salt and pepper, and beat in 2 well-beaten egg yolks. Blend well. Remove from the fire until ready for use. This is the sauce.

SECOND Melt about 2 ounces of butter in a skillet. Gently fry ½ pound mushrooms and 2 whole minced shallots (or 1 small, minced onion) in the butter until tender but not too dark in color. See to it that the mushrooms retain their shape.

THIRD Skin and boil 1 dozen tiny white boiling onions. When soft but not mushy, drain. Add the cooked mushrooms (and any of the frying-butter that may be left), the minced shallots or onion, and the tiny boiling onions to 2 cups of crab meat (fresh preferred).

FOURTH Add ½ cup of sherry. Then pour on the sauce. Fold the sauce in very, very carefully so as not to break up the pieces of crab meat. Shake the pot rather than handle the crab meat. If you *must* handle it, use a fork instead of a clumsy kitchen spoon.

FIFTH Heat slowly but *do not boil*. When well heated, set in a buttered pie dish and cover with Parmesan cheese and a few thin slices of butter. Place under the broiler and *watch* while it browns on top. Place a napkin on a platter, set the pie plate on the napkin, and serve bubbling hot.

CRAWFISH, SHRIMP, OR LOBSTER SUPERB

[*Pre-heat oven to 400°*]

empty shells of 100 crawfish, *or* 50 shrimp, *or* 4 lobsters
1 pound butter
1 quart broth (½ chicken broth, ½ consommé)
dash of Maggi *or* Kitchen Bouquet

1 tablespoon butter
1 heaping tablespoon flour
½ cup cream
dill, chopped fine *or* chives, chopped fine
cooked rice *or* barley

SERVES 6

To Prepare Sauce Start the Day Before

FIRST   Remove boiled crawfish, shrimp, or lobster from the shells. Set in refrigerator. Place the empty shells on a cookie sheet and set in a 400° oven for an hour until almost powder dry.

SECOND   Remove shells from the oven. When cool enough to handle, grind to a fine powder in the meat-grinder.

THIRD   Melt 1 pound of butter in a deep iron skillet. When thoroughly melted dump in the powdered shells and stir until all the butter is absorbed. Slowly add 1 quart of hot broth (½ chicken broth and ½ consommé) and a dash of Maggi or of Kitchen Bouquet. Stir until the butter floats to the top. Skim the butter into a bowl alongside the skillet. Stir and skim. Add more broth from time to time, until all the butter has been skimmed into the bowl.

FOURTH   Strain remaining broth in the skillet into a second bowl. When sufficiently cooled place both bowls in refrigerator overnight.

To Make the Sauce

FIRST   Blend 1 tablespoon melted butter with 1 heaping tablespoon flour until smooth. Slowly add 2 cups of the prepared broth to the butter and flour, and stir until thick and smooth. Add ½ cup of the butter you have skimmed from the skillet. Blend well and add

½ cup cream. If flavor is not strong enough, add additional skimmed butter. Any remaining butter may be used in sauces or in soups.

SECOND Stir in chopped dill or chopped chives as preferred. Heat crawfish, shrimp, or lobster in this sauce but do not boil.

THIRD Place hot boiled rice or barley on warm platter. Pour shellfish and sauce over rice or barley. Serve very hot.

NOTE The use of shrimp or lobster, although delicious, is for a conservative. Unless you have known the high adventure of packing off the entire family with a picnic basket to the banks of the nearest sweet-water stream where you catch the greedy crawfish with the uncomplicated aid of string and horse liver, you will never thoroughly appreciate this magnificent, original recipe.

DEVILED CLAMS, GRANDMÈRE

[*Pre-heat oven to 400°*]

1 large onion	1 cup cream
2 inner stalks of celery	4 well-beaten egg yolks
2 ounces of butter	¼ cup chives *or* spring onions
20 clams	buttered crumbs
salt and pepper	paprika

SERVES 6

FIRST Chop 1 large onion and 2 inner stalks of celery. Render 2 ounces butter in skillet. Brown the chopped onion and celery in the butter until glazed. Chop 20 clams and add to the onion and simmer. Salt and pepper to taste.

SECOND Stir in 1 cup cream, and when it boils turn off the fire. Stir in 4 well-beaten egg yolks and ¼ cup minced chives or spring onions.

THIRD Fill individual ramekins or baking shells quite full. Cover with buttered crumbs and bake in a 400° oven until brown and bubbling hot. Remove and sprinkle with paprika.

BAKED LOBSTER
[*Pre-heat oven to 400°*]

2 ounces butter
lobster liver
lobster coral (roe)
Worcestershire sauce

chopped chives *or* onions
4 teaspoons white wine *or* sherry
1 can drained mussels
2 split live lobsters

SERVES 4

FIRST Cream 2 ounces butter with the liver of the lobsters and any available lobster coral (roe) until smooth. Add Worcestershire sauce, chopped chives or onions, and 4 teaspoons white wine or sherry. If sherry is used, be sure to "flame" it first. (Heat, then set fire with match and allow it to burn out.)

SECOND Drain 1 can of mussels and fold carefully into the creamed mixture. Spread over the top of the lobster meat and fill the crevice in the shell. Bake in 400° oven from 12 to 15 minutes, depending on size of the lobster.

NOTE During baking time, prop lobsters so that they will not tilt and lose the butter mixture.

BROILED LIVE LOBSTER WITH PINK LOBSTER BUTTER
[*Pre-heat broiler for 30 minutes*]

3 live broiling-lobsters
½ pound butter
salt and pepper

2 lemons
Pink Lobster Butter (page 211)

SERVES 6

FIRST Have fish market split 3 live broiling lobsters in half. Spread each half with ¼ pound very soft butter. Salt and pepper, and sprinkle each half generously with lemon juice.

SECOND Place the lobster halves under the broiler, pre-heated for 30 minutes, and broil until done. The timing process of the broiling

SEAFOOD

will vary according to the size of the lobster and the heat of the oven. When they appear to be ready, slightly lift the meat of one half with a fork, and investigate the "doneness" of the underneath side. When ready, serve sizzling hot with Pink Lobster Butter (page 211).

LOBSTER THERMIDOR

[*Pre-heat oven to 450°*]

2 freshly cooked lobsters (2 pounds each)
3 ounces butter
⅔ cup Cream Sauce (page 203)
1 pint cream
1 tablespoon dry mustard
1 tablespoon butter

1½ cups Hollandaise Sauce I (page 207)
1 overflowing teaspoon tarragon vinegar
1 teaspoon chopped parsley
2 lemons, quartered
grated Parmesan cheese (optional)

SERVES 4

FIRST Remove the meat of 2 two pound lobsters and cut into cubes. Render 3 ounces butter in a good-sized skillet. Toss the lobster meat into the butter and simmer for a few minutes.

SECOND Make ⅔ cup Cream Sauce (page 203). Stir in 1 pint cream and add to lobster a little at a time.

THIRD Cream 1 tablespoon dry mustard with 1 tablespoon butter and add to sauce. Blend well, shaking skillet back and forth. Remove from flame and cool a little.

FOURTH Make 1½ cups Hollandaise Sauce I (page 207) and stir in 1 overflowing teaspoon tarragon vinegar and 1 teaspoon chopped parsley. Stir into lobster until the whole is well blended. Pack the 4 lobster shells with the meat of the lobster. Distribute any leftover sauce evenly over the lobster meat. Set the filled shells in a 450° oven for 5 to 10 minutes. Serve hot and bubbling with quartered lemons on the side.

NOTE If desired, the filled lobsters may be sprinkled with Parmesan cheese before setting them in the oven.

FRIED SHRIMP

1 pound fresh shrimp
1 large onion
whole cloves
1 lemon
sprigs of parsley
salt and pepper

bread crumbs
2 beaten eggs
oil for frying
1 large tomato
tartar sauce

SERVES 4

FIRST Boil 1 pound fresh shrimp for about 15 minutes in water with 1 large onion stuck with whole cloves, 1 lemon cut into quarters, several sprigs of parsley, salt, and pepper.

SECOND Remove the shells from shrimp and carefully remove black line from the backs. Dip each shrimp separately in bread crumbs, then in 2 beaten eggs, and again in bread crumbs. Fry until golden in deep fat. Drain on paper and serve on a round platter around a large tomato scooped out and filled with tartar sauce.

NOTE In the winter, when tomatoes are not so easily available, simply pour the sauce into a small round serving-bowl.

SHRIMP JAMBALAYA

1 large onion
3 cloves garlic
1 green pepper
2 stalks celery
3 sprigs parsley
2 tablespoons bacon fat
1 can tomato sauce

salt and pepper
pinch of thyme
1½ pounds large shrimps
2 ounces butter
1 pound rice
large oysters (optional)

SERVES 8

FIRST Chop 1 large onion, 3 cloves garlic (very, very fine), 1 green pepper, 2 stalks celery, and 3 sprigs parsley. Fry all together in 2 tablespoons rendered bacon fat until soft, being careful not to char.

SECOND Add 1 can tomato sauce. Stir well and season to taste with salt, pepper, and a pinch of thyme.

THIRD Cut 1½ pounds large shrimps into halves the length of each shrimp. Fry the shrimps in 2 ounces rendered butter until they start to curl. Add to the sauce mixture and simmer for half an hour.

FOURTH Boil 1 pound rice until soft. Rinse with cold water. Mix the shrimps and sauce with the rice. Large oysters, cut up, may be added to the sauce just before mixing with the rice. Heat and serve.

NOTE This is better the second day reheated.

SEAFOOD GOULASH

½ onion
½ clove garlic
1 green pepper
2 ounces butter
1 pound large scallops

2 cans tomato soup
1 pound raw shrimps (shells removed)
2 dozen large oysters
rice *or* toast fingers

SERVES 6

FIRST Lightly fry ½ onion, ½ clove garlic, and 1 green pepper (all chopped very fine) in 2 ounces butter. When onions have begun to glaze add 1 pound large scallops and simmer. Turn and simmer again until cooked.

SECOND Heat 2 cans tomato soup. Add the scallop mixture. Boil 1 pound shrimps (shells removed) in the soup until tender. Just before serving, drop in 2 dozen large oysters and cook for about 2 minutes (no longer). Serve over rice or in soup plates with toast fingers.

OYSTER PATTIES

2 dozen medium-sized oysters
½ cup milk
3 tablespoons butter
2 tablespoons flour
1 cup milk
cayenne pepper

salt
2 egg yolks
3 tablespoons brandy
4 patty shells
chopped parsley

SERVES 4

FIRST Heat 2 dozen medium-sized oysters in a pan with ½ cup of milk over a slow fire until the edges curl. Then cut each oyster into four pieces, discarding the hard core.

SECOND Render 3 tablespoons butter. Remove from the fire and work in 2 tablespoons flour until no lumps remain. Return to the fire and gradually add 1 cup of milk, a little at a time, stirring constantly in order to keep the white sauce very smooth. Add any oyster juice you may have and season with a pinch of cayenne pepper and salt to taste. Stir until smooth and thick. Remove from fire and cool a little.

THIRD Beat 2 egg yolks until light and add to the white sauce. Reheat over a slow fire and stir constantly until thick. Incorporate the oyster pieces in the sauce and add 3 tablespoons of the very best brandy. Fill warm, flaky patty shells. Sprinkle with chopped parsley and serve.

SCALLOPED OYSTERS VIRGINIA

[*Pre-heat oven to 400°*]

1 pint oysters
3 slices toasted white bread
butter

salt and pepper
Worcestershire sauce
4 slices bacon

SERVES 4

FIRST Drain the juice from 1 pint oysters. Cut 3 slices toasted white bread into little squares.

SECOND Butter a 1-quart glass baking-plate. Put in a layer of oysters with some salt, pepper, butter, and a little Worcestershire sauce. Next add a layer of toasted bread squares. Top with second layer of oysters and then bread squares until the dish is full. Cover with 4 slices bacon.

THIRD Place in a 400° oven until the oysters are done and the bacon is brown and crisp.

SEAFOOD

BASTED TUNA SQUARES

1 large can best tuna
½ green pepper
1 can anchovy fillets
small amount pimiento
1 hard-boiled egg
½ cup mayonnaise

¼ cup chili sauce
¼ cup ketchup
4 pieces white bread
¼ cup melted butter
¼ cup Worcestershire sauce

SERVES 4

FIRST Chop together the contents of 1 large can best tuna, ½ green pepper, 1 can anchovy fillets, a small amount of pimiento, and 1 hard-boiled egg.

SECOND Blend ½ cup mayonnaise, ¼ cup chili sauce, and ¼ cup ketchup.

THIRD Fry 4 pieces of white bread in ¼ cup melted butter. Cover the fried bread with the tuna mixture. Put mayonnaise sauce and ¼ cup Worcestershire sauce over the squares and baste.

BROOK TROUT IN AN ASPIC POND

PART I

6 trout
3 pints water
1 quartered lemon
1 quartered onion
parsley

celery
1 large carrot
pepper and salt
1 wineglass white wine
1 tablespoon tarragon

SERVES 6

To prepare the trout:

FIRST Place 6 trout in 3 pints water with 1 quartered lemon, 1 quartered onion, some parsley, a little celery, 1 large carrot cut into pieces, pepper, salt, 1 wineglass white wine, and 1 tablespoon tarragon. Simmer gently for about half an hour. To facilitate your handling the trout in removing, permit water to cool a little.

SECOND Remove the trout very carefully so as not to tear skin or break off heads or tails. This process is somewhat difficult, but the proper utensil in which to boil the trout will greatly help (see note). Place the trout on a fairly large round serving platter.

THIRD Strain the water in which the fish was cooked and cool to room temperature. It should measure somewhat more than a quart.

PART II

raw carrots	water cress
turnips	2 envelopes gelatin
radishes	½ cup warm water
beet slices	Cold Mustard Sauce (page 202)

To prepare the pond:

FIRST Decorate the fish platter with small flowers cut out of raw carrots, turnips, radishes, and beet slices. The stems and leaves of the flowers are of water cress. This process is a challenge to your ingenuity and imagination, and practice makes perfect. Before starting, just remember to keep your "flowers" small—never larger than an inch across.

SECOND Soak 2 envelopes of gelatin in ½ cup warm water. Dissolve over hot water (page 280) and add to the strained fish water. (The French call it "court bouillon.") Pour the liquid with care over the trout and "flowers." As you pour, the aspic will disturb the position of the decorations, but they will readjust themselves as they settle.

THIRD The only difficult part is in carrying the platter to the refrigerator. Be certain that you have made room for it ahead of time and are sure that the platter fits into the allotted space. Serve with Cold Mustard Sauce (page 202).

NOTE Instead of cooking the trout in a deep pot, use your enamel roasting-pan. If necessary, set it over two burners, one under either end of the pan. The shallowness of this utensil makes it much simpler to remove the trout when they are done.

EIGHTEEN SMALL CRÊPES FILLED

[*Pre-heat oven to 350°*]

1 can Maine clams
1 small can red salmon
½ can mushroom soup
½ teaspoon black pepper
1 tablespoon minced chives *or* green onions
1 tablespoon sherry
1 teaspoon flour
18 small Crêpes (page 345)
1 cup heavy cream
2 egg yolks
1 tablespoon chopped parsley

SERVES 9

FIRST Heat 1 can Maine clams and juice, 1 small can red salmon, ½ can mushroom soup, ½ teaspoon black pepper, 1 tablespoon minced chives or green onions, and 1 tablespoon sherry. Rub in 1 teaspoon flour to thicken.

SECOND Fill 18 small Crêpes (page 345) with this mixture. Roll each filled Crêpe in turn and place one next to the other in a buttered baking-dish.

THIRD Beat 1 cup heavy cream with 2 egg yolks until thick. Pour over the filled Crêpes. Sprinkle with tablespoon chopped parsley and set in 350° oven for 15 or 20 minutes.

FILLETS OF SOLE FLORENTINE

[*Pre-heat oven to 375°*]

1 cup Creamed Spinach (page 186)
6 fillets of sole (*or* flounder)
salt and pepper
2 ounces butter
½ cup minced mushrooms
½ cup freshly grated Parmesan cheese
1 cup Marie's Cream Sauce (page 203)

SERVES 6

FIRST Prepare 1 cup Creamed Spinach (page 186), spread it evenly on a flat well-buttered glass oven dish. Cover with 6 fillets of sole and sprinkle with salt and pepper.

SECOND Render 2 ounces butter in a skillet and add ½ cup minced mushrooms. Simmer until soft. Then pour the butter and mushrooms over the fillets.

THIRD Stir 3 tablespoons of freshly grated Parmesan cheese into 1 cup of Marie's Cream Sauce (page 203) and add plenty of pepper and salt. Pour sauce over the mushrooms and top the dish with the remaining Parmesan cheese. Bake in a 375° oven for half an hour.

NOTE If fillets of sole are not available, fillets of flounder may be used.

FILLETS OF SOLE MARGUERY
[Pre-heat oven to 375°]

8 fillets of sole	2 tablespoons butter
salt	2 tablespoons flour
juice of 1 lemon	4 ounces sweet butter
8 large shrimps	½ cup heavy cream
8 mushrooms	cayenne pepper
8 oysters	buttered parsley potato balls
Sauterne wine (best quality)	

SERVES 8

FIRST Salt 8 fillets of sole, fold with the ends tucked under, and place in a buttered shallow baking-dish. Sprinkle with the strained juice of 1 lemon and garnish each fillet with 1 large cooked shrimp, 1 cooked mushroom, and 1 raw oyster. Almost cover the fillets with a Sauterne wine of the best quality. Cover dish with buttered paper and place in a 375° oven to poach for not longer than 15 minutes.

SECOND Remove from oven. Keep fillets well covered and warm. Carefully pour juice into a casserole and reduce by boiling to about one third. Melt 2 tablespoons butter and rub in 2 tablespoons flour. Add the reduced juice to this paste and stir until smooth. Boil briskly for a few minutes, stirring well. Remove from fire. At this point turn on the broiler and allow to pre-heat.

THIRD Lightly stir in 4 ounces sweet butter with a wooden spoon, one small lump at a time. Add ½ cup unflavored heavy cream. Season with a pinch of cayenne pepper and salt to taste.

FOURTH Arrange the fillets on the center of a silver platter with the oysters, shrimps, and mushrooms. Pour sauce over all and place under the broiler for a minute or two to lightly brown. Put small, cooked potato balls that have been buttered and strewn with chopped parsley around the fish.

FILLETS IN PARCHMENT PAPER CASES

[*Pre-heat oven to 400°*]

6 parchment paper bags (see Note)
6 fillets of flounder
salt and pepper
pinch of thyme

6 pieces cold, cooked ham, ¼″ thick
18 good-sized cooked mushrooms
3 teaspoons minced parsley
½ cup melted butter
juice ½ lemon

SERVES 6

FIRST Butter 6 fairly thick fillets of flounder and sprinkle each with pepper, salt and a pinch of thyme. Place each fillet on a piece of cold, cooked ham, about ¼″ thick, trimmed to fit the shape of the fillets. Put 3 mushrooms (and a sprinkling of minced parsley) on top of each fillet. Place each unit on an individual sheet of parchment paper. Fold and turn the paper along the edges to prevent the escape of any of the juices.

SECOND Place the cases in a pan and brush each with melted butter. Bake 15 minutes in a 400° oven and serve each on individual plates without removing the bags. Serve with ½ cup melted butter mixed with the juice of ½ lemon.

NOTE This was first served us on the Italian Riviera. The intensity of the flavor is a great surprise to all. Parchment paper may be purchased in the better hardware stores.

FILLETS OF SOLE IN PARMESAN CHEESE
[*Pre-heat oven to 375°*]

2 cups grated Parmesan cheese
2 beaten egg yolks
dash of cayenne pepper
6 small fillets of sole
2 tablespoons butter

2 tablespoons flour
1½ cups milk
1 tablespoon heavy cream
1 teaspoon lemon juice
1½ cups grated Parmesan cheese

SERVES 6

FIRST Mix ½ cup grated Parmesan cheese with 2 beaten eggs. Add dash of cayenne pepper to 6 small fillets of sole. Lay the fillets on a greased baking-pan and cover with the egg mixture. Cover the dish with greased paper and bake in 375° oven for about 20 minutes.

SECOND Melt 2 tablespoons butter in the top of a double boiler and rub in 2 tablespoons flour until smooth. Gradually add 1½ cups milk, stirring constantly until mixture thickens. Add 1 tablespoon heavy cream and 1 teaspoon lemon juice. Remove paper from top of fillets and pour sauce over them, topping with 1½ cups grated Parmesan cheese and return to oven to brown. Do not leave in oven longer than 10 minutes or sauce will curdle.

NOTE If you prefer a very dark somewhat soft "Au gratin" top, set the dish under a pre-heated broiler instead of in the oven. But be sure to leave the door open. Watch it!

FILLETS OF SOLE QUEEN VICTORIA
[*Pre-heat broiler*]

4 carrots
parsley
2 large onions
salt and pepper
fish trimmings for stock (bones, heads, *or* tails)
2 cups water
1 cup fish stock
1 wineglass white wine (Chablis preferred)

1 tablespoon brandy
butter
2 tablespoons heavy cream
8 slices truffles
8 fillets of sole
milk
Parmesan cheese
puff paste *or* toast points

SERVES 8

FIRST Make a stock of 4 cut-up carrots, plenty of parsley, 2 large sliced onions, salt, pepper, some fish trimmings, and 2 cups of water. Boil for 35 minutes.

SECOND Strain the stock and measure out 1 cup, to which add 1 wineglass of white wine and 1 tablespoon of brandy. Stir in 1 teaspoon of butter and 2 tablespoons of heavy cream. If available, add 8 slices of truffles chopped fine. Simmer over a low fire.

THIRD Dip 8 fillets of sole in milk, then fry lightly in butter. Place them in a buttered glass oven-proof dish. Pour the sauce over them and scatter with grated Parmesan cheese. Place under a pre-heated broiler for a few minutes. Keep the broiler door open and watch carefully while the dish glazes. Serve, if possible, with bits of puff paste or, if more convenient, with toast points.

FILLETS OF SOLE WITH HAM

[*Pre-heat oven to 400°*]

4 slices baked ham
4 fillets of sole
4 small boiled onions
2 tomatoes
2 ounces butter

chopped parsley
¼ cup sherry
½ cup cream
1 tablespoon bread crumbs

SERVES 4

FIRST Butter an oven-proof glass pie plate generously. Set 4 slices of baked ham on bottom of dish. Cover each slice with a fillet of sole. Put in 4 small boiled onions and 2 skinned tomatoes (previously stewed in 2 ounces of butter). Add chopped parsley to taste.

SECOND Combine ¼ cup sherry and ½ cup cream with the butter in which the tomatoes were stewed. Pour this sauce over the fish and top with 1 tablespoon bread crumbs. Set the dish in a 400° oven for 10 minutes. At the end of that time, cover with an inverted pie plate and continue to cook for another 20 minutes, or until done.

NOTE If you poach the fillets in a little hot water with butter, salt, cloves, lemon juice and onion before assembling the dish, time may be cut in half. French bread is delicious with this, as the sauce must not be ignored.

FILLETS OF SOLE WITH RIESELING
[*Pre-heat oven to 400°*]

6 fillets of sole
2 finely minced shallots (*or* 1 small chopped onion)
salt and pepper

1 cup Rieseling wine
½ cup heavy cream
2 tablespoons butter
¾ cup seedless grapes

SERVES 6

FIRST Wipe 6 fillets of sole with a damp cloth. Grease a baking-pan and sprinkle the pan with 2 finely minced shallots (or 1 small chopped onion) and salt and pepper.

SECOND Place the fillets on top of the shallots. Cover with 1 cup of Rieseling wine and bake in a 400° oven for 10 minutes.

THIRD Drain the fish, place on a serving-dish and set in oven to keep warm. Add ½ cup heavy cream and 2 tablespoons of butter to the wine. Cook over a low heat, stirring occasionally, for ten minutes.

FOURTH Pour the sauce over the fish and sprinkle with ¾ cup seedless grapes.

FILLETS OF SOLE WITH WHITE WINE
[*Pre-heat oven to 250°*]

4 large fillets of sole
chopped shallots or green onions
3 tablespoons sliced cooked mushrooms
1¼ cup dry white wine
¾ cup water

2 tablespoons butter
2 tablespoons flour
juice of ½ lemon
¼ pound butter
salt and white pepper
cooked shrimp and oysters

SERVES 4

FIRST Take four large fillets of sole and arrange them in a flat buttered baking-dish. Sprinkle with chopped shallots or green onions and 3 tablespoons sliced cooked mushrooms. Cover with ¾ cup dry white wine and ¾ cup water. Bring to a boil and simmer for 4 or 5 minutes.

SECOND Remove fish to suitable serving-dish, and place in warming-oven at slow heat. Strain broth into a saucepan and reduce by boiling to one cup. Render 2 tablespoons butter in a separate pan and rub in 2 tablespoons flour until paste is smooth. Add the cup of broth, a little at a time, stirring constantly until smooth. Add ½ cup dry white wine, juice of ½ lemon, ¼ pound butter, beaten in until thoroughly combined, salt, and white pepper to taste.

THIRD Surround fish with warm cooked shrimp and a few lightly poached oysters. Pour sauce over all.

SALMON MOUSSE

[*Pre-heat oven to 350°*]

1½ pounds salmon
2 egg whites
salt, pepper, and a dash of cayenne

1 pint heavy cream
Sauce Mousseline (page 213)

SERVES 6

FIRST Put 1½ pounds salmon through a meat grinder 4 times. Pound with a masher. Then add 2 egg whites stiffly beaten but not dry. Add salt, pepper and a dash of cayenne. Then gradually pour in 1 pint of heavy cream.

SECOND Drop 1 tablespoon of this mixture into boiling water for about 3 minutes as a test. If, at the end of this time, it is too hard in the cooking, add more cream to the mixture. If too soft, add more beaten egg white.

THIRD Put the mixture in a mold, preferably one shaped like a fish, and cover with brown paper. Set the mold in a flat pan of boiling water and place in a 350° oven for about 18 or 20 minutes. Unmold and serve with Sauce Mousseline (page 213).

SALMON MOUSSE DE BEAUZON

2 tablespoons gelatin
scant ½ cup cold water
⅓ cup lemon juice
2 cups flaked, cold, cooked fresh salmon
1 heaping teaspoon grated onion
2 tablespoons capers

2 tablespoons Worcestershire sauce
1 cup mayonnaise
Tabasco to taste
salt
water cress
1 dozen large split shrimp
Cucumber Sauce (page 205)

SERVES 6

FIRST Soak 2 tablespoons gelatin in ½ scant cup cold water for 5 minutes. Dissolve over hot water. Add ⅓ cup lemon juice. Cool.

SECOND Mix 2 cups flaked, cold, cooked fresh salmon, simmered in herbs and water, 1 heaping teaspoon grated onion, 2 tablespoons capers, 2 tablespoons Worcestershire sauce, 1 cup mayonnaise, and Tabasco and salt to taste. Fold in the cooled gelatin, blend thoroughly. Place in a mold, and put in refrigerator until set.

THIRD Unmold on a bed of fresh green water cress, garnish with with 1 dozen large split shrimp and serve with Cucumber Sauce (page 205).

NOTE If you find the given amount of gelatin makes the Mousse too stiff for your taste, cut the gelatin to 1½ tablespoons. It is all a matter of preference.

SHAD-ROE RING

[*Pre-heat oven to 350°*]

1 shad-roe
1 grated onion
4 egg yolks
salt and pepper

4 egg whites
1 pint heavy cream
Hollandaise Sauce (page 207)
bacon

SERVES 6

FIRST Mash 1 raw shad-roe and mix with 1 grated onion, 4 egg yolks and salt and pepper to taste.

SECOND   Beat 4 egg whites until stiff. Beat 1 pint heavy cream until stiff. Fold into the raw mixture, not both at the same time however, first the egg whites, and then the cream folded in at the last. Put in a buttered ring mold in a warm pan of water and place in a 350° oven. Bake until set, or until a knife comes out clean.

THIRD   Serve with Hollandaise Sauce (page 207) on a platter with plenty of crisp bacon, either crumbled or left whole, decorating the ring.

SWEDISH FISH

3 to 4 pounds raw cod *or* halibut
1 egg
1 quart milk
salt, pepper, and pinch of nutmeg

bacon fat
tomato sauce (any good commercial brand)

SERVES 8

FIRST   Bone and skin 3 to 4 pounds raw cod or halibut. Put through the meat-grinder 3 times.

SECOND   Add 1 beaten egg to the fish. Beat well. Add 1 quart milk, a little at a time. Beat well after each addition, and beat at the end until the fish is light and fluffy and thick enough to stay together. Add salt, pepper, and a pinch of nutmeg.

THIRD   Drop mixture from a tablespoon into hot, fairly deep bacon fat and fry until well done. Drain on paper. Serve with tomato sauce.

WHITEBAIT FRIED   *Marie's*

[*Pre-heat oven to 275°*]

oil for frying
2 pounds whitebait
½ cup flour
salt, pepper, and paprika

1 large bunch parsley
lemons
tartar sauce or Paprika Butter (page 210)

SERVES 6

FIRST Heat oil in deep frying-pan. While oil is heating, prepare two pounds of whitebait.

SECOND Place whitebait in large paper bag with ½ cup flour, salt, pepper, and paprika. Shake the bag vigorously to coat the fish. Place fish in frying-basket, and before plunging into oil, shake to remove any excess flour. Plunge basket into smoking oil and fry fish to a deep, crisp brown.

THIRD Spread paper towels or napkins in oven. Drain fish on these and keep warm. Fry one large bunch of parsley until crisp. Drain parsley, place on hot platter, top with fish surrounded with quartered lemons. Serve with bowl of tartar sauce or Paprika Butter (page 210).

Chapter V: *Poultry*

And we meet with champagne and a chicken at last!

LADY MARY WORTLEY MONTAGU   (*1690–1762*)

CHICKEN

A Bird in Tarragon Cream
Baked Broilers in Cream
Budapest Chicken Paprika
Buttery Chickens
Capon par Excellence
Chicken à la King, Lily
Chicken Blintzes, Sylvia
Chicken Breasts on the Wing
Chicken in Custard and Rice
Chicken in Garlic Cream
Chicken Georgia
Chicken Malibu
Chicken Mervyn
Chicken Normande
Chicken Romanoff
Chicken Timbale
Cutlets Kiev
Danish Chicken
Fricassee of Chicken, Espagnole
Parisian Chicken Croquettes
Poulet à l'Archiduc
Two Chickens in White Wine
Young Chicken in Burgundy

CHICKEN LIVERS

Chicken Livers on Artichoke Hearts
Chicken Liver Pâté, Paul
Chicken Liver Ring

DUCK

Duckling with Sour Red Cherries
Duck Fredericka
Duck Pickings San Vicente
Duck Superb

PHEASANT

Pheasant Knopf
Pheasant Knopf in Gravy Aspic
Pheasant in Sour Cream
Young Pheasant with Raisin Purée

SQUAB

Broiled Squab in Brandy
Squabs in Marjoram
Stuffed Squabs
Wild Rice Stuffing

TURKEY

Turkey Cutlets, Nela
Turkey in Yellow Cream Sauce
Turkey Stuffing, Peter

A BIRD IN TARRAGON CREAM

five-pound roasting-chicken, young hen, or capon
salt, pepper
5 tablespoons tarragon (fresh preferred)
3 carrots
2 stalks celery
parsley
2 medium onions
4 tablespoons butter
3 tablespoons flour
1 wineglass white wine
1 cup chicken broth
1 cup cream
2 beaten egg yolks
cooked potato balls

SERVES 6

FIRST Rub a five-pound roasting-chicken, young hen, or capon inside and out with salt, pepper, and 2 tablespoons tarragon. Cut up 3 good-sized carrots, 2 stalks of celery, parsley, and 2 medium onions. Set the chicken and vegetables into a stew pot, cover with water, and cook slowly until tender. Be sure *not* to *overcook*, as the bird must be very juicy.

SECOND Skin the bird very carefully without tearing the meat. Leave whole and let stand in its own juices, well covered.

THIRD Render 4 tablespoons butter. Rub in 3 tablespoons flour until paste is smooth. Gradually add 1 wineglass white wine and 1 cup of strained chicken broth. Add 2 tablespoons tarragon and cook slowly. Turn the flame down and gradually add 1 cup warm cream, salt and pepper to taste, and 2 beaten egg yolks. Keep flame low and stir constantly. When the sauce thickens, remove from fire and pour it over the chicken (left whole and set in a deep dish). Spoon some of the sauce over the bird and sprinkle with 1 tablespoon tarragon. Put cooked potato balls (as many as desired) around the chicken into the sauce. Carve the bird in the dish, covering each portion with the sauce. Garnish each portion with cooked potato balls and serve. If you prefer, you may use white rice in a separate dish instead of the potato balls.

NOTE This dish came from the Latin Quarter in Paris, where in the 1920's, in the smallest places for the smallest prices, the quality of the food was the highest.

BAKED BROILERS IN CREAM

3 broilers, split
salt and pepper
flour

6 teaspoons butter
1 cup rich cream
half milk, half cream (optional)

SERVES 6

FIRST Split 3 broilers and season them with salt and pepper. Place them on a buttered baking-pan. Then sprinkle with flour and put a teaspoon of soft butter on each half. Cover them with 1 cup of rich cream. Let stand in the refrigerator overnight.

[*Pre-heat oven to 400°*]
SECOND Three quarters of an hour before serving, set the baking-pan in a 400° oven for about 15 minutes, or until well browned.

THIRD At the end of 15 minutes reduce the temperature to 350°, cover the pan tightly, and continue to cook for another half hour.

NOTE The cream will be absorbed by the chickens while baking. If necessary, add a small amount of half milk, half cream during the baking period.

BUDAPEST CHICKEN PAPRIKA ("Paprikas—Csirke")
Marie's

¼ pound butter
6 large brown onions
2 tablespoons paprika
1 teaspoon sugar
salt and pepper

3 two-pound broilers
flour
2 cups strong consommé
1½ cups heavy cream
cooked noodles

SERVES 6

FIRST Render ¼ pound butter in largest skillet. Chop 6 large brown onions and fry lightly until light gold but not brown. When they have begun to glaze, rub in 2 tablespoons paprika and 1 teaspoon of sugar. Salt and pepper 3 two-pound broilers. Cut each broiler into quarters, flour well, and fry slowly and lightly in the paprika butter for ten minutes on each side. Keep your fire moderate so as not to char the onions.

POULTRY 89

SECOND Add 2 cups strong consommé and stew the chickens in this for 20 minutes, turning them several times. Now add 1½ cups heavy cream, blending into the sauce by tipping the skillet back and forth. Simmer all together until the sauce thickens a little.

THIRD Remove from fire and skin each quarter carefully. Drain the sauce into a bowl, forcing the onions through a sieve. Wash the skillet so that no particles remain. (The sauce must be smooth and rich in texture and color.) Pour the sauce back in the skillet, taste for flavor, and add more cream and paprika if desired. Stir away all lumps. Then place the chicken pieces in the sauce, baste, and heat thoroughly without boiling. Serve on a hot round plate over a bed of buttered noodles or with a surrounding wreath of loose noodles. Pour some of the sauce over the chicken and serve the rest in a gravy boat.

NOTE Nothing is more delicious than this typical Hungarian Chicken Paprika. You will not find it difficult to prepare, and far less difficult to enjoy! Be fussy in the quality of paprika you select. Marie's Spätzle (page 165) may be used in place of the noodles.

BUTTERY CHICKENS

[*Pre-heat oven to 500°*]

3 small broilers (1½ to 2 pounds each)
butter *or* chicken fat
salt, pepper

flour
¾ pound butter
3 tablespoons chopped chives *or* green onions

SERVES 6

FIRST Rub 3 small broilers (left whole) with soft butter or chicken fat and sprinkle generously with salt, pepper, and flour. Stuff each chicken with ¼ pound butter and 1 tablespoon chopped chives or green onions.

SECOND Tie up the legs of each chicken and roast in a 500° oven for 15 minutes. Then turn down the heat to 400° and roast for 30 minutes more.

CAPON PAR EXCELLENCE

FROM THE MEDITERRANEAN

[*Pre-heat oven to 300°*]

¼ pound butter
⅛ pound salt pork, diced
1 fat capon
3 large carrots
6 small white onions stuck with cloves
marjoram *or* thyme
3 stalks celery
3 large sprigs of parsley
12 whole peppercorns

2 cans consommé
1 minced clove garlic
2 bay leaves
2 cans bouillon
dry white wine
salt
young vegetables to taste
Hollandaise sauce (optional)
½ cup heavy cream (optional)

SERVES 6

FIRST Render in a heavy pot ¼ pound butter and ⅛ pound salt pork cut into pieces. Place a fat capon in this and brown all over, turning from side to side. Remove capon and place in a slow oven to keep warm while the following "vegetable bed" is prepared: 3 large carrots cut into pieces, 6 small white onions stuck with cloves, a scattering of marjoram or thyme, 3 cut-up stalks of crisp celery, 3 sprigs of parsley, and a dozen peppercorns.

SECOND Place capon on top of the "vegetable bed." Add 2 cans of consommé, 1 minced clove garlic, and 2 bay leaves. Cover and put on a low flame until liquid is reduced one half. Carefully skim off fat and fill pot once more, this time with 2 cans bouillon and same amount of dry white wine. Salt well, replace cover, and stew slowly until done.

THIRD Remove capon skin. Carve bird into tidy pieces, place on a hot platter, and cover with some of the well-strained juices. Garnish with young vegetables, such as peas, baby carrots, baby lima beans, parsley potato balls.

NOTE In the Mediterranean restaurant where we first enjoyed this splendid dish, the final serving was accompanied by a bowl of Hollandaise sauce, strongly flavored with lemon juice and combined at the moment before serving with half a cup of heavy cream whipped to a froth. This really makes it a feast but is hardly necessary in following this recipe for everyday use.

CHICKEN À LA KING, LILY

1½ cups cut-up roasted chicken
2 tablespoons butter
2 tablespoons flour
1 cup hot chicken broth
1 cup hot evaporated milk
1 tablespoon onion juice

salt, white pepper
1 egg yolk
2 tablespoons sherry
½ cup cooked fresh mushrooms
1 teaspoon chopped parsley

FIRST Cut up 1½ cups roasted chicken into attractive pieces. (Never chop or mince.) Set aside.

To make your sauce, render 2 tablespoons butter in a skillet and rub in 2 tablespoons flour to make a smooth paste. Gradually add 1 cup hot chicken broth blended with 1 cup hot evaporated milk and stir until it thickens. Stir in 1 tablespoon onion juice and salt and pepper to taste. Simmer over a low fire, but not for long. Watch to keep it smooth.

SECOND Beat 1 egg yolk with 2 tablespoons sherry and add slowly to the sauce, stirring constantly. From this time on, never allow the sauce to get too hot or it will curdle.

THIRD Submerge the chicken in the sauce with ½ cup cooked fresh mushrooms. Scatter with 1 teaspoon chopped parsley and serve.

NOTE #1 This chicken à la king may be served in the center of a dish with crisp toast points surrounding it and a dash of paprika on top to give it a festive look. Please do not be tempted to pour it on top of toast squares unless you have a hankering for soggy bread. It may be served, if you hurry it to the table, inside puff-paste shells, provided they are thoroughly warm before filling and provided you know an excellent baker who will sell you some worth eating, or provided you have the will to follow Miggie's recipe for Puff-Paste Cases (page 409). They are, of course, far superior to any you can buy.

NOTE #2 Should you happen to have a little Hollandaise left over from the night before, try blending it with your sauce before adding the chicken. You will have a golden delight that will mystify your guests. I have never known anyone to discover the answer to this golden secret.

CHICKEN BLINTZES, SYLVIA

(12 blintzes)

THE FILLING

2 ounces butter	5 celery stalks
2 onions	½ pound mushrooms
½ green pepper	3-pound roasted chicken

SERVES 6

FIRST Render 2 ounces butter in a skillet. Slice very fine, 2 onions, ½ green pepper, and 5 celery stalks. Slice ½ pound fresh mushrooms. Place them all in the melted butter and fry lightly until the onions and celery are glazed and the mushrooms and peppers softened without being too soft.

SECOND Cut a 3-pound roasted chicken into ¼-inch cubes. Combine with the cooked vegetables. Set aside while preparing the batter for the Blintzes.

THE BATTER

1 cup milk	½ cup sifted flour
2 eggs	½ teaspoon salt
1 ounce butter, melted	

FIRST Combine 1 cup milk with 2 eggs and 1 ounce butter, melted. Add ½ cup sifted flour and ½ teaspoon salt. Beat until smooth.

SECOND Butter a small skillet very lightly. Pour in a small amount of batter, as for Crêpes Suzette (pages 345–6). Fry on one side only. When bubbly, turn out on a clean cloth, brown side up.

[*Pre-heat oven to 300°*]
THIRD   Fill with the chicken mixture and roll with the ends turned in. Place on a dish and pour Rich Cheese Sauce (page 204) over them. Bake in a 300° oven for 45 minutes.

[*Pre-heat broiler*]
FOURTH   Remove from the oven and place under the broiler for a few seconds until nicely browned.

CHICKEN BREASTS ON THE WING

6 chicken breasts with wing bones left attached
salt, pepper
6 slices ham
soft butter
2 beaten eggs

sifted bread crumbs (very, very fine—almost dust)
½ pound melted butter
paprika
fresh water cress

FIRST   Ask your butcher to remove 6 breasts of chicken from 3 fat fryers, taking off wing tips but leaving the main wing bone attached to each breast. Then have him pound each breast with the flat side of his cleaver.

SECOND   Sprinkle the 6 breasts with salt and pepper. Cut 6 slices of ham the approximate size and shape of the chicken breasts. Spread and seal them together with soft butter.

THIRD   Now dip each unit in 2 beaten eggs and drag lightly across a pastry board covered with sifted bread crumbs that are very, very fine—almost dust.

FOURTH   Heat ½ pound butter in a large skillet until bubbling. Fry these breaded chicken breasts lightly, first on one side, then on the other. Serve them very hot with all the remaining butter poured over them. Garnish with a sprinkling of paprika and fresh sprigs of water cress.

NOTE   This recipe came from a small Italian restaurant in Paris incongruously named San Francisco! The place is so small, the tables all too few, always jam-packed and always serving incredibly delicious and original food.

CHICKEN IN CUSTARD AND RICE

[*Pre-heat oven to 350°*]

½ cup rice
1½ cups chopped cooked chicken
1½ cups sliced mushrooms
⅛ lb. butter
salt, pepper
¼ teaspoon marjoram

parsley *or* chives (*or* both)
½ cup slivered blanched almonds
2 eggs
1 cup cream
½ cup chicken broth

SERVES 6

FIRST Drop ½ cup washed rice, a little at a time, into boiling salted water. Boil for about 20 minutes, or until tender. Drain and rinse in cold water.

SECOND Butter a casserole generously. Fill with alternate layers of 1½ cups cooked rice, 1½ cups chopped cooked chicken, and 1½ cups of sliced mushrooms lightly fried in ⅛ pound of butter. The mushrooms will be the top layer. Sprinkle each layer with salt, pepper, ¼ teaspoon of marjoram, chopped parsley, chopped chives and ½ cup of slivered almonds.

THIRD Beat 2 eggs into 1 cup of cream and ½ cup of chicken broth. Set on a moderate flame and stir until the mixture thickens and coats the spoon. Pour this sauce over the layers. Cover the casserole, stand it in a pan of warm water, and bake for 30 minutes in a 350° oven.

NOTE The sauce should seep throughout the casserole. Pour it in slowly and try to distribute it carefully.

CHICKEN IN GARLIC CREAM

cooked noodles *or* boiled white rice
5-pound roasting-chicken *or* fat capon
2 onions
2 whole cloves
thyme, sage (fresh preferred)
6 ounces butter
2 chopped white onions
3 level tablespoons flour

1 cup cream
2 cups strained chicken broth
2 minced, crushed cloves garlic
4 egg yolks
salt, white pepper
½ pound mushrooms
½ cup best sherry
paprika
chopped parsley

SERVES 6

FIRST Before starting with your chicken, boil noodles or white rice and put aside. Salt five-pound roasting-chicken or fat capon inside and out. Place in pot with water and 2 onions cut into quarters. Stick 2 whole cloves into 2 of the onion quarters, add some thyme and sage (fresh preferred). Simmer gently for 1½ to 2 hours, depending on the size and the tenderness of the bird. Do not boil hard, as the meat must not shrink.

SECOND When the chicken is cooked, start the sauce by melting 4 ounces of butter in a pan and adding 2 chopped white onions. Cook very slowly until the onions are barely soft. Remove from the fire and rub in 3 level tablespoons of flour and stir to a smooth paste. Return to the fire and gradually stir in 1 cup of cream combined with 2 cups of strained chicken broth. Continue to stir until the sauce thickens, but *do not boil!*

THIRD *Mince* then thoroughly crush 2 cloves of garlic. Add to the sauce and stir for several minutes over an exceedingly low flame. Remove from the flame and beat in 4 egg yolks, one at a time. Season to taste with salt and white pepper. Now *strain* the sauce.

FOURTH Skin and cut the chicken or capon into shapely pieces. Place them in the sauce and put the pan on a very slow fire. (It is best to use your largest skillet, where you will be able to baste the chicken pieces from time to time with the sauce.)

FIFTH Render 2 ounces of butter in a skillet. When bubbling hot, add ½ pound of fresh mushrooms (including the chopped-up stems). Cook, turning every now and then with a spatula, until softened. Pour in ½ cup of best sherry and stir until blended. Pour the entire contents of the skillet into a saucepan with the cooked noodles or boiled white rice. Use a fork and mix together. Heat altogether for a moment. Then make a nest of the noodles or rice on a hot serving-platter and set the chicken and garlic cream sauce in the center. Garnish lightly with paprika and chopped parsley. Serve immediately.

NOTE I have always envied my friend, Muriel Oakes Ames. She knew the Latin Quarter of Paris as most Americans only know the

Rue de la Paix. She took a group of her friends to dine one night somewhere in a neighborhood she knew and loved best. I shall always regret that I can't remember the name of the restaurant, but I do remember that we descended three or four steps to a dark, dingy little place where taxi drivers and petty merchants were breaking crisp French bread on the red and white checkered tablecloths and drinking the ruby red Vin du Pays. I don't suppose I shall ever forget that dinner. I present to you their magnificent Chicken in Garlic Cream and only regret that I shan't be with you to share your pleasure in your very first attempt.

WARNINGS 1. Do not boil your chicken or capon too fast or too long. If you do, the meat will shrink and be dry.
2. Once the cream and the egg yolks are added to the sauce, never leave it unwatched on the flame. Above all, never let it get too hot. If you do, it will curdle and that's the sad end of that!
3. If it's a chicken you choose to prepare, try to get a large, fat roasting-chicken. Most hens in the market are rather too old to do this recipe justice. The old girls have to be cooked too long, which is quite against the rules. If you do use a hen, be sure she's got some life left in her. When boiled chicken was served at home, my father used invariably to inquire: "Did this one vote for Lincoln?" It's not a bad idea to ask your poultry man just that.

CHICKEN GEORGIA

two 3- to 3½-pound fryers
flour, pepper, and salt
¼ pound butter
½ cup olive oil

marjoram *or* summer savory
2 ounces butter
tiny spring potatoes *or* potato balls
1 cup pecans

SERVES 6

FIRST Cut up 2 fat fryers, 3 to 3½ pounds in weight, and rub each piece thoroughly with flour, salt, and pepper.

SECOND Heat ¼ pound butter and ½ cup olive oil in a large skillet. Lightly fry the chicken pieces in this fat until brown on both sides. Sprinkle with marjoram or summer savory, according to preference. Turn down the flame, cover skillet, and simmer gently until chicken is tender. Place on very hot platter.

THIRD On top of chicken, toss tiny spring potatoes (or potato balls), previously boiled, skinned, and heated in 2 ounces melted butter until lightly browned. Add 1 cup pecans that have been warmed in the butter when the potatoes have been removed.

CHICKEN MALIBU

[*Pre-heat the broiler*]

2 broilers (2 pounds each)	1 cup heavy cream
1 cup brandy	chicken livers
¾ pound butter	chopped chives *or* parsley
salt, pepper, paprika	

SERVES 6

FIRST Sprinkle two 2-pound broilers with ¼ cup good brandy. Take a soft, clean, dry cloth and wipe the broilers with the brandy. *Do not wash them with water.*

SECOND Melt ½ cup of butter in a saucepan. Place the chickens in a dripping- or baking-pan, cover them with the melted butter, and add ¼ cup of brandy. Place under a pre-heated broiler. Broil until the chickens are half done, basting every now and then.

THIRD While still under the broiler, pour ¼ cup of brandy over the chickens. Watch, and when the brandy catches fire, remove from the broiler, allowing the brandy to burn itself out undisturbed. Add salt, pepper and paprika and return to the broiler to finish broiling.

FOURTH Melt ¼ pound of butter in a skillet. Turn the fire down to moderate and stir in 1 cup of heavy cream. Do not neglect to watch this. Stir every now and then. Do not let it boil.

FIFTH Mash a few chicken livers as thoroughly as possible with a fork. Stir the mashed livers into the sauce. Remove the chickens from the broiler, cut into six pieces each, and place on a serving-platter in the warming-oven until ready.

SIXTH Slightly cool the dripping-pan juice and strain. Remove the sauce from the fire and gradually add the strained juice, stirring all the while. Add ¼ cup brandy. Pour over the chicken and serve quickly. Just before serving, sprinkle the chicken with chopped chives or parsley.

WARNINGS 1. If the drippings are too hot when added to the sauce, the sauce is very likely to curdle, which spoils its creamy effect. It will taste the same but be far from appetizing to the eye. 2. Finish your sauce quickly, so that the chicken pieces do not have to stay too long in the warming-oven. They are supposed to be juicy and succulent, and if left too long they may scorch and dry out.

CHICKEN MERVYN

2 three-pound fryers
chicken fat *or* butter
salt, pepper, seasoning salt
1 #2 can Maine blueberries

¼ cup sugar
¼ cup Jamaica rum
chopped, fresh water cress
browned potato balls

SERVES 6

FIRST Split 2 three-pound fryers in half down the back, rub each with chicken fat or butter and season with salt, pepper and seasoning salt. Let stand several hours in the refrigerator.

[*Pre-heat broiler*]

SECOND Broil in pre-heated broiler for 15 minutes. Baste with the rendered fat several times during the cooking time.

THIRD Heat the contents of one #2 can Maine blueberries, with ¼ cup sugar, ¼ cup Jamaica rum and the drippings in the broilers. Stir until it just reaches the boiling point. Do not boil. Remove from fire and pour over the chickens (they may be quartered before placing on serving dish). Sprinkle the dish generously with chopped, fresh water cress. Surround with browned potato balls.

CHICKEN NORMANDE

[*Pre-heat oven to 375°*]

4-pound chicken
salt
¼ pound butter

1 pound cooking-apples
1 teaspoon sugar
1 wineglass cider

SERVES 4

FIRST Sprinkle a 4-pound disjointed chicken with salt. Then fry lightly in ¼ pound rendered butter.

SECOND Place chicken and butter in a glass baking-dish with 1 pound peeled and sliced cooking-apples sprinkled with 1 teaspoon sugar. Add one wineglass cider. Cover dish and set in a 375° oven.

THIRD Cook until chicken is done (about 45 minutes). Wrap a napkin around the baking-dish and serve.

NOTE Applejack or cider liqueur may be substituted for the cider.

CHICKEN ROMANOFF

1 cold boiled chicken (approximately 6 pounds)
4 ounces sherry wine
4 cups Cream Sauce (page 203)
salt and pepper

25 white cherries (pitted)
½ cup Hollandaise Sauce I (page 207)
½ cup whipping cream

SERVES 6

FIRST Cut 1 cold boiled chicken, weighing approximately 6 pounds, into even dice. Place these pieces in a pan and cover with 4 ounces of sherry wine. Heat slowly until the sherry wine is reduced by one half.

[*Pre-heat broiler*]

SECOND Mix the chicken with 3 cups of Cream Sauce (page 203) and season to taste with salt and pepper. Place the mixture in a chafing dish or in a large skillet. Distribute 25 white, pitted cherries evenly on top of the prepared chicken. Heat thoroughly.

THIRD Combine ½ cup Hollandaise Sauce I (page 207) with ½ cup whipping cream and the remaining cup of Cream Sauce I. Pour on top of chicken. Place under the broiler until golden brown. Watch carefully as this will only take a few minutes.

NOTE In trying to emulate this superb dish I do not cut my chicken pieces into such small dice that they cannot be appreciated. I believe that you will agree that "Emperor" Mike Romanoff does well to honor the kingly and queenly representatives of the motion picture screen with royal dishes such as this!

WARNING In placing a chafing dish or a skillet under the broiler, protect the handle against scorching. A small, wet rag will do the trick.

CHICKEN TIMBALE

2 uncooked breasts of 4-pound chicken	pinch of pepper
	2 egg yolks
1 tablespoon butter	1 pint heavy cream
1 teaspoon salt	Mushrooms Edwine (page 181)

SERVES 6

FIRST Put 2 uncooked breasts of 4-pound chicken through the meat-chopper twice. Then put through the potato-ricer or strainer.

SECOND Cream 1 tablespoon butter with the chicken. Add teaspoon of salt, pinch of pepper, and 2 lightly beaten egg yolks. Mix well until completely blended and place in coldest part of refrigerator for 20 minutes.

THIRD Whip 1 pint heavy cream until stiff. Place in coldest part of refrigerator for 15 minutes.

[*Pre-heat oven to 375°*]

FOURTH Butter ring mold or individual timbale molds. Blend chicken mixture with whipped cream and fill mold. Place mold in pan of warm water and bake in 375° oven for 20 minutes. Unmold onto warm platter and fill center of ring or surround individual timbales with Mushrooms Edwine (page 181).

NOTE If a large ring is desired, double the recipe. It is not necessary to serve this timbale with the mushrooms. It is delicious by itself with the accompaniment of Hollandaise Sauce (page 207). Roast the rest of the chicken and use in such dishes as Baked Eggs in Spinach Boxes (page 54) or Poached Eggs à la Hash (page 55).

CUTLETS KIEV

1 pound butter
1 clove mashed garlic
2 tablespoons chopped chives
2 tablespoons chopped parsley
salt, pepper
breasts of 2 roasting-chickens
flour

2 beaten eggs
1 cup sifted bread crumbs
oil
parsley, water cress, *or* carrot greens
mashed potatoes

SERVES 8

FIRST Cream 1 pound butter with 1 mashed clove of garlic, 2 tablespoons chopped chives, 2 tablespoons chopped parsley, and pepper and salt to taste. Set in refrigerator. When butter is hardened, measure into 8 separate amounts and roll each to the approximate length of your middle finger.

SECOND Carefully remove the breasts from 2 roasting-chickens. Skin carefully and separate each breast into 2 separate fillets (8 portions in all). Place each fillet between 2 sheets of wax paper and flatten with a meat-pounder—the thinner the better.

THIRD Salt and pepper each fillet. Place one of the butter rolls on top of each, roll lightly, and tuck ends in. Sprinkle sparingly with flour and dip each rolled fillet into 2 beaten eggs. Then roll lightly over 1 cup sifted bread crumbs and fry until amber-colored in moderately hot oil. Remove and drain on paper towels. Tuck a sprig of parsley, water cress, or carrot tops in the top of each and serve quickly with a dish of moist mashed potatoes.

WARNINGS 1. Be sure not to have your fat too hot; otherwise the crumbs will fry dark before the breasts have had a chance to cook through.

2. When you first prick them with your fork, watch out! The butter jumps out at you in a hot, aromatic stream!

DANISH CHICKEN

4-pound roasted chicken
2 tablespoons butter
3 tablespoons flour
1 cup consommé or 1 cup strained chicken broth

1 cup Hollandaise Sauce (page 207) (omit lemon)
1 or 2 tablespoons freshly grated horseradish
salt, pepper, and sugar to taste
boiled rice

SERVES 4 GENEROUSLY

FIRST Skin and carve a 4-pound roasted chicken into attractive portions. Keep warm on a hot serving-platter while making the sauce.

SECOND Render 2 tablespoons butter and rub in 3 tablespoons flour until smooth. Cook for 1 minute, then gradually add 1 cup boiling consommé or 1 cup strained chicken broth. Slowly add 1 cup Hollandaise Sauce (page 207) made without any lemon juice. Stir in 1 or 2 tablespoons freshly grated horseradish and salt, pepper, and sugar to taste.

THIRD Surround chicken with boiled rice. Pour sauce over and serve.

FRICASSEE OF CHICKEN, ESPAGNOLE

1 fat stewing-hen
salt, pepper
½ cup vegetable shortening
1 tablespoon chopped onion
herbs (parsley, tarragon, marjoram, and bay leaf)

1 tablespoon flour
1 wineglass dry white wine
1 quart chicken broth
saffron, nutmeg
1 cup cooked young peas
cooked brown rice

SERVES 6

FIRST Cut up 1 fat stewing-hen. Season with salt and pepper. Melt ½ cup vegetable shortening in a large skillet. Arrange the pieces of chicken in the skillet together with 1 tablespoon chopped onion and mixed herbs (parsley, tarragon, marjoram, and bay leaf). Turn the pieces several times. When chicken begins to brown, sprinkle with 1 tablespoon flour. Add 1 wineglass dry white wine. Simmer slowly until liquid is slightly reduced.

SECOND Add 1 quart chicken broth and allow chicken to simmer until tender, skimming carefully from time to time. Add a pinch of saffron and a pinch of nutmeg. When ready to serve, place the pieces of chicken on a hot platter, strain the sauce over all, scatter with 1 cup cooked young peas, and garnish with heaps of cooked brown rice.

PARISIAN CHICKEN CROQUETTES

1 pound cooked chicken	7 egg yolks
½ pound cooked mushrooms	butter
½ pound cooked ham	flour
truffles	pepper, salt
salt, pepper	finely sifted bread crumbs
2 tablespoons chives *or* spring onions	fat
1 cup Sauce Allemande (page 212)	Tomato Sauce, White Sauce, *or* Mushroom Sauce
	parsley

SERVES 6

FIRST Remove all skin and tendons from 1 pound of cooked chicken meat and dice into tiny pieces. Cut ½ pound cooked mushrooms and ½ pound cooked ham into equally small pieces. Chop a few truffles. Combine, scatter with salt, pepper, and 2 tablespoons minced chives or spring onions, and add 1 cup thick Sauce Allemande (page 212).

SECOND Set over very low flame and stir until somewhat dry. Remove from fire and mix in 4 beaten egg yolks. Pour into a glass dish, thoroughly buttered on all sides. Butter top of mixture with very soft butter to prevent caking. Place in refrigerator until thoroughly chilled.

THIRD Separate into pieces, each the size of half a 4-ounce cube of butter. Roll on a lightly floured board and shape into croquettes. Dip into 3 beaten egg yolks seasoned with salt and pepper, then into finely sifted bread crumbs. Drop into hot fat and fry until golden brown. Drain on paper towels and place on hot platter. Serve with tomato sauce, Cream Sauce (page 203), or Creamed Mushrooms (page 181). Garnish with parsley.

POULET À L'ARCHIDUC
[*Pre-heat oven to 325°*]

3½-pound chicken
3 tablespoons butter
3 tablespoons olive oil
1 jigger brandy
1 jigger whisky
1 jigger port wine

2 egg yolks
2 cups heavy cream
salt, pepper
2 ounces butter
cooked rice

SERVES 4 GENEROUSLY

FIRST   Cut one 3½-pound chicken as if for fricassee and fry in 3 tablespoons butter and 3 tablespoons olive oil until well browned. Put chicken in well-covered hot dish and set in a 325° oven to keep warm.

SECOND   Pour fat out of pan. Into same pan put 1 jigger brandy, 1 jigger whisky, and 1 jigger of port wine. Roll pan back and forth to loosen the juices that have remained in pan. Then simmer lightly to reduce the liquors to approximately ⅓ original amount.

THIRD   Beat 2 egg yolks with 2 cups heavy cream and salt and pepper to taste. Heat over a very low flame until it begins to slightly thicken. Add 2 ounces butter. When well blended, add reduced liquors, stir together, and pour over chicken. Serve with rice to do justice to the sauce.

NOTE   Never, under any circumstances, allow the sauce to boil!

TWO CHICKENS IN WHITE WINE
[*Pre-heat oven to 275°*]

two 3½-pound chickens
pepper, salt, marjoram
½ cup olive oil
½ cup butter
½ pound mushrooms
2 tablespoons chopped shallots *or* onions (*or* 1 clove garlic)

2 wineglasses dry white wine
2 jiggers brandy
2 tablespoons tomato purée
¼ teaspoon sugar
½ cup boiling water
2 tablespoons chopped parsley

SERVES 8

FIRST Cut two 3½-pound chickens into pieces as for fricassee. Season with pepper, salt, and marjoram. Fry until cooked through in ½ cup olive oil and ½ cup butter. Remove from skillet and place in covered dish in 275° oven to keep warm.

SECOND Simmer ½ pound mushrooms with 2 tablespoons chopped shallots or onions (or 1 chopped clove of garlic) until cooked through in the fat in which the chicken was fried. Add 2 wineglasses of dry white wine and 2 jiggers of brandy. Turn up the fire and cook rapidly for 5 minutes.

THIRD Stir in 2 tablespoons tomato purée, ¼ teaspoon sugar, and ½ cup boiling water. Turn flame down and simmer for several minutes until well combined. Sprinkle with 2 tablespoons chopped parsley and pour over the chicken.

YOUNG CHICKEN IN BURGUNDY

[*Pre-heat oven to 275°*]

3½-pound chicken
flour, salt, pepper
½ cup butter
⅛ pound diced salt pork
12 small mushrooms
6 small white onions

1½ cups red burgundy wine
herbs (parsley, chives, tarragon, and bay leaf)
3 tablespoons flour
¾ cups water

SERVES 4 GENEROUSLY

FIRST Cut up 3½-pound chicken as for fricassee. Roll each piece in flour seasoned with salt and pepper. Fry pieces lightly in ½ cup rendered butter until browned. Remove chicken from frying-pan. Render ⅛ pound diced salt pork in the butter in the same pan. Cook 12 small mushrooms and 6 small white onions in this fat. Place chicken on top of mushrooms and onions, cover with 1½ cup red burgundy wine, and simmer for 30 minutes.

SECOND Add small bunch of herbs (parsley, chives, tarragon, and bay leaf). Cover again and simmer 40 minutes more, or until tender. Remove chicken to a hot platter and keep warm in a 275° oven.

THIRD Make a smooth paste of 3 tablespoons flour and ¾ cup water. Add gradually to liquid and vegetables in the skillet, stirring well after each addition until completely blended. When all is added, simmer 5 minutes, stirring constantly. Pour over chicken and serve.

NOTE If fresh herbs are not obtainable, the dried variety may be used instead.

CHICKEN LIVERS ON ARTICHOKE HEARTS

6 cooked artichoke hearts
6 cooked chicken livers
Mushrooms Edwine (page 181)
paprika
toast points

SERVES 6

FIRST Place 6 cooked artichoke hearts on individual serving-plates. Cover each with 1 cooked chicken liver cut into 6 slices. Cover the whole with 1 recipe Mushrooms Edwine (page 181).

SECOND When ready to serve, sprinkle with paprika. Serve with crisp toast points. Above all, serve hot.

CHICKEN-LIVER PÂTÉ, PAUL

[*Pre-heat oven to 250°*]

1 pound ground chicken livers
½ pound pork sausage
salt, pepper
½ cup minced parsley
1 cup chopped celery
2 onions
1 tablespoon prepared salt seasoning
pinch of cloves
1 whole beaten egg
¼ pound bacon
raw strips bacon
French bread

SERVES 6

FIRST Cut 1 pound of chicken livers into small pieces, then grind them in the meat-chopper, using as fine a knife in the chopper as possible. Mix with ½ pound ground pork sausage.

SECOND Season with salt, pepper, ½ cup minced parsley, 1 cup chopped celery, and 2 onions chopped very fine. Add 1 tablespoon prepared salt seasoning, a pinch of cloves, and 1 whole beaten egg. Beat the mixture until everything is well combined.

THIRD Render ¼ pound of bacon and drain on paper towels. Pour the drippings into the liver mixture and crumble the fried bacon into tiny bits. Add the bacon and work the mixture until the bacon fat is thoroughly incorporated.

FOURTH Set the mixture in a glass baking-dish, either flat or casserole-shaped, cover the top with a few raw strips of bacon, and set in a 250° oven to bake for about 2 hours. Cool. Set in refrigerator, and when thoroughly chilled, remove the bacon strips that have been placed on top of the paté, turn out onto a platter, and serve with toasted or fresh French bread.

NOTE Rendered chicken fat or lard (about ¼ pound) may be used instead of the bacon drippings. Dehydrated onions and parsley may be used instead of the fresh, but the flavor will not be quite so keen.

CHICKEN-LIVER RING

½ pound *fresh* chicken livers
5 eggs, slightly beaten
½ pint cream

¼ teaspoon salt
greens of spring onions *or* chives

SERVES 6 GENEROUSLY

FIRST Soak ½ pound fresh raw chicken livers in cold water for half a day. Dry, then mash through a strainer.

SECOND Mix the strained livers with 5 slightly beaten eggs and ½ pint of cream. Beat well and add ¼ teaspoon salt.

[*Pre-heat oven to 350°*]

THIRD Grease ring form and cut tops of spring onions or, better still, chives until very fine. Place in bottom of form and cover with liver mixture. Steam for 20 minutes in a pan of warm water in a 350° oven.

NOTE This is particularly delicious with a filling of Creamed Mushrooms in the center (page 181).

DUCKLING WITH SOUR RED CHERRIES

1 young duck
salt, pepper, marjoram
2 cups strained chicken broth
1 wine glass sweet sherry *or* Madeira

½ teaspoon arrowroot
2 tablespoons butter
2 tablespoons flour
2 cups canned, sour red cherries

SERVES 4

FIRST Rub 1 young duck inside and out with salt and pepper. Season with salt, pepper, and marjoram. Set in a heavy stew pot with 2 cups strained chicken broth. Cover and simmer lightly for 45 minutes or 1 hour, depending on the size of the bird.

[*Pre-heat oven to 275°*]

SECOND Add 1 wineglass of sweet sherry or Madeira and ½ teaspoon arrowroot diluted in a little cold water. Boil for 3 minutes. Remove the duck from the broth, then remove the skin. Carve into nice pieces. Place on a serving-platter and keep warm in the oven.

THIRD Render 2 tablespoons butter and rub in 2 tablespoons flour. Add to the broth as a thickening, stirring constantly. Add 2 cups of drained, canned, sour red cherries to the gravy and pour over the duck. Serve very hot.

DUCK FREDERICKA

1 duck
salt, pepper
1 onion
1 herb bouquet (sage, 2 bay leaves, marjoram, basil)
dry red wine

½ cup olive oil
1 clove garlic
boiled wild rice
Fresh Peas in Sour Cream (page 184)

SERVES 4

FIRST Cut 1 duck as for fricassée. Clean pieces with a damp cloth, dry with a dry cloth, and salt and pepper. Set them in a deep mixing-bowl and add 1 chopped onion and 1 herb bouquet (sage, 2 bay leaves, marjoram, and basil). Cover the whole with dry red wine and let stand for 24 hours.

SECOND Remove duck pieces and brown in ½ cup olive oil with 1 bruised clove of garlic. When the pieces are brown, cover with the wine sauce in which they have soaked. Place in a casserole and simmer at slow heat on top of stove until done.

THIRD Remove pieces of duck to a hot platter, strain the sauce over them, and serve with boiled wild rice and fresh Peas in Sour Cream (page 184).

DUCK PICKINGS SAN VICENTE

[*Pre-heat oven to 450°*]

all the pickings from the left-over carcass of a roast duck (no skin)
1 or 2 raw duck livers
1 small onion, minced
½ cup cooked creamed spinach
1 teaspoon butter, melted
1 strip fried bacon, minced

1 thick slice raw chopped eggplant
salt, pepper, paprika
marjoram
4 tablespoons duck gravy *or* stock
butter
1 scant cup grated nippy yellow cheese

SERVES 4

FIRST Put all the pickings of a left-over carcass of 1 roast duck (no skin) and 1 or 2 raw duck livers through the meat-grinder together with 1 small onion, minced.

SECOND Add ½ cup cooked creamed spinach, 1 teaspoon melted butter, 1 strip fried minced bacon, and 1 thick slice raw chopped eggplant. Mix well and add salt, pepper, paprika, and pinch of marjoram. Moisten with 4 tablespoons duck gravy or stock.

THIRD Put a thin slice of butter in the bottom of individual baking-dishes. Measure duck mixture evenly in the dishes, but do not fill to full measure—leave about ¼ inch on top for the cheese. Cover with individual tops or greased paper to prevent drying, and place in a 450° oven for about 15 minutes.

FOURTH Remove from oven. Remove tops and scatter evenly with the contents of 1 scant cup grated nippy yellow cheese. Place under broiler flame for 5 minutes, or until cheese is glazed and smooth. Watch this process through open broiler door. Before serving, sprinkle paprika on top of each dish.

NOTE Chicken, turkey, or squab left-overs may be treated in the same way. This dish may be served in a casserole if preferred.

DUCK SUPERB *Marie's*

2 ducks, each about 4 or 4½ pounds dressed	1 strip bacon
	1 cube sugar
2 tablespoons chicken fat *or* butter	whole peppercorns
salt	1 wineglass white wine
4 slices onion	1 cup water
1 small clove garlic	

SERVES 8

FIRST Smear a Dutch oven lightly with 2 tablespoons chicken fat or butter. Put in 2 dressed ducks, salt well, and add 4 slices onion, 1 small clove of garlic, 1 strip bacon, 1 cube sugar, and whole peppercorns to taste. Add 1 wineglass white wine and 1 cup water. Cook until almost done, turning the ducks now and again.

SECOND Remove the skin from the ducks, carve into attractive pieces, and return to the Dutch oven to keep warm.

GRAVY

1 tablespoon chicken fat *or* butter	gravy from the ducks
1 tablespoon flour	few drops gravy concentrate (optional)
½ cup consommé	
1 cup sliced mushrooms	½ cup white wine *or* sherry
1 tablespoon Worcestershire sauce	

FIRST To make the gravy, render 1 tablespoon chicken fat or butter and rub in 1 tablespoon flour. Gradually add ½ cup consommé, 1 cup sliced mushrooms, 1 tablespoon Worcestershire sauce.

and the strained gravy from the ducks. Simmer until the mushrooms are done. If the gravy is insufficiently dark in color, add a few drops of gravy concentrate.

SECOND When ready to serve, add ½ cup white wine or sherry, bring to a rapid boil and remove from the fire.

GARNISH

2 dozen button mushrooms	1 tablespoon cream
1 tablespoon butter	duck gravy
1 small tin paté de fois gras	24 pitted green olives

FIRST Simmer 2 dozen finely chopped button mushrooms in 1 tablespoon butter. Stir in the contents of 1 small tin paté de fois gras and 1 tablespoon cream. The mixture must be moist and smooth. If necessary work in a small amount of the duck gravy. Stuff 24 stoned green olives with this mixture.

SECOND Place the pieces of duck on a warm platter with some of the prepared gravy and garnish with mushrooms and the stuffed olives. Serve the rest of the gravy in a gravy boat or bowl.

PHEASANT KNOPF

[*Pre-heat oven to 550°*]

1 pheasant	3 sliced celery stalks
5 tablespoons butter	4 sprigs parsley
salt, pepper	½ cup chicken broth
6 slices bacon	1 cup claret wine
1 sliced carrot	2 ounces currant jelly

SERVES 4

FIRST Grease 1 pheasant with 4 tablespoons creamed butter. Place 1 tablespoon butter inside the pheasant and sprinkle the outside with salt and pepper. Drape 6 slices of bacon over the bird and place in a small roasting-pan on top of a bed of the following vegetables: 1 sliced carrot, 3 sliced celery stalks, and 4 sprigs of parsley.

SECOND Add ½ cup chicken broth and 1 cup claret wine. Place in a 550° oven for 20 minutes. Turn oven down to 350°, cover the roasting-pan, and cook for half an hour. Remove the cover from the roasting-pan and return the heat to 550°. Brown for 10 minutes. Baste three times during the last 10 minutes.

GRAVY Strain the pan gravy and mix with 2 ounces of melted currant jelly. Serve very hot in a separate bowl.

NOTE See Pheasant in Gravy Aspic (page 112) for an excellent method of preparing any left-over pheasant.

PHEASANT KNOPF IN GRAVY ASPIC

left-over pheasant	¼ cup cold water
water cress	1 cup left-over gravy
½ envelope gelatin	Pheasant Knopf (page 111)

FIRST Remove bones from any left-over pheasant. Lay it on a small platter deep enough to hold the jellied gravy to be made. Decorate with tiny sprigs of water cress.

SECOND Soak ½ envelope gelatin for 5 minutes in ¼ cup cold water and dissolve over boiling water. Heat 1 cup gravy and stir in the gelatin. Pour over pheasant, cool, and place in refrigerator to set.

NOTE This is to be used with left-over pheasant and pheasant gravy from the recipe Pheasant Knopf (page 111).

PHEASANT IN SOUR CREAM

½ cup olive oil	1 cup dry white wine
young pheasant	1 teaspoon dried thyme
salt, pepper	boiled small new potatoes (optional)
flour	
1 large white onion	paprika (optional)
1 cup sour cream	chopped parsley (optional)

SERVES 4

FIRST Set ½ cup olive oil to heat in a Dutch oven or deep earthenware casserole over a low flame. Carve 1 young pheasant into quarters. Season the pieces with salt and pepper and dredge with flour. Place them in the heated oil. Cook them carefully, first one side, then on the other. They must *not* brown.

SECOND Add 1 large white onion sliced into coarse pieces. Add 1 cup sour cream and 1 cup dry white wine. Sprinkle the dish with 1 teaspoon dried thyme. Cover the pot and simmer gently for about 45 minutes, turning the pieces of pheasant every now and then.

THIRD Boiled new potatoes may be added to the top of the dish just before serving. In this case, dash them with paprika and sprinkle them lightly with chopped parsley.

NOTE Should your pheasant be brought to you with his feathers still on, and you are having a difficult time removing them, this dish may be prepared by simply removing feathers and skin together.

YOUNG PHEASANT WITH RAISIN PURÉE

[Pre-heat oven to 350°]

young pheasant	½ cup sherry
brandy	1 cup chicken broth
½ lemon	1 cup seeded raisins
salt, pepper	2 tablespoons sugar
nutmeg	pheasant liver
4 slices bacon	½ cup chicken broth
2 thin slices ham	parsley
1 tablespoon melted butter	

SERVES 4

FIRST Wash 1 young pheasant with a cloth wet with brandy, dipping the cloth several times and not sparing the brandy. Rub the bird, inside and out, with ½ lemon and allow to dry. Season with salt, pepper, and a pinch of nutmeg. Stuff the inside of the bird with 4 slices of bacon and 2 thin slices of ham.

SECOND Cover the bottom of a roasting-pan with 1 tablespoon melted butter combined with ½ cup of sherry and ½ cup of chicken broth. Place the pheasant in this pan and set in a 350° oven. Baste frequently. When it begins to brown, cover.

THIRD Cook 1 cup seeded raisins in salted water until tender. Add 2 tablespoons sugar and press through a sieve. Set aside. Cook the pheasant liver for 5 minutes in ½ cup chicken broth. Mash and set aside.

FOURTH Remove the bacon and ham from the inside of the bird, put through the meat-grinder, and place in a pan with the mashed liver and all the remaining broth. Heat well. Serve the bird garnished with parsley and with a side dish containing the gravy. Just before serving, spread the raisin purée thickly on top of the gravy. Serve with mashed potatoes.

BROILED SQUAB IN BRANDY

3 jumbo squabs
bacon fat
salt, pepper, marjoram
2 ounces butter
½ pound fresh mushrooms

few drops gravy concentrate
¼ cup best brandy
browned potato balls
chopped parsley

SERVES 6

FIRST Have your poultryman split 3 jumbo squabs down the back and prepare them for the broiler. Grease them generously with bacon fat and sprinkle them liberally with salt, pepper, and marjoram. Set aside in the kitchen for at least one hour before broiling.

[*Pre-heat the broiler*]

SECOND The mushrooms may be prepared while the squabs are waiting. Wash and dry carefully. Remove the caps and reserve the stems for another occasion. Melt 2 ounces of butter in a skillet and fry the mushroom caps lightly. Allow them to brown, but do not permit them to lose their well-rounded shape. Turn off the flame and return your attention to the squabs.

THIRD Pop the squabs into the broiler, which must be very hot indeed. Broil them first on one side until deep gold in color, then turn and broil them on the other side. Baste them with the seasoned grease that will have poured into the well of the broiler. Do this several times (at least three times) on each side. Turn again, watch, and do not allow any scorching.

FOURTH Reheat the mushrooms add a few drops of gravy concentrate, 2 tablespoons bacon fat and ¼ cup the best brandy. Shake the skillet well. Remove the squabs to a warm platter and pour the gravy over the birds. Surround them with browned potato balls and sprinkle the whole with chopped parsley. Serve immediately while very hot.

SQUABS IN MARJORAM

[*Pre-heat oven to 500°*]

4 fat squabs	1 cup water
2 ounces soft butter	3 ounces butter
salt and pepper	squab livers
marjoram	tart jelly
squabs' gizzards, hearts and necks	

SERVES 4

FIRST Smear 4 fat squabs inside and out with 2 ounces soft butter, salt and pepper. Sprinkle profusely with marjoram inside and out.

SECOND Simmer the squabs' gizzards, hearts, and necks in 1 cup water and 1 ounce butter. At the same time lightly fry the squab livers in 2 ounces butter. When the gizzards, hearts, and necks are cooked through, add the livers with the butter in which they were fried. Set this aside on a very low flame. Use as a basting for the squabs.

THIRD Set squabs in a 500° oven for 20 minutes. Reduce the heat to 350° and cook for half an hour or more, basting frequently with the broth. The squabs may remain in the oven for less than the allotted time, but not for more. They are intended to be crisp on the outside and to remain juicy, even slightly pink, on the inside.

FOURTH Mash the squab livers and add them to the natural pan gravy. Serve very hot with a side dish of tart jelly, such as currant or plum.

NOTE Wild Rice Stuffing (page 116) may be used if desired. Personally I find the squabs remain juicier without stuffing of any sort.

STUFFED SQUABS

4 squabs	4 chicken livers
butter	milk
salt, pepper	

FIRST Ask your butcher to remove the breast bones of 4 squabs. Rub each squab inside and out with soft butter and season with salt and pepper. Set in the refrigerator for 24 hours.

SECOND Soak 4 chicken livers in a little milk for 24 hours. Lightly season with salt and pepper.

[*Pre-heat oven to 450°*]

THIRD Stuff each squab with 1 chicken liver. Bake in a 450° oven for 15 minutes. Reduce heat to 350° and continue baking for an additional half hour, basting every 10 minutes with the drippings in the pan and, if necessary, a little butter melted in a cup of boiling water.

WILD-RICE STUFFING

1½ cups wild rice	½ teaspoon poultry seasoning
3 tablespoons cubed salt pork	3 ounces melted butter
3 tablespoons chopped onion	½ pound chopped cooked mushrooms
1½ tablespoons minced parsley	
1 teaspoon marjoram	¼ cup coarsely chopped pecans

FIRST Wash 1½ cups wild rice several times in cold water. Cover with three inches salted boiling water and boil hard for 20 minutes. Stir occasionally during boiling. Drain and return to pot. Shake dry over a low flame.

SECOND Render 3 tablespoons cubed salt pork in a skillet. Add 3 tablespoons chopped onions and fry until lightly browned.

THIRD Add onions and rendered salt pork to the rice. Combine 1½ tablespoons minced parsley, 1 teaspoon marjoram, ½ teaspoon poultry seasoning, 3 ounces melted butter, ½ pound chopped cooked mushrooms, and ¼ cup coarsely chopped pecans and add to rice.

NOTE This recipe is sufficient to stuff 6 squabs or 1 large roasting-chicken or capon.

TURKEY CUTLETS NELA

2 pounds raw breast of turkey	salt, pepper
3 slices bread	chopped chives
milk	flour
3 eggs	¼ pound butter

SERVES 6

FIRST Put 2 pounds raw breast of turkey through the meat-grinder. Combine with 3 slices bread soaked in a little milk and 3 beaten eggs. Flavor with pepper, salt, and chopped chives to taste.

SECOND Shape the paste into cutlets, roll in flour, and fry lightly in ¼ pound rendered butter.

NOTE Mrs. Artur Rubinstein's delicious cutlets are equally good made with chicken breast.

TURKEY IN YELLOW CREAM SAUCE

3 cups cooked turkey	2 cups Yellow Cream Sauce (page 204)
¼ cup best sherry	2 slices white toast
1 cup button mushrooms	
salt, white pepper	

SERVES 6

FIRST Cut 3 cups cooked turkey into half-inch pieces. Put into a saucepan with ¼ cup best sherry and 1 cup cooked button mushrooms. Season with salt and white pepper.

SECOND Pour 2 cups Yellow Cream Sauce (page 204) over turkey mixture. Shake the pan over low flame so sauce will cover every piece of meat. Do not allow the sauce to become too hot or it will separate.

THIRD Pour into the center of a hot round platter and surround with 3 pieces toasted white bread, crusts removed and each cut into 4 diagonal points.

TURKEY STUFFING PETER

turkey giblets
2 large onions
¼ pound butter
1 bunch celery (medium)
1 bunch parsley (medium)
1 bell pepper
1½ pounds pork sausage meat

1 teaspoon sage
1 teaspoon thyme
4 cups bread crumbs
salt, pepper
1 egg
1 cup milk

FIRST Put turkey giblets on to boil for half an hour with a little celery. Reserve the broth for basting the turkey, cut the giblets into small pieces and set aside.

SECOND Chop 2 large onions and brown lightly in ¼ pound rendered butter.

THIRD Chop one bunch celery, 1 bunch parsley and 1 bell pepper. Mix with 1½ pounds pork sausage meat and add to browned onions. Then add 1 teaspoon sage, 1 teaspoon thyme, 4 cups bread crumbs and salt and pepper to taste.

FOURTH Beat 1 egg with 1 cup milk. Use this to moisten dressing. Add cut-up giblets. Mix well.

NOTE This makes sufficient dressing for a medium-sized turkey.

Chapter VI: *Meats*

But we hae meat and we can eat

Sae let the Lord be thankit.

Robert Burns: *Grace before Meat,* 1795

BEEF

Beef Casserole
Beef Stew Bourguignonne
Beef Stew with Tomato Sauce
Beef Stew in 6 Minutes
Beef Tongue with Raisins, Prunes
   and Almonds
Bœuf à la Mode Margot
Broiled Steak with Roquefort Cheese
Economical Country Casserole
Fillets of Beef Rapallo
Frankfurters in Casserole
Grenadine of Beef
Meat Balls
   with Buttermilk
   in Mushroom Stems Sauce
   Swedish
Race Horse Steaks
Sirloin Strips the Magnificent
Steaks Brizola
Thin Tenderloin Steaks

HAM

Baked Virginia Ham
Ham Butt (with Sauerkraut and
   Salami)
Ham Decorated for a Buffet Table
Ham Steak from Virginia
Tenderized Ham with Apricots

LAMB

Lamb Chops, Wendy
Lamb Stew Dellarobbia
Rack of Spring Lamb
Stuffed Lamb Chops

PORK

Chop Suey
Polish Pâté, Rubinstein
Pork Chops in Gravy

VEAL

Calves' Brains au Beurre Noir
Calves' Liver in Sour Cream
Hungarian Stew
Stuffed Breast of Veal
Veal Casserole with Sour Cream
Veal Chops in Tomato Sauce
Veal Cutlets in Sherry
Veal Cutlets Vienna (Wiener
   Schnitzel)
Veal Kidneys in Brandy Sauce
Veal Kidneys in White Wine with
   Mushrooms

BEEF CASSEROLE

3 pounds top round steak
flour, pepper, salt, paprika,
    gravy-seasoning salt, cayenne
bacon fat
2 cloves garlic *or* 1 onion
hot water

2 cups fresh peas
2 bunches spring onions (green)
2 cans button mushrooms
1 cup chili sauce
marjoram
1 cup good red wine

SERVES 6

FIRST Take 3 pounds top round steak, cut into small pieces, roll each piece in flour, pepper, salt, paprika, gravy-seasoning salt, and a pinch of cayenne; then brown in bacon fat together with 2 minced cloves of garlic or 1 onion chopped fine.

SECOND Place the meat, and scrape the fat in which meat was browned, into a deep casserole or Dutch oven. Pour hot water into the pan to remove all the bits of meat and seasoning; add to casserole with sufficient additional water to bring the liquid to the level of the meat. Cook until almost tender.

THIRD Add 2 cups fresh peas, cook another 10 minutes, then add 2 bunches spring onions with tails cut partly off, 2 cans button mushrooms, 1 cup chili sauce, salt, pepper and marjoram. Stir chili sauce with the rest of the gravy and cook until done, being careful not to cook too much for the sake of the vegetables, especially the green onions which must be added last. Just before serving add 1 cup good red wine.

NOTE This excellent beef casserole has several advantages. First, it will beautifully absorb any left-over vegetables or small amounts of cooked spaghetti, macaroni, or diced potatoes as well as, or in addition to, the ingredients mentioned in the recipe. Then, too, it permits the hostess to join her guests with perfect poise and absolute ease during the cocktail period.

BEEF STEW BOURGUIGNONNE

12 small cubes salt pork (approximately ¼ pound)
12 small white onions
2 pounds round steak cut into 2-inch pieces
1½ tablespoons flour

salt, pepper, thyme, marjoram
1 cup burgundy wine
1 cup bouillon *or* water (bouillon preferred)
12 small potato balls
½ pound sliced mushrooms

SERVES 6

FIRST Fry 12 small cubes of salt pork and 12 small white onions in a hot skillet until brown. When browned, remove and set aside.

SECOND Fry 2 pounds round steak, cut up into 2-inch pieces, in the same skillet until brown on all sides. Sprinkle beef with 1½ tablespoons flour, mixed with 1 generous pinch of salt, pepper, thyme, and marjoram.

THIRD Put the meat in a heavy saucepan (iron preferred) and add 1 cup of burgundy wine (domestic will do) and 1 cup of bouillon or water (bouillon preferred). Cover closely and cook for five hours as slowly as possible.

FOURTH Three quarters of an hour before serving, add the strained browned onions and cubes of salt pork to the beef, along with 12 small, uncooked potato balls and ½ pound uncooked sliced mushrooms.

NOTE The flavor is improved if the stew is prepared in the morning and reheated. The sauce should be thick and dark brown. Serve with crusty French bread, red wine, and a tart green salad and pretend that you are dining under the stars in Montmartre!

BEEF STEW WITH TOMATO SAUCE

3 pounds stewing-beef
flour
¼ pound butter
3 onions, cut into small pieces
1 cup boiling water
salt and pepper

1 bunch carrots, cut into even slices
12 small white whole onions
1 can tomato sauce *or* tomato concentrate
additional boiling water

SERVES 6

FIRST Cut all fat away from 3 pounds of stewing-beef. Do not wash the meat. Wipe and blot dry with paper towels. Put on bread board and cover thoroughly with flour, rubbing with hands.

SECOND Render ¼ pound butter in a deep iron skillet and brown the meat on all sides. When brown, cut up 3 onions into small pieces and add to meat. Cook again until onions are lightly browned. Then add 1 cup boiling water, plenty of salt and pepper, cover tightly, and let simmer for approximately two hours.

THIRD Add 1 bunch carrots, cut up into even slices, 12 small whole white onions, and cook about twenty minutes. Add 1 can tomato sauce, or if a stronger flavor is desired, 1 can of tomato concentrate, and sufficient additional boiling water to cover meat. Keep well stirred and cook until done.

NOTE This is a simple dish to prepare, but the combination of the ingredients affords a wonderful rich color to the gravy, unlike the usual beef stew. One of its practical advantages is that it can be made ahead of time and reheated just before serving.

BEEF STEW IN SIX MINUTES

3 club steaks (ask for minute steaks) 1 inch thick
salt, pepper, paprika
flour

¼ pound butter
½ cup best sherry
water cress

FIRST Remove all fat and gristle from 3 club steaks. Then cut into one-inch pieces. Roll pieces in salt, pepper, paprika and flour.

SECOND Render ¼ pound butter in a skillet over a moderate flame, add meat and ½ cup best sherry. Cover the skillet and cook for exactly six minutes. Serve immediately on a round dish, surround by sprigs of crisp water cress. Mashed potatoes make an excellent addition.

NOTE There is no reason why this recipe could not be used to good advantage with left-over pieces of steak or roast beef. However, these pieces must be very tender.

BEEF TONGUE WITH RAISINS, PRUNES AND ALMONDS

1 fresh beef tongue
2 onions, sliced
2 bay leaves
3 sprigs parsley
½ lemon, sliced
6 whole peppercorns
1 tablespoon salt
1 teaspoon black pepper
1 tablespoon butter
1 teaspoon flour

½ cup tarragon or cider vinegar
¼ cup red wine
½ cup sugar
¼ teaspoon ground cloves
¼ teaspoon cinnamon
¼ teaspoon spices mixed
½ cup seedless raisins
1 cup soaked prunes
¼ cup blanched almonds

FIRST Wipe one fresh beef tongue with a damp cloth. Place in a good-sized pot and cover with cold water. Add 2 sliced onions, 2 bay leaves, 3 sprigs of parsley, ½ sliced lemon, 6 whole peppercorns, 1 tablespoon salt, and 1 teaspoon black pepper.

SECOND Bring to a gentle boil, then simmer between 2 and 3 hours, depending on size and tenderness of tongue. Test with a fork. As long as it feels hard, it is *not* done. When tender, remove from liquid, pull off skin, and return to pot to cool in its own water.

THIRD Melt 1 tablespoon butter. Rub in 1 teaspoon flour and gradually add ½ cup tarragon or cider vinegar and ¼ cup red wine, stirring constantly until thickened. Add ½ cup sugar, stir once more, then add the following spices: ¼ teaspoon ground cloves, ¼ teaspoon cinnamon, and ¼ teaspoon mixed spices.

FOURTH Warm ½ cup seedless raisins, 1 cup soaked prunes, and ¼ cup blanched almonds in this sauce. Place tongue in an iron pot or large, deep skillet and pour sauce over the tongue. Simmer very slowly for half an hour, turning tongue occasionally and basting every few minutes with the sauce. Serve, carved into even slices on a hot platter, surrounded and strewn with the raisins, prunes, and almonds.

NOTE If you have a little extra time, remove the prune pits and stuff the prunes with additional blanched almonds.

BŒUF À LA MODE MARGOT   Mrs. Julian Street

4- or 5-pound chunk or rump beef, bottom round, or any other available cut that will do for pot roast
1 pint red wine
1 small bay leaf
¼ teaspoon oregano
pinch thyme
8 peppercorns
vegetable oil or fat
2 cups strong beef stock or 1 can undiluted bouillon
2 or 3 bouillon cubes
¼ cup good brandy
2 diced onions
3 carrots, cut up fine
2 or 3 sprigs parsley
handful celery leaves
1½-2 pounds cracked soup bones
2 bunches carrots
16 small white onions
6 branches celery
2 generous tablespoons butter or margarine
flour or arrowroot (optional)

SERVES 6

FIRST Have your butcher lard with hard suet a 4- or 5-pound chunk of rump beef, bottom round, or any other available cut that will do for pot roast. Place this meat in a deep glass or earthenware container and pour the following over it: 1 pint of red wine, to which has been added, 1 small bay leaf, ¼ teaspoon oregano, a pinch of thyme, and 8 peppercorns. Marinate for 24 hours, turning the meat occasionally.

SECOND Four hours before serving, remove the meat from the marinade (reserve the marinade), dry thoroughly, and brown well in hot vegetable oil or fat. While the beef is browning, add the following to the marinade: 2 cups of strong beef broth, or 1 can of undiluted beef bouillon and 2 bouillon cubes. Heat the marinade to the boiling point.

THIRD Place the beef on a trivet in an earthenware soup kettle or deep casserole. Pour over it ¼ cup good brandy and light. When the brandy is burned out, pour the boiling marinade over the roast. Add 2 diced onions, 3 carrots cut very fine, 2 or 3 sprigs of parsley, a handful of celery leaves, and 1½-2 pounds of cracked soup bones. Seal the cover on with waxed paper and simmer slowly for about three hours.

FOURTH An hour and a half before serving prepare 2 bunches of carrots, each cut lengthwise into quarters or eighths, 16 small white onions left whole, and 6 branches of celery cut to match the carrots in size. Render 2 generous tablespoons butter or margarine in a saucepan and add the carrots. Cook them very slowly for ten minutes. Now add the onions and the celery, continuing to cook them very slowly, turning frequently so that they do not brown but become slightly softened.

FIFTH Three quarters of an hour before serving remove the meat and the soup bones. Strain the sauce. Replace the meat in the kettle and add the vegetables and the strained liquid. Taste and season. Add 1 more bouillon cube if extra flavor and salt are necessary. Cover again and continue simmering until done.

SIXTH A few minutes before serving transfer a portion of the sauce to a small saucepan; thicken for gravy with flour or arrowroot rubbed in carefully until well blended. Serve the meat on a platter surrounded by the vegetables and serve the gravy separately in a sauce boat.

NOTE Strain the balance of the sauce and set aside to jell for future use. This may be poured into small mounds, to be turned out and served with the cold sliced meat as a left over.

BROILED STEAK WITH ROQUEFORT CHEESE

[*Pre-heat broiler for 30 minutes*]

¼ pound Roquefort cheese
¼ cup cream
2 tablespoons Worcestershire sauce

2 two-inch club steaks (bones removed)
salt and pepper

SERVES 4 GENEROUSLY

FIRST Cream ¼ pound Roquefort cheese with ¼ cup cream and 2 tablespoons Worcestershire sauce. Work until mixture is smooth.

SECOND Broil 2 two-inch club steaks on one side until brown. Salt and pepper. Turn the steaks and cover the uncooked sides thickly with the Roquefort paste. Broil again until brown. Serve very hot.

MEATS

ECONOMICAL COUNTRY CASSEROLE

[*Pre-heat oven to 350°*]

3 pounds potatoes
salt, pepper to taste
1 small branch celery
1 green pepper

3 medium onions
1½ pounds ground round steak
1-pound can solid-pack tomatoes

SERVES 6

FIRST Butter a casserole. Slice in a layer of potatoes from a total quantity of 3 pounds and season with salt and pepper. Cover the potatoes with ⅓ of a branch of celery, coarsely chopped, and ⅓ of 1 green pepper, finely sliced, and 1 medium onion thinly sliced. Season.

SECOND Cover these vegetables with a layer of ground round steak. Season meat, repeat layers until casserole is almost filled. (Three layers in all.)

THIRD Pour the contents of 1-pound can of solid-pack tomatoes over top layer of ground round steak and bake in 350° oven for an hour and a half.

FILLETS OF BEEF RAPALLO

[*Pre-heat broiler for 20 minutes*]

2 ounces butter
1 small onion
1 box mushrooms
6 center slices, 1 inch thick, from a whole tenderloin of beef
Salt, pepper, paprika
6 slices bread, 1 inch thick

Butter
Sage, thyme, and/*or* marjoram leaves
6 cold boiled potatoes
melted butter, flavored with herbs

SERVES 6

FIRST Render 2 ounces butter in a skillet and slightly brown 1 small minced onion. When onion is brown, add 1 box fresh mushrooms, turn down flame, and allow to simmer slowly.

SECOND Cut 6 even slices, 1 inch thick, from center of a whole tenderloin and rub each slice with salt, pepper, and paprika. Cut six 1-inch slices bread from a loaf of white bread and shape with a sharp kitchen knife to exact shape of tenderloin slices, then butter thickly on each side. Press a leaf of any preferred fresh herb (thyme, sage, or marjoram) on to each buttered slice of bread. Arrange tenderloin and bread slices alternately on a skewer long enough to handle the whole and long enough to balance ends on the rims of a well-buttered dripping-pan. (See note.)

THIRD Take 6 cold boiled potatoes, cut into slices, and drop into dripping-pan. Pour additional butter over them and balance the skewer with the alternate slices of meat and bread on the ends of the dripping-pan. Place under a very hot broiler and broil for 15 minutes, basting now and again with melted butter flavored with mixed herbs of the variety used on the bread slices.

FOURTH When meat is done, remove the potatoes with a broad spatula to a hot platter, pour a little melted butter over them, then hold the skewer over the potatoes and carefully push the meat and bread off on the top of the potatoes. Empty the mushrooms and contents of skillet over all. Replace under broiler to reheat for 1 minute. Serve quickly.

NOTE A skewer long enough to accommodate the slices of tenderloin and bread and at the same time long enough to permit its ends to rest on either end of a dripping-pan is not the simplest thing in the world to find. I know because I spent the better part of a week, darting in and out of hardware stores, looking. My search came to an end when a bright young man in one of the stores suggested I buy a 10-cent length (the exact length required) of heavy wire and allow him to straighten it and file one end to a point. This particular wire is the approximate circumference of a #8 knitting-needle.

FRANKFURTERS IN CASSEROLE
[*Pre-heat oven to 400°*]

1 pound frankfurters
1 quart sauerkraut

2 cups sour cream
paprika

SERVES 6

FIRST Peel and quarter 1 pound frankfurters. Mix with 1 quart sauerkraut. Heat in a 400° oven in a buttered casserole.

SECOND Add 2 cups sour cream and coat with paprika.

[*Pre-heat broiler*]
THIRD Just before serving, place under the broiler to brown the top.

NOTE Be sure to serve crisp, hot, buttered French bread with this delectable supper dish.

GRENADINE OF BEEF

[*Pre-heat oven to 450°*]

6 slices tenderloin of beef ½″ thick (out of the center of tenderloin)	2 ounces butter
	2 tablespoons Madeira wine
	3 tablespoons glaze (page 206)
salt and pepper	Mushroom Stems Sauce (page 209)

SERVES 6

FIRST Cut six slices, about ½″ thick, out of the center cut (the thickest part) of the tenderloin. Ask your butcher to lard each slice with tiny strips of salt pork or suet. Season with salt and pepper.

SECOND Render 2 ounces butter, brush each slice generously with the butter and place them in a pan in a hot oven (450°) for 8 minutes. Remove from oven and pour off fat. Combine 2 tablespoons Madeira wine and 3 tablespoons Glaze (page 206) and baste tenderloin slices. Return to oven for 2 minutes, basting once again before removing.

THIRD Arrange on a hot serving-dish and pour Mushroom Stems Sauce (page 209) around them.

BUTTERMILK MEAT BALLS

1 pound ground round steak	¼ cup olive oil
1½ cups buttermilk	1 cup sour cream
½ cup fresh rye-bread crumbs	4 tablespoons sherry
salt, pepper, flour	buttered noodles *or* rice
2 ounces butter	paprika

SERVES 6

FIRST Combine 1 pound of the best, freshly ground round steak with 1½ cups buttermilk and ½ cup fresh rye-bread crumbs. Season with salt and pepper and shape into meat balls. Roll in a scant amount of flour.

SECOND Render 2 ounces of butter in ¼ cup olive oil until hot. Fry the meat balls lightly on both sides. Be sure not to get them too well done or they will be dry.

THIRD Combine 1 cup sour cream with 4 tablespoons sherry. Pour over the meat balls and shake the pan from side to side. Remove the meat balls with a spatula and serve on top of a bed of buttered noodles or white boiled rice, according to preference. Pour the sauce over all and sprinkle with a dash of paprika.

NOTE If preferred, this mixture need not be shaped into meat balls, but may be poured on top of noodles or rice.

MEAT BALLS IN MUSHROOM-STEMS SAUCE
[*Pre-heat broiler*]

¼ pound butter
1 medium onion, well chopped
½ cup chopped parsley
stems from 1 pound of fresh mushrooms

salt, pepper
2 pounds ground round steak
1 beaten egg
¼ pound butter, melted
½ cup sour cream (optional)

SERVES 8

FIRST Render ¼ pound butter in skillet. Add 1 medium onion, well chopped, ½ cup chopped parsley, and the chopped raw stems of 1 pound of fresh mushrooms. Sprinkle with salt and pepper and stir back and forth with a spatula. Allow to simmer on a medium flame while preparing the meat balls.

SECOND Take 2 pounds *freshly* ground round steak (twice through the butcher's machine), place in a bowl, salt and pepper generously, and work in 1 well-beaten egg. Shape the balls large enough for an individual serving. Place in broiling-pan, pour ½ cup melted butter over them, and set close under broiler flame. Baste every few minutes with butter in the pan. Do not turn.

THIRD When the meat balls are well browned on top but still juicy and rare inside, remove to platter and pour mushroom-stems onion sauce over each. Serve immediately.

NOTE If desired, a sour-cream version of the mushroom-stems sauce may be used instead. This recipe will teach you never again to discard mushroom stems.

SWEDISH MEAT BALLS

½ pound pork
½ pound beef
½ pound veal
salt, pepper, nutmeg
2 medium-sliced onions
2 ounces butter
1 cup milk
¾ cup beer
3 eggs
2 pieces zweiback
Spaghetti and Spaghetti Sauce (page 159)

SERVES 6

FIRST Have your butcher put ½ pound pork, ½ pound beef, and ½ pound veal through his meat-grinder twice. Add salt, pepper, and pinch of nutmeg.

SECOND Lightly fry 2 medium-sliced onions in 2 ounces butter. Add to meat.

THIRD Combine 1 cup milk with ¾ cup beer and 3 beaten eggs. Soak 2 pieces of zweiback in this liquid and add to meat, mixing thoroughly.

FOURTH Shape meat balls with the help of a teaspoon. Let them stand half an hour. Then drop them in the skillet in which the onions were cooked and fry lightly on both sides. Serve with Spaghetti and Spaghetti Sauce (page 159).

RACE-HORSE STEAKS

12 very, very thin slices club steak (commonly known as "minute" steaks)
¼ pound butter
¼ cup chopped parsley *or* chives

SERVES 6

FIRST The only trick to complete success in this original and very delicious meat recipe is in getting your butcher to understand what you want. Ask him to bring out a piece of loin and have him place the club or "minute" steak on his slicing-machine. It is sliced raw as though it were a piece of cold luncheon meat, and sliced thin, thin, thin—exactly as though you were buying sliced roast beef at the delicatessen. Have the twelve slices, boneless of course, put on waxed paper, about three to a sheet, and covered with another sheet until the process is complete. Do not permit the raw beef slices to be piled one on top of another, as they stick and may tear when you try to separate them at home. The business of getting what you want is the only complication. The rest is easy, and the results superlative!

SECOND Render ¼ pound butter in a large skillet, scatter in ¼ cup chopped parsley or chopped chives or both. Gently lay the slices, a few at a time, in the butter. Fry them lightly, barely long enough to change their color, turn and do the same thing on the other side. Keep the finished steaks warm in the oven, ready to be served on a serving-platter.

THIRD When all the steaks are fried, pour the butter and herbs on top of the platter. Hurry to the table! Two per person is nothing, nothing at all!

NOTE Remember, *THIN!*

SIRLOIN STRIP THE MAGNIFICENT
[*Pre-heat broiler 30 minutes*]

1 sirloin strip	½ cup melted butter
olive oil	gravy extract
salt, pepper	water cress

SERVES 12

FIRST Have your butcher bone out a whole sirloin strip from a loin of beef. This is the sirloin used for club steaks, T-bone steaks, and porterhouse steaks. Ask for it left whole by itself trimmed off the bone and without the tenderloin.

MEATS 133

SECOND Rub the meat on both sides with olive oil. Salt and pepper generously. Brown all around in a red-hot skillet.

THIRD Place in a very hot pre-heated broiler for 15 minutes on each side.

FOURTH Remove from broiler and place in oven. Turn indicator to 400° and roast for five minutes.

FIFTH Pour off any juice left in the broiler, mix with ½ cup melted butter and enough gravy extract to give a rich color. Place meat on platter, pour juice over roast, decorate with water cress, and send to the carver.

STEAKS BRIZOLA

6 slices of raw prime ribs of beef   salt, pepper
¼ pound butter   2 tablespoons chopped parsley

SERVES 6

FIRST Ask your butcher to cut 6 slices of raw prime ribs of beef, quite, quite thin. Have him sandwich each slice between layers of paper and then flatten them with the side of his cleaver.

SECOND Sprinkle the slices lightly with salt and pepper on both sides. Set them aside for a few minutes while you put your largest skillet on the flame. Having heated it very thoroughly, render ¼ pound of butter.

THIRD Into this butter place the slices of beef, one at a time. Fry them carefully, first on one side then on the other, but do not fry them too long as they must remain slightly pink. Remove them to a platter, keeping the first ones warm in a heating oven until they are all prepared. Just before serving, sprinkle with 2 tablespoons of chopped parsley and pour over the slices the darkened butter in which they have fried. Hurry to the table with a side dish of "Per-taters!" (Page 195.)

THIN TENDERLOIN STEAKS

6 tenderloin steaks
6 squares butter (1 heaping teaspoon each)
3 tablespoons chopped parsley

1 recipe Mushrooms Edwine (page 181)
1 recipe Sauce for Meats (page 212)

SERVES 6

FIRST Have your butcher cut 6 tenderloin steaks, about $\frac{1}{2}$ inch thick, and place each one between two sheets of waxed paper and slap with the flat side of his cleaver. This will spread them and thin them out. Have some fat left on each steak.

SECOND Place the steaks directly into a piping-hot skillet and brown them quickly on both sides. The fat on the steaks will render, and the steaks will fry in their own fat.

THIRD Place on a platter and just before serving, put 1 square of butter (heaping teaspoon) on top of each steak. Sprinkle with an even distribution of 3 tablespoons of chopped parsley. Ring the steaks with 1 recipe of Mushrooms Edwine (page 181) and serve with 1 recipe Sauce for Meats (page 212) in a side bowl or sauce boat.

BAKED VIRGINIA HAM

1 Virginia ham
1 cup brown sugar
2 tablespoons molasses

1½ cups bread crumbs
whole cloves

FIRST Scrub 1 Virginia ham on top and bottom. Place in a large roasting-pan and cover with water. Let soak all night.

SECOND Next morning wash ham in cold water. Then place in roasting-pan, skin side down, and cover with fresh cold water and bring to a boil on slow fire. Cook until done or until bottom bone comes off by itself. Let soak overnight again, this time in the juice in which it was cooked.

[*Pre-heat oven to 275°*]

THIRD Next morning pull off the skin and cut away any excess fat. Mix 1 cup brown sugar with 2 tablespoons molasses. Rub this mixture over the ham "good and thick." Put 1½ cups bread crumbs on top of the ham, and stick with whole cloves. Bake in a 275° oven until brown and crust has formed.

NOTE This recipe comes from Helen whose home is in Richmond, Virginia. Helen is a natural born Virginia cook, a statement of fact that all Virginians realize incorporates the highest praise. All the Virginia recipes in this book are hers.

HAM BUTT WITH SAUERKRAUT AND SALAMI

[*Pre-heat oven to 350°*]

1½ pounds garlic salami
1 quart sauerkraut
¼ pound salt pork
chicken fat *or* butter
1 ham butt (with plenty of meat and not too much fat left on it)
1 cup sliced onions

1 cup sliced carrots
1 teaspoon whole peppercorns
aniseed to taste
1 small bunch parsley
1 handful celery tops
2 bay leaves
consommé
white wine

SERVES 8

FIRST Scrub a whole 1½-pound piece of garlic salami under the cold water tap with a stiff brush. Wash 1 quart sauerkraut in a collander in cold running water. Cut ¼ pound salt pork into small pieces. Now grease a Dutch oven with chicken fat or butter. Cover bottom with half the amount of sauerkraut. Put in a ham butt, with plenty of meat and not too much fat left on it. Add the garlic salami (left whole) and ¼ pound salt pork cut into small pieces.

SECOND Cover with 1 cup sliced onions, 1 cup sliced carrots, 1 teaspoon whole peppercorns, and top with the second half of the sauerkraut. Scatter aniseed to taste on top. Cover with a small bunch of parsley, a handful of celery tops, and 2 bay leaves.

THIRD Fill until covered with half consommé and half white wine. Rub the inside of the cover of the Dutch oven with chicken fat or butter, and close. Place in a 350° oven for 4 hours, turning the oven up to 400° for the last thirty minutes. Serve the sauerkraut in a loose ring on a hot platter with the meat in the center.

HAM DECORATED FOR A BUFFET TABLE
[*Pre-heat oven to 350°*]

2 envelopes gelatin
½ cup cold water
1 quart mayonnaise
1 tenderized ham, roasted in a 350° oven for 1½ hours, then skinned and cooled

ripe olives
raw carrot slices
water cress sprigs

FIRST Soak 2 envelopes gelatin in ½ cup cold water. Let stand 5 minutes, then dissolve over hot water (page 280). Cool a little, then blend with 1 quart mayonnaise.

SECOND As soon as mayonnaise is blended with gelatin, use it to cover 1 tenderized ham that has been roasted in a 350° oven for 1½ hours, then skinned and cooled. Work quickly before it solidifies. While the mayonnaise is *still soft*, decorate the ham with "black-eyed Susan petals" made of slices of large ripe olives. Use tiny rounds of carrots for the hearts of the flowers. Push these gently into the mayonnaise cover, then arrange the sprigs of water cress as stems and leaves.

NOTE White daisies may be used, with the help of slices of raw turnips. Once the decorations are on, don't leave it too long in the refrigerator as the water cress will become dehydrated and have a limp and weary appearance.

HAM STEAK FROM VIRGINIA

1 large thick slice smoked ham
2 ounces butter
2 tablespoons brown sugar

½ cup sherry
1 teaspoon flour
2 tablespoons water

SERVES 3

FIRST Brown one large thick slice smoked ham in 2 ounces butter until brown on both sides. Remove to platter.

SECOND Put 2 tablespoons brown sugar and ½ cup sherry into skillet in which ham was browned. Melt sugar in wine over a slow fire. Mix one teaspoon flour with 2 tablespoons water. Add to sauce and let cook slowly until slightly thickened, stirring constantly.

THIRD Place ham in the sauce and let simmer about 5 minutes on each side.

TENDERIZED HAM WITH APRICOTS
[*Pre-heat oven to 500°*]

1 tenderized ham	½ pound brown sugar
1 large can of whole apricots	ground cloves (optional)

FIRST Ask your butcher to remove the skin from a tenderized ham and to score the fat in an attractive pattern.

SECOND Set the ham in a large roasting-pan. Open 1 large can of whole apricots. Drain the fruit and pour the juice carefully over the scored fat.

THIRD Spread ½ pound of brown sugar over the top of the fat, and if you wish, sprinkle the sugar generously with ground cloves. Set the ham in a pre-heated 500° oven, for 20 minutes. Remove the ham from the oven for a few minutes.

FOURTH Turn the heat down to 350°. Garnish the top of the ham with the whole apricots, inserting each one into the top of the ham fat with the help of a toothpick. Return to the oven and baste every ten minutes for an hour.

LAMB CHOPS, WENDY

6 small loin lamb chops	2 bruised peppercorns
sherry	heaping teaspoon dry mustard
red wine	salt, pepper
1 onion, chopped	1 heaping tablespoon butter
1 shallot *or* 1 clove garlic	

SERVES 6

FIRST Place 6 small loin lamb chops in a shallow pan and cover with sherry and red wine.

SECOND Chop 1 onion and 1 shallot or 1 clove of garlic. Bruise 2 whole peppercorns. Add 1 heaping teaspoon of dry mustard and season with salt and pepper. Add to the sherry and red wine and soak the chops in this marinade for about an hour and a half. Turn several times.

[*Pre-heat the broiler*]

THIRD Broil the chops, but not too close to the flame. Strain the marinade, reserving several tablespoons of the liquid and all strainings. Baste with the rest of the liquid, twice on each side, while the chops are in the oven.

FOURTH Render 1 heaping tablespoon butter in a small frying-pan. Add the strainings from the marinade and lightly fry. Add the reserved liquid and a few tablespoons of any liquid in the broiler. Spoon this mixture over each chop just before sending to the table.

LAMB STEW DELLAROBBIA

1 whole shoulder of lamb	3 large stalks of celery
flour	1 cup coarsely chopped parsley
salt and pepper	4 turnips
paprika	summer savory
½ cup oil *or* bacon fat	bay leaf
4 large onions	1 can tomatoes (large)
1 can consommé	gravy concentrate
2 cans onion soup	fresh vegetables
4 large carrots	

SERVES 12

FIRST Have butcher cut a whole shoulder of lamb into 2-inch chunks. Remove as much of the fat as possible and roll each piece in flour generously combined with salt, pepper, and paprika.

SECOND Render ½ cup oil or bacon fat in a large iron skillet. Brown the pieces of lamb on all sides, turning them with a narrow spatula. Remove meat and fat to a Dutch oven. Cut 4 large onions into small pieces, cook with meat until onions are glazed and slightly brown. (Never let them burn—keep turning with spatula.) Then add 1 can consommé and 2 cans of onion soup. Bring to a simmer. Add 4 large carrots, 3 large stalks of celery chopped, 1 cup coarsely chopped parsley, 4 turnips, and summer savory, bay leaf, salt, pepper, and paprika to taste. Cover and allow to simmer for an hour. Add 1 large can tomatoes, liquid and all. Stir thoroughly with a large spoon. Cover again and simmer on a low flame until meat is tender.

THIRD Remove meat to a very large hot platter and keep warm in a slow oven. Strain gravy and darken with a few drops of gravy concentrate. Pour some of the gravy over the meat, but not too much—it must not run into the wreath of vegetables. Pour the rest into a gravy boat. Surround the stew with even mounds of preferred vegetables—diced carrots, baby limas, fresh peas, baby onions, cauliflower flowerlets, turnip balls, potato balls. Plan your vegetables as though you were forming a beautiful and colorful wreath. Dab the mounds of vegetables with bits of butter and sprinkle here and there very lightly with paprika. Serve hot, accompanied by the gravy.

NOTE This recipe presupposes that you prefer clear gravy. If not, crush some of the vegetables that have cooked with the stew through a strainer into the gravy. This, of course, gives more body to the gravy but affects the clarity. This is a better-than-average stew, but its enjoyment depends a great deal on your artistic conscientiousness in forming a colorful wreath of vegetables around the meat.

RACK OF SPRING LAMB

[*Pre-heat oven to 500°*]

1 rack of spring lamb (both legs and part of the loin left attached)
prepared mustard
flour, salt, pepper

marjoram
mint
gravy concentrate
Chive Potatoes (page 193)

SERVES 12

FIRST When spring lamb is in the market, ask your butcher to find you a carcass where the legs will not weigh more than 4 pounds each. Ask him to cut the carcass halfway up the back and to trim the legs as usual. Have him skin the lamb unless it is very young.

SECOND Rub the rack, top and bottom, with any favorite prepared mustard, flour, salt, pepper, marjoram, and mint. Set in a preheated 500° oven for 30 minutes. At the end of that time, turn the heat down to 300° and roast for another $2\frac{1}{2}$ hours. Baste once every half hour. Remove some of the fat from the gravy, add a few drops of gravy concentrate to darken, and serve surrounded by Chive Potatoes (page 193).

NOTE It is highly unlikely that your roasting-pan is large enough to accommodate a rack of spring lamb. Do as we do: take the broiler pan out of the broiler and set the lamb on that. In most broilers the well in the front of the broiling pan helps with the basting.

STUFFED LAMB CHOPS
[Pre-heat broiler for 20 minutes]

6 double rib lamb chops ($1\frac{1}{2}''$ thick)	2 ounces of butter
2 minced cloves of shallots *or* 3 minced green onions	salt, pepper
	1 teaspoon lemon juice
6 chicken livers	6 large mushroom caps
	parsley

SERVES 6

FIRST Have your butcher trim 6 double rib lamb chops approximately $1\frac{1}{2}''$ thick each and ask him to make a deep incision in the side of each chop.

SECOND For the stuffing, lightly fry 2 minced cloves of shallots or 3 minced green onions with 6 chicken livers in 2 ounces butter until cooked through but not browned. When cooked, mash with a fork, season with salt, pepper, and 1 tablespoon lemon juice. Stuff the chops.

THIRD Broil the stuffed chops. Arrange on hot platter. Top each chop with a fried mushroom cap and garnish with parsley.

CHOP SUEY

4 tablespoons oil
1½ pounds lean pork
3 cups water
2 medium onions
2 stalks celery
2½ cups bean sprouts

1½ cups small mushrooms
5 tablespoons soy sauce
2 tablespoons molasses *or* 2 tablespoons brown sugar
Chinese noodles

SERVES 6

FIRST Heat 4 tablespoons oil in skillet. If it starts to smoke, turn the heat down. While oil is heating, cut 1½ pounds lean pork into small pieces. Brown pork in the oil, but keep the pieces tender—not hard. Cover meat with 3 cups water and simmer for 20 minutes.

SECOND Add 2 medium onions chopped, 2 stalks celery cut into very small pieces, 2½ cups bean sprouts, 1½ cups small mushrooms, 5 tablespoons soy sauce, 2 tablespoons molasses or 2 tablespoons brown sugar. Cook for 15 minutes longer, turning occasionally with a kitchen spoon. Serve very hot in nests of Chinese noodles heated in the oven.

POLISH PÂTÉ, RUBINSTEIN

[*Pre-heat oven to 400°*]

2 pounds shoulder of pork
6 onions
2 bay leaves
2 pounds unsliced calves' liver
¼ pound butter

2 whole eggs
nutmeg
marjoram
pepper and salt
½ to 1 pound raw bacon

SERVES 12

FIRST Roast 2 pounds shoulder of pork in a 400° oven with 6 quartered onions, 2 bay leaves, and a little water.

SECOND A half hour before pork is completely roasted, add 2 pounds unsliced calves' liver and ¼ pound butter. Baste four times while cooking. When meats are done, set aside to cool.

THIRD Cut pork and liver into pieces and work through a meat-grinder. Do this twice— first, with the grinder's largest knife, second, with a smaller one.

FOURTH Strain all the fat and the cooked onions through a strainer into a bowl. Mix this purée with the meat. Add 2 well-beaten eggs. Beat the mixture. Add the seasonings, ground nutmeg, marjoram, pepper, and salt—all to taste—and mix again.

FIFTH Line a fairly large, deep Pyrex baking-dish with raw bacon strips. The bacon must be arranged so that the ends hang over the top edge of the dish. Pour in the mixture and fold the hanging ends of bacon on top. Cover top with additional strips of bacon and set in 400° oven for about half an hour. Remove and cool to room temperature. Then set in refrigerator and serve very cold.

NOTE Use as a luncheon meat, or cut to fit pieces of buttered rye toast and serve as an incomparable hors d'oeuvre.

PORK CHOPS IN GRAVY

6 thick pork chops
3 tablespoons flour
2 cups milk
2 large onions

thyme, sage
2 bay leaves
salt, pepper

SERVES 6

FIRST Place 6 thick pork chops in an iron skillet and brown crisply. Remove the chops to a side platter, leaving the rendered fat in the pan.

SECOND Remove the skillet from the fire and add 3 tablespoons of flour, rubbing until free of all lumps. Gradually add 2 cups of milk, stirring constantly to be sure the sauce is very smooth. Return the chops to the skillet, being sure that the gravy is sufficient to cover the chops. Replace the skillet on the fire.

THIRD Cut up 2 large onions into slices and add to the gravy. Season to taste with thyme, sage, 2 bay leaves, salt, and pepper.

Cook slowly for 1½ hours, uncovered. Remove the bay leaves and serve.

NOTE The exact amount of gravy required will vary with the size and thickness of your chops. The important thing to remember is that the chops must be *covered* by the gravy.

CALVES' BRAINS AU BEURRE NOIR

6 calves' brains
½ lemon
salted cold water
salted boiling water
1 tablespoon lemon juice
¼ pound butter, melted
pepper and salt

2 tablespoons lemon juice
capers to taste
½ cup browned butter
thin slices of lemon
additional capers
2 chopped hard-boiled eggs
chopped parsley

SERVES 6

FIRST Clean 6 calves' brains of all membranes. Soak in salted cold water with ½ lemon for about an hour. Rinse and inspect to be certain all membranes have been removed.

SECOND Cover with salted boiling water. When the water begins to simmer, add 2 tablespoons lemon juice. Continue to simmer gently for about 20 or 30 minutes, then blanch in cold water.

THIRD Lightly fry the brains in ¼ pound of melted butter, sprinkle with pepper and salt, and add 2 tablespoons lemon juice and capers to taste. When lightly browned on both sides (to the point of being almost crisp), turn the flame down to its very lowest, to keep the brains warm, while you melt ½ cup of butter in another skillet. Brown the butter over a quick flame until it is almost black. This suggestion does not, of course, mean that you are to burn the butter. There is a moment in the process of browning when it turns a rich brown-black color, at which point it is ready.

FOURTH Place the brains on a small hot platter, cover them with the butter in which they were fried, then pour over the black butter. Decorate the dish with thin slices of lemon, more capers, and 2 chopped hard-boiled eggs, sprinkled on top of the brains, and with chopped parsley for flavor and color.

NOTE I find, to my regret, that many of my countrymen know very little about the deliciousness of calves' brains. They certainly deserve proper appreciation, as they have a very delicate flavor. If you like sweetbreads, you will like calves' brains even better.

CALVES' LIVER IN SOUR CREAM

½ cup vegetable shortening
½ cup butter
3 brown onions
6 nice slices calves' liver

salt, pepper, paprika
1 cup sour cream
¼ cup chopped chives

SERVES 6

FIRST Render ½ cup vegetable shortening and ½ cup butter in a large skillet. Chop 3 brown onions and stew them in the fat until golden but never brown. Scatter 6 nice slices of calves' liver with salt, pepper, and paprika. Cook them in the fat, turning from side to side until brown but not cooked through, leaving a little pink inside.

SECOND Turn off the flame, pour 1 cup sour cream over the liver slices, stir, and shake the pan until the cream is thoroughly mixed with the fat and the onions. Sprinkle with ¼ cup chopped chives. Shake the pan once more, then set the liver on a hot platter, pouring the sauce over the slices.

HUNGARIAN STEW

1½ pounds veal steak
¼ cup flour
3 tablespoons shortening
1 clove garlic
2 tablespoons minced onion
1 tablespoon parsley

½ teaspoon salt
¼ teaspoon paprika
¼ teaspoon celery salt
1 cup boiling water
½ cup sour cream

SERVES 4

FIRST Cut 1½ pounds veal steak into one-inch pieces and roll in ¼ cup flour.

SECOND Melt 3 tablespoons shortening in frying-pan, add one crushed clove of garlic, and cook 3 minutes. Discard garlic, add 2 tablespoons minced onions and the veal. Brown well together. Add one tablespoon parsley, ½ teaspoon salt, ¼ teaspoon paprika, ¼ teaspoon celery salt, and 1 cup boiling water. Simmer 1 hour.

THIRD Add ½ cup sour cream, shake the pan, then cook 10 minutes more. Serve with mashed potatoes.

STUFFED BREAST OF VEAL OR LAMB *Marie's*

1 boned breast of veal *or* lamb	1 turnip
salt and pepper	1 stalk celery
1 pound pork sausage, ground	2 crumbled bay leaves
½ pound fresh veal, ground	parsley
1 cup fresh bread crumbs	sprinkling of thyme
1 medium onion, finely chopped	8 *or* 10 whole peppercorns
¼ teaspoon sage	¼ pound butter
3 onions	2 cups water
3 carrots	gravy concentrate

SERVES 6

FIRST Choose a breast of boned young veal or lamb and have butcher flatten it with the side of his cleaver. Salt and pepper the meat. Spread with a mixture of 1 pound ground pork sausage, ½ pound fresh ground veal meat, 1 cup fresh bread crumbs, 1 medium onion, finely chopped, and ¼ teaspoon sage. Roll tight and tie in several places. Cut up 3 onions, 3 carrots, 1 turnip, 1 stalk of celery and add 2 crumbled bay leaves, a little parsley, a sprinkling of thyme, and 8 or 10 whole peppercorns. Cover the bottom of a deep pan with the vegetables.

SECOND Render ¼ pound butter. When sizzling hot, brown the meat on all sides, turning it several times. When this is done set the meat on top of the vegetables and pour the remaining butter on top. Add 2 cups water, cover with a double layer of wax paper, and cover pan tightly with a lid. Cook very slowly until done—approximately two hours. Strain gravy, darken with a few drops of gravy concentrate, set meat on a hot platter, cut and remove the string. Pour some of the gravy over the meat and the rest into a gravy boat and serve.

VEAL CASSEROLE WITH SOUR CREAM

6 strips bacon
2 pounds stewing-veal
2 large onions, thinly sliced
½ lb. mushrooms

1 cup white wine
2 cups sour cream
paprika

SERVES 6

FIRST   Render 6 strips bacon until crisp. Drain on paper and set aside. Cut 2 pounds stewing-veal into two-inch pieces, then braise in the rendered bacon fat. Add 2 large onions, thinly sliced, ½ lb. mushrooms, 1 cup white wine, and 2 cups sour cream. Stir well. Cook slowly until the onions have lost their crispness.

SECOND   Pour into a buttered casserole, coat top with paprika and the 6 slices bacon, crumbled. Simmer gently until the meat is done. Place under the broiler to make the top crisp and bubbly.

VEAL CHOPS IN TOMATO SAUCE *Marie's*

6 veal chops
salt, pepper, paprika
juice of 1 lemon
prepared mustard
flour
2 eggs, beaten

1 cup fine, sifted bread crumbs
vegetable oil *or* fat
water cress
2 cups tomato sauce
1 cup sliced cooked mushrooms

SERVES 6

FIRST   Get your butcher to trim 6 young veal chops. Sprinkle them generously with salt, pepper, and paprika, then sprinkle on both sides with the juice of 1 lemon. Rub in some prepared mustard, scatter with flour, dip in 2 beaten eggs, and cover with fine, sifted bread crumbs. Fry in medium-hot fat until golden brown. Drain on kitchen towels and place on hot platter with water cress garnishes.

SECOND   Heat 2 cups tomato sauce and incorporate 1 cup sliced cooked mushrooms. Pour over chops and serve.

NOTE

1. Do not have the butcher cut the chops too thick.
2. If you prefer, sauce may be served separately.
3. Be sure the fat is not too hot; otherwise the crumbs will fry dark brown before the meat has had a chance to cook through.

VEAL CUTLETS IN SHERRY

2 pounds very thin veal cutlets
salt, pepper, paprika
1½ cups freshly grated Parmesan cheese
¼ cup olive oil
1 mashed clove garlic

1 cup very dry sherry
2 cups freshly cooked and buttered peas
little additional grated Parmesan cheese

SERVES 6

FIRST Order 2 pounds of veal cutlets and have the butcher pound them very, very thin with the flat side of his cleaver. Cut them into individual portions, add salt, pepper and paprika. Then scatter each portion with an equal share of 1½ cups freshly grated Parmesan cheese. Pound the cheese gently into both sides of the meat with a wooden meat-pounder.

SECOND Heat ¼ cup of olive oil and 1 mashed clove of garlic in a large skillet. Quickly fry the cutlets on both sides until appetizingly brown. Cover with 1 cup of very dry sherry, rapidly bringing to a boil.

THIRD Remove to a hot platter, drain the sauce over them, and cover with 2 cups of freshly cooked and buttered peas. Sprinkle the peas with a little added grated Parmesan cheese.

NOTE Be certain that the cutlets remain juicy! Fried and buttered noodles make a nice bed on which to place these cutlets. However, when this dish was served us on the Mediterranean, the cutlets concealed a fragrant bed of Mario's Risotto (page 156).

VEAL CUTLETS VIENNA *Wiener Schnitzel*

3 very thin slices leg of young veal
salt, pepper, flour
2 whole eggs, beaten
sifted, dry bread crumbs
vegetable shortening
2 chopped hard-boiled eggs

6 very thin slices of lemon
 (skinned)
6 rolled anchovies with capers
12 slices of pickled beets
parsley

SERVES 6

FIRST This famous Viennese dish can be made or ruined by your choice of meat at the butcher shop. The veal must be pale in color, and the cutlets cut from the leg in the thinnest manner possible. Once home, place each cutlet between two pieces of wax paper and pound until it flattens out. Cut each cutlet into individual portions, at least two to each cutlet.

SECOND Salt, pepper, and scatter each with a little flour. Beat two whole eggs in a soup plate just long enough to be combined. Take each cutlet at one end and drag through the beaten egg, first on one side, then on the other. Place on a board lightly scattered with sifted, dry bread crumbs. Scatter more bread crumbs over cutlets, pat them in, and proceed in this manner until all are prepared. Let them stand while heating the shortening.

THIRD Melt enough vegetable shortening in largest skillet so that it is approximately one inch deep. Do not add the cutlets until the fat is smoking hot. Then fry them no more than *one minute* on each side. Drain on paper towels on both sides. Place on a very hot platter and garnish with two chopped hard-boiled eggs, 6 very thin slices of skinned lemon, 6 rolled anchovies with capers, 12 slices of pickled beets, and sprigs of parsley. Serve at once.

NOTE This fine Old World dish requires only a few words of warning. 1. Young veal, cut very thin, then flattened. 2. Crumbs, well sifted. (Big crumbs make a lumpy, thick crust.) Scattering must be delicate and smooth. 3. Fat must be hot enough to fry quickly—remember, they are very thin but must still be kept juicy. If you have two large skillets, so much the better—fry the cutlets all at one time; it is bad for them to stand and wait. No matter what you do, never keep them hot in the oven—this dries them out, and that is disastrous! Remember these few things, and proceed with all the confidence of an accomplished Viennese chef!

VEAL KIDNEYS IN BRANDY SAUCE

3 veal kidneys
pepper and salt
5 tablespoons butter
1 wineglass brandy

1 teaspoon dry mustard
juice of ¼ lemon
¼ cup chives

FIRST Season 3 veal kidneys with salt and pepper. Brown in a casserole with 4 tablespoons butter over a very hot flame. Place casserole in a 350° oven for about 15 minutes. Remove the kidneys from the casserole to a hot plate and cover well.

SECOND Remove from oven and return casserole to flame, pour in 1 wineglass of brandy. Cook until liquid is reduced by one half. Cut kidneys into small slices, season again with pepper and salt, and cover with hot plate.

THIRD To the brandy add 1 teaspoon dry mustard and 1 tablespoon butter cut into small bits. Add kidney slices to the sauce and heat without boiling. Remove from flame. Just before serving on a very hot platter, stir in the juice of ¼ lemon and sprinkle with ¼ cup chopped chives. Serve with warm French bread.

VEAL KIDNEYS IN WHITE WINE WITH MUSHROOMS

2 ounces butter
2 veal kidneys
2 tablespoons flour
½ cup white wine (see Note below)

½ pound mushrooms
salt
¼ cup heavy cream
chopped parsley

SERVES 4

FIRST Render 2 ounces of butter in a skillet. Cut 2 veal kidneys into pieces about the size of quarter dollars. Dredge them with 2 tablespoons of flour, then set them to fry lightly in the rendered butter until the raw look has disappeared. Do not cook too long or they will be dry.

SECOND Add ½ cup of white wine, blend well, and cook gently for a moment or two. Add ½ pound of mushrooms cut into slices. Continue to cook over a low flame for 10 minutes.

THIRD Sprinkle with salt to taste. Just before serving, stir in ¼ cup of heavy cream. Sprinkle generously with chopped parsley and serve with warm toast.

NOTE This recipe, which came to me from the countryside outside Paris, calls for a very dry white wine. Chiefly recommended is Meursault or Montrachet which are "Bourgognes Blancs." It is further recommended that the rest of the wine be consumed along with this delicious dish.

Chapter VII: *Starches*

To strive and compete

Eat of the wheat.

To outrun the mice,

Eat of the rice.

OLD JINGLE

ITALIAN DISHES

Gnocchi Gruyère with Sour Cream
Gnocchi with Cream Sauce
Gnocchi with Parmesan
Lasagne
Risotto
  Mario's
  with Sausages
Spaghetti
  al Dente with Spaghetti Sauce,
    Edwin
  Green
  Nests

RICE DISHES

Fried Philippine Rice
Spanish Rice

ASSORTED STARCH DISHES

French Toast with French Bread
Hominy, Tomato and Cheese Soufflé
Macaroni Ring of Plenty
Marie's Spätzle
Schupfnudeln or Bubbenspritze

NOODLE DISHES

Noodle Ring
Noodles with Cottage Cheese
Skillet Noodles

GNOCCHI GRUYÈRE WITH SOUR CREAM

½ pound grated Swiss cheese
1 cup heavy sour cream
4 egg yolks

salt, pepper (*or* dry mustard)
3 tablespoons flour
butter

SERVES 6

FIRST Mix ½ pound Swiss cheese with 1 cup of heavy sour cream, 4 egg yolks, salt, pepper (or dry mustard), and 3 tablespoons of flour. Mix well until thoroughly blended.

SECOND Lightly butter a frying-pan. Place spoonfuls of this mixture into the pan and fry until golden brown, first on one side and then on the other.

GNOCCHI WITH CREAM SAUCE

1 quart milk
1 quart water
1 heaping cup white corn meal
1 heaping cup farina

salt
Marie's Cream Sauce (page 203)
grated Parmesan cheese
grated yellow cheese

SERVES 6

FIRST Cook 1 quart milk, 1 quart water, 1 heaping cup white corn meal, 1 heaping cup farina, and salt to taste in the top of a double boiler for 3 hours, stirring occasionally.

SECOND At the end of 3 hours remove the cereal to a long, shallow pan to cool. When it has cooled to room temperature, place in refrigerator until chilled. Remove from refrigerator, turn out on a board, and cut into small rounds with a cutter.

[*Pre-heat oven to 325°*]

THIRD Place a layer of these gnocchi in a baking-dish, cover with Marie's Cream Sauce (page 203) and sprinkle generously with grated Parmesan cheese. Repeat the operation, sprinkle with grated Parmesan cheese again, and top with grated yellow cheese. Bake in a 325° oven for 1 hour.

NOTE In this recipe, as in all others calling for grated Parmesan cheese, freshly grated is preferred.

GNOCCHI WITH PARMESAN CHEESE

½ cup butter
½ cup cornstarch
½ cup farina *or* Italian semolina
½ teaspoon salt
4 cups hot milk

4 beaten egg yolks
1 cup grated Parmesan cheese
butter
additional Parmesan cheese

SERVES 6

FIRST Melt ½ cup butter in a large double boiler. Mix ½ cup cornstarch with ½ cup farina (or Italian semolina) and ½ teaspoon salt. Add to the melted butter. Stir thoroughly and gradually add 4 cups hot milk. Remove top of double boiler, place directly on the flame, and stir with vigor until the mixture is very thick. Return to double boiler and cook three minutes *exactly*. Remove from fire.

SECOND Beat in 4 well-beaten egg yolks and 1 cup grated Parmesan cheese. Blend well. Pour into a flat dish or onto a bread board. It is not necessary to grease the dish or board as the mixture will not stick. Spread mixture about ½ inch thick.

[*Pre-heat oven to 450°*]

THIRD When very cold, cut into 2-inch squares. Butter an oblong, flat, glass baking-dish and cover the bottom with the squares (but do not have them touching each other). Put a dot of butter on each square and sprinkle generously with additional grated Parmesan cheese. Add another layer, repeating the butter and the cheese. Cook in a 450° oven for about 15 minutes.

ITALIAN LASAGNE
PART I
MEAT BALLS

½ loaf stale French bread
1 clove garlic
parsley

4 eggs
1½ pounds ground lean beef

SERVES 12

FIRST Soak ½ loaf stale French bread in water. Squeeze out the water *thoroughly*. Add 1 clove of garlic, minced very fine, finely chopped parsley, 4 whole eggs, and 1½ pounds ground lean beef. Mix together very thoroughly in a large bowl.

SECOND Make tiny meat balls (about the size of a fingernail) —the smaller, the better. Place on greased platters until ready for use.

PART II
SAUCE

3 pounds tomatoes (*or* 1 large can)	1 cup olive oil
1 teaspoon sugar	2 cans tomato paste
½ onion	1 teaspoon salt

FIRST Cut up 3 pounds tomatoes (or 1 large can) into small pieces and stew with 1 teaspoon sugar until completely done.

SECOND Fry ½ onion in 1 cup olive oil. Remove onion when almost black. Fry meat balls in the onion-flavored olive oil. Remove to large stew pan.

THIRD Add 2 cans tomato paste to the olive oil in the skillet, stir until smooth. Then place the stewed tomatoes in a sieve, and work them through the sieve into the skillet. Cook thoroughly.

FOURTH Add 1 teaspoon salt and pour the sauce into the stewpan over the meat balls. Cook slowly for one hour, adding water if the sauce thickens.

PART III
THE LASAGNE AND COMBINING

2 pounds Lasagne (wide noodles)	½ pound freshly grated Parmesan cheese
1 pound Mozzarella cheese	
1 pound Ricotta cheese	

FIRST Boil salted water in a large pan. Cook 2 pounds of Lasagne (broad Italian noodles) for 12 minutes, stirring constantly. During the boiling process, if necessary add a little boiling water to keep the noodles from sticking. Drain when done.

[*Pre-heat oven to 350°*]

SECOND Pour some sauce into a large roasting-pan. Then make layers thus: sauce (aforementioned) *without* meat balls, strips of Lasagne, Mozzarella cheese, Ricotta cheese, Parmesan cheese (grated), sauce *with* meat balls distributed evenly. Repeat until all the materials are used. Bake in a 350° oven for about 20 minutes. As soon as the dish comes out of the oven, serve immediately.

NOTE Practically all the ingredients for this recipe will have to be secured at an Italian grocery store. Find one! It's worth it!

MARIO'S RISOTTO

¼ cup dried mushrooms
1 can consommé
1 medium onion, chopped
½ cup olive oil
1 cup rice
1 can tomato sauce (optional)

1 can chicken broth
salt, pepper, nutmeg
1 cup cooked ham, chopped
1½ cups grated Parmesan cheese
grated Parmesan cheese (additional)

FIRST Soak ¼ cup dried mushrooms for several hours in 1 can consommé.

SECOND Fry 1 chopped medium onion in ½ cup olive oil until light gold. Use a Dutch oven or a large, deep skillet.

THIRD Pour in 1 cup rice, a little at a time. Allow the rice to turn light brown in the oil. Add the consommé in which the mushrooms have been soaking, 1 can of tomato sauce (optional), and 1 can of chicken broth. Season with a light sprinkling of salt, pepper, and nutmeg. Turn down the flame and simmer, stirring occasionally. Continue to simmer until the rice has absorbed all the liquid.

FOURTH Cut the drained mushrooms into small pieces, mix with the rice, with a fork (never a spoon). Add 1 cup of cooked ham, chopped into small pieces, and 1½ cups of grated Parmesan cheese.

[*Pre-heat oven to 350°*]
FIFTH Cut a piece of brown wrapping-paper large enough to cover the top of the skillet and yet turn down an inch along the sides. Tie this paper to the skillet with a piece of string. Cut a hole (about 1½″) in the center of the paper. Place in a 350° oven for about 20 minutes. Remove the paper and serve the Risotto with additional grated Parmesan cheese.

NOTE This Risotto is delicious and may be served, if preferred, without the tomato sauce, and with any number of ingredients incorporated according to taste: chicken livers, chopped crisp bacon, cooked spring peas, pieces of shrimp, etc., etc. It is the perfect Sunday-night supper dish.

RISOTTO WITH SAUSAGES

¼ lb. butter
¼ cup olive oil
1 medium onion
1½ cups rice
2 quarts chicken broth

1 pound cooked mushrooms
½ pound chicken livers (optional)
1 dozen skinless frankfurters
grated Parmesan cheese

SERVES 12

FIRST Render ¼ pound butter in a large skillet. Add ¼ cup olive oil and 1 medium onion minced.

SECOND When the onions are glazed, put 1½ cups of rice in the skillet and fry slowly until the kernels start to turn light gold. Then add 2 quarts boiling chicken broth. Boil gently until the rice is soft but not mushy.

THIRD When the rice is cooked (but remember, not mushy), add 1 pound cooked mushrooms, ½ pound cooked chicken livers (optional), and 1 dozen skinless frankfurters cut into half-inch pieces. Place all this in an earthenware casserole and sprinkle the mixture freely with grated Parmesan cheese.

[*Pre-heat the oven to 300°*]
FOURTH Remove the casserole to the kitchen table. Cover the top with waxed paper large enough to hang down on the sides. Tie

down with a strong string. Cut a hole in the center of the paper (approximately 1½″) to permit the steam to escape. Place the casserole in a 300° oven and bake for half an hour. Remove from the oven and take off the paper. Serve very hot, with a side bowl of freshly grated Parmesan cheese.

NOTE Incorporate the mushrooms, livers, and frankfurters with a fork. A spoon is likely to crush the rice.

SPAGHETTI AL DENTE

½ pound long-strand spaghetti *or* spaghettini (the same, but thinner)
¼ pound butter
grated Parmesan cheese

1 recipe Spaghetti Sauce, Edwin (page 159)
additional grated Parmesan cheese

SERVES 4

FIRST Bring generously salted water to a full boil in your largest pot. Place ½ pound long-strand spaghetti (or, spaghettini) into the water. Let it slide in gradually, being sure not to break the strands. Cook for 12 minutes (no more, no less) over a high flame. The time is measured from when the spaghetti is put into the water.

SECOND Drain spaghetti in the colander. Have a small pot of boiling water at hand. Pour over the spaghetti through the colander. Drain well and return to the large pot in which it was cooked. Add ¼ pound butter cut into several pieces. Turn the spaghetti in the butter, with the help of a kitchen fork, until all the butter is melted and the strands of the spaghetti are well coated.

THIRD Toss the buttered spaghetti onto a hot platter and cover the top generously with freshly grated Parmesan cheese. Serve very quickly accompanied by Spaghetti Sauce, Edwin and additional Parmesan cheese. The secret of this recipe is in the timing.

NOTE It is best to serve the spaghetti on a flat meat platter rather than in a bowl. The confines of the bowl presses the spaghetti down and tends to make it gummy.

SPAGHETTI SAUCE, EDWIN

½ cup olive oil
1 tin tomato paste
1 tin boiling water
¼ teaspoon thyme
Salt, paprika, and onion salt to taste

2 ounces butter
¼ pound very lean ground round steak
1 tablespoon good meat sauce
Parmesan cheese freshly grated

FIRST Mix ½ cup olive oil, 1 tin tomato paste, the same tin full of boiling water, ¼ teaspoon thyme, and salt, paprika, and onion salt to taste in a large-sized skillet. Simmer, well covered, for half an hour. Stir occasionally.

SECOND Add 2 ounces butter to the sauce and stir well until melted. Then add ¼ pound very lean ground round steak. Stir until the meat is well distributed. Replace cover and simmer again for 15 minutes more, always on a very low flame.

THIRD Just before serving, stir in 1 tablespoon of any preferred meat sauce. Pour a quarter of this spaghetti sauce over the spaghetti. Serve the remaining sauce in a separate bowl to serve as an accompaniment to the spaghetti, along with a bowl of freshly grated Parmesan cheese.

NOTE For a recipe to use with left-over spaghetti and left-over spaghetti sauce, see Spaghetti Nests (page 160).

GREEN SPAGHETTI

½ pound butter
1 clove garlic
1 pound spaghetti
4 ounces grated Parmesan cheese

1½ cups finely chopped fresh parsley
additional grated Parmesan cheese

SERVES 8

FIRST Melt ½ pound butter in a small pot. Add 1 clove of garlic, minced very fine. Simmer together until the butter is very lightly browned. Strain through a fine strainer to remove all particles of garlic. Set the butter aside.

SECOND Cook 1 pound spaghetti in boiling salted water for exactly 12 minutes after the spaghetti has been put in the water. Immediately the 12 minutes are over, drain in a colander and run cold water through it. Return to pot.

THIRD Scatter 4 ounces freshly grated Parmesan cheese and 1½ cups finely chopped fresh parsley over the spaghetti. Pour the butter over all, and turn over and over with the help of two large kitchen forks. Serve as hot as possible, accompanied by a bowl of freshly grated Parmesan cheese.

NOTE In tossing the spaghetti just before serving, do *not* use spoons. Two large kitchen forks are ideal for this purpose.

SPAGHETTI NESTS

6 round rolls
soft butter
spaghetti (left-over)

Spaghetti Sauce (page 159)
freshly grated Parmesan cheese

SERVES 6

FIRST Warm 6 round rolls in the oven. Cut off the tops and scoop out the soft insides. Butter the rolls and fill with left-over spaghetti (well warmed).

SECOND Pour a small amount of Spaghetti Sauce (page 159) (well warmed) over the top of the rolls. Sprinkle a generous amount of grated Parmesan cheese over each. Do not use too much sauce as these rolls are to be eaten by hand.

NOTE These spaghetti-stuffed rolls are a saga of Broadway in the twenties. Three struggling actors, (now all successful stars) in their early beginnings, shared one portion of spaghetti at midnight, after the evening's performance. This is the way they made it stretch. Even today they find it, perhaps not quite so expedient, but certainly every bit as delicious!

NOODLE RING

[*Pre-heat oven to 350°*]

¼ pound broad noodles
3 tablespoons butter, melted
2 tablespoons flour
½ cup light cream *or* milk
salt and pepper

4 egg yolks
4 egg whites
¼ cup parsley, chopped very fine
paprika

SERVES 6

FIRST Cook ¼ pound broad noodles in 3 quarts boiling, salted water until soft, but not too soft. Drain and rinse in cold water.

SECOND Melt 3 tablespoons butter. Remove from flame and rub in 2 tablespoons flour. Return to the fire and gradually add ½ cup light cream or milk, a little at a time, stirring constantly. Add salt and pepper rather generously. Cool slightly.

THIRD Add 4 beaten egg yolks. When thoroughly blended, fold in the drained noodles.

FOURTH Beat 4 egg whites until stiff and fold into the mixture with a gentle hand. Sprinkle in ¼ cup parsley, chopped very fine. Fold carefully so as to distribute as evenly as possible. Pour into a well-buttered ring mold, set the mold in a pan of hot water, and bake in a 350° oven for approximately thirty minutes. Unmold and sprinkle with paprika.

NOTE The center of this ring may be filled with any creamed dish, such as sweetbreads, crab, lobster, hard-boiled eggs, or filled with vegetables, such as peas or peas and carrots mixed. For variety in making the sauce, try using sour cream instead of sweet.

NOODLES WITH COTTAGE CHEESE

[*Pre-heat oven to 350°*]

3 cups medium noodles
1 cup creamed cottage cheese
2 packages cream cheese
1 cup sour cream

¼ teaspoon salt
¼ teaspoon pepper
spring onions
½ cup grated Parmesan cheese

SERVES 6

FIRST Cook 3 cups medium noodles in salted water until tender but not soft. Drain well. Keep warm.

SECOND Mash 1 cup creamed cottage cheese with 2 packages cream cheese and 1 cup of sour cream. Mix with the noodles. Add ¼ teaspoon salt and ¼ teaspoon pepper.

THIRD Chop spring onions (any desired amount) and mix with the noodles with the help of a fork, using a light hand. Place in a well-buttered baking-dish. Sprinkle the top evenly with ½ cup grated Parmesan cheese. Bake in a 350° oven for half an hour. Serve in the baking-dish.

NOTE A two-quart glass baking casserole lends itself well to this.

SKILLET NOODLES

1 package medium noodles	3 cups *tiny* white-bread croutons
8 ounces butter	2 ounces of shredded almonds
4 medium onions, chopped	additional butter, if required
vegetable shortening	

SERVES 6

FIRST Boil 1 package medium noodles in salted water until done but not too soft. Drain, then fry lightly in 4 ounces melted butter.

SECOND Chop 4 medium onions and simmer until glazed in vegetable shortening. Mix with the fried noodles.

THIRD Fry 3 cups tiny white-bread croutons and 2 ounces blanched and shredded almonds in 4 ounces melted butter until nicely browned. Toss on top of the noodles and pour over additional butter if required.

NOTE Croutons are tiny squares of bread fried until brown on all sides in butter. The croutons and the almonds may be served on top of the noodles or scattered throughout with the aid of two large serving forks.

FRIED PHILIPPINE RICE

1 cup rice
2 tablespoons butter
2 tablespoons soy sauce

½ cup chopped scallions
touch of minced garlic

SERVES 6

FIRST A pot with a thick bottom is necessary for this dish. Pour in 1 cup boiling water and add, little by little, 1 cup rice. Once the water comes to a boil again, turn the flame *very* low and simmer until done. Watch for burning and for sticking and be certain that the flame is at its lowest.

SECOND When the rice is done, drain and allow it to cool. Fry it in 2 tablespoons butter. Add 2 tablespoons soy sauce, ½ cup chopped scallions, and a touch of minced garlic.

SPANISH RICE

1 cup rice
2 tablespoons butter
1 onion, chopped
1 green pepper, chopped
1 small stalk celery, chopped

¼ pound fresh mushrooms, cut into pieces
4 large ripe tomatoes, cut into pieces
salt and pepper
grated Parmesan cheese

SERVES 6

FIRST Boil 1 cup rice until well cooked. Put in strainer to drain thoroughly.

SECOND Render 2 tablespoons butter. Add 1 onion, 1 green pepper, 1 small stalk of celery, ¼ pound mushrooms, 4 large, ripe tomatoes, all chopped into small pieces. Season with salt and pepper. Cook until well blended and until the vegetables are tender.

THIRD Stir the rice into the vegetables. Heat well in the skillet. Serve with a side dish of grated Parmesan cheese.

FRENCH TOAST WITH FRENCH BREAD

4 slices stale French sour-dough bread
2 beaten eggs
½ cup cream
3 ounces butter

FOR 4

FIRST Dip 4 slices stale French sour-dough bread until thoroughly soaked in 2 eggs beaten with ½ cup cream.

SECOND Melt 3 ounces butter. Fry the soaked bread slices brown on one side, then brown on the other. Serve at once with warm maple syrup.

NOTE This happened quite by accident one midnight when we entered the house hungry and upon examining the bread box found it empty of the usual store bread. The stale French sour-dough bread was all that the larder offered. We were most grateful for the omission. So will you be, if you will follow this recipe.

HOMINY, TOMATO AND CHEESE SOUFFLÉ

[*Pre-heat oven to 350°*]

2 heaping cups cooked hominy
salt, paprika
1 tablespoon melted butter
1 tablespoon Worcestershire Sauce
1 cup tomato sauce (canned)
1 cup grated American cheese
2 egg yolks
2 egg whites

SERVES 6

FIRST Put 2 heaping cups cooked hominy into a mixing-bowl and mash with a fork to remove all lumps. Add salt and paprika to taste, 1 tablespoon melted butter, 1 tablespoon Worcestershire Sauce, 1 cup tomato sauce (canned), 1 cup grated American cheese, and 2 well-beaten egg yolks. Mix well.

SECOND Beat 2 egg whites until stiff. Fold into mixture and turn into a buttered 2-quart baking-dish. Bake in a 350° oven until well risen and nicely browned.

MACARONI RING OF PLENTY

[*Pre-heat oven to 375°*]

1½ cups cooked macaroni
1 cup diced cheese
1 cup soft bread crumbs
1 tablespoon minced parsley
3 tablespoons minced pimiento (optional)
3 tablespoons melted vegetable shortening
1 tablespoon minced onion
1 cup scalded milk
2 well-beaten eggs
1 tablespoon salt
¼ teaspoon black pepper
paprika
chopped parsley

SERVES 6

FIRST Mix 1½ cups cooked macaroni with 1 cup diced cheese, 1 cup soft bread crumbs, 1 tablespoon minced parsley, 3 tablespoons minced pimiento (optional), 3 tablespoons melted vegetable shortening, and 1 tablespoon minced onion. Mix well.

SECOND Beat 1 cup scalded milk with 2 well-beaten eggs. Add 1 tablespoon salt and ¼ teaspoon black pepper. Blend the milk with the macaroni mixture.

THIRD Butter a ring form generously. Pour the macaroni mixture into the ring and bake for 35 minutes in a 375° oven. Unmold, sprinkle with paprika and chopped parsley.

MARIE'S SPÄTZLE

1½ cups flour
¼ teaspoon salt
2 eggs
½ cup milk
½ cup water
¼ pound butter
bread crumbs (optional)

SERVES 6

FIRST Place 1½ cups sifted flour and ¼ teaspoon salt in a bowl. Beat 2 eggs with ½ cup milk and ½ cup water. Combine with flour. Mixture must be smooth but not firm.

SECOND Cut mixture into small pieces about 1 inch long and the approximate width of your little finger. Cut directly from the mixing-board into boiling salted water. Boil the tiny "spätzle" for a few minutes. Then drain in a colander and pour cold water over them. Drain again.

THIRD Brown spätzle in hot skillet in ¼ pound butter. Add brown buttered crumbs, if desired.

NOTE These were a great favorite of my grandmother's and of Marie's. It is a popular central European dish and is served with great success with pot roast, boiled chicken, and stews of any kind.

SCHUPFNUDELN OR BUBBENSPRITZE *Marie's*

1 cup mashed potatoes
1 beaten egg
pinch of salt
1 teaspoon soft butter

1 cup of flour
vegetable shortening *or* oil
salt

SERVES 6

FIRST Mix 1 cup mashed potatoes with 1 beaten egg, a pinch of salt, 1 teaspoon soft butter, and 1 cup of flour. Blend well.

SECOND Roll into thin rolls, 3 inches long and ½ inch wide.

THIRD Fry the little rolls in deep fat, either melted vegetable shortening or oil. Drain and salt. Serve hot.

Chapter VIII: *Vegetables and Potatoes*

Sonny Bunny had a Doctor

Who was very, very wise.

He could tell what you'd been eating

Just by looking at your eyes.

"Sonny," he'd say, "if you want

To grow to be a great big man,

Drink all the milk and

Eat all the green string beans you can."

NURSERY RHYME

THE PREPARATION OF VEGETABLES

ARTICHOKES
Artichokes Filled with Mushrooms
Artichoke Hearts
Artichoke Hearts Parisian

ASPARAGUS
Asparagus Almondine and Variations
   Hollandaise
   Mousseline
   Parmesan
Asparagus Soufflé

Beans, *Black in Rum*

BEETS
Harvard Beets
Polish Beets

Cabbage, *Red*

Carrots, *Glazed*

Celery *in Consommé*

CORN
Baked Corn
Corn on the Cob, Country Style
Corn Ring
Virginia Corn Fritters

MUSHROOMS
Creamed Mushrooms
Mushrooms Edwine
Mushrooms Marie

Onions, *French Fried*

Parsnips *in Parmesan*

PEAS
French Peas in a Lettuce Bowl
Peas and Sour Cream

Sauerkrauts, *Three*

SPINACH
Creamed Spinach
Creamed Spinach, Baked

SQUASH
Squash Purée
Squash with Shredded Almonds
Zucchini Shredded with Sour Cream

STRING BEANS
Whole String Beans with Crumbed
   Brown Butter and Variations
   Hollandaise
   Almondine
   Chopped Pecans

Tomatoes, *Hot and Raw*

POTATOES
Baked Herb Potatoes
Bird's Nest
Creamed Potatoes
Edwin's Potatoes au Gratin
Filled Oranges, Sweet Southern Style
Four Ways of Preparing Spring Potatoes
   in Salted Jackets
   with Chopped Greens
   with Parmesan Cheese
   Leftovers
"Pertaters"!
Potato Charlotte
Potato Crumples
Potato Pancakes

VEGETABLES AND POTATOES

THE PREPARATION OF VEGETABLES

ARTICHOKES With a kitchen shears cut off each thorn at the end of each leaf. Soak the artichokes for at least an hour in cold water lightly salted. When ready to cook, plunge into salted boiling water. Prick heart, on under side of the artichoke, while cooking to see if tender. Do not overcook.

ASPARAGUS Peel the last inch or inch and a half of the asparagus removing the tip end. This peeled portion of the vegetable may not be edible, but it makes an excellent portion to use as a "holder" when dipping the asparagus into the sauce. Wash each individual spear under the cold-water tap to remove all grit. If the asparagus must wait before cooking, stand in two or three inches of cold water. The bottom part of a double boiler makes an excellent receptacle for this purpose. When ready to cook, plunge into salted boiling water. I find a roasting-pan (where the asparagus can lie flat) an excellent receptacle. For additional directions see Asparagus Almondine (page 174).

BEETS Remove the greens, but not too close to the flesh of the beet, otherwise it will bleed while cooking and lose much of its flavor. When beets have cooked for a while in salted boiling water, they will have to be peeled. The peeling slips away very easily. Return to the water and continue to boil until soft, but of course not too soft as all vegetables suffer by overcooking.

CARROTS Carrots should be scraped with a sharp knife or a parer. They may be sliced, cut lengthwise into strips, diced, or left whole. At all events they must be covered with a damp cloth until ready to plunge into salted boiling water with a pinch of sugar added. If the damp cloth is not used and they are left to stand for any length of time, they will dehydrate and be tasteless.

CELERY Celery must be cleaned of all strings before being cut up for cooking. It must also be washed very carefully to remove all sand or grit that may have worked its way between the stalks. Do not cook celery in too much water. It is a moist vegetable in itself and loses its flavor if too much water is used.

CORN Remove the husks of fresh corn on the cob. Keep some of the husks to use as a bed on which to lay the corn during the cooking process. Remove the corn silk and cut off the ends of the husks with a bread knife, which serves as an excellent saw. Scrub the ears under a tap of running water with a rough brush to rid them of all corn silk. Then set aside until ready to cook in lightly salted water (a very small amount is all that is necessary, particularly if the corn is young, which of course it should be). The water must be boiling, and I have found it advantageous to add about half a cup of milk to the water just before dropping the corn onto the bed of husks. Young corn can be ruined by overcooking. Five minutes should be enough if the corn is very young and fresh.

MUSHROOMS Wash the mushrooms in a colander under a tap of running water, carefully inspecting each head in turn and rubbing all grit away with the ball of the thumb. Drain thoroughly and blot the tops gently with a soft cloth. Remove the stems and slice or mince these for immediate use or set aside in the refrigerator for future use. I never peel mushrooms unless they show spoiled or dried spots.

ONIONS Onions must be peeled before preparing. The chief concern in preparing onions is to be certain you spare yourself as much of the torture of the "weeping" that ensues from slicing, chopping or cutting them. I have tried taking everyone's advice. I have sliced them under cold water, chopped them in a covered container, I have looked like a mad woman, holding a slice of bread between my teeth, or like a horse with half a raw apple held jauntily between my jaws. I have still wept as though my last friend had left this world. The best and most effective method I have been able to discover is to tie a dish towel tightly around my face, just under the eyes. This gives you the appearance of some sort of bandit, but *is* effective and saves the day as far as the "weeps" are concerned.

PARSNIPS Parsnips are prepared like carrots for cooking.

PEAS Peas must be young! Shell them and set them in a bowl until ready for use. If you do not plan to use them immediately, place a wet, cold cloth over the bowl, but do not under any circumstances let them stand in water. My mother had a friend who used to plunge the empty pods into salted boiling water and then boil them until they were quite limp. She would then remove the pods and use the water in which the pods had been cooked to cook the peas themselves. It is quite extraordinary what a strong "pea" flavor it gives to this delicious vegetable.

RED CABBAGE Red cabbage must be firm, and the outer leaves must be bright in color. Cut the head in quarters and remove the heavy veins. Discard them, then shred the rest of the leaves on a coarse shredder. The outer head, before cutting, may be washed under running water. I do not advise washing the shreds. Cook in salted boiling water with a pinch of sugar.

SAUERKRAUT The basic sauerkraut for use in these recipes may be purchased at delicatessen stores.

SPINACH The most important thing in the preparation of spinach for cooking is twofold: first, be certain the leaves are fresh and crisp, and second, be certain that they are thoroughly cleaned before setting on the fire. Some cooks advocate seven separate waters. I have usually found that four or five are sufficient. The only qualification here is that the kitchen sink or basin in which the spinach is washed must be thoroughly rinsed and wiped clean after each washing, otherwise the grit that has dropped off the leaves will settle right back on them again. It is unnecessary and unwise to add additional water in the cooking. The water left on the leaves after the final rinsing should be sufficient.

SQUASH Summer squash needs only to be washed and have the bud ends cut away, If they are very young (the best way), they may be boiled whole. If heavier, cut into halves or quarters. Zucchini are usually left whole and boiled until tender but not too soft. It is best to cut them into various shapes for different purposes after cooking. However, if it is to be cooked again in a sauce or in a casserole for instance, be *sure* that it is not cooked too much the first time.

STRING BEANS String beans must be crisp and fresh, preferably small rather than large and thick. If the seeds have developed inside, the beans themselves are almost certain to be tough. If the beans are to be served whole, snip off both ends of each bean, remove any strings and tie them in small bunches before plunging into salted boiling water. If the beans are French style I cannot say enough about cutting them up fine. It makes all the difference in their flavor. If you use a bean-slicer, which helps a great deal in saving time, do take a little bit more time and examine the slices, particularly of the larger beans. If they are very long and extra wide, split them in half with a sharp kitchen knife. It is well worth the extra effort.

TOMATOES Wipe the tomatoes clean with a damp cloth. Plunge them into steaming water, remove after a moment, and pare them carefully with the tip of a paring knife. Remove the stem ends and set aside until ready to use. Should you be rushed and wish to peel a tomato in a hurry, stick a fork into the end of the tomato and hold it over a flame on the stove, turning it first on one side then on the other. This causes the skin to crack and makes it easy to remove.

POTATOES As soon as potatoes are peeled they tend to turn brown. They should therefore be allowed to stand in cold water in order to prevent oxidation from taking place. However, they should not to allowed to stand too long. It is best to prepare them immediately before cooking. If you wish to have boiled potatoes in the refrigerator for a hurry-up plate of lyonnaise or buttered, sliced, or creamed potatoes, boil them first in their jackets. They hold their shape better that way.

ARTICHOKES FILLED WITH MUSHROOMS

6 good-sized artichokes paprika
1 recipe Mushrooms Edwine
   (page 181)

SERVES 6

FIRST Boil 6 good-sized artichokes until tender but not too mushy and soft. Drain well on a soft kitchen towel.

SECOND Remove most of the center to form a hollow shell, but be certain to allow a double row of leaves to remain. Scrape the artichoke hearts free of all fuzz.

THIRD Set the "artichoke boxes" on a serving platter and fill to the brim with 1 recipe of Mushrooms Edwine (page 181). Sprinkle lightly with paprika and serve very hot.

ARTICHOKE HEARTS

6 artichoke hearts
2 tablespoons butter
2 tablespoons flour

2 cups rich milk
salt
½ cup grated Parmesan cheese

SERVES 6

FIRST Boil six artichokes in salted water until soft (approximately half an hour). When cool enough to handle, pull off all leaves, rub the ends of the large leaves, clean the hearts of all fiber and set the hearts on a flat glass baking-dish buttered rather generously.

SECOND Render two tablespoons butter in a pan and rub in 2 tablespoons flour until quite smooth. Gradually add 2 cups rich milk, continuing to stir until very smooth. Add salt to taste, the scraped artichoke, and ½ cup grated Parmesan cheese. Stir until well blended and pour over the artichoke hearts. Set dish under the broiler until nicely browned. Serve immediately.

NOTE This dish may be combined with slices of cold ham and used as a luncheon dish.

ARTICHOKE HEARTS PARISIAN

[*Pre-heat oven to 400°*]

6 cooked hearts of artichokes
¼ cup finely chopped mushrooms
1 tablespoon pâté de foie gras
¼ cup Madeira wine

¼ cup beef stock *or* consommé
1 tablespoon butter
salt, pepper

SERVES 6

FIRST Place 6 cooked artichoke hearts in a baking-pan, sprinkle with ¼ cup finely chopped mushrooms and a bit of pâté de foie gras in the center of each (1 tablespoon in all).

SECOND Add ¼ cup Madeira wine and ¼ cup beef stock or consommé. Dot each heart with butter (1 tablespoon altogether) and sprinkle with salt and pepper. Place in a 400° oven for 15 minutes.

NOTE The original French recipe called for a choice of truffles or mushrooms. Good luck in finding the truffles!

ASPARAGUS ALMONDINE

¼ pound butter
¼ cup slivered almonds
juice of ½ lemon

2 pounds asparagus
salt

SERVES 6

FIRST Render ¼ pound butter in a skillet and brown until dark but not black. Fry ¼ cup finely slivered almonds in the butter. Add the juice of ½ lemon to the butter.

SECOND Boil 2 pounds asparagus in slightly salted water until soft, but not too soft (about 20 minutes, depending on the thickness of the asparagus).

THIRD Drain the asparagus, lay the spears evenly on a flat, hot platter, pour the brown butter over them, and sprinkle with the almonds. Salt very lightly.

NOTE 1. This almond butter also lends itself excellently to string beans and to cauliflower.

2. I have found from experience that the most effective way to cook asparagus is to lay them flat covered with slightly salted water in a roasting-pan. Set the roasting pan if necessary over two burners and cover until the water comes to a boil. Once the water is boiling, the cover may be removed. This method cooks the asparagus evenly and makes it simple to remove without breaking any heads. Do not pour the asparagus out of the water, but, with a spoon or spatula lift onto a flat platter to drain. Drain them thoroughly of all water;

otherwise need I warn you your sauce will be ruined! Asparagus is equally delicious served with Hollandaise Sauce (page 207), Sauce Mousseline (page 213), or with drawn butter and a thick covering of grated Parmesan cheese.

ASPARAGUS SOUFFLÉ

2 tablespoons butter
2 tablespoons flour
1 cup cream (or ¾ cup cream and ¼ cup milk)
4 beaten egg yolks
1 cup cooked green asparagus tips
salt, pepper
4 egg whites

SERVES 6

FIRST Melt 2 tablespoons of butter, then remove from the fire. Rub in 2 tablespoons of flour until completely free from lumps. When well blended, add 1 cup of cream (or ¾ cup cream and ¼ cup milk). Stir constantly until thickened. Boil over lowest possible flame for two minutes, stirring constantly. Cool.

[*Pre-heat oven to 325°*]

SECOND When well cooled, add 4 well-beaten egg yolks and 1 cup of cooked green asparagus tips. Season with salt and pepper to taste.

THIRD Beat 4 egg whites until stiff. Fold into the mixture with a gentle hand. Pour into a 1-quart greased, glass baking-dish. Place baking-dish in pan of hot water and bake in a 325 oven for approximately thirty minutes.

NOTE Any cooked vegetable, meat or sea food may be used in place of the asparagus. This is a particularly useful recipe for the use of left-overs.

BLACK BEANS IN RUM

1 pound black beans
1 large onion
2 cloves garlic
3 stalks celery
1 minced carrot
small herb bouquet
salt, freshly ground black pepper
3 tablespoons butter
2 jiggers rum
sour cream

SERVES 8

FIRST Soak 1 pound black beans overnight in cold water.

SECOND Next morning add 1 large onion, 2 cloves of garlic finely minced, 3 stalks of celery, 1 minced carrot, 1 small herb bouquet, salt and freshly ground pepper to taste. Simmer slowly until, as the old recipe would have it, "The beans will split when blown upon."

[*Pre-heat oven to 350°*]

THIRD Put the beans in a bean pot or casserole, juice and all. Add 3 tablespoons butter and a jigger of good dark rum. Cover and bake in a 350° oven until the beans are tender. The baking time is indefinite, as black beans vary. When done add another jigger of rum and serve piping hot with cold sour cream.

NOTE A far cry from the Boston baked beans of our Yankee ancestors!

HARVARD BEETS

scant ⅓ cup vinegar
scant ⅓ cup water
½ cup sugar
1 tablespoon cornstarch

1 tablespoon cold water
¼ tablespoon salt
pepper
cooked sliced beets

FIRST Boil scant ⅓ cup vinegar and scant ⅓ cup water together. Add ½ cup sugar and thicken with 1 tablespoon cornstarch mixed with 1 tablespoon cold water. Add ¼ tablespoon salt and pepper to taste.

SECOND Pour this brine over cooked sliced beets. Bring to a quick boil, remove from fire, and serve hot.

POLISH BEETS

12 small, young beets
1 tablespoon cider vinegar
1 tablespoon tarragon vinegar
2 tablespoons sugar
3 tablespoons olive oil

salt, pepper
1 tablespoon flour
1 tablespoon lemon juice
½ cup sour cream

SERVES 4

FIRST Boil 12 small, young beets. Skin and slice them.

SECOND Blend 1 tablespoon cider vinegar, 1 tablespoon tarragon vinegar, 2 tablespoons sugar, 2 tablespoons olive oil, and salt and pepper to taste. Add to beets.

THIRD Heat 1 tablespoon olive oil in a saucepan and rub in 1 tablespoon flour. When smooth, add 1 tablespoon lemon juice and then the beet mixture. Fold in ½ cup sour cream. Heat well (do not boil) and serve.

RED CABBAGE *Marie's*

1 head red cabbage
4 level tablespoons sugar
1 level tablespoon salt
½ cup cider vinegar
4 tablespoons chicken *or* goose fat

2 ounces butter
2 *or* 3 sour apples
red wine
juice ½ lemon (optional)

SERVES 6

FIRST Slice 1 head red cabbage as for cole slaw. Place in a pot without any water. Add 4 level tablespoons sugar, 1 level tablespoon salt and ½ cup cider vinegar. Allow to stand for ½ hour.

SECOND Melt 4 tablespoons chicken or goose fat and 2 ounces butter. Stir into the cabbage. Peel 2 or 3 sour apples, cut into eighths, and place on top of the cabbage. Cover and let simmer slowly.

THIRD When the cabbage starts to shrink add a little warm water and cook slowly for an hour and a half. Add a tumbler of red wine. Add more salt and pepper and the juice of ½ lemon. (This is optional.)

NOTE This cabbage should be limp and moist. It is delicious with pot roast. Equally good the next day.

GLAZED CARROTS

2 bunches very young carrots
¼ pound butter

½ cup chopped parsley
salt

SERVES 6

FIRST Boil 2 bunches very young whole carrots in salted water.

When cooked and cool enough to handle, cut each carrot into pieces about one inch long.

SECOND Render ¼ pound butter in a pot. Drop the carrots into the melted butter and sprinkle with ½ cup chopped parsley. Shake the pot until the carrots are covered with the butter and the bits of parsley adhere to the carrots. Serve slightly salted and very hot.

NOTE Under no circumstances stir the carrots with a fork or spoon. They must be left alone—whole and unbroken—and the method described will do the trick.

CELERY IN CONSOMMÉ

3 stalks hearts of celery
1 can consommé *or* bouillon
1 tablespoon butter
paprika

SERVES 6

FIRST Cut 3 stalks hearts of celery lengthwise into 4 pieces each.

SECOND To 1 can consommé or bouillon add an equal amount of water (if you have chosen a concentrate variety) and bring to a simmer. Add 1 tablespoon butter.

THIRD Pour half the amount of broth into a flat sauce pan and add the celery. Bring to a boil and cook until tender. Serve on a flat vegetable dish (as for asparagus) adding the reserved broth. Sprinkle lightly with paprika.

NOTE If the broth should boil away during cooking, use some of the reserved.

BAKED CORN

1½ cups milk
2 level tablespoons melted butter
1 teaspoon salt
⅔ cup yellow cornmeal
1 teaspoon baking powder
2 eggs
1 small onion, chopped very fine
4 slices crisp bacon, crumbled
6 ears of fresh corn

SERVES 6

FIRST Heat 1½ cups milk. Add 2 level tablespoons melted butter and 1 teaspoon salt. Cool.

[*Pre-heat oven to 350°*]

SECOND Sift ⅔ cup yellow cornmeal with 1 teaspoon baking powder. Add to milk. Beat 2 eggs. Mix with 1 small onion chopped very fine and 4 pieces of crisp bacon crumbled into bits. Stir, then add fresh corn cut off 6 cobs and stir again until all is well blended.

THIRD Place in a well-buttered casserole or baking-dish without covering for 45 minutes in a 350° oven until nicely browned.

NOTE In the absence of fresh young corn, frozen or canned may be used, but believe me it's not as juicy. If you run across an advertisement for a waterground cornmeal, get some. It is a new experience for cornmeal enthusiasts.

CORN ON THE COB COUNTRY STYLE

6 ears fresh young corn   **salt**

SERVES 6

FIRST After having removed the husks of 6 ears of fresh young corn and scrubbed them clean of all silk, place a bed of half the husks in the bottom of a large pot.

SECOND On top of the husks place the corn and pour into the pot no more than 2 inches of boiling slightly salted water. Cover the pot and steam for no longer than five minutes.

NOTE Most of the flavor is boiled away by the average cook. This method preserves the flavor and is the finest method of cooking corn on the cob I have found. A little milk may be added to the water if desired. It heightens the flavor.

CORN RING

[*Pre-heat oven to 350°*]

2 cups fresh corn (*or* canned whole corn)
1 cup soft bread crumbs
¼ teaspoon celery salt
1 tablespoon chopped onion
2 beaten eggs

3 tablespoons melted butter
⅓ cup milk
vegetable for center of ring (peas, limas, etc.)
2 teaspoons chopped parsley
paprika

SERVES 6

FIRST Mix 2 cups fresh corn (or canned whole corn) with 1 cup soft bread crumbs, ¼ teaspoon celery salt, and 1 tablespoon chopped onion.

SECOND Beat 2 eggs with 3 tablespoons melted butter. Beat with ⅓ cup milk until blended. Add to corn mixture.

THIRD Rinse a ring mold in cold water. Dry, then grease with soft butter. Pour mixture into the mold. Set the mold in a pan of hot water and place in a 350° oven. Bake for half an hour.

FOURTH Remove from oven but do not remove from water. Allow mold to stand in water for five minutes after taking out of oven. Run a knife around the edges and unmold on a hot platter. Fill the center with fresh peas, tiny limas, or any preferred small vegetable. Sprinkle with 2 teaspoons chopped parsley and paprika.

VIRGINIA CORN FRITTERS

2 cups fresh cooked corn
1 cup milk
2 egg yolks

1 cup sifted flour
2 teaspoons baking powder
2 egg whites

SERVES 6

FIRST Add 2 cups fresh cooked corn to 1 cup of milk. Beat in 2 egg yolks.

SECOND Sift 1 cup of flour. Measure and resift twice with 2 teaspoons baking powder. Combine with the milk mixture and beat until thoroughly blended.

VEGETABLES AND POTATOES

THIRD Beat 2 egg whites until stiff. Fold them in with a gentle hand to the batter. Fry at once on a hot, greased griddle and serve at once.

NOTE The younger the corn you use, the more delicate your fritters will be. 2 cups of cornmeal may be substituted for the fresh corn.

CREAMED MUSHROOMS

4 ounces butter
1 pound fresh mushrooms
½ cup flour
1 cup cream

1 cup sour cream
salt, pepper
¼ cup chopped parsley
¼ cup sherry

SERVES 6

FIRST Render 2 ounces butter in a skillet. Remove the stems of 1 pound of fresh mushrooms. Wash the mushrooms, dry, and fry lightly in the rendered butter until soft, but not so soft as to lose their shape. Set aside in the butter.

SECOND Render 2 ounces butter in a sauce pan and remove from fire. Rub in ½ cup of flour, stirring and rubbing constantly until a smooth paste has been achieved.

THIRD Gradually add 1 cup of cream, stirring constantly until smooth. Add 1 cup of sour cream, stirring again. Season with salt and pepper and sprinkle in ¼ cup chopped parsley. Heat thoroughly, stirring to keep smooth. Just before serving, stir in ¼ cup sherry and the contents of the skillet in which the mushrooms have cooked. Serve over toast.

MUSHROOMS EDWINE

¼ pound butter
1 onion
1 pound mushrooms
2 tablespoons flour
1 cup consommé

salt, pepper
1 cup sour cream
1 cup best sherry
minced chives *or* chopped parsley
white toast

SERVES 6

FIRST Melt ¼ pound butter in skillet. Chop 1 onion and the stems from 1 pound mushrooms. Set in skillet with melted butter and the caps of the mushrooms and cook until onion is light gold, keeping skillet covered.

SECOND Add 2 tablespoons flour, sprinkling carefully over onion and mushrooms. Stir in 1 cup consommé and add salt and pepper to taste. Cover again and simmer for 20 minutes.

THIRD Add 1 cup sour cream and 1 cup best sherry, stirring carefully until smooth. Sprinkle in minced chives or chopped parsley to taste. Heat thoroughly, stirring constantly.

NOTE Serve immediately on white toast with the crusts removed

MUSHROOMS MARIE

1 pound fresh mushrooms	juice of 1 lemon
1½ tablespoons butter	flour
1½ tablespoons chicken fat	½ cup consommé
2 finely chopped onions	½ cup cream
1 teaspoon finely chopped parsley	salt, pepper

SERVES 6

FIRST Clean 1 pound fresh mushrooms and slice very fine.

SECOND Render 1½ tablespoons butter and 1½ tablespoons chicken fat in a saucepan with 2 finely chopped onions and 1 teaspoon finely chopped parsley. Let simmer. Add the mushrooms and the juice of 1 lemon and continue to simmer until the mushrooms have absorbed the liquid. Then dust with a little flour.

THIRD Gradually add ½ cup consommé, stirring until it thickens. Continue to cook slowly for 15 minutes. Before serving, add ½ cup cream and season with salt and pepper to taste.

NOTE These mushrooms make a delicious vegetable and are not to be confused with mushroom sauce. They are a splendid vegetable, especially when served with steak or chops.

FRENCH-FRIED ONIONS

3 extra large onions salt, pepper, paprika
milk vegetable shortening *or* oil
flour

SERVES 6

FIRST Remove peels and cut 3 extra large onions into ¼ inch slices across. Soak in milk to cover for half an hour.

SECOND Drain and roll in flour seasoned with salt, pepper, and paprika. Drop onion slices into deep hot fat (375°). Fry until golden brown. Drain on paper towels, salt, and serve.

NOTE The slices may be separated into rings if preferred.

PARSNIPS IN PARMESAN

6 boiled, thick parsnips grated Parmesan cheese
2 ounces butter paprika
salt, pepper

SERVES 6

FIRST Cut off the narrow ends from 6 boiled, thick parsnips and slice the tops in half.

SECOND Render 2 ounces butter in a skillet. Place the pieces of parsnips in the butter and fry lightly until slightly brown on one side. Season with salt and pepper. Turn and fry lightly on the other side.

THIRD Turn once again and sprinkle with grated Parmesan. Cook until the cheese blends with the butter. Place on a flat serving-dish and pour the butter over the parsnips. Sprinkle lightly with paprika and serve hot.

NOTE Artichoke hearts also lend themselves beautifully to this treatment.

FRENCH PEAS IN A LETTUCE BOWL

12 small boiling onions
4 ounces butter
½ head lettuce (or scooped center of large lettuce)
1 teaspoon sugar

salt, pepper
4 pounds shelled young peas
1 large firm head lettuce
½ cup crisp bacon bits

SERVES 6

FIRST Boil 12 small, boiling onions in a little water until soft. Set aside, retaining water.

SECOND Render 2 ounces butter in a skillet. Break ½ head lettuce into pieces and smother in the melted butter. Add 1 teaspoon of sugar and salt and pepper to taste.

THIRD Put in 4 pounds shelled young peas, the cooked onions, and the water in which the onions were cooked. Cover the skillet and cook about 15 or 20 minutes, depending on the freshness of the peas.

FOURTH If too much juice remains, pour some off. Add 2 ounces butter. Shake the skillet until the butter is melted and thoroughly distributed throughout the peas.

FIFTH Scoop out the center of a large firm head of fresh, uncooked lettuce. Fill the hollow center with the cooked peas and serve quickly. If the peas stand, they have a tendency to shrink. Just before serving, sprinkle with ½ cup crisp bacon bits.

PEAS AND SOUR CREAM

3 pounds fresh peas
1 tablespoon melted butter

1 cup sour cream
chopped mint *or* chives (optional)

SERVES 4

FIRST Boil 3 pounds fresh peas in as little lightly salted boiling water as possible. The cooking time cannot be accurately estimated, since it depends entirely on the freshness and the size of the peas. But for very young peas, ten minutes should suffice.

VEGETABLES AND POTATOES

SECOND Drain the peas and put them back in the pot with 1 tablespoon of butter. Shake the pot *over* the flame—not *on* it—until all the peas are coated with the melted butter.

THIRD Add 1 cup of sour cream to the peas and fold in quickly until well distributed. It is not necessary to heat the cream. The peas will be hot, the cream cool. It makes a very novel combination of temperatures and of flavors. Sprinkle, if you like, with chopped mint or chopped chives. In any case, serve immediately.

THREE SAUERKRAUTS *Marie's*

2 pounds sauerkraut
1 piece roast-pork fat *or* soup-meat fat (about ¼ pound)
1 sour apple, peeled and sliced
1 wineglass white wine *or* a demi-tasse cup vinegar
Juice of ½ lemon
½ teaspoon caraway seed

SERVES 6

FIRST Place 2 pounds sauerkraut in a small amount of boiling water. Cook until the kraut is fairly clear.

SECOND Add a piece of roast-pork fat or soup-meat fat and 1 sour apple peeled and sliced. Cook for 2 hours.

THIRD Add 1 wineglass white wine or one demi-tasse cup vinegar, the juice of ½ lemon, and ½ teaspoon caraway seeds. Stir and serve.

II

2 pounds sauerkraut
1 tablespoon beef fat
1 finely chopped medium-sized onion
flour
½ teaspoon sugar
1 large sour apple

FIRST Boil 2 pounds sauerkraut for 2 hours in a small amount of water.

SECOND Render 1 tablespoon beef fat in a skillet. Fry 1 finely chopped medium-sized onion in the fat and rub in a dusting of flour. Simmer until the onions are light gold in color. Sprinkle in ½ teaspoon sugar. Then combine the contents of the skillet, fat and all, with the sauerkraut.

THIRD Cut up 1 large sour apple, add to the sauerkraut, and cook for 15 minutes longer.

III

2 pounds sauerkraut
3 tablespoons bacon drippings
1 small chopped onion

2 large sour apples, peeled and cut into eighths
flour

FIRST Render 3 tablespoons bacon drippings in a saucepan. Add 1 small chopped onion and let simmer until light gold in color.

SECOND Add 2 pounds sauerkraut, 2 large sour apples peeled and cut into eighths, and ½ cup water. Let simmer for 2 hours.

THIRD Dust with a little flour a short time before serving. Turn the flour into the kraut to blend it well. Cook for a few more minutes, then serve.

CREAMED SPINACH

3 pounds spinach
2 heaping tablespoons butter
1½ tablespoons flour

1 cup milk
salt, pepper
2 tablespoons cream

SERVES 6

FIRST Cook 3 pounds spinach in a very little salted water. Drain thoroughly and place in a colander, pressing and rubbing until the spinach is mashed through. Strain off any remaining liquid.

SECOND Melt 2 heaping tablespoons butter and rub in 1½ tablespoons flour, stirring until smooth. Gradually stir in 1 cup milk, stirring constantly until sauce thickens. Season with salt and pepper.

THIRD Fold the spinach pureé into the cream sauce and cook together for a few minutes. At the last, add 2 tablespoons cream. Stir well and serve.

BAKED CREAMED SPINACH

[*Pre-heat oven to 375°*]

1 cup heavy cream
¾ cup freshly grated Parmesan cheese
3 cups cooked chopped spinach

½ teaspoon salt
pepper to taste
nutmeg

SERVES 6

FIRST Whip 1 cup heavy cream until stiff. Fold in ½ cup freshly grated Parmesan cheese. Fold cream and cheese mixture into 3 cups chopped cooked spinach. Blend well. Season with ½ teaspoon salt and pepper and nutmeg to taste.

SECOND Butter a glass oven-proof pie plate. Fill the plate with the spinach. Sprinkle with ¼ cup freshly grated Parmesan cheese and bake until slightly brown in a 375° oven.

SQUASH PURÉE

2 pounds summer squash
1 large onion
2 ounces butter

salt, pepper
grated Parmesan cheese (optional)

SERVES 6

FIRST Cut young summer squash into quarters. Boil with 1 large onion, also cut into quarters. Salt to taste.

SECOND When the squash is tender, remove and discard the onion. Place the squash in a sieve and drain thoroughly. Press it lightly to remove any excess water. (Squash has a tendency to sponge up water). Rub through the sieve into a bowl. Mash with a potato-masher and stir in 2 ounces of butter. Season to taste.

NOTE Parmesan cheese may be sprinkled on top if desired.

SQUASH WITH SHREDDED ALMONDS

2 pounds small, young summer squash
½ small onion, finely minced
2 ounces butter (*or* 3 tablespoons bacon drippings)
salt, pepper
1 cup sour cream
1 tablespoon flour
¼ cup almonds, blanched and slivered
chopped parsley, chives, *or* spring onions

FIRST Boil 2 pounds small, young summer squash in salted water until cooked but not too soft.

SECOND Fry ½ finely minced small onion in 2 ounces butter (or 3 tablespoons bacon drippings) until slightly yellow. Add to the squash and season with salt and pepper.

THIRD Heat 1 cup sour cream. Rub 1 tablespoon flour with a small amount of the cream. Stir into the whole, a little at a time. Add ¼ cup blanched and slivered almonds. Stir until the sauce thickens, pour over the squash, and garnish with chopped parsley, chives, or spring onions.

ZUCCHINI SHREDDED WITH SOUR CREAM

2 pounds zucchini
1 tablespoon melted butter
1 cup sour cream
paprika

SERVES 6

FIRST Coarsely shred 2 pounds fresh uncooked zucchini and boil in a small amount of salted boiling water for no more than 5 or 6 minutes. Drain very thoroughly.

SECOND Add 1 tablespoon melted butter and fold in 1 cup sour cream. Warm gently, being careful not to curdle the cream. Sprinkle with paprika and serve.

NOTE You may vary this recipe by pouring ¼ cup melted butter over the cooked shreds of zucchini and tossing well with chopped parsley, or by sprinkling ¼ cup grated Parmesan cheese over the vegetable. In either case, of course, omit the sour cream.

WHOLE STRING BEANS

[*With Crumbed Brown Butter*]

2 pounds string beans
¼ pound butter
½ cup sifted bread crumbs

salt, pepper
paprika

SERVES 6

FIRST Prepare 2 pounds of string beans, leaving them whole. Boil, in as little salted hot water as possible, until soft but still slightly firm.

SECOND Set the well-drained string beans the length of a serving platter, like asparagus. Keep warm while quickly preparing the butter sauce.

THIRD Render ¼ pound butter in a small sauce pan. Add ½ cup sifted bread crumbs—stirring until the crumbs are well soaked and slightly browned. Pour evenly over the beans on the platter. Sprinkle with salt, pepper, and paprika.

NOTE Whole String Beans are also very effectively served with Hollandaise Sauce (page 207), Almondine Sauce (page 201), or with brown butter and coarsely chopped pecans.

TOMATOES HOT AND RAW

2 pounds firm tomatoes
2 ounces butter

salt

SERVES 6

FIRST Skin 2 pounds firm tomatoes. Cut the four sides off each tomato, so that each resembles a somewhat square box. Scoop out the seeds.

SECOND Quarter each tomato and set in a stew pan with 2 ounces butter and salt to taste.

THIRD Heat the tomatoes, stirring constantly in the butter. When heated through (less than 5 minutes), serve them immediately.

> *Pray for peace and grace and spiritual food,*
> *For wisdom and guidance, for all these are good,*
> *But don't forget the potatoes.*
>
> —Prayer and Potatoes
> JOHN TYLER PETTEE (*1822–1907*)

BAKED HERB POTATOES

[*Pre-heat oven to 450°*]

6 baking-potatoes	1 tablespoon chopped chives *or* spring onions
1 teaspoon salt	1 tablespoon tarragon
1 teaspoon pepper	1 teaspoon sweet basil
¼ pound butter	1 tablespoon chopped parsley
½ cup cream	

SERVES 6

FIRST Bake 6 potatoes for about 45 minutes in a 450° oven.

SECOND When baked, cut off top third of potatoes and scoop out all the insides of the potatoes into a good-sized bowl. Mash with a potato-masher until all the lumps are removed.

THIRD Put 1 teaspoon salt, 1 teaspoon pepper, and ¼ pound butter into the bowl. Work the butter and seasonings into the potatoes. Pour in ½ cup cream, little by little. Beat until smooth. The mixture must be smooth and a little creamy—if necessary, use a little more cream. This mixture must be less firm than the usual "stuffed baked potatoes."

FOURTH Add 1 tablespoon chopped chives or spring onions. Mix. Add 1 tablespoon tarragon and 1 teaspoon sweet basil. Mix. Add 1 tablespoon chopped parsley. Mix. Fill the potato shells with the creamy mixture. Place under the broiler for a few moments to brown very lightly. Serve.

BIRD'S NEST

½ cup chopped cooked bacon, ham, *or* salami
4 cups raw shredded potatoes

2½ onions
salt, pepper, paprika
oil

SERVES 6

FIRST Chop enough cooked bacon, ham, or salami to fill ½ cup. Set aside.

SECOND Shred enough raw potatoes to fill 4 cups. Keep these raw shreds in a bowl filled with water until ready for use. This will prevent discoloration.

THIRD Chop 2½ onions. Drain potatoes and mix with onions. Add salt, pepper, and paprika to taste.

THIRD Heat oil in largest skillet available. When hot, dump potatoes into the oil, pat them down gently with a spatula, and allow to fry at a high speed until the potatoes at the bottom of the skillet are well browned and crisp. Turn down the heat so as not to scorch. Distribute the chopped bacon, ham, or salami evenly over the top of the "bird's nest." Fold over in half, as for an omelet.

NOTE When the potato is brown on one side, instead of folding over like an omelet, you may turn and brown on the other side like a pancake.

CREAMED POTATOES *Marie's*

1 pound boiled new potatoes
salt
1 heaping tablespoon butter
1 heaping tablespoon flour
½ can consommé

½ cup milk
2 tablespoons cream
1 tablespoon finely chopped parsley

SERVES 4

FIRST While they are still warm, slice 1 pound new potatoes, previously boiled and peeled. Salt them and put aside.

SECOND Render 1 heaping tablespoon butter and rub in 1 heaping tablespoon flour. Mix ½ can consommé with ½ cup milk. Gradually add to the paste and stir until smooth and thick. Add 2 tablespoons cream and 1 tablespoon finely chopped parsley. Pour over potatoes.

EDWIN'S POTATOES AU GRATIN
[*Pre-heat oven to 450°*]

6 firm medium-sized boiled potatoes
¼ pound butter

2 cups grated Parmesan cheese
1 cup heavy cream
1 tablespoon butter

SERVES 6

FIRST Cut 6 medium-sized boiled potatoes into even cubes. (These potatoes must be firm, not crumbly.) Place a layer of these on the bottom of a flat, thickly buttered glass baking-dish. Cover with thin slices of ¼ pound butter. Sprinkle with ½ cup grated Parmesan cheese, on first layer. Repeat twice, using 1½ cups of Parmesan cheese in all.

SECOND Pour 1 cup heavy cream over all. Dot with 1 tablespoon butter, and place in a 450° oven until the cream bubbles.

THIRD Remove and sprinkle with ½ cup of Parmesan cheese. Place under the broiler until well browned. Wrap a napkin around the dish. Set on a tray or platter and serve.

FILLED ORANGES SWEET SOUTHERN STYLE
[*Pre-heat oven to 450°*]

3 large oranges
4 medium sweet potatoes *or* yams
1 tablespoon grated orange peel
½ teaspoon nutmeg
1 tablespoon sugar
1 teaspoon salt

1 tablespoon butter
⅓ cup light cream
chopped pulp of 3 oranges
½ teaspoon vanilla extract
1 tablespoon butter
marshmallows (optional)

SERVES 6

FIRST Cut 3 large oranges in half. Scoop out carefully, reserving the shells for cups. Flute or scallop the edges with a scissors or a very sharp knife.

SECOND Mash 4 boiled medium sweet potatoes or yams. Add 1 tablespoon grated orange peel, ½ teaspoon nutmeg, 1 tablespoon sugar, 1 teaspoon salt, 1 tablespoon butter, ⅓ cup light cream, and the chopped pulp of the 3 oranges. Beat until light and well blended and add ½ teaspoon vanilla extract.

THIRD Heap the mixture lightly into the orange cups and dot with 1 tablespoon butter. Place in a 450° oven for 5 or 10 minutes.

NOTE For those who associate marshmallows with yams or sweet potatoes, shove one whole marshmallow deep down into the potato mixture before setting in the oven.

FOUR WAYS OF PREPARING SPRING POTATOES

I

2 pounds young spring potatoes   butter
salt

FIRST Boil 2 pounds young spring potatoes in their jackets in salted water. When soft, drain and return to the same pot in which they were boiled. Salt them heavily.

SECOND Set them on a very low flame and shake the pot again and again until all the potatoes are caked with salt and are very thoroughly dry. Serve very hot with plenty of fresh butter on the side.

II

2 pounds spring potatoes   chopped parsley, chives or spring
2 ounces butter   onions

FIRST Boil 2 pounds young spring potatoes in their jackets in salted water until done. Drain well. When cool enough to handle, remove the jackets with the help of a small paring-knife.

SECOND Melt 2 ounces butter in a skillet. Bounce the potatoes in the butter, shaking the pot back and forth until the potatoes are well covered with the butter. Sprinkle them generously with chopped parsley, or, even better, with chopped chives or spring onions, until well coated.

III

2 pounds young spring potatoes
¼ cup butter
¼ cup vegetable shortening

Parmesan cheese
black pepper, salt, paprika

FIRST Boil 2 pounds young spring potatoes in their jackets in salted water until done. Drain well. When cool enough to handle, remove jackets with the help of a small paring-knife.

SECOND Render ¼ cup butter and ¼ cup vegetable shortening in a skillet. When bubbling hot, brown the skinned potatoes in the fat, first on one side, then on the other.

THIRD Drain well and cover with Parmesan cheese and a sprinkling of salt and pepper. Garnish each potato with a dash of paprika.

IV

left-over young spring potatoes
2 ounces butter

salt, pepper, paprika
chopped parsley *or* watercress

FIRST Slice left-over boiled young spring potatoes with or without their jackets. Fry them rapidly in 2 ounces butter until lightly browned.

SECOND Sprinkle the potato slices with salt, pepper, and a dash of paprika. Cover them with the butter in which they were fried and sprinkle them freely with coarsely chopped parsley or watercress.

"PERTATERS"!

2 pounds potatoes
¼ pound butter
3 egg yolks
1 teaspoon salt

¼ teaspoon white pepper
1 cup cream
large lump butter
paprika

SERVES 6

FIRST Peel, then boil 2 pounds potatoes in salted water until soft but not too crumbly and mushy. Force through the ricer into a comfortably large mixing-bowl.

SECOND Melt ¼ pound butter and pour into the potatoes. Mix well. Beat in 3 egg yolks, one at a time, and continue to beat. Add 1 teaspoon salt and ¼ teaspoon of white pepper. Beat.

THIRD Add 1 cup cream and beat until smooth and very creamy. There must be no signs of dryness, flakiness, or, heaven forbid, lumps. Place the mashed potatoes in the top of a *large* double boiler. Keep warm, turning the potatoes every now and then to insure even distribution of the heat. Just before serving, place a large lump of butter in the middle of the top and sprinkle lightly with paprika.

NOTE Whether at home or whether in the elegant dining room of the Majestic Hotel in Paris, whenever my very small daughter saw these (her particular brand of mashed potatoes) arriving on the scene, she would regale the assembled company with the jubilant childish scream of: "PERTATERS"!

POTATO CHARLOTTE

[*Pre-heat oven to 400°*]

6 grated potatoes
1 teaspoon salt
3 beaten eggs
2 tablespoons uncooked farina *or* Cream of Wheat

juice of 1 medium onion
3 tablespoons rendered chicken fat *or* butter
paprika
1 tablespoon minced parsley

SERVES 6

FIRST Grate 6 potatoes. Add 1 teaspoon of salt, 3 well-beaten eggs, 2 tablespoons uncooked farina or Cream of Wheat, and the juice of 1 medium onion.

SECOND Render 3 tablespoons chicken fat or butter. Grease muffin tins with the rendered fat, distributing it evenly. Heat the fat in the muffin tins until it is bubbling.

THIRD Fill the muffin tins with the mixture and bake in a 400° oven for one hour. Turn out onto a platter and sprinkle with paprika and 1 tablespoon minced parsley. Serve quickly.

POTATO CRUMBLES

10 heaping tablespoons mashed potatoes
2 heaping tablespoons flour
salt, pepper

7 eggs
oil *or* vegetable fat

SERVES 6

In the Morning

FIRST Measure out 10 heaping tablespoons mashed potatoes into a mixing-bowl. Add 2 heaping tablespoons flour and season with salt and pepper to taste.

SECOND Beat in 7 eggs, one at a time, incorporating each in turn before adding another. Place the bowl in the refrigerator all day.

Before Serving

THIRD Heat some oil or vegetable fat until very hot. Drop the batter, a teaspoon at a time, into the oil, being careful not to let it drip in gradually as the shape of the finished product will be affected by the manner in which the batter is dropped into the fat.

FOURTH Drain on paper towels, or brown wrapping paper, sprinkle generously with salt, and place in a serving-bowl. Keep warm in the oven until the last moment before serving.

NOTE This is a Belgian recipe—wonderful with fried chicken or roast of beef.

POTATO PANCAKES

[*Pre-heat griddle*]

2 cups raw grated potatoes
3 eggs
1 scant teaspoon baking powder
2 tablespoons flour

1 teaspoon salt
¼ cup chopped chives
¼ cup chopped parsley

SERVES 4 TO 6

FIRST Grate 2 cups raw potatoes. Drain to remove all liquid.

SECOND Beat 3 whole eggs very well and mix with 1 scant teaspoon baking powder, 2 tablespoons flour, and 1 teaspoon salt. Add to the potatoes.

THIRD Chop ¼ cup chives and ¼ cup of parsley as fine as possible. Stir the greens into the batter.

FOURTH Drop the batter onto the pre-heated griddle with a soup spoon. The charm of these pancakes is that they must be very thin and not too large in diameter. They are particularly delicious with pot roast. Once the potatoes are grated, work quickly. Remember they turn brown when exposed to the air.

Chapter IX: *Sauces*

FOR USE WITH MEATS, FISH, POULTRY,
VEGETABLES, AND EGGS

Epicurean cooks sharpen with cloyless sauce his appetite.

WILLIAM SHAKESPEARE: *Antony and Cleopatra,*

Act II, Scene i

SAUCES

Almondine Sauce
Bahama Sauce for Fish
Bread Sauce with Poultry or Game
Cold Mustard Sauce
Cream Sauces
  Cream Sauce
  Marie's Cream Sauce
  Rich Cheese Sauce
  Yellow Cream Sauce
Cucumber Sauce
Curry Sauce
Glaze for Meats and Fowl
Hollandaise I

Hollandaise II Very Rich
Horseradish Mold
Mushroom Stems in Sherry Sauce
Mushroom Stems and Tomato Sauce
Paprika Butter
Pink Lobster Butter
Raisin Sauce for Cold Fish
Sauce Allemande
Sauce for Meats
Sauce Mousseline
Sauce Tartar
Steak Butter

ALMONDINE SAUCE

¼ pound butter
¼ cup slivered almonds
juice of ½ lemon

FIRST Render ¼ pound of butter in a skillet and brown until dark but not black. Fry ¼ cup finely slivered almonds in the butter. Squeeze the juice of ½ lemon and add to the butter.

NOTE This butter-almond sauce lends itself excellently to string beans and to cauliflower.

BAHAMA SAUCE FOR FISH

1 cup sour cream
½ cup Bahama mustard
¼ cup chopped parsley

FIRST Mix 1 cup sour cream with ½ cup Bahama mustard, stirring until thoroughly blended.

SECOND Chop ¼ cup parsley very fine and stir into the cream and mustard. Heap the sauce into a bowl and set in refrigerator until ready to serve.

NOTE Excellent with cold fish of any sort or cold eggs.

BREAD SAUCE WITH POULTRY OR GAME

1 cup milk
2 whole cloves
1 small onion
1¼ cups fresh bread crumbs
salt, pepper
1 thin slice butter (¼ ounce)
1 tablespoon heavy cream

FIRST Pour 1 cup milk into a saucepan. Stick 2 whole cloves in one small onion, add to the milk, and bring to a boil.

SECOND Add 1¼ cup bread crumbs and simmer gently for about 20 minutes. Remove the onion. Add salt and pepper to taste.

THIRD   Stir in 1 thin slice butter (¼ ounce) and 1 tablespoon heavy cream. Heat well and serve.

NOTE   This is an excellent example of the famous English bread sauce that the British serve with chicken and other kinds of fowl. It may be an innovation to most Americans, but, believe me, a very pleasant one.

COLD MUSTARD SAUCE
[for cold fish and eggs]

Gulden's mustard   mayonnaise

NOTE   The recipe for this excellent sauce is incorporated in a story. A number of years ago I spent some time in Palm Beach. Some friends were kind enough to take me to dine one evening at an outdoor restaurant where very excellent and very imaginative food was served. We ordered cold Pompano, and the sauce that was served with it was of a most beautiful texture and color. Very, very smooth in texture, "café au lait" in color. I asked the head waiter to inquire of the chef how the sauce was made, but the head waiter just greeted my inquiry with a haughty smirk and informed me that that particular sauce was one of the precious assets of the restaurant. I could scarcely blame the chef for wanting to keep his secret, but the next week when I returned I pressed my suit. This evening the head waiter was in an excellent mood indeed, owing, I have always suspected, to his having imbibed rather indiscreetly before the evening's work had begun. At all events when I asked him again (with the added emphasis of a slight remuneration), he broke down and leaned over to whisper as though he were giving away some great state secret: "Just mix Gulden's mustard and a tart mayonnaise together, half and half. Set it in the refrigerator for about an hour before serving." And there you have it. I have been known to vary it at times by using more or less mustard; and sometimes, depending on what it is to garnish, I add ½ teaspoon of dry mustard for added zest.

CREAM SAUCE

¼ pound quartered mushrooms
2 cups cold milk
salt and pepper
½ minced small onion

¼ pound butter
3 tablespoons flour
2 egg yolks
2 egg whites

FIRST Place ¼ pound quartered mushrooms, 2 cups cold milk, salt, pepper, and ½ minced small onion in the top of a double boiler. Cook together over a medium flame for half an hour.

SECOND Melt ¼ pound butter. Remove from flame and rub in 3 tablespoons flour. Stir in 2 beaten egg yolks.

THIRD Add the first mixture to the second, a little at a time, blending each addition thoroughly before adding more. When it is all blended, place on the fire, stirring constantly and rapidly until the mixture is thickened, but not too thick.

FOURTH Beat 2 egg whites very stiff. Add to the sauce, stirring the whites in rapidly and thoroughly. Serve very hot over fish, chicken, turkey, or eggs.

MARIE'S CREAM SAUCE

2 ounces butter
½ cup flour
1 cup cream

1 cup milk
salt, pepper
¼ cup chopped parsley

FIRST Render 2 ounces of butter in a sauce pan. Remove from the fire and rub in ½ cup of flour, rubbing thoroughly to remove all lumps.

SECOND Gradually add 1 cup of cream, a little at a time, stirring until smooth and creamy. Add 1 cup of milk and continue to stir until smooth again. Season with salt and pepper to taste.

THIRD Fold in ¼ cup of chopped parsley.

RICH CHEESE SAUCE

1 heaping tablespoon flour
1 ounce butter
1½ cups milk
½ pound grated sharp Cheddar cheese

2 tablespoons sherry
salt, pepper
paprika (optional)

FIRST Brown 1 heaping tablespoon flour in a skillet with 1 ounce of butter.

SECOND Add 1½ cups milk, a little at a time, stirring constantly until a smooth paste has been achieved.

THIRD Stir ½ pound grated sharp Cheddar cheese into the paste, and when melted, remove from the fire and add 2 tablespoons sherry. Season with salt and pepper. Paprika may be added if you like. Serve with Chicken Blintzes, Sylvia.

YELLOW CREAM SAUCE

1 ounce butter
2 tablespoons flour
1½ cups hot cream
salt and pepper to taste

½ cup Hollandaise Sauce I (page 207)
2 beaten egg yolks

FIRST Render 1 ounce butter. Remove from flame and rub in 2 tablespoons flour. Gradually add 1½ cups hot cream and salt and pepper to taste. Stir constantly until thickened.

SECOND Stir in ½ cup Hollandaise Sauce I (page 207) over a low flame. As soon as it is well blended remove from fire.

THIRD Stir in 2 beaten egg yolks. Return to a low flame for half a minute, stirring constantly. Serve at once over chicken, turkey, fish, or eggs.

CUCUMBER SAUCE

[*for cold fish*]

1 cup mayonnaise
1 cup sour cream
1 teaspoon dry mustard

2 cucumbers, chopped
1 drop green coloring
2 tablespoons chopped chives
   or parsley

FIRST Mix 1 cup mayonnaise with 1 cup sour cream. Stir until well blended.

SECOND Remove a small amount of the mixture and stir with 1 teaspoon of dry mustard until thoroughly dampened and smooth. Return to the rest of the mixture and add 2 chopped cucumbers.

THIRD Stir in 1 drop of green vegetable coloring and continue to stir until the sauce takes on a very pale even green hue. Fold in 2 tablespoons of chopped chives or chopped parsley.

CURRY SAUCE

[*with meat, fowl, or sea food*]

3 ounces butter
2 large onions
3 tablespoons curry powder
2 tablespoons flour

1½ cups chicken broth
1 cup cream
½ cup milk
condiments (see below)

FIRST Render 3 ounces butter in a large skillet. Lightly fry over a moderate flame 2 large onions, chopped into small pieces, until golden-colored but not brown. With the flat of a large spoon rub in 3 tablespoons curry powder and 2 tablespoons flour. Stir until you have a smooth paste. Then gradually add 1½ cups chicken broth, 1 cup cream, and ½ cup milk. Mix well, stirring until sauce thickens.

SECOND Pour into this sauce, chicken, lamb, shrimp, crab, lobster, or turkey cut into good-sized pieces (never chopped or minced). These all make delectable selections. Simmer in sauce for 10 minutes on a low flame. Now empty contents of skillet over a bed of *flaky* rice. Serve it *hot*, accompanied by a selection of the following condiments: Chutney, chopped nuts, chopped crisp bacon, grated coconut, minced green onions, minced raw onion, shredded pineapple, chopped apple, chopped hard-boiled eggs, raisins soaked in wine, and bananas fried in butter and strewn with cinnamon and cloves.

NOTE A great deal too much has been said about preparing curries. This simple, splendid recipe was given me by an English friend who had lived a great many years in India. Here are just a few things to consider: 1. The quality of the curry powder. Only the best imported curry powder will do. The amount given in this recipe makes a hearty dish, but if you can take it and want to go "native," use more. 2. Have your sauce (which is of major importance in a curry) *smooth*. 3. The rice! Anyone who is not willing to turn out a beautiful flaky rice had better not try a curry recipe at all. 4. Use imagination in the presentation of your condiments. The more the merrier, although it is not necessary to use more than four or five at a time. But please remember that the chutney is never to be omitted, and, here again, only the best will do. Treat yourself to a condiment dish (a dish that is divided into sections and that will hold a good number of condiments at one time). They are usually found in Chinese shops. Of course this is not absolutely necessary, but does add to the charm of the whole. Above all, remember to smirk at anyone who tells you about the perfect curry they turn out by merely adding curry powder to their pet white sauce!

GLAZE FOR MEATS AND FOWL
[*for giving them that finished, professional appearance*]

1 quart consommé **1 heaping tablespoon arrowroot powder**

FIRST Bring 1 quart consommé to a boil and continue to boil until the original amount is reduced to about one-third.

SECOND Place 1 heaping tablespoon arrowroot powder in a tea cup. Spoon several tablespoons boiling broth into the powder and carefully stir together until no lumps remain. Little by little stir the moist arrowroot into the broth and stir.

THIRD Stirring constantly bring to a boil until thick and glossy. Remove from fire and cool. Apply with a clean pastry brush. After the glaze has been applied set the meat or fowl in the refrigerator to allow the glaze to set.

NOTE Many markets carry arrowroot powder; failing this it may be purchased at druggists.

HOLLANDAISE I

¼ pound butter
1 teaspoon lemon juice
salt, pepper, and a pinch of cayenne pepper
3 egg yolks
¼ cup cream (approximately)

FIRST Fill a large skillet about half full with hot water. Place a flat-bottomed earthenware bowl in the skillet and let it warm. Do not permit the water to boil.

SECOND Cut ¼ pound butter into three even pieces. Place the first piece in the bowl with 1 teaspoon strained lemon juice, salt, pepper, and a pinch of cayenne pepper. When the butter has melted, add 3 egg yolks. As soon as the eggs have been added, whisk with a flat wire hand whip until the mixture thickens (about five minutes).

THIRD Add the second piece of butter. Continue to whisk until the butter has merged with the egg mixture and the whole has thickened again. Add the third piece of butter. Continue to whisk until this butter has merged with the rest. *Under no circumstances ever stop whisking.*

FOURTH The mixture should now be very thick. Gradually add approximately ¼ cup cream a very little at a time, whisking all the time. The amount of the cream may be judged by how thick or how flowing you wish the sauce to be. When the desired amount of cream has been added, whisk a little more. Then remove bowl from the skillet. *It is not necessary to serve this sauce immediately.* This is its great advantage. If it cools, set in the hot water in the skillet again and whisk a few moments before serving.

NOTE This is a very *reliable* and simple Hollandaise to make. If there is any left over it will keep very well in the refrigerator and may be used again by repeating the process of whisking in a bowl. Set in a skillet half filled with hot water. When reheating add a little more cream, as standing in the refrigerator tends to thicken the sauce. Left-over Hollandaise may be used to great advantage with Creamed Turkey (page 117), chicken, or eggs.

HOLLANDAISE II

[very rich]

6 egg yolks
1½ pounds melted sweet butter
salt and cayenne pepper to taste
6 drops lemon juice

FIRST Place 6 egg yolks and ¼ cup cold water in a deep pot. Place the pot in a pan of hot water over a moderate flame, being sure the water does not boil. Stir constantly and rapidly with a hand wire whip until the consistency of mayonnaise has been achieved (about 5 minutes). Remove from fire.

SECOND Slowly add 1½ pounds melted sweet butter to the egg mixture, a tablespoon at a time. Add salt, cayenne pepper to taste, and 6 drops of lemon juice. Stir constantly. For extra smoothness, put through a fine strainer.

NOTE Anyone who has ever made Hollandaise knows that the most important warning one can give a beginner is to keep constantly stirring and never to let it get too hot—that *is*, unless you want scrambled eggs!

HORSERADISH MOLD

[*excellent with roast beef*]

1 envelope gelatin
¼ cup cold water
1 cup heavy cream
2 egg whites

½ cup finely grated fresh horseradish
¼ cup red pickled horseradish
1 teaspoon salt
1 small onion

FIRST Soak 1 envelope gelatin in ¼ cup cold water for five minutes. Dissolve over boiling water. Cool.

SECOND Whip 1 cup heavy cream. Beat 2 egg whites until stiff. Fold into whipped cream.

THIRD Mix ½ cup finely grated fresh horseradish with ¼ cup red pickled horseradish, 1 teaspoon salt, and 1 small grated onion. Fold into the whipped cream.

FOURTH Stir in the cooled dissolved gelatin. Pour the whole into a rinsed mold and place in refrigerator until set.

MUSHROOM STEMS IN SHERRY SAUCE

1 medium-sized onion, chopped very fine
stems of ½ pound mushrooms
chopped parsley

¼ pound butter
salt, pepper
½ teaspoon paprika
2 tablespoons sherry

FIRST Chop 1 medium-sized onion until very fine in a wooden chopping-bowl or on a wooden bread board. Chop the stems of ½ pound mushrooms on top of, and along with, the already chopped onion. Cut in some parsley with kitchen shears and continue to chop everything together.

SECOND Melt ¼ pound butter in a skillet. Add the onion, mushroom stems, and parsley. Salt and pepper to taste. Stir with a spatula, turning the vegetables about. When the onions have begun to glaze, turn the fire down and cover the skillet. Continue to simmer until the vegetables are quite soft. At this point the sauce is done. At the end, stir in ½ teaspoon paprika and 2 tablespoons of sherry.

NOTE Here are some of the different ways in which this sauce may be used:

1. Combined with ground meat for meat balls.
2. As a sauce on top of meats.
3. In omelettes.
4. Over shirred or scrambled eggs.
5. Spread on toast with hard-boiled eggs on top.
6. As an appetizer on toast rounds, either hot or cold. (In this case, it is extremely good served in a cold mound, surrounded by pieces of crisp toast.)

MUSHROOM STEMS AND TOMATO SAUCE

stems of 1 pound fresh mushrooms
2 leeks (whites only), chopped
¼ pound butter

½ large can solid pack tomatoes (reserve ½ amount juice)
salt, pepper, and paprika
½ cup pecans, chopped coarsely

FIRST Chop the stems of 1 pound fresh mushrooms and the whites only of 2 leeks and simmer lightly until soft in ¼ pound of rendered butter in a good-sized skillet.

SECOND Add ½ large can solid pack tomatoes, together with one-half the amount of juice in the can. Crush the tomatoes while stirring. Salt and pepper to taste and add a dash of paprika. At the last, stir in ½ cup coarsely chopped pecans.

NOTE This is splendid with fish or over meat balls.

PAPRIKA BUTTER

¼ pound butter
1 teaspoon paprika

½ teaspoon white wine
½ teaspoon lemon juice

FIRST Cream ¼ pound butter with 1 teaspoon paprika until soft and creamy. Add ½ teaspoon white wine and ½ teaspoon lemon juice. Continue to cream. Place in a small bowl or cup and chill.

SECOND Unmold on a plate surrounded by parsley and serve with hot fish.

PINK LOBSTER BUTTER

lobster coral
2 tablespoons butter
½ pound sweet butter
juice of ½ lemon

½ teaspoon paprika
½ cup chopped chives *or* spring
   onions
few drops red vegetable coloring

FIRST Fry lightly in 2 tablespoons of butter all the lobster coral you have been able to get. Cool and set aside.

SECOND Cream ½ pound sweet butter until soft and creamy. Mix in the coral until well blended. Then add juice of ½ lemon, ½ teaspoon paprika, ½ cup chopped chives or spring onions, and a few drops of red vegetable coloring until a delicate pink.

THIRD Place in serving-bowl and set in refrigerator until ready to serve.

RAISIN SAUCE FOR COLD FISH

2 cups raisins
1½ cups water
1 tablespoon sugar
1 tablespoon flour
salt, pepper, paprika
8 egg yolks

½ cup lemon juice
1½ cups raisin juice
½ cup fish stock
1 teaspoon butter
4 tablespoons cream

FIRST Poach 2 cups raisins in 1½ cups water for about 15 minutes. Cool.

SECOND Mix 1 tablespoon sugar, 1 tablespoon flour, salt, pepper, and paprika together. Add 8 egg yolks. Cream mixture together.

Add ½ cup lemon juice. Cream again. Add 1½ cups raisin juice (water in which raisins were poached) and cream again. Add ½ cup fish stock and cream again.

THIRD Cook in a double boiler until it thickens. Add 1 teaspoon butter. Cool. Before serving, add 4 tablespoons cream. Garnish the fish of your choice with 2 cups of poached raisins, pour the sauce over the fish, and serve.

NOTE Particularly good with cold boiled halibut or salmon.

SAUCE ALLEMANDE

2 ounces butter	2 egg yolks
3 tablespoons flour	1 tablespoon mushroom sauce *or* juice
1½ cups chicken broth	
½ cup cream	¼ teaspoon lemon juice

FIRST Render 2 ounces of butter. Remove from the fire and rub in 3 tablespoons of flour.

SECOND Gradually add 1½ cups of chicken broth and stir until it thickens.

THIRD Beat ½ cup cream with 2 egg yolks. Add to the sauce and stir until it thickens. Stir in 1 tablespoon mushroom sauce or mushroom juice (either bottled or homemade) and ¼ teaspoon lemon juice. Stir until smooth. Strain.

NOTE Mushroom juice may be made at home by soaking 1 commercial package of dried mushrooms in ¼ cup cold water for several hours.

SAUCE FOR MEATS

¼ pound butter	1 tablespoon paprika
½ cup cream	pepper, salt
¼ cup any good commercial meat sauce	¼ cup chives, cut fine (*or* ¼ cup parsley, cut coarsely)

FIRST Melt ¼ pound butter. Add ½ cup cream, ¼ cup any good commercial meat sauce, and 1 tablespoon paprika, pepper, salt, and ¼ cup chives cut fine (or parsley cut coarsely). Blend well.

SECOND Simmer and serve hot with steak or leg of lamb.

NOTE Any left-over sauce added to clear pan gravy makes a superb meat gravy with a very provocative flavor.

SAUCE MOUSSELINE

¼ pound butter
4 egg yolks
1 cup cream

salt, pepper
juice of ½ lemon

FIRST Melt ¼ pound of butter in the top of a double boiler. Beat 4 egg yolks and add to the melted butter, beating constantly with a wire whisk until thickened.

SECOND Add 1 cup of cream, a little at a time. Season with salt and pepper and continue to beat until smooth and somewhat thick. At this point add the juice of ½ a lemon.

WARNING This sauce may be kept warm in the top of the double boiler, but never allowed to get hot. Like Hollandaise, if it *must* stand a short while, it must be whisked, and although it remains standing over the hot water in the under part of the double boiler, the flame must be turned off. It is unexcelled with boiled fish, such as halibut or salmon.

SAUCE TARTAR

2 tablespoons minced green onions
1 tablespoon minced sour pickles
1 tablespoon minced sweet pickles

½ teaspoon Tabasco sauce
1 pint mayonnaise
1 tablespoon capers

FIRST Mince 2 tablespoons green onions, 1 tablespoon sour pickles and 1 tablespoon sweet pickles.

SECOND Stir ½ teaspoon Tabasco sauce into 1 pint mayonnaise. Stir in the minced ingredients and 1 tablespoon capers.

NOTE Use a mayonnaise that is not sweet. This is wonderful with fish.

STEAK BUTTER

¼ peeled clove garlic
¼ pound butter
1 teaspoon minced chives *or* spring onions
1 teaspoon minced herbs (savory, *or* basil, marjoram, *or* dill, etc.)

1 teaspoon lemon juice
½ teaspoon hickory salt
black pepper, freshly ground
salt
1 teaspoon paprika

FIRST Cut ¼ peeled clove garlic. Rub small bowl with the garlic and discard the garlic. Place ¼ pound butter in the garlic flavored bowl and cream it thoroughly until it is of a soft and satiny consistency.

SECOND When butter is thoroughly creamed, blend in 1 teaspoon minced chives or spring onions, 1 teaspoon of any preferred herb (savory, basil, marjoram, dill, etc.), 1 teaspoon lemon juice, ½ teaspoon hickory salt, freshly ground black pepper, salt to taste, and 1 teaspoon paprika. Work well together.

THIRD When the steaks are removed from the broiler, spread with steak butter. Keep butter at room temperature. Do not chill before using.

NOTE This excellent steak butter is just as delicious when served on any other broiled meat or fish. Just spread on the meat to be used when the meat is sizzling hot. Hickory salt may be found anywhere where preserved herbs are sold.

Chapter X: *Salads*

Oh, herbaceous treat!

'Twould tempt the dying anchorite to eat;

Back to the world he'd turn his fleeting soul,

And plunge his fingers in the salad bowl;

Serenely full the epicure would say,

"Fate cannot harm me,—I have dined today."

SYDNEY SMITH

A Receipt for a Salad, 1810

SALADS

NOTES ON SALAD MAKING

SALADS USING VEGETABLES, TOMATOES AND POTATOES

Celery Hearts in Tarragon Vinegar
Celery Root Sticks in Mustard Marinade
Celery Root with Pears
Cucumber Boats
Cucumbers in Sour Cream or French Dressing
Double Cole Slaw
Hot Potato Salad
Ice Cold Cauliflower
Large Beets Sliced with Spring Onions
Russian Salad
Spinach Salad, Dave Chasen
String Bean Salad
Tomatoes in Marinade
Tomato Towers
Tomatoes Stuffed with Smoked Salmon
Vegetable Salad, Diddie
Zucchini Canoes

SALADS USING SEAFOOD

Green Goddess Salad
Herring Salad
Herring Salad with Fruits and Endive
Sardine Salad
Seafood Salad Knopf
Shrimp, Crab, Lobster Salad

SALADS USING MEATS OR FOWL

Beef Salad
Chicken Salad, Diddie
Endive with Breast of Turkey
Salad Greens with Chicken Livers
Sweetbread Salad

SALADS USING FRUITS

Bunches of Grapes
Cantaloupe Balls in a Nest

SALAD RINGS

Beet Ring
Borsch Ring
Cucumber Ring
Lime Ring
Pineapple Ring
Relish Ring
Tomato Aspic Ring

SALADS USING GREENS

Chiffonade Salad
Company Salad, Josephine
Field Salad
French or Belgian Endive
Garden Salad and Sour Cream
Romaine Amsterdam
Salade au Pernod
Tossed Salad with Pecan Nut Balls

GARNISHES FOR SALAD

Cream Cheese Balls and Variations
  in Minced Ham
  in Minced Tongue
  in Shredded Swiss Cheese
  in Caviar
  in Chives
  in Raw Chopped Onion
Roquefort Cheese Balls in Paprika

SALADS

SALAD DRESSINGS

Boiled Salad Dressing
French Dressing
French Dressing, George Fitzmaurice
Mayonnaise Marguerite

Mayonnaise with Horseradish
Roquefort Dressing I
Roquefort Dressing II
Russian Dressing
Thousand Island Dressing
Vinaigrette

NOTES ON SALAD-MAKING

1. Salad greens must be thoroughly washed and dried. Anyone who has a wire basket such as the French use to shake the water off the salad greens is way ahead of the game. They may be purchased in most of the leading hardware stores in New York City.

2. French dressing is *not* French dressing when sugar is used. Sweet dressings may have their place, but not when the recipe calls for a French dressing.

3. To vary a French dressing, the addition of well-beaten egg is a pleasing novelty.

4. A dab of whipped cream topped with a maraschino cherry on any salad is strictly tea-room or drugstore-counter food.

5. Anyone who has a plot of ground and who does not avail himself of the pleasant surprise enjoyed only by those who have tasted garden greens is never going to know what a real garden salad can taste like. Grow: Boston, Butter Ball . . . Bib . . . Corn Salad. . . . Romaine. . . . New York head. . . . King Salad, etc., etc. Seeds are available in all garden seed stores.

6. It is always best to use more French dressing than less. When the leaves are turned in the dressing, they must all be well covered. If there is dressing left in the bottom of the bowl, pour it in a jar. It may be used again. If it is not "strong" enough, it may be "freshened."

7. For recipes requiring the use of gelatin, note instructions at the beginning of the Dessert chapter.

CELERY HEARTS IN TARRAGON VINEGAR
[French hors d'oeuvres salad]

4 hearts celery	pimiento
tarragon vinegar	2 tablespoons chopped chives

SERVES 6

FIRST Cut 4 hearts celery into even quarters. Place in salted water to cover and simmer until done. Drain and cool.

SECOND Place in a shallow dish long enough to allow the hearts to lie flat and evenly. Cover with tarragon vinegar and place in the refrigerator.

THIRD When ready to serve, pour off the vinegar, drape each heart with a long narrow slice of pimiento, and sprinkle the whole with 2 tablespoons chopped chives.

CELERY ROOT STICKS IN MUSTARD MARINADE
[French hors d'oeuvres salad]

1 large celery root (celeriac)	2 tablespoons vinegar
¼ cup olive oil	½ teaspoon salt
¼ cup French mustard (Dijon type preferred)	cayenne pepper

SERVES 6

FIRST Peel and blanch 1 large celery root in salted boiling water for about five minutes. Drain and cool. Chill in refrigerator.

SECOND Cut into sticks the size of a kitchen match. This will take a little patience.

THIRD Beat ¼ cup olive oil with ¼ cup French mustard (Dijon type preferred) and 2 tablespoons vinegar. Add ½ teaspoon salt and a dash of cayenne pepper. Just before serving, pour this dressing over the celery-root sticks, turning the sticks over and over until all are well covered by the dressing. Serve quickly as the oil has a tendency to separate.

CELERY ROOTS WITH PEARS

3 celery roots (celeriac)
1 head lettuce
6 pears

½ cup Thousand Island Dressing (page 250)
lemon juice

SERVES 6

FIRST Pare, then boil 3 celery roots in salted water until done. Cool. Slice evenly, about ¼ inch thick. Chill until ready to serve.

SECOND Tear 1 head of lettuce by hand. Use as a bed for 6 large quartered pears and the chilled celery roots. Cover the whole with ½ cup Thousand Island Dressing (page 250).

NOTE As soon as each pear is peeled sprinkle with lemon juice to prevent the fruit from turning brown.

CUCUMBER BOATS

3 long, firm cucumbers
2 large avocados
2 grapefruit
3 tomatoes

black olives
¾ cup French Dressing (page 247)

SERVES 6

FIRST Peel 3 cucumbers. Cut lengthwise in halves and soak in well-salted cold water for at least an hour. Remove from the water, rinse thoroughly under running water, and drain.

SECOND Cut thin slivers from the bottom of the cucumber halves so that they will stand without toppling. Scoop out most of the pulp of the cucumber, leaving a shell. Fill each "boat" with alternate thin slices made to fit of 2 large avocados, 2 grapefruit and 3 tomatoes. Arrange these slices evenly and attractively, for the appearance of this salad adds greatly to its enjoyment.

THIRD When ready to serve, dress the tops of the "boats" with tidy wedges of black olives and ¾ cup of tangy French Dressing (page 247). Set on lettuce leaves and serve very cold.

CUCUMBERS IN SOUR CREAM OR FRENCH DRESSING

4 cucumbers
salt
1 cup sour cream

2 tablespoons chopped chives
black pepper

SERVES 6

FIRST Pare and thinly slice 4 cucumbers. Salt the slices on a good-sized plate. Place another plate on top of them and weigh down with a pressing-iron or something equally heavy.

SECOND Two hours later remove the weight and the top plate and rinse the cucumber slices in fresh water. Drain thoroughly and store in refrigerator.

THIRD When ready to serve, fold in 1 cup of sour cream until the slices are all well covered. Dress the dish with 2 tablespoons chopped chives and a generous sprinkling of black pepper.

NOTE This is particularly well suited as an accompaniment for cold fish. The cucumbers may be covered with ½ cup of French Dressing (page 247) instead of the sour cream if preferred.

DOUBLE COLE SLAW

½ head firm white cabbage
½ head firm red cabbage
anise seeds

black pepper
½ cup French Dressing (page 247)

SERVES 6

FIRST Shred ½ head firm white cabbage and ½ head firm red cabbage. Sprinkle with anise seeds and black pepper. Pour on ½ cup French Dressing (page 247) and turn the cabbage in the dressing a number of times.

SECOND Allow to marinate in the refrigerator for at least an hour before serving. Just before serving, turn in the dressing once again.

HOT POTATO SALAD

2 pounds new potatoes
6 slices bacon
1 medium onion
¼ cup wine vinegar
2 cups sour cream

salt, black pepper
celery seed
¼ cup minced chives *or* spring onions

SERVES 8

FIRST Boil 2 pounds new potatoes in their jackets in salted water. Do not let them get too soft.

SECOND While the potatoes are cooking, prepare the sauce as follows: Fry 6 slices bacon until crisp. Break into moderate-sized pieces. Fry 1 finely chopped medium onion in the bacon drippings until golden. Strain and mix with the bacon. Stir ¼ cup wine vinegar into 2 cups sour cream. Add salt, black pepper, and celery seed to taste. Fold in the chopped onions and bacon.

THIRD Peel and slice the cooked potatoes. Drop the warm sliced potatoes into the sour-cream sauce, turning several times with spoon and fork. Sprinkle the top of the salad with ¼ cup minced chives or spring onions.

NOTE Prepare the sauce while the potatoes are boiling. Since this is a hot potato salad, the sauce must be ready when the potatoes are done.

ICE-COLD CAULIFLOWER

1 large head cauliflower
1 head lettuce

½ cup French Dressing (page 247)
paprika

SERVES 6

FIRST Cook 1 large head cauliflower in salt water. Drain, cool, then chill in refrigerator.

SECOND Separate lettuce leaves and place them in a salad bowl in the shape of a nest. Set the cauliflower inside the nest and pour over it ½ cup French Dressing (page 247). Sprinkle with paprika.

NOTE The French sometimes serve this with mayonnaise. We prefer it with the tart dressing. In either case, serve it very cold.

LARGE BEETS SLICED WITH SPRING ONIONS
[*French hors d'oeuvres salad*]

2 cans large sliced beets
¼ cup minced spring onions
¼ cup tarragon vinegar
½ cup olive oil

black pepper, salt
celery salt
onion salt

SERVES 6

FIRST Drain 2 cans large sliced beets. Place them in a flat serving-dish and add ¼ cup minced spring onions. Chill in the refrigerator.

SECOND Beat ¼ cup tarragon vinegar with ½ cup olive oil, black pepper, salt, celery salt, and onion salt to taste. Pour over the beets and serve.

RUSSIAN SALAD

1 cup carrots
1 cup beets
1 small cauliflower
1 cup asparagus tips
1 cup fresh green peas
1 cup French style string beans
3 artichoke hearts

1 head lettuce
½ cup chili sauce
1 cup mayonnaise
juice of ½ lemon
½ teaspoon paprika
½ teaspoon celery salt
tarragon

SERVES 6

FIRST Cook each vegetable separately. Be careful not to overcook them—they must on no account be mushy. Dice 1 cup carrots and 1 cup beets. Separate the flowerlets of 1 small cauliflower. Measure out 1 cup asparagus tips, 1 cup fresh green peas, and 1 cup French style green beans. Cut 3 artichoke hearts into pieces.

SECOND Carefully open a head of lettuce without breaking the

SALADS 223

leaves from the core. Place this loosened head of lettuce in the center of a round platter. Arrange each vegetable separately in small mounds surrounding the head of lettuce.

THIRD Cover the vegetables and the lettuce with the following dressing: mix ½ cup chili sauce with 1 cup mayonnaise, the juice of ½ lemon, ½ teaspoon paprika, and ½ teaspoon celery salt. Mix well, and add ½ teaspoon salt and a pinch of tarragon.

NOTE The beauty of this salad is entirely up to the ingenuity of the cook. It can be made to look like a colorful bouquet, but it is not one of those gaudy salads given to looks alone. It is wholesome and most satisfying.

SPINACH SALAD, DAVE CHASEN

1 pound fresh very young spinach   ½ cups French Dressing (page 247)
4 slices bacon

SERVES 6

FIRST Sort 1 pound fresh very young spinach, choosing only the most tender leaves. Remove all the stems, wash well, and drain.

SECOND Fry 4 slices bacon until crisp. Crumble thoroughly and add to the spinach. Add ½ cup French Dressing (page 247) and toss until everything is well covered with the dressing and the bacon bits are well distributed throughout.

NOTE Do not allow this salad to stand. Have it well chilled. The main precaution, of course, is to see that the spinach leaves are young—the younger, the better.

STRING-BEAN SALAD

1 pound whole fresh, young string beans   3 hard-boiled eggs
½ cup French Dressing (page 247)   almonds
   paprika

SERVES 4

FIRST Cook 1 pound whole fresh, young string beans (the salad can be no better than the quality of the string beans) for about twenty minutes in as little salted water as possible. Cool and place in the refrigerator until chilled.

SECOND When ready to serve, place in a salad bowl and add ½ cup French Dressing (page 247), turning the beans in the dressing until thoroughly coated. Decorate with wedges of 3 hard-boiled eggs and thin slivers of crisp peeled almonds. Sprinkle very lightly with paprika.

NOTE A splendid variation of this is the addition of a liberal quantity of chopped fresh parsley and 2 tablespoons of minced raw onion.

TOMATOES EN MARINADE
[*A French hors d'oeuvres salad*]

4 large tomatoes	2 tablespoons chopped chives
½ cup French Dressing (page 247)	2 tablespoons chopped parsley
	black pepper

SERVES 6

FIRST Peel and slice 4 large tomatoes. Place on a flat serving-dish, the slices overlapping one another. Pour over them ½ cup French Dressing (page 247).

SECOND Sprinkle evenly with 2 tablespoons chopped chives, 2 tablespoons chopped parsley, and a generous shaking of black pepper, preferably freshly ground.

TOMATO TOWERS

6 large tomatoes	6 slices ham
salt and peppre	6 hard-boiled eggs
mayonnaise	12 anchovy fillets
6 slices liver sausage	chopped parsley
	water cress

SERVES 6

FIRST Peel and slice 6 large tomatoes each into three even pieces.

SECOND Place 6 slices tomato on six individual plates, sprinkle with salt and pepper, and spread thinly with mayonnaise. Top each with a slice liver-sausage, then another slice tomato. Sprinkle again with salt and pepper and spread thinly with mayonnaise.

THIRD Proceed as before, this time with 6 slices of ham (cut to fit), 6 more slices of tomato, pepper, salt, and thinly spread mayonnaise; then finally tidy slices of hard-boiled eggs (6 eggs in all). Top each "tomato tower" with a cross made of 2 fillets of anchovies. Add a generous dab of mayonnaise, sprinkle with chopped parsley, and decorate with sprigs of water cress. Serve very cold.

NOTE In order to avoid any confusion, here is the order in which the tower is built:

1 slice tomato	1 slice tomato
salt and pepper	salt and pepper
thinly spread mayonnaise	thinly spread mayonnaise
1 slice liver sausage	1 hard-boiled egg, cut into slices
1 slice tomato	2 crossed anchovy fillets
salt and pepper	generous dab of mayonnaise
thinly spread mayonnaise	chopped parsley
1 slice ham, cut to fit	sprigs water cress

TOMATOES STUFFED WITH SMOKED SALMON

6 good-sized tomatoes	1 cup Thousand Island Dressing
6 stuffed eggs (page 51)	(page 250)
12 slices smoked salmon	caviar (optional)

SERVES 6

FIRST Dip 6 good-sized tomatoes into boiling water and skin them. Then cut off the top and hollow slightly. Place in refrigerator until ready to serve.

SECOND Tuck the ends of 12 even slices smoked salmon (2 for each tomato) in the center of the tomatoes, allowing them to hang down on either side. Set 6 stuffed eggs (page 51) in the center of the tomatoes, thereby securing the ends of the salmon.

THIRD Cover the tops (except for the stuffed eggs) with 1 cup Thousand Island Dressing (page 250). Serve very cold.

NOTE If you have any caviar, dot the top of each stuffed egg with a small amount.

VEGETABLE SALAD DIDDIE

2 envelopes gelatin
½ cup cold water
2 cups clear chicken broth
½ cup cooked carrots
½ cup cooked string beans

½ cup cooked peas
½ cup chopped raw celery
½ cup cooked corn
1 head lettuce
½ cup mayonnaise

SERVES 8

FIRST Soak 2 envelopes gelatin in ½ cup cold water for five minutes. Dissolve over hot water.

SECOND Add the dissolved gelatin to 2 cups clear chicken broth. Add to the liquid the following vegetables: ½ cup cooked carrots, ½ cup cooked string beans, ½ cup cooked peas, ½ cup chopped raw celery, and ½ cup cooked corn. Pour it all into a ring mold.

THIRD When ready to serve, unmold and fill the center of the ring with the leaves of ½ head lettuce turned in ½ cup mayonnaise. Form a wreath around the ring with the leaves of the second half of the head of lettuce, also turned in mayonnaise. If desired, serve with extra mayonnaise.

ZUCCHINI CANOES

6 long, firm zucchini
¼ cup olive oil
4 tablespoons vinegar
dry mustard

salt, pepper
2 hard-boiled eggs
6 lettuce leaves
paprika

SERVES 6

FIRST Boil 6 long, firm zucchini in salted water until cooked but left a little firm. Cool. Cut each zucchini into four long sections or "canoes."

SECOND Make a salad-dressing with ¼ cup olive oil, 4 tablespoons vinegar, a pinch of dry mustard, and salt and pepper to taste. Beat until well blended. Chop 2 hard-boiled eggs very fine and add to the dressing.

THIRD Place a large lettuce leaf on six individual salad plates. Lay four zucchini "canoes" on each, cover with dressing, and sprinkle with paprika. Serve very cold.

GREEN GODDESS SALAD

8 or 10 anchovy fillets	1 tablespoon tarragon vinegar
1 small onion	salad greens (romaine, chicory, escarole)
2 sprigs parsley	
fresh tarragon leaves	crab (optional)
1 bunch fresh chives	shrimp (optional)
3 cups mayonnaise	

SERVES 8

FIRST Chop 8 or 10 anchovy fillets with 1 small onion.

SECOND Chop 2 sprigs parsley, a few fresh tarragon leaves (or preserved, if necessary), and 1 bunch fresh chives. After these herbs are finely chopped, mash them together.

THIRD Combine the chopped anchovy fillets, chopped onion, and the mashed herbs with 3 cups mayonnaise and add 1 tablespoon tarragon vinegar.

FOURTH Mix this dressing with salad greens (romaine, chicory, and escarole) in a garlic-rubbed bowl. Serve immediately.

NOTE Crab or small shrimp may be added to the salad.

HERRING SALAD *Marie's*

4 salt herrings
½ pound roasted veal
3 cooked beets
3 boiled potatoes
5 *or* 6 sour apples
1 small bunch of celery
1 bottle vinegar pickles (5 ounces)
1 garlic-flavored dill pickle
⅛ pound sardellen *or* anchovies

5 hard-boiled eggs
1 cup olive oil
½ cup tarragon vinegar
1½ tablespoons onion juice
powdered cloves
salt, black pepper
pickled beets
capers

SERVES 12

FIRST Carefully remove all the bones from 4 salt herrings. Cut the herring into *small* pieces and place into a large mixing bowl. Cut ½ pound roasted veal into *small* pieces. Cut up into small pieces: 3 cooked beets, 3 boiled potatoes, 5 or 6 sour apples, 1 small bunch celery, 1 5-ounce bottle vinegar pickles, and 1 garlic-flavored dill pickle. *Mince* ⅛ pound sardellen or anchovies *with* 1 hard-boiled egg. Toss everything together into the mixing-bowl and mix well.

SECOND Beat 1 cup olive oil with ½ cup tarragon vinegar. Whip in 1½ tablespoons onion juice, pinch of powdered cloves, and a generous shake of salt and black pepper. Pour this dressing over the herring salad and mix until everything is well dampened with the dressing. Stand in refrigerator all day or overnight.

THIRD When ready to serve, decorate with 4 quartered hard-boiled eggs, sliced pickled beets, and a scattering of capers. Cut several thin slices of toast into wedged-shaped pieces and surround the salad on a serving-platter.

NOTE Any left-over Herring Salad is almost certain to enchant your guests if served on rye-bread rounds as an appetizer.

HERRING SALAD WITH FRUITS AND ENDIVE

1 pound marinated herring (with sour-cream sauce and onions)
4 pears
3 tart apples

¾ pound French *or* Belgian endive
¼ cup seedless raisins
½ cup French Dressing (p. 247)

SERVES 6

FIRST Cut 1 pound marinated herring into 1-inch pieces. Cut up

4 pears, 3 tart apples, and ¾ pound French or Belgian endive. The endive must be cut first into long pieces and then cut across into one-inch pieces. Toss everything together into a salad bowl.

SECOND Add ¼ cup seedless raisins. Then add ½ cup French Dressing (page 247), mixed with the sour-cream sauce and onions in which the herring has been marinated. Serve very cold.

NOTE This happened all by accident. It sounds odd, but was the hit of the party! If you find it difficult to believe, try it and see!

SARDINE SALAD

4 skinless and boneless sardines	1 head lettuce
½ cup olive oil	1 head romaine
¼ cup cider vinegar	2 tablespoons chives
pepper, salt	paprika

SERVES 6

FIRST Crush 4 skinless and boneless sardines with ½ cup olive oil. Add the oil, a little at a time. Add ¼ cup cider vinegar and pepper and salt to taste. Mash through a strainer.

SECOND Stir the sardine dressing until well blended, then pour over the separated leaves of 1 head lettuce and the cut leaves of 1 head romaine. Sprinkle the finished salad with 2 tablespoons chives and with sufficient paprika to color lightly.

SEA-FOOD SALAD KNOPF

2 boiled crabs	¼ cup prepared mustard
1 boiled lobster	½ cup mayonnaise
6 boiled shrimp	¼ cup ketchup
1 firm avocado	4 tomatoes
½ head lettuce	4 hard-boiled eggs
1 tablespoon minced chives	paprika
salt, black pepper, celery salt	capers (optional)

SERVES 6

FIRST Pick over meat from 2 boiled crabs, 1 boiled lobster, and 6 boiled shrimps. Cut into medium pieces and place in a large mixing-bowl.

SECOND Dice 1 firm avocado, shred ½ head of lettuce, and mix all together. Then sprinkle with 1 tablespoon minced chives. Season with salt, black pepper, and celery salt to taste.

THIRD Mix ¼ cup prepared mustard with ½ cup mayonnaise and ¼ cup ketchup until well blended. Fold the sauce into the sea-food mixture. Continue to fold until the sea food is well covered with the sauce.

FOURTH Press the whole with a large kitchen spoon into a smaller bowl and set it in the refrigerator until ready to serve. Unmold onto a serving-platter and garnish with a ring made of 4 quartered tomatoes. Cover the mounded salad with slices of 4 hard-boiled eggs set closely together. Sprinkle the egg slices lightly with paprika.

NOTE Some people don't like capers, but if you do, place one between each slice of hard-boiled egg. It gives the whole a very professional garnish and a festive look. Do not let this salad stand around the kitchen. Serve it when it is very cold.

SHRIMP, CRAB, OR LOBSTER SALAD

1 quart shrimp, crab, *or* lobster meat	½ cup mayonnaise
1 tablespoon chopped chives	4 tablespoons tarragon vinegar
1 tablespoon capers	1 teaspoon chopped tarragon
salt, black pepper	3 hard-boiled eggs
	paprika

SERVES 6

FIRST Pick over 1 quart shrimp, crab, or lobster meat, but do not cut or shred too small, as the flavor is best retained when the pieces are reasonably large. Sprinkle 1 tablespoon chopped chives and 1 tablespoon capers on the sea food. Season with salt and black pepper to taste.

SECOND Combine ½ cup mayonnaise with 4 tablespoons tarragon vinegar and 1 teaspoon chopped tarragon. Fold into the sea food. Garnish with narrow, canoe-shaped wedges of 3 hard-boiled eggs and a sprinkling of paprika.

NOTE This salad is excellent in itself molded on lettuce leaves or used as a filling in the center of a ring. There is no reason why it couldn't be tried occasionally as a mixed sea food salad, using all three—shrimp, crab, *and* lobster.

BEEF SALAD

2 pounds boiled beef
4 boiled potatoes
1 onion
4 frankfurters
¼ pound Italian salami
2 sour pickles
2 hard-boiled eggs
½ head lettuce

salt, black pepper, paprika
¾ cup olive *or* "salad oil"
½ cup vinegar
½ cup mayonnaise
lettuce leaves
4 hard-boiled eggs
16 anchovy fillets

SERVES 12

FIRST Chop or shred 2 pounds boiled beef into fine little pieces. Chop together 4 boiled potatoes, 1 onion, 4 frankfurters, ¼ pound Italian salami, 2 sour pickles, 2 hard-boiled eggs, and ½ head lettuce. Mix well and add a generous shake of salt, black pepper, and paprika.

SECOND Mix ¾ cup olive or "salad oil" with ½ cup vinegar and ½ cup mayonnaise until smooth. Pour onto beef salad and toss until the mixture is thoroughly coated with the dressing. Place in refrigerator to marinate overnight or all day.

THIRD Serve on a platter and surround with lettuce leaves. Set 4 quartered hard-boiled eggs on the lettuce leaves, topping each wedge with an anchovy fillet.

CHICKEN SALAD DIDDIE

1 large roasted chicken
1 cup chopped celery
¼ cup capers
4 sliced hard-boiled eggs
3 tomatoes
celery seed
salt, black pepper

mayonnaise

Garnish:
water cress
3 tomatoes
4 hard-boiled eggs
paprika

SERVES 6

FIRST Cut up 1 large roasted chicken. Remove all skin and tendons and leave the pieces in chunks. Under no circumstances chop small.

SECOND Mix chicken pieces with 1 cup chopped celery, ¼ cup capers, 4 sliced hard-boiled eggs, and 3 tomatoes peeled and cut up. Add celery seed, salt, and black pepper.

THIRD Fold in mayonnaise to taste. Place the chicken salad on a serving-platter and surround with a wreath of water cress. Top the water cress with alternate quarters of 3 firm tomatoes and the quarters of 4 hard-boiled eggs. Sprinkle the salad and the eggs lightly with paprika. Serve very cold.

NOTE Many people will tell you that a stewing-hen will do. But it depends what you are after. If it is primarily flavor, then do, by all means, use a roasting-chicken, and do not roast it until it is dry as a bone. Also be sure you do not chop it up into little pieces. As I say, if its flavor you are after, let it be enjoyed.

ENDIVE WITH BREAST OF TURKEY

2 slices cooked breast of turkey
1 pound French *or* Belgian endive
1 hard-boiled egg

½ cup French Dressing blended with ¼ teaspoon dry mustard
paprika

SERVES 6

FIRST Cut 2 slices of cooked breast of turkey into long, thin slivers. Separate the leaves of 1 pound French or Belgian endive lengthwise into sections, as you would celery hearts. Chop 1 hard-boiled egg.

SECOND Set the sections of endive on individual salad plates. Divide the slivers of turkey breast evenly. Pour on ½ cup French Dressing blended with ¼ teaspoon dry mustard and sprinkle each salad with the chopped egg. Add a sprinkling of paprika.

NOTE Smoked turkey or cold roast chicken may be used in this fashion.

SALAD GREENS WITH CHICKEN LIVERS

salad greens to taste
3 to 4 chicken livers
2 tablespoons chicken fat *or* butter
marjoram

minced chives
½ cup French Dressing (page 247)
paprika

SERVES 6

FIRST Separate the leaves of salad greens and toss into a bowl.

SECOND Lightly fry 3 or 4 very fresh chicken livers in 2 tablespoons chicken fat or butter. Remove from the skillet, drain, and cool. Sprinkle with marjoram and minced chives.

THIRD Cut the chicken livers into small pieces, but do not mince. Combine them with the salad greens. Add ½ cup French Dressing (page 247), and turn the whole until thoroughly blended. Dot with paprika.

SWEETBREAD SALAD

[*A French hors d'oeuvres salad*]

2 pairs boiled sweetbreads
¼ firm head lettuce
½ cup mayonnaise
capers

paprika
green olives and sweet pickles, sliced

SERVES 4

FIRST Cut 2 pairs boiled sweetbreads into even slices. Shred ¼ firm head lettuce. Make a bed of the lettuce and place the slices of sweetbreads on top. Cover with ½ cup mayonnaise.

SECOND Scatter capers on top, sprinkle with paprika, and decorate with slices of green olives and sweet pickles. Serve very cold.

NOTE This is the original recipe the French use on their fabulous hors d'œuvres tray; but, for those who prefer it, a tart French Dressing (page 248) may be used instead of the mayonnaise.

BUNCHES OF GRAPES

3 large Bartlett pears
juice of ½ lemon
2 packages cream cheese
4 tablespoons cream

1 teaspoon vanilla
1 tablespoon sugar
6 large leaves (grape, if possible)
seedless grapes

SERVES 6

FIRST Pare and core 3 large Bartlett pears. Cut the pears in even halves and sprinkle with the juice of half a lemon to prevent their discoloration.

SECOND Cream 2 packages cream cheese with 4 tablespoons cream. Add 1 teaspoon vanilla for flavor and 1 tablespoon sugar to sweeten. Work this until smooth.

THIRD Place a large flat leaf on each individual salad plate. On each leaf place half a pear, cut side *down*. Conceal the pear half entirely with a thick covering of creamed cheese. Cover the cheese as closely as possible with seedless grapes. Each half pear will give the appearance of a small bunch of grapes.

NOTE If you like the idea, the cavity in the underside of the pear may be filled with any preferred tart jelly.

CANTALOUPE BALLS IN A NEST

1 large solid head lettuce
1 ripe cantaloupe

1 ripe avocado
½ cup French Dressing (page 247)

SERVES 4

FIRST Remove the center of 1 large solid head lettuce. Scoop out enough balls from 1 ripe cantaloupe to half fill the center of the lettuce. Scoop out sufficient balls from 1 ripe avocado to finish filling center of the lettuce.

SECOND Pour ½ cup French Dressing (page 247) over the whole. Serve with a knife, with which to cut the lettuce, and a spoon, with which to scoop out the balls of melon and avacodo.

BEET RING

2 cans small beets
1 envelope gelatin
¼ cup cold water

½ cup chopped celery
2 tablespoons sugar
1 tablespoon horseradish

SERVES 6

FIRST Boil the juice from 2 cans small beets with a little water. Add 1 envelope of gelatin that has soaked for 5 minutes in ¼ cup cold water. Stir until dissolved in boiling juice. Cool.

SECOND Add ½ cup chopped celery, 2 tablespoons sugar, 1 tablespoon horseradish, and the contents of 2 cans small beets. Mix together and place in a cold ring mold. Place in refrigerator until set. Serve with any preferred salad in the center of the ring, using the salad dressing best suited to your choice of salads.

BORSCH RING

1 quart borsch
2 envelopes gelatin
½ cup cold water

2 cups sour cream
6 spring onions

SERVES 6

FIRST Heat 1 quart borsch. Soak 2 envelopes gelatin in ½ cup cold water for 5 minutes. Dissolve in hot borsch. Pour into a small ring mold. Cool. Place in refrigerator to set.

SECOND Unmold when ready to serve. Fill the center with 2 cups of sour cream combined with 6 coarsely chopped spring onions.

NOTE Prepared borsch may be bought in most delicatessen stores.

CUCUMBER RING

1½ envelopes gelatin	½ teaspoon salt
½ cup cold water	1 large cucumber
½ cup sugar	1 green pepper
¼ cup lemon juice	1 onion
½ cup vinegar	3 celery stalks
2 cups hot water	3 cabbage leaves

SERVES 6

FIRST Soak 1½ envelopes gelatin in ½ cup cold water. Allow to stand while the next step is being prepared.

SECOND Combine ½ cup sugar with ¼ cup lemon juice, ½ cup vinegar, and 2 cups hot water. Bring to a boil and add ½ teaspoon of salt. Dissolve the gelatin in the boiling mixture. Allow the mixture to stand until it thickens.

THIRD Once the mixture has begun to thicken, put the following ingredients through the food-chopper: 1 large cucumber, 1 green pepper, 1 onion, 3 celery stalks, 3 cabbage leaves. Add to the liquid mixture and place in a mold. This is delicious with crab, lobster, or shrimp. Serve with mayonnaise or any preferred cold sauce.

LIME RING

2 packages lime Jello	almonds
2 cans grapefruit segments	lettuce
2 large avocados	mayonnaise

SERVES 6

FIRST Dissolve 2 packages of lime Jello in the juice from 2 cans grapefruit segments. Pour half the Jello in a ring mold and place in the refrigerator to set.

SECOND Arrange 2 cans grapefruit segments, 2 large avocados sliced, and a few slivered white almonds on top of the set Jello. Add the second half of the Jello and replace the mold in the refrigerator.

THIRD When ready to serve, unmold on a bed of lettuce leaves with a wreath of lettuce leaves surrounding the ring and a generous amount of mayonnaise in a nest of lettuce leaves in the center.

PINEAPPLE RING

1 envelope gelatin
¼ cup cold water
¼ cup lemon juice
¼ cup sugar

1 cup shredded pineapple
1 cup chopped celery
chicken, crab, *or* fruit salad

SERVES 6

FIRST Soak 1 envelope gelatin in ¼ cup cold water and dissolve over hot water. Add ¼ cup vinegar, ¼ cup lemon juice, and ¼ cup sugar.

SECOND Drain 1 cup shredded pineapple, mix with 1 cup chopped celery, and add to liquid. Place in a ring mold and set in refrigerator overnight or all day.

THIRD When ready to serve, unmold and fill center with chicken, crab, or fruit salad.

RELISH RING

1 can shredded pineapple
1 package lemon Jello

1 package lime Jello
1 medium jar Indian relish

SERVES 6

FIRST Mix pineapple juice from 1 can shredded pineapple with sufficient water to make 4 cups. Dissolve 1 package lemon Jello and 1 package lime Jello in the liquid.

SECOND Add 1 can shredded pineapple (drained of juice) and 1 medium jar of Indian relish. Pour into a ring mold and set in refrigerator until firm.

NOTE This ring may be filled with any preferred filling, but it is especially good filled with a combination of sliced avocados and segments of grapefruit, using a tart French Dressing to contrast with the sweet flavor of the Jello ring.

TOMATO-ASPIC RING

2 envelopes gelatin
½ cup cold water
1 quart tomato juice
½ cup chopped celery
¼ cup Worcestershire Sauce
1 teaspoon celery salt
1 teaspoon salt

½ teaspoon black pepper
4 hard-boiled eggs
lettuce
paprika
chicken salad, cole slaw *or* potato salad

SERVES 6

FIRST Soak 2 envelopes of gelatin in ½ cup cold water. Dissolve over hot water.

SECOND Combine 1 quart tomato juice, ½ cup chopped celery, ¼ cup Worcestershire Sauce, 1 teaspoon celery salt, 1 teaspoon salt, and ½ teaspoon black pepper. Add the dissolved gelatin. Pour into a ring mold and set in refrigerator until firm.

THIRD Just before serving, unmold and surround with a ring of 4 quartered hard-boiled eggs on a wreath of lettuce leaves. Sprinkle the eggs with paprika and fill the center of ring with any desired filling—chicken salad, cole slaw, or potato salad. Serve very cold.

CHIFFONADE SALAD

2 hard-boiled eggs
2 large cooked beets
3 sprigs parsley
6 sprigs water cress

½ cup French Dressing (page 247)
1 head lettuce

SERVES 6

FIRST Chop together 2 hard-boiled eggs, 2 large cooked beets, 3 sprigs parsley, and 6 sprigs water cress. Marinate in ½ cup of French Dressing (page 247).

SECOND When ready to serve, tear apart 1 head lettuce and place in a salad bowl. Pour the dressing over the lettuce and toss until well distributed. Serve very cold.

COMPANY SALAD JOSEPHINE

1 head lettuce
1 head chicory
1 head romaine
½ bunch water cress
1 hard-boiled egg

½ cup French Dressing (page 247)
chopped parsley and chives
½ pound Swiss cheese

SERVES 8

FIRST Loosen the leaves of 1 head lettuce and tear them in half. Cut off the dark parts of 1 head chicory, using only the very light. Cut in two the light leaves of 1 head romaine. Toss lettuce, chicory, and romaine with ½ bunch of water cress (sprigs only) in a salad bowl.

SECOND Crush 1 hard-boiled egg to a paste in ½ cup French Dressing (page 247). Add chopped parsley and chives to taste. Allow to stand before using, but stir thoroughly when ready to pour into salad.

THIRD Cut ½ pound Swiss cheese into long slender pieces approximately the size of a kitchen match. Toss into salad bowl. Pour on French Dressing and turn with fork and spoon until the salad is thoroughly covered with the dressing.

FIELD SALAD

young garden salad greens
½ cup French Dressing (page 247)

3 hard-boiled eggs

SERVES 6

FIRST Wash and dry young garden salad greens and toss in a salad bowl. Pour over them ½ cup French Dressing (page 247), turning the greens in the dressing until well covered.

SECOND Slice 3 hard-boiled eggs and add to the salad. Turn them several times, not minding if some of the yolk blends with the dressing. Serve immediately.

FRENCH OR BELGIAN ENDIVE

1 pound French *or* Belgian endive	½ cup French Dressing (page 247)
celery seed	¼ teaspoon dry mustard
black pepper	

SERVES 6

FIRST Separate the leaves of 1 pound ice cold French or Belgian endive. (If you cut it, you will have to serve it immediately; otherwise it will turn brown.)

SECOND Sprinkle the endive with celery seed and black pepper. Pour over it ½ cup French Dressing (page 247), seasoned with ¼ teaspoon dry mustard (French mustard may be used, if preferred). Serve on individual plates.

GARDEN SALAD WITH SOUR CREAM

1 large cucumber	2 zucchini
1 bunch radishes	1 small head cauliflower
1 bunch spring onions	1 cup sour cream
2 peeled tomatoes	lettuce leaves
2 large, scraped carrots	

GARNISH

6 tablespoons sour cream	capers (optional)
paprika	

SERVES 6

FIRST Slice 1 large cucumber, 1 bunch radishes, 1 bunch spring onions, 2 peeled tomatoes, 2 large, scraped carrots, and 2 zucchini. Separate the flowerlets from a small head of cauliflower. Cover all these vegetables with 1 cup sour cream. Turn again and again until well covered by the cream.

SECOND Arrange lettuce leaves on individual plates and place the vegetables in cream in even portions on the lettuce leaves. Top each portion with additional sour cream, about 1 tablespoon a portion. Sprinkle with paprika. Decorate with capers if desired. Serve very cold.

ROMAINE AMSTERDAM

2 heads romaine ½ pound best Roquefort *or* Blue cheese

SERVES 6

FIRST Separate the leaves of 2 heads romaine, leaving each separate leaf whole. Wash, dry and chill well.

SECOND Serve these leaves of romaine without any dressing. Pass ½ pound best Roquefort or Blue cheese in a separate dish. Tuck the cheese generously onto the leaves of romaine, along the vein of each leaf. Then pick the leaf up in your hand and eat, starting at the top, as though eating a sandwich.

SALADE AU PERNOD

½ teaspoon salt
½ teaspoon dry mustard
1 tablespoon chopped parsley
1 tablespoon chopped chives
1 slice toast

½ clove garlic
1 cup olive oil
½ cup Pernod
fresh salad greens

SERVES 6

FIRST Combine ½ teaspoon salt, ½ teaspoon dry mustard, 1 tablespoon chopped parsley, and 1 tablespoon chopped chives.

SECOND Rub 1 slice toast with the cut side of ½ clove of garlic. Cut toast into cubes. Discard the garlic and add the bread cubes to the seasonings.

THIRD Mix 1 cup olive oil with ½ cup Pernod. Combine with the seasonings and bread cubes. Shake well and serve over fresh salad greens. Turn the greens over and over in the dressing.

NOTE I don't even blush when I admit that I turn my salad with my bare hands. My mother's fabulous cook, Marie, used always to say that no matter how excellent your kitchen implements, "There is no substitute for the human hand." If ever there was a true word spoken! . . .

TOSSED SALAD WITH PECAN NUT BALLS

1 head lettuce	2 tablespoons chopped water cress
1 head chicory *or* escarole	½ cup French Dressing (page 247)
1 head romaine	
2 tablespoons chopped chives	1 recipe Pecan Nut Balls (page 242)
2 tablespoons chopped parsley	

SERVES 6

FIRST Tear 1 head lettuce by hand. Cut the best leaves of 1 head chicory or escarole and 1 head of romaine. Toss together in a large salad bowl and sprinkle the greens with 2 tablespoons each of chopped chives, chopped parsley, and chopped water cress.

SECOND Add ½ cup French Dressing (page 247), turning the greens in the dressing over and over again. Set in the refrigerator until ready to serve.

THIRD After the greens have been given a final turning, and just before serving, distribute Cream Cheese Pecan Nut Balls (page 242) on top of the salad bowl.

CREAM CHEESE BALLS AND VARIATIONS

2 packages cream cheese   ½ cup chopped pecans

SERVES 6

FIRST Cut 2 packages cream cheese into 12 even pieces. Grease the palms of the hands with butter. Roll each ball between the palms until quite smooth and round.

SECOND Chop ½ cup pecans until very, very fine. Scatter the chopped nuts on a bread board. Roll each cheese ball over and over in the chopped nuts until entirely covered.

SALADS

VARIATIONS:
Cream Cheese Balls Rolled in Minced Ham
Cream Cheese Balls Rolled in Minced Tongue
Cream Cheese Balls Rolled in Shredded Swiss Cheese
Cream Cheese Balls Rolled in Caviar
Cream Cheese Balls Rolled in Chives
Cream Cheese Balls Rolled in Raw Chopped Onions

ROQUEFORT CHEESE BALLS

½ lb. Roquefort cheese
2 tablespoons cream

paprika

SERVES 6

FIRST Mash ½ lb. Roquefort cheese together with 2 tablespoons cream until slightly softened.

SECOND Divide the cheese into even sections, the size being a matter of preference. Pick them up one at a time and roll them between the buttered palms of your hands.

THIRD Put some paprika on a flat plate and roll each ball around and around in the paprika until thoroughly coated. Toss on top of a green salad and serve with well-heated crackers.

Salad-Dressings

Mayonnaise . . . one of the sauces which serve the French in place of a state religion.

AMBROSE BIERCE: *The Devil's Dictionary*, 1906

SALAD-DRESSINGS

Boiled Salad-Dressing
French Dressing
  George Fitzmaurice
Mayonnaise Marguerite
  with Horseradish

Roquefort
  Dressing I
  Dressing II
Russian Dressing
Thousand Island Dressing
Vinaigrette

BOILED SALAD-DRESSING

3 eggs
1 teaspoon dry mustard
½ cup sugar
½ cup vinegar
¼ cup water

salt
1 tablespoon flour
1½ tablespoons butter
¾ cup milk

FIRST Beat 3 eggs. Add 1 teaspoon dry mustard, ½ cup sugar, ½ cup vinegar, and ¼ cup water. Blend well. Salt to taste. Then add 1 tablespoon flour, 1½ tablespoons butter, and ¾ cup milk.

SECOND Place on the fire and stir constantly until smooth and thick. Allow to cook several minutes, stirring all the while. Cool. Serve cold.

FRENCH DRESSING

½ cup tarragon vinegar
1 cup olive oil
1 teaspoon dry mustard
½ teaspoon Worchestershire sauce
½ teaspoon salt

½ teaspoon black pepper (freshly ground preferred)
¼ teaspoon celery seed
2 cubes ice

FIRST Place ½ cup tarragon vinegar in a bowl and add 1 cup of olive oil, beating it in gradually.

SECOND Combine 1 teaspoon dry mustard, ½ teaspoon Worcestershire sauce, ½ teaspoon salt, ½ teaspoon black pepper, and ¼ teaspoon of celery seed. Add to the liquid and beat with a fork until thoroughly blended.

THIRD Add 2 cubes ice and beat for a few seconds. Set in the refrigerator until thoroughly chilled. Just before throwing over the greens, beat again.

NOTE A generous sprinkling of chopped chives and chopped parsley makes an excellent addition to this dressing. They must be added last—just before pouring the dressing over the greens.

FRENCH DRESSING GEORGE FITZMAURICE

2 teaspoons salt
1 teaspoon black pepper
1 teaspoon Dijon mustard
3 teaspoons tarragon vinegar
3 teaspoons red wine

1 cup best olive oil
1 tablespoon chopped onion
1 clove garlic (optional)
chopped parsley

FIRST Rub 2 teaspoons salt and 1 teaspoon pepper with 1 teaspoon Dijon mustard.

SECOND Stir in 3 teaspoons tarragon vinegar and 3 teaspoons red wine. Gradually add 1 cup best olive oil. Beat constantly with a fork while the oil is being added. Add 1 tablespoon chopped onion; 1 clove minced, bruised garlic (optional) and chopped parsley.

NOTE Toss the salad greens in the dressing over and over so that each leaf turns a little limp and is thoroughly coated. The French always tell you to—"Fatiguez la salade" which literally translated means "tire the salad."

MAYONNAISE MARGUERITE

1 cut clove garlic (optional)
½ teaspoon sugar
1 teaspoon dry English mustard
1 teaspoon salt

2 egg yolks
4 tablespoons lemon juice
2 cups olive oil

FIRST Rub a small mixing-bowl with one cut clove of garlic (optional). Mix ½ teaspoon sugar, 1 teaspoon of dry English mustard, and 1 teaspoon of salt.

SECOND Add 2 egg yolks and beat thoroughly. Beat 2 tablespoons lemon juice into the eggs.

THIRD Add 2 cups of olive oil alternately with 2 tablespoons of lemon juice, a very little of each at a time, beating vigorously after each addition. Continue to beat until the mixture is thick and very, very smooth. Chill in refrigerator until ready to serve.

SALAD-DRESSINGS

MAYONNAISE WITH HORSERADISH

1 cup mayonnaise
3 tablespoons horseradish

2 tablespoons tarragon

FIRST Mix 1 cup of mayonnaise with 3 tablespoons of horseradish. Stir well.

SECOND Stir in 2 tablespoons tarragon. Set in refrigerator and serve ice cold.

ROQUEFORT DRESSING I

½ pound Roquefort *or* Blue cheese
½ teaspoon salt

½ teaspoon paprika
6 tablespoons vinegar
6 tablespoons olive oil

FIRST Mash ½ pound Roquefort or Blue cheese in a bowl. Add ½ teaspoon salt, ½ teaspoon paprika, 6 tablespoons vinegar, and 6 tablespoons olive oil. Work until very smooth—the smoother, the better.

SECOND Push through a fine strainer and use at once. If you prefer to make this dressing ahead of time, place in refrigerator in a jar, being certain to shake well before using.

NOTE There are various variations of this dressing. Perhaps the most successful is the addition of ¼ cup heavy cream and 2 tablespoons chopped chives, or 1 tablespoon onion juice. Another venture into the realm of imagination is to substitute 6 tablespoons port wine for 6 tablespoons vinegar.

ROQUEFORT DRESSING II

¼ pound Roquefort cheese
2 tablespoons cream
1 cup French Dressing (page 247)

¼ teaspoon paprika
1 teaspoon mayonnaise

FIRST With a fork crush ¼ pound Roquefort cheese to a paste. Then smooth with 2 tablespoons cream.

SECOND Slowly beat cheese into 1 cup French Dressing (page 247) using a hand wire whisk. When well blended, add ¼ teaspoon paprika and 1 teaspoon mayonnaise. Place in refrigerator.

THIRD Whisk sharply just before serving. Pour over salad greens and serve quickly.

RUSSIAN DRESSING

1 cup mayonnaise
¼ cup chili sauce
¼ teaspoon salt
½ teaspoon paprika
1 teaspoon tarragon vinegar

1 teaspoon finely chopped green pepper (optional)
1 teaspoon finely chopped pimiento (optional)
3 tablespoons heavy cream
capers (optional)

FIRST Combine 1 cup of mayonnaise, ¼ cup chili sauce, ¼ teaspoon salt, ½ teaspoon paprika, and 1 teaspoon of tarragon vinegar in a mixing-bowl. 1 teaspoon finely chopped green pepper and 1 teaspoon finely chopped pimiento may be added if desired.

SECOND Just before serving, whip 3 tablespoons heavy cream until stiff and fold into the dressing.

NOTE Capers may be substituted for the green peppers and pimientos.

THOUSAND ISLAND DRESSING

1 cup mayonnaise
½ cup chili sauce
1 tablespoon lemon juice

salt, black pepper
¼ teaspoon dry mustard

FIRST Blend 1 cup mayonnaise with ½ cup chili sauce. Stir in 1 tablespoon lemon juice.

SECOND Season with salt, black pepper, and ¼ teaspoon of dry mustard. Place in refrigerator until ready to serve.

VINAIGRETTE

4 hard-boiled eggs
½ cup sliced pickles, chopped fine
1 teaspoon dry mustard
salt, black pepper

¼ teaspoon marjoram
½ teaspoon tarragon
¼ cup wine vinegar
¼ cup brine from pickle bottle
½ cup olive oil

FIRST Chop 4 hard-boiled eggs and ½ cup sliced pickles until very fine. Mix thoroughly and season with 1 teaspoon dry mustard, salt, black pepper, ¼ teaspoon marjoram, and ½ teaspoon tarragon.

SECOND Combine ¼ cup wine vinegar, ¼ cup brine from the pickle bottle, and ½ cup olive oil. Stir this combination with the egg mixture. Place in refrigerator for several hours before using. Stir well before serving.

NOTE Serve with cold asparagus, cold artichokes, or cold hearts of celery.

Chapter XI: *Cheese Dishes*

An apple-pie without some cheese

Is like a kiss without a squeeze.

OLD ENGLISH RHYME

CHEESE DISHES

SWISS RECIPES

SWISS TOASTS (CROUTES)

Croutes Emmental
Croutes Vaudoises
Croutes Oberland
Croutes Bonne-Femme

FONDUES

Fondue Neuchateloise
Fontina
Bouchees "Golden Buck"
Old French Fondue

SOUFFLÉS

Chaeswaehe (Cheese Pie)
Cheese Charlotte
Ramequin
Swiss Soufflé

MEATS

Ham Roulades with Swiss Mornay Sauce
Piccata
Stuffed Veal Cutlets

VEGETABLES

Egg plant au Gratin
Cauliflower Bernese
Stuffed Potatoes
Stuffed Tomatoes
Swiss Chard Stalks

SALADS

Salade Bonne Femme
Salade Bruxelloise
Salade au Tomates
Tomates Fribourgeoises

A VARIETY OF OTHER CHEESE RECIPES

Bologna Éclairs, Jonathan
Cheese Balls
Cheese Casserole with Hard-Boiled Eggs and Tomato Sauce
Crêpes Farcies
Fried Camembert
Gay Nineties Rarebit
Hostess Tartlets
Midnight Sandwiches
Simple Cheese Tartlets
Swiss Tartlets
Truffes Vertes
Waffle Sandwiches

CHEESE DISHES

A SERIES OF AUTHENTIC AND DISTINGUISHED CHEESE RECIPES OF SWITZERLAND

It is with infinite pride that I present the next group of cheese recipes with the permission of the Switzerland Cheese Association, whose wonderful recipes were first brought to my attention during the World's Fair in 1940.

To identify the true imported Swiss cheese, the Swiss have stamped the word "Switzerland" on the rind. I suggest that you do what you can about finding this splendid product, known as Switzerland Swiss.

CROUTES EMMENTAL
[*Crusts Emmental Fashion*]

½ pound grated Swiss cheese
2 egg yolks
1 medium onion, chopped fine
2 egg whites
12 slices bread
¼ pound butter, melted

SERVES 6

FIRST Grate ½ pound Swiss cheese and mix with 2 egg yolks and 1 medium onion chopped fine.

SECOND Beat 2 egg whites until stiff. Fold gently into the mixture until well blended. Spread the mixture evenly on 12 slices bread.

THIRD Fry the bread slices, spread sides first, in ¼ pound melted butter until golden brown. Turn slices and fry other sides until golden brown.

CROUTES VAUDOISES
[*Crusts Vaudois Fashion*]
[*Pre-heat oven to 450°*]

6 slices white bread
½ cup dry white wine
3 ounces melted butter
¼ cup flour
½ cup milk
½ cup cream
½ cup grated Swiss cheese
2 egg yolks
salt, pepper, nutmeg, paprika
1 heaping tablespoon butter, cut into lumps

SERVES 6

FIRST Soak 6 slices white bread in ½ cup dry white wine. Place carefully in a well-buttered glass pie plate and sprinkle with 2 ounces melted butter.

SECOND Melt 1 ounce of butter, remove from fire, and rub in ¼ cup flour until completely free of lumps. Return to fire and, little by little, add ½ cup milk and ½ cup cream. Stir constantly until thickened.

THIRD Stir in ½ cup grated Swiss cheese. Beat in 2 egg yolks, and stir constantly until thick and smooth. Season with salt, pepper, nutmeg, and paprika. Pour this sauce over the bread. Top with 1 heaping tablespoon butter cut into lumps. Brown in a hot oven. Serve very hot and bubbling.

CROUTES OBERLAND

[*Crusts Mountaineer Fashion*]

[*Pre-heat oven to 450°*]

1 slice buttered toast	1 thick slice Swiss cheese (size of toast)
1 thick slice cooked ham (size of toast)	1 fried, poached, *or* scrambled eggs

SERVES 1

FIRST Cover 1 slice of buttered toast with 1 thick slice cooked ham the size and shape of the toast. Cover the ham with a thick slice of Swiss cheese (same size) and brown in a 450° oven.

SECOND When serving, top with 1 fried, poached, or scrambled egg.

NOTE This recipe can, of course, be prepared for as many as required. With an accompaniment of a green salad this makes a splendid luncheon or light dinner.

CROUTES BONNE FEMME

[*Pre-heat oven to 450°*]

3 shallots *or* 1 medium-sized onion, finely chopped
6 ounces butter
½ cup shredded ham
½ pound fresh mushrooms
½ cup flour

1 cup milk
1 cup cream
salt, pepper
6 slices buttered toast
6 thick slices of Swiss cheese
½ cup grated Swiss cheese

SERVES 6

FIRST Stew 3 finely chopped shallots (or 1 finely chopped medium-sized onion) in 4 ounces melted butter. Add ½ cup shredded ham and ½ cup quartered fresh mushrooms. Simmer until tender and free of moisture. Keep flame low, being careful not to scorch.

SECOND Make a cream sauce by melting 2 ounces of butter, removing it from the fire, and rubbing ½ cup flour until completely free of lumps. Return to the fire and add 1 cup of milk and 1 cup of cream, a little at a time. Add salt and pepper and stir constantly until it thickens. When thick, add the mushroom-ham mixture, stirring it into the sauce until well blended.

THIRD Arrange 6 slices of buttered toast not too close together in a large, buttered baking-dish. Top the toasts with 6 thick slices of Swiss cheese. Now pour the prepared sauce between the toasts and sprinkle with ½ cup grated Swiss cheese. Brown the whole in a 450° oven and serve piping hot.

FONDUE NEUCHÂTELOISE

[*Melted Cheese Neuchâtel Fashion*]

½ pound grated Swiss cheese
1 tablespoon flour
1 cut clove garlic
1 cup dry white wine

salt, pepper, nutmeg
3 tablespoons kirsch
cubes of sour-dough French bread

SERVES 4

FIRST Dredge ½ pound grated Swiss cheese thoroughly with 1 tablespoon flour.

SECOND Rub a cooking casserole or a saucepan with 1 cut clove garlic. Add a cup of dry white wine and bring almost to a boiling point. Add the grated cheese and stir constantly with a fork until the cheese is all melted. Add salt, pepper, and nutmeg to taste.

THIRD When the Fondue starts to boil, add 3 tablespoons of kirsch. Serve quickly, bringing it cooking hot to the table, over an an alcohol lamp, on an electric plate, or in a chafing-dish. Pass a dish or bread basket full of fair-sized cubes of sour-dough French bread, instructing the guests to spear each cube in turn, to dip it into the Fondue, and to eat it while still very hot.

NOTE This dish can establish your reputation as a very special chef. Remember only to keep the Fondue warm. Pouring it into individual cups or plates is a temptation, but *disastrous*, as it *very* quickly becomes gummy. This is a recipe well worth trying, if only for the reputation it will bring you!

FONTINA

[*Melted Cheese Valois Fashion*]

1 tablespoon butter	1 pound grated Swiss cheese
3 level tablespoons flour	salt, pepper, nutmeg
2 cups milk	cubes of sour-dough French bread

SERVES 4

FIRST Melt 1 tablespoon butter in a saucepan. Add 3 level tablespoons flour and blend well. Stir in 2 cups of milk, a little at a time. When the milk is all added and it has been brought gradually to a boil, add 1 pound grated Swiss cheese, stirring constantly with a *fork* until melted. Add salt, pepper, and nutmeg to taste.

SECOND Serve, cooking hot at the table, over an alcohol lamp, an electric plate, or in a chafing-dish. Pass a dish or bread basket full of fair-sized cubes of sour-dough French bread, instructing the guests to spear each cube in turn and to dip it into the Fontina and devour it while still very hot.

NOTE See the note on Fondue Neuchâteloise (page 257).

BOUCHÉES

[*Golden Buck*]

6 Patty Shells (page 409) *or*
6 slices toast
1 recipe Fondue (page 257) *or* Fontina (page 258)

6 poached eggs
1 cup shredded cooked ham
½ cup shredded cooked mushrooms

SERVES 6

FIRST Fill 6 Patty Shells (page 409) or cover 6 slices toast with 1 recipe Fondue (page 257) or Fontina (page 258).

SECOND Top with 6 poached eggs and garnish with 1 cup of shredded cooked ham and ½ cup shredded cooked mushrooms. Serve very hot.

NOTE If preferred, the Fondue or Fontina may be poured over the poached eggs and the trimmings of ham and mushrooms.

OLD FRENCH FONDUE

[*An Ancient Recipe*]

12 eggs
¾ pound grated Swiss cheese
scant ½ pound butter

salt
½ teaspoon black pepper
hot, crisp, buttered toast

SERVES 6

FIRST Break 12 eggs into a saucepan before setting pan on the stove. Beat them well and add ¾ pound grated Swiss cheese and a scant ½ pound butter. Set on a low flame and continue to beat until the butter and the cheese are incorporated.

SECOND Turn the mixture with a spatula until it is sufficiently thick and soft. Add a good pinch salt and ½ teaspoon black pepper. Serve on warm plates with hot, crisp, buttered toast.

NOTE The amount of the salt is to be decided upon by the individual cook. A lot depends on the cheese. For your entertainment I submit the original, old recipe translated from the French: Weigh the number of eggs that you want to use according to the numbers of diners. Then take a good piece of cheese from the Alpine regions, weighing one third, and a piece of fresh butter, weighing one sixth, of the total weight. Break the eggs into a clean casserole and beat them well, after which add the butter and the cheese. Place the casserole on a quiet fire and turn with a flat spoon or knife until the Fondue is sufficiently thickened and softened to be ready to present. Add a pinch of salt and a goodly measure of pepper, which is one of the positive elements of this recipe. Serve on slightly heated plates.

CHAESWAEHE

[*Pre-heat oven to 400°*]

1 recipe for Pie Pastry (page 408)
milk
½ pound Swiss cheese, grated *or* shredded

1 tablespoon flour
1 cup cream *or* milk
3 well-beaten eggs
pepper, salt

SERVES 6

FIRST Line a 9-inch glass pie plate with 1 recipe for Pie Pastry (page 408). Brush the dough with milk and fill it with ½ pound finely grated or shredded Swiss cheese.

SECOND Combine 1 tablespoon flour with 1 cup cream or milk. Add 3 well-beaten eggs and season the mixture with pepper and salt. Pour this over the grated cheese in the pie shell.

THIRD Bake the pie 15 minutes in a 400° oven. Reduce the heat to 300° and bake an additional 30 minutes, or until a knife inserted in the center of the pie comes out quite clean. Serve hot or cold.

NOTE This makes an excellent dish for luncheon served with a green salad.

IMPORTANT Follow the baking directions carefully and do not overbake!

CHEESE CHARLOTTE

[Pre-heat oven to 350°]

3 tablespoons butter
3 egg yolks
1½ tablespoons flour
2 cups diced white bread
milk
½ pound shredded Swiss cheese

salt, nutmeg
½ cup heavy cream (*or* evaporated milk)
bread slices soaked in milk (approximately 6)
3 egg whites

SERVES 6

FIRST Beat 3 tablespoons butter with 3 egg yolks and 1½ tablespoons flour.

SECOND Soak 2 cups diced white bread in milk until well moistened. Add to the egg mixture. Add ½ pound shredded Swiss cheese and salt and nutmeg to taste. Then add ½ cup heavy cream (or evaporated milk) and mix well.

THIRD Butter a deep baking-dish. Line with approximately 6 bread slices soaked in milk. Beat 3 egg whites until stiff, then fold gently into the cheese mixture. Pour the mixture into the baking-dish and bake in a 350° oven for 30 minutes. Serve very hot.

RAMEQUIN

[Pre-heat oven to 350°]

½-inch slices Swiss cheese
slices white bread
2 eggs

2 cups milk
salt, nutmeg

SERVES 4 TO 6

FIRST Butter a deep glass baking-dish and fill alternately with ½-inch slices Swiss cheese and slices white bread. The cheese slices should overlap the bread slices by about half an inch.

SECOND Beat 2 eggs with 2 cups milk. Add salt and nutmeg to taste and pour over the filling.

THIRD Place the baking-dish in a pan of hot water and bake in a 350° oven for about 30 minutes. Serve hot.

SWISS SOUFFLÉ

[*Pre-heat oven to 350°*]

2 ounces butter
½ cup flour
1 cup milk
¼ teaspoon salt
nutmeg

3 egg yolks
½ pound grated Swiss cheese
1 level teaspoon cornstarch
3 egg whites

SERVES 6

FIRST Melt 2 ounces butter in a saucepan. Remove from flame and stir in ½ cup flour, rubbing it in until entirely free of lumps and until the paste is quite smooth. Return to the fire and stir in 1 cup warm milk, a little at a time, stirring constantly until thick. Add ¼ teaspoon salt and a pinch nutmeg. Beat until absolutely smooth, remove from fire, and *cool slightly*.

SECOND Add 3 beaten egg yolks, ½ pound grated Swiss cheese, and 1 level teaspoon cornstarch. Beat again until smooth.

THIRD Beat 3 egg whites until stiff and fold gently into the cheese mixture. Butter a baking-dish that has been dusted with flour. Then fill the dish with the cheese mixture and set in a 350° oven until it has risen. Serve quickly and very hot. Like all soufflés this must be served immediately.

HAM ROULADES

[*Pre-heat oven to 350°*]

6 thick slices boiled ham
1 recipe stiff Mornay Sauce (page 263)
½ cup canned tomato sauce

light cream
½ cup grated Swiss cheese
2 ounces melted butter

SERVES 6

FIRST Cover 6 thick slices boiled ham with half a recipe stiff Mornay Sauce (page 263). Roll up and fasten the slices with a toothpick.

SECOND Butter a flat, glass baking-dish and cover the bottom dish with ½ cup canned tomato sauce. Arrange the roulades (rolled slices) in the dish.

THIRD Thin the second half of the Mornay Sauce with a little light cream. Pour this over the roulades and sprinkle with ½ cup grated Swiss cheese and 2 ounces melted butter. Bake in a 350° oven until brown on top (about 15 minutes).

SWISS MORNAY SAUCE

4 tablespoons butter	2 egg yolks
8 tablespoons flour	cayenne pepper
1¾ cups milk	1 cup small cubes Swiss cheese

FIRST Melt 4 tablespoons butter in a saucepan. Remove from fire and rub in 8 tablespoons flour.

SECOND Gradually add 1¾ cups boiling milk, a little at a time, stirring constantly to keep very smooth and creamy. Simmer for 10 minutes. *Cool.*

THIRD Beat in 2 egg yolks. Add a pinch cayenne pepper and 1 cup small cubes Swiss cheese.

NOTE If you wish to have the cheese completely incorporated with the rest of the sauce, the saucepan may be returned to the fire, where the mixture should be constantly stirred until the cubes are melted. Otherwise, leave them as they are without returning to the stove.

PICCATA

[Veal Cutlets with Cheese]

6 small veal cutlets
salt
2 beaten eggs

1 teaspoon flour
½ cup grated Swiss cheese
¼ pound butter

SERVES 6

FIRST Have your butcher cut 6 small, very thin veal cutlets. Ask him to beat the cutlets until very thin. Salt them.

SECOND Beat 2 eggs until well blended. Thicken with 1 teaspoon flour and add ½ cup grated Swiss cheese. Dip the cutlets in this mixture on both sides until well covered.

THIRD Fry on both sides in ¼ pound melted butter. Serve with spaghetti or macaroni.

STUFFED VEAL CUTLETS

6 small veal cutlets
salt
6 slices Swiss cheese (1 ounce each)

flour
2 beaten eggs
finely sifted bread crumbs
¼ pound butter *or* oil

SERVES 6

FIRST Have your butcher cut 6 small, very thin veal cutlets. Ask him to beat the cutlets until very thin. Salt them.

SECOND Cover half of each cutlet with 1-ounce slice Swiss cheese, and fold over the other half. Seal the edges by pressing.

THIRD Dip the cutlets, first in flour, then in 2 beaten eggs, and lastly in finely sifted bread crumbs. Fry them in ¼ pound melted butter or in deep oil. Serve with a sharp green salad.

EGG PLANT AU GRATIN

[*Pre-heat oven to 350°*]

1 large eggplant
¼ pound butter

thin slices Swiss cheese
salt, pepper

SERVES 6

FIRST   Cut 1 eggplant into ¼-inch slices. Soak in salt water for 20 minutes. Scald in boiling water, drain, and dry.

SECOND   Fry the slices lightly in ¼ pound melted butter. Arrange the slices in layers in a buttered baking-dish with alternate layers of thin slices of Swiss cheese. Sprinkle with salt and pepper between the layers. Bake in a 350° oven until the cheese begins to melt.

THIRD   Turn the heat up and brown under the broiler and serve at once.

CAULIFLOWER BERNESE

[*Pre-heat oven to 400°*]

1 large cauliflower
½ pound grated Swiss cheese
½ cup rye-bread crumbs
1½ cups cream *or* milk

3 egg yolks
salt, pepper, nutmeg
2 ounces melted butter

SERVES 6

FIRST   Boil 1 cauliflower until tender in salted water. Drain and place in a shallow, buttered baking-dish.

SECOND   Combine ½ pound grated Swiss cheese with ½ cup rye bread crumbs. Mix with 1½ cups cream or milk and beat in 3 egg yolks. Season with salt, pepper, and nutmeg. Pour mixture over cauliflower.

THIRD   Sprinkle with 2 ounces melted butter and brown in the oven.

STUFFED POTATOES
[Pre-heat broiler]

6 baked potatoes
grated Swiss cheese
cooked, chopped mushrooms (approximately ½ pound)
chopped, boiled ham (approximately ½ pound)
¼ cup chopped chives
4 egg yolks
salt, pepper
cream *or* milk
grated Swiss cheese
small lumps butter

SERVES 6

EXPLANATORY NOTE   It is impossible to give the exact amounts of the ingredients in this recipe since everything depends on the size of your baked potatoes. The approximations will help you, however, to follow the original recipe so that the results will be satisfactory.

FIRST   Cut 6 baked potatoes in half lengthwise and scoop out the centers. Save the shells to be stuffed later. To 10 parts of potato (measure in measuring-cup) add 8 parts of grated Swiss cheese, 4 parts cooked, chopped mushrooms (approximately ½ pound), 4 parts chopped, boiled ham (approximately ½ pound), ¼ cup chopped chives, egg yolks (2 yolks to half pound potato, probably 4 yolks), and salt and pepper. Combine all this and add just enough cream or milk to make a moist and smooth mixture. Be certain that you use enough so as to be sure it is really *moist*.

SECOND   Fill the potato shells generously with this mixture. Sprinkle with grated Swiss cheese and dot with small lumps of butter. Brown quickly under the broiler. Serve at once.

NOTE   Do not leave the potatoes under the broiler too long, the filling must remain *moist*. Too much heat will dry them out.

STUFFED TOMATOES
[Pre-heat oven to 350°]

6 large tomatoes
½ pound grated Swiss cheese
2 egg yolks
½ cup heavy cream (*or* evaporated milk)
curry powder
3 tablespoons finely sifted bread crumbs
3 tablespoons melted butter

SERVES 6

FIRST Cut 6 large, solid tomatoes in half. Hollow out the center, leaving a wall at least ¼ inch thick.

SECOND Combine ½ pound grated Swiss cheese, 2 beaten egg yolks, ½ cup heavy cream (or evaporated milk), and curry powder to taste. Fill the tomatoes with this mixture.

THIRD Sprinkle the tomatoes with 3 tablespoons finely sifted bread crumbs and 3 tablespoons melted butter. Bake in a 350° oven until the tomatoes are tender.

SWISS-CHARD STALKS

[*Pre-heat oven to 350°*]

2 pounds Swiss-chard stalks
juice of half lemon
1 cup grated Swiss cheese
¼ cup meat sauce *or* gravy
2 ounces butter

SERVES 6

FIRST Cut 2 pounds Swiss-chard stalks into 1 inch pieces. Boil until tender in salt water to which the juice of half lemon has been added.

SECOND Grate 1 cup Swiss cheese. Fill a buttered vegetable dish with alternate layers of stalks and grated cheese.

THIRD Sprinkle the dish with ¼ cup meat sauce or gravy and 2 ounces browned butter. Set in 350° oven only long enough for the cheese to melt.

SALADE BONNE FEMME

1 cup *tiny* cubes Swiss cheese
4 large boiled potatoes
½ cup chopped celery (knobs and stalks)
¼ cup chopped nuts
½ cup mayonnaise
1 tablespoon prepared mustard
1 teaspoon Worcestershire sauce

SERVES 6

FIRST Cut up 1 cup Swiss cheese into tiny cubes. Pare 4 large boiled potatoes and cut into cubes. Chop ½ cup celery (both knobs and stalks) ¼ cup nuts. Toss all these ingredients together in a bowl.

SECOND Mix ½ cup mayonnaise with 1 tablespoon any preferred prepared mustard and 1 teaspoon of Worcestershire sauce. Blend well and pour over the potato-and-cheese salad, turning it over and over until all the ingredients are well covered with the dressing.

SALADE BRUXELLOISE

½ pound French endive
½ pound Swiss cheese
½ cup mayonnaise

1 teaspoon prepared mustard
juice 1 lemon
¼ cup heavy cream

SERVES 4 TO 6

FIRST Separate the leaves of ½ pound French endive and cut into inch-long pieces. Cut ½ pound Swiss cheese into tiny cubes and add to the endive.

SECOND Combine ½ cup mayonnaise with 1 teaspoon prepared mustard, the juice of 1 lemon, and ¼ cup heavy cream beaten until stiff. Pour over the endive and cheese. Set in the refrigerator and serve very cold.

SALADE AU TOMATES

1 cup very small cubes Swiss cheese
1 cup small cubes fresh tomatoes
1 finely chopped small onion

salt, pepper, nutmeg, cayenne pepper
½ cup mayonnaise

SERVES 4

FIRST Combine 1 cup very small cubes Swiss cheese and 1 cup small cubes fresh tomatoes. Add 1 finely chopped small onion and season with salt, pepper, nutmeg, and cayenne pepper.

SECOND Add ½ cup mayonnaise, turning the "salade" over and over until everything is well coated.

TOMATES FRIBOURGEOISES

[Stuffed Tomatoes Fribourg Fashion]

½ pound Swiss cheese cut into *tiny* cubes
4 large boiled potatoes cut into *tiny* cubes
salt, pepper

1 finely chopped small onion
½ cup sharp French Dressing (page 247)
6 medium-sized tomatoes
½ cup mayonnaise

SERVES 6

FIRST Combine ½ pound tiny cubes Swiss cheese with 4 large, boiled potatoes cut into tiny cubes. Season with salt and pepper. Add 1 finely chopped small onion and ½ cup sharp French Dressing (page 247). Mix well.

SECOND Peel and scoop out 6 medium-sized tomatoes. Season lightly with salt and pepper. Fill with the cheese-potato mixture. Garnish each with an equal share of ½ cup mayonnaise.

BOLOGNA ÉCLAIRS JONATHAN

12 slices bologna sausage

1 pint cottage cheese with chives

SERVES 6

FIRST Cover 12 slices bologna sausage with 1 pint cottage cheese with chives.

SECOND Roll each slice up loosely and secure with a toothpick.

NOTE My youngest son, Jonathan, loves to eat! Sometimes the poor lad must diet. Going to grammar school, taking your lunch and trying to do without sandwiches, is quite a weighty problem for one of tender years and a hearty appetite. The Bologna Éclairs are entirely his own invention to fill his school box. The rest of us like them at any time, any place, especially on Sunday nights with a cheese platter and a tossed green salad.

CHEESE BALLS

1½ cups grated Cheddar cheese
1 tablespoon flour
2 tablespoons sherry
¼ teaspoon salt
½ teaspoon black pepper

cayenne pepper
3 egg whites
finely sifted bread crumbs
oil

FIRST Mix 1½ cups grated Cheddar cheese with 1 tablespoon flour, 2 tablespoons sherry, ¼ teaspoon salt, ½ teaspoon black pepper. And a tiny pinch cayenne pepper.

SECOND Beat 3 egg whites until firm. Blend with a gentle hand into the cheese mixture. Roll carefully into balls about the size of a quarter dollar. Roll each ball into finely sifted bread crumbs until well covered.

THIRD Fry the cheese balls in deep oil or vegetable shortening. Do not have the fat too hot or the crumbs will cook to a deep brown before the cheese cooks through. Drain on paper towels or brown wrapping-paper. Serve very hot.

NOTE Test the heat of the oil with one ball before proceeding with the others. Brown grocery bags, split open and laid flat on the kitchen table, make excellent "brown wrapping-paper" on which to drain after frying.

CHEESE CASSEROLE WITH HARD-BOILED EGGS AND TOMATO SAUCE *Marie's*

[*Pre-heat oven to 400°*]

2 ounces butter
½ cup flour
1 cup cream
1 cup milk
pepper, salt

6 hard-boiled eggs
½ pound Cheddar cheese
1 can tomato sauce
thin slices additional butter
toast

SERVES 6

FIRST Melt 2 ounces butter. Remove from the fire and rub in ½ cup flour. Return to fire and gradually stir in 1 cup cream and 1 cup milk. Season with pepper and salt to taste.

SECOND Butter a deep glass baking-dish and cover the bottom of the dish with some of the white sauce. Slice 6 hard-boiled eggs and place a layer of these egg slices on top of the white sauce. Cover the egg slices with thin slices of Cheddar cheese. Salt and pepper the cheese and eggs, then cover them with canned tomato sauce. Repeat this entire process until the baking-dish is almost filled. This will require ½ pound Cheddar cheese and 1 can tomato sauce.

THIRD Add the last of the white sauce, topping with thin slices of additional butter. Place in a 400° oven for 20 minutes. Serve the dish bubbling hot with hot, buttered toast.

CRÊPES FARCIES

1 recipe Crêpes Suzette (page 345)
12 finger-sized pieces Swiss cheese
2 beaten eggs
bread crumbs
oil

SERVES 6

FIRST Fry 1 recipe Crêpes Suzette (page 345) in smallest skillet. Keep warm in oven until ready to fill.

SECOND Roll 12 finger-sized pieces Swiss cheese into the pancakes and secure with toothpicks.

THIRD Roll the filled pancakes, first in 2 beaten eggs, then in finely sifted bread crumbs. Fry in a deep fat. Serve them quickly while still very hot.

NOTE These may be served with a green salad for luncheon. By following this recipe exactly, but making very small, miniature filled pancakes, they may be also served with great effect as hors d'œuvres.

FRIED CAMEMBERT CHEESE

1 whole firm Camembert cheese
2 ounces soft butter

finely sifted bread crumbs
melted butter

SERVES 6

FIRST Take 1 whole firm Camembert cheese, preferably one that is a little hard, not too soft and ripe. Carefully remove the outer skin. Cream the cheese together with 2 ounces soft butter. Shape carefully into small hamburger-shaped patties.

SECOND Cover each patty with finely sifted bread crumbs and fry in hot melted butter until brown on both sides. Serve very hot on a warm plate as an accompaniment to a cold, crisp salad.

NOTE For a stronger Camembert flavor, the skin need not be removed.

GAY NINETIES RAREBIT

3 tablespoons butter
3 tablespoons flour
¾ teaspoon salt
cayenne pepper
½ cup milk
¼ cup best sherry

1½ cups shredded Cheddar cheese
1 overflowing cup beer *or* ale
6 pieces crisp toast *or* English crumpets

SERVES 6

FIRST Heat the top of a large double boiler. Melt 3 tablespoons butter. Rub in 3 tablespoons flour and season with ¾ teaspoon salt and a tiny pinch cayenne pepper. Gradually pour in ½ cup of milk, stirring constantly until thick. Then, little by little, add ¼ cup best sherry. Stir once more until thick and smooth.

SECOND Drop in 1½ cups shredded, well-aged cheddar cheese. Stir occasionally until melted and smooth. Gradually stir in an overflowing cup beer or ale. Serve piping hot over 6 pieces of crisp toast or well-toasted hot English crumpets.

CHEESE DISHES

NOTE This may be served from a chafing-dish and ladled onto the toast or crumpets.

HOSTESS TARTLETS

1 cup flour
½ teaspoon salt
1 teaspoon sugar
4 tablespoons butter
2 tablespoons water

4 eggs
1 cup grated Swiss cheese
1 teaspoon flour
salt, pepper, nutmeg
¾ cup milk

APPROXIMATELY 15 TARTLETS

FIRST Sift 1 cup flour. Measure and resift with ½ teaspoon salt and 1 teaspoon sugar. Then work in 4 tablespoons butter and about 2 tablespoons water. Let the dough stand in the refrigerator for about an hour.

[*Pre-heat oven to 400°*]

SECOND Roll out and cover buttered tartlet forms or the backs of *small* muffin tins. Pierce the bottoms of the tarts. Bake in a 400° oven until golden.

THIRD Mix 4 eggs with 1 cup grated Swiss cheese until completely blended. Add 1 teaspoon flour and salt, pepper, and nutmeg to taste. Thin with ¾ cup cold milk and beat well. Fill tarts ⅔ full of this mixture. Bake 12 to 15 minutes in a 400° oven.

MIDNIGHT SANDWICHES

[*Pre-heat broiler*]

6 slices white bread
soft butter
6 quarter-inch slices American *or* Cheddar cheese

6 thick slices fresh tomatoes
12 slices bacon

SERVES 6

FIRST Toast 6 slices white bread on one side only. Trim the edges of the bread. Butter on each untoasted side.

SECOND Cover the 6 buttered slices toast with 6 thick (about ¼ inch) slices Cheddar or American cheese. Then cover with 6 thick slices fresh tomatoes.

THIRD Set two slices bacon, criss-cross fashion, on top of each sandwich. Place the sandwiches under the pre-heated broiler until the bacon is crisp and the cheese is melted.

SIMPLE CHEESE TARTLETS
[Pre-heat oven to 400°]

1 recipe Pie Crust (page 408) 1 recipe custard filling for Cheese
grated Swiss cheese Pie (page 260)

FIRST Line tartlet forms or the back of muffin tins with 1 recipe Pie Crust (page 408). Cover each tartlet before baking with 1 tablespoon shredded Swiss cheese. Bake in a 400° oven until light gold.

[Reduce oven to 350°]

SECOND Fill each tartlet ⅔ full of the custard mixture described under Cheese Pie (page 260) and bake the tartlets in a 350° oven until a knife inserted in the center of a tartlet comes out quite clean. Serve hot or warmed over.

NOTE Excellent for afternoon tea. The amount of Swiss cheese is not given as it depends entirely on how many tartlets are required. Each tartlet calls for 1 tablespoon grated Swiss cheese.

SWISS TARTLETS
[Pre-heat oven to 450°]

12 three-inch tartlets (page 448) 1 teaspoon chopped, fried onion
¼ pound grated Swiss cheese salt, pepper
1 egg scant ½ cup light cream

FIRST Bake 12 three-inch tartlets as per recipe and instructions for Strawberry Tartlets (page 448).

SECOND Cream ¼ pound grated Swiss cheese with 1 well-beaten egg. Add 1 teaspoon chopped, fried onion. Salt and pepper to taste and beat in a scant ½ cup light cream.

THIRD Fill the tartlets with this mixture and bake quickly in a 450° oven. Serve at once—the tartlets should be moist and warm. Do not allow them to dry out.

TRUFFES VERTES

½ cup grated Swiss cheese
2 ounces soft butter
1 egg yolk
1 teaspoon dry mustard (*or* any prepared mustard)

salt, pepper, nutmeg
½ cup very finely chopped ham
finely chopped chives *or* parsley

FIRST Cream ½ cup Swiss cheese with 2 ounces soft butter. Work in 1 egg yolk until well blended. Then season with 1 teaspoon dry mustard (or any prepared mustard), salt, pepper, and nutmeg. Work in ½ cup very finely chopped ham.

SECOND Form balls the size of marbles and roll them in finely chopped chives or parsley. Serve on rounds of toast or, quite simply, by themselves.

WAFFLE SANDWICHES

[*Pre-heat waffle iron*]

12 thin slices white sandwich bread
butter

6 quarter-inch slices American sandwich cheese

SERVES 6

FIRST Cut the crusts from 12 thin slices white sandwich bread. Butter each slice. Make sandwiches with ¼-inch slices of American sandwich cheese.

SECOND Place one sandwich in the waffle iron. Press the lid down hard on top of the sandwich, holding it there until it stays down without pressure. The purpose of this is to have the sandwich as thin and flat as possible.

THIRD Open the lid of the waffle iron. If the sandwich sticks to the iron, the tip of a knife will remove it easily. Continue in this manner until all six sandwiches are done.

Chapter XII: *Desserts*

The daintiest last, to make the end most sweet.

WILLIAM SHAKESPEARE: *King Richard II*, Act I

INSTRUCTIONS ON THE USE OF GELATIN

CHEESE DESSERTS

Cheese Blintzes
Cheese Cake Irene
Cœur à La Crème
Refrigerator Cheese Cake
Rum Cheese Pie
Top Secret

CHOCOLATE DESSERTS

Black Chocolate Dessert Cake
Chocolate Bavarian Cream
Chocolate Date Cake with Whipped Cream
Chocolate Ice Box Cake
Chocolate Roll I
Chocolate Roll II
Chocolate Soufflé (cold)
Chocolate Soufflé (hot)
Devil's Food Cake as a Box
"Korsu Cake"
Molded Chocolate Hidden Away
Molded Chocolate Pudding, Marie
Petits Pots au Chocolat
Têtes de Negres

CUSTARDS

Crême Brulée, June Platt
Custard White or Amber
Indian Pudding Custard

MOLDED DESSERTS

Cold Rice Pudding in a Mold
English Gooseberry Fool
Fruit Salad in Layer Cake
Ginger Cream
Macaroon Fluff
Maple Mousse

Molded Eggnog Pudding
Orange Cream
Peach Cream
Peppermint Stick Cream
Punch Bavarian
Rote Greutze
Rum Bavarian
Wine Jelly

WITH ICE CREAM OR WHIPPED CREAM

Apricot Ice Box Cake
Cornucopias
Cream Puffs and Eclairs
Coconut Torte, Lashanska
Ice Box Pudding Parfait
Mishmash Meringue
Orange Cream with Cake
Profiterolles
"Rien de Tout"
Sponge Cake Ring
Sponge Cake Surprise
Queen's Delight

SIX HOT DESSERTS

Apple Charlotte
Beignets Soufflés
Boothbay-Blueberry Betty
Kaiserschmarren
Sabayon
Puff Omelette, Edwin

FRUIT TORTES

Applesauce Torte
Blackbread Cherry Torte
Grandmother's Three Tortes
   Lemon with Meringue
   Strawberry with Cream Sauce
   Huckleberry or Blueberry with Whipped Cream

ICE CREAMS

Cranberry Cream
Lemon Ice Cream in Lemon Shells
Mousse au Chocolat, Lashanska
Rummy Coffee Ice Cream
Vanilla Ice Cream
    New York's Best Vanilla Ice Cream
    Old Vienna Vanilla Ice Cream
    Vanilla Ice Cream with Anisette and Coconut

NUT DESSERTS

Chestnut Desserts (Marrons)
    Marrons Purée (Chestnut Purée)
    Marrons Purée en Meringue (in Meringue)
    Marrons Purée sous Chocolat (Under Chocolate)
    Marrons Purée with Marguerites
Date and Walnut Torte
Nut Torte
Peanut Brittle Dessert

PANCAKES AND CREPES

Apple Pancake
Crêpes au Kirsch
Crêpes Suzette
Little Jelly Pancakes
Maple Pancake Dessert, Elizabeth

PUDDINGS

Cake Pudding, Marie
Rice Pudding, Norma
Rice Pudding Round Table
Ten Victorian Puddings
    Chocolate Cream
    Coffee
    Fruit Juice
    Hazelnut Cream
    Lemon (or Orange)
    Punch
    Rum
    Vanilla Cream
    Wine

DESSERT SAUCES

Apricot Sauce
Caramel Sauce
Chocolate Sauce I
Chocolate Sauce II
Crême d'Isigny
Custard Cream Sauce
Foamy Sauce
Fruit Custard Sauce
Hard Sauce
Peach Sauce
Pineapple Cream Sauce
Vanilla Sauce I
Vanilla Sauce II with Rum
Warm Wine Sauce
Wine Froth Sauce

INSTRUCTIONS ON THE USE OF GELATIN

In many of the recipes in this Dessert Chapter, you will find the following instructions:

"Soak 1 envelope of gelatin in ¼ cup of water" or "Soak 2 envelopes of gelatin in ½ cup of water." This process is accomplished by tearing open the envelope of gelatin, pouring the powdered gelatin into a measuring cup, measuring out the prescribed amount of water, and stirring it smooth with a teaspoon. Allow it to "soak" for five minutes.

Further instructions may follow to:

"Dissolve the gelatin over hot water until it clarifies." This is accomplished by taking a small saucepan or skillet and filling it the depth of about two inches with hot water. Set the gelatin in the measuring cup into this water and bring the water in the pan or skillet to a boil. Stir the gelatin occasionally with a teaspoon. This process will clarify, or melt the soaked gelatin. After having been removed from the water and allowed to stand a little in the measuring cup until cooled, it is now ready to be added to cold or lukewarm mixtures.

When the dessert mixture is hot, soaked gelatin may be dissolved by stirring it into the hot mixture. Stir hard to be sure that the gelatin is thoroughly absorbed in the mixture.

CHEESE BLINTZES

1½ cups flour
½ teaspoon salt
3 eggs
1½ cups milk
melted butter
1 pound moist cottage cheese

2 tablespoons sugar
1 egg
oil
apricot jam
sour cream

FIRST Sift 1½ cups flour. Measure and resift twice with ½ teaspoon salt.

SECOND Beat 2 whole eggs and mix with 1½ cups of milk. Gradually combine with the sifted flour until well blended. The batter must have the appearance of heavy cream or canned milk. If necessary add a little more milk. *Put through a fine sieve.*

THIRD Heat smallest frying-pan (about 6 inches in diameter), grease it scantily with melted butter, and pour in just enough batter to cover the bottom of the pan. This is achieved by tilting the pan back and forth off the flame. The proper amount will be quickly ascertained, but a large soup spoon will usually take care of a six inch skillet. When pancake pulls away from the sides, remove to a warm plate *without frying on the other side.* Continue until all are ready to be filled.

FOURTH Put 1 pound moist cottage cheese through a strainer and mix with 2 tablespoons sugar and 1 beaten egg. Beat together until smooth and well blended. Place a heaping tablespoon of this filling on each pancake. Roll and tuck the ends under. Press the ends down so that filling cannot escape. Place in refrigerator for several hours.

FIFTH Heat some oil, a little less than two inches deep, in a frying-pan until hot. Fry rolls until golden brown, turning carefully so that they brown on both sides. Drain on paper towels or brown paper. Keep each batch warm in the oven while the others are being prepared. When they are all done, serve immediately with apricot jam and a bowl of chilled sour cream.

NOTE This famous old recipe from Central Europe is little known to most Americans. Once you have achieved the knack of it, it is no more difficult to prepare than any other little pancake. If apricot jam is not your favorite, any other jam is acceptable. Apricot just happens to be traditional.

CHEESE CAKE IRENE

LINING FOR SPRING FORM

¼ **pound butter**
¾ **box zwieback**
⅓ **cup sugar**

2 **tablespoons cinnamon**
soft butter

SERVES 8

FIRST Stir ¼ pound melted butter into ¾ box zwieback rolled and sifted into fine crumbs. Add ⅓ cup sugar and 2 tablespoons cinnamon.

SECOND Butter bottom and sides of spring form. Press the moist crumbs against the sides and bottom of the form until they stick in place. Use too little rather than too much. Reserve a few of the crumbs to use as a light sprinkling on top of the cake.

THE CAKE

6 egg yolks
¾ cup sugar
2 pounds double cream cheese
2 tablespoons flour
juice 2 lemons
grated rind 2 lemons
1 cup heavy cream
6 egg whites
powdered sugar

FIRST Beat 6 egg yolks with ¾ cup sugar until light. Mash 2 pounds double cream cheese with a fork and add to the egg mixture. Blend well.

SECOND Stir in 2 tablespoons flour and the juice and grated rind of 2 lemons. When well blended pour in 1 cup of heavy cream. Mix thoroughly.

THIRD Beat 6 egg whites until stiff but not dry. Fold in with a gentle hand. Do not stir. Pour into the lined spring form, sprinkle top with the reserved crumbs, and set in a *cold* oven. Turn oven to 375° and bake about 1 hour. Test with a straw in the center of the cake. When done, turn off heat and open the oven door. Remove cake after 15 minutes. When cooled to room temperature, run a knife along side of cake, then remove the edge of the spring form. Set cake on a serving plate (leave bottom of spring form under cake). Sprinkle generously with powdered sugar and serve.

WARNING Do not place in refrigerator.

NOTE Double cream cheese is to be found at most delicatessens. It can be made at home by creaming cream cheese with heavy cream. Proportionately: 1 package cream cheese to 2 tablespoons heavy cream. Remembering that the recipe calls for 2 pounds of double cream cheese, care must be taken to make enough of the mixture to weigh an equivalent amount. June Platt asked me to demonstrate the preparation of this recipe, then published it in her "Party Cook Book" (Houghton Mifflin), where she called it "a cheese cake sublime." I take especial pleasure in presenting this recipe to you.

CŒUR A LA CRÈME

1 pound double cream cheese (see note page 282)
1 tablespoon powdered sugar

Strawberry Preserves (page 449)
unsalted crackers

FIRST Combine 1 pound double cream cheese with 1 tablespoon powdered sugar.

SECOND Line a heart-shaped mold with cheese cloth. Pack the cheese tightly into the mold. Chill thoroughly overnight in the refrigerator.

THIRD When ready to serve, unmold, peel off the cheese cloth, and serve with Strawberry Preserves (page 449) and unsalted crackers.

NOTE This typical French dish makes an excellent substitute for dessert. The amounts used in this recipe will vary, of course, according to the size of your mold.

REFRIGERATOR CHEESE CAKE

CRUST

¼ pound soft butter
½ cup sugar

2 cups finely crushed cornflakes
1 teaspoon cinnamon

SERVES 6 TO 8

FIRST Cream ¼ pound butter with ½ cup sugar until smooth. Then mix well with 2 cups finely crushed cornflakes. Sprinkle in 1 teaspoon cinnamon.

SECOND Butter a 9-inch spring form to make the crumb mixture stick to the bottom and the sides. Press the crumb mixture onto the bottom of the spring form, then sparingly onto the sides, reserving a little for the top.

FILLING

2 tablespoons gelatin
½ cup cold water
3 egg yolks
½ cup sugar
½ cup milk

5 packages cream cheese
grated rind and juice 1 lemon
½ teaspoon salt
½ cup heavy cream
3 egg whites

FIRST Soften 2 tablespoons gelatin in ½ cup of cold water and dissolve over hot water.

SECOND Beat 3 egg yolks slightly and combine with ½ cup sugar and ½ cup milk. Cook in a double boiler for 3 minutes, stirring occasionally. Add the melted gelatin, stirring well until thoroughly blended. Add this mixture gradually to 5 packages mashed cream cheese. Beat in the grated rind and the juice of 1 lemon. Add ½ teaspoon salt.

THIRD Whip ½ cup heavy cream and fold into cheese mixture. Whip 3 egg whites until stiff and fold into cheese mixture. Pour the entire mixture into the spring form and sprinkle the remaining crumbs over the top. Chill in refrigerator until firm.

RUM CHEESE PIE

[*Pre-heat oven to 275°*]

½ recipe zwieback crust—see Cheese Cake Irene (page 281)
2 packages cream cheese
1¼ cup heavy cream

3 eggs
¾ cup sugar
¼ teaspoon salt
4 tablespoons rum
½ teaspoon grated lemon rind

SERVES 6

FIRST Butter a glass pie dish. Then lightly and *not* thickly press in ½ recipe for zwieback crust—see Cheese Cake Irene—(page 281). Set aside until ready to be filled.

SECOND Blend 2 packages cream cheese with 1¼ cups cream. Mash with a fork and then beat with a rotary beater until completely smooth.

THIRD Beat 3 eggs with ¾ cup sugar until fluffy. Add ¼ teaspoon salt, 4 tablespoons rum, and ½ teaspoon grated lemon rind. Beat with the eggs until thick and smooth. Combine with cheese mixture. Beat again with the rotary beater until absolutely smooth. Pour into crumb crust and bake in a 275° oven until set. Serve very cold.

NOTE A few crumbs may be reserved to sprinkle on top of the pie if desired. This is the usual garnish, but I find that a sprinkling of rum on top just before serving is a more novel presentation.

TOP SECRET

[Pre-heat oven to 350°]

CRUST

14 graham crackers	¼ pound butter

SERVES 6

FIRST Crumble 14 graham crackers with your hands. Then run over them with rolling-pin.

SECOND Melt ¼ pound butter and combine with crumbs. While still warm, press the mixture into a lightly buttered pie plate to form a crust. Reserve a few crumbs to sprinkle over the top of the pie.

THE FILLING

5 packages cream cheese	2 eggs
½ cup light cream	2 teaspoons vanilla
½ cup sugar	1 teaspoon almond extract

FIRST Cream 5 packages cream cheese and ½ cup light cream. Beat well and work until absolutely smooth. Add ½ cup sugar and beat again. Add 2 whole eggs and beat hard and very thoroughly.

SECOND Add 2 teaspoons vanilla and 1 teaspoon almond extract. Beat once more. Then pour into crust. Bake in a 350° oven for 20 minutes.

THE TOPPING

1 cup sour cream	1 teaspoon vanilla
1 tablespoon sugar	½ teaspoon almond extract

FIRST Mix 1 cup sour cream, 1 tablespoon sugar, 1 teaspoon vanilla, and ½ teaspoon almond extract, using a rotary beater.

SECOND When the pie has been in the oven exactly 20 minutes, remove, cover with topping, and return to the oven immediately for an additional 5 minutes. Allow to cool completely before serving. Just before serving, sprinkle lightly with the reserved crumbs.

NOTE Two words of caution: 1. When setting the crumb mixture into the pie plate, butter the plate sufficiently to help the crumbs to adhere. Make the crust thin.
2. Use a rather large pie plate—otherwise the filling will run over when the sour cream is added.

BLACK CHOCOLATE DESSERT CAKE

[*Pre-heat oven to 375°*]

¼ pound butter	1¾ cups pastry flour
1½ cups sugar	1 teaspoon baking soda
3 eggs	¼ teaspoon salt
4 squares cooking chocolate	1 cup milk

GARNISH

1 cup heavy cream	1 square cooking chocolate
½ cup sugar	1 teaspoon vanilla

SERVES 8

FIRST Cream ¼ pound butter with 1½ cups sugar until fluffy. Beat in 3 eggs.

SECOND Set 4 squares cooking chocolate in the oven to soften. Cool before using. Add to butter mixture. Beat well.

THIRD Sift 1¾ cups pastry flour. Measure and resift twice with 1 teaspoon baking soda and ¼ teaspoon salt. Add alternately to the batter with 1 cup of milk. Bake in a square cake tin for 20 minutes in a 375° oven.

FOURTH When the cake is cool, split in half and ice, inside and out, with 1 cup heavy cream whipped stiff, sweetened with ½ cup sugar, and flavored with 1 square of melted cooking chocolate and 1 teaspoon vanilla.

CHOCOLATE BAVARIAN CREAM

2 cups milk	4 egg whites
⅔ cup sugar	1 cup heavy cream
4 squares cooking chocolate	1 tablespoon vanilla
2 envelopes gelatin	

GARNISH

1 cup heavy cream	1 tablespoon vanilla
¼ cup sugar	chocolate bits

FIRST Scald 1½ cups milk. Add ⅔ cup sugar and stir until dissolved. Add 4 squares cooking chocolate and stir until dissolved.

SECOND Add 2 envelopes gelatin to ½ cup cold milk. Soak 5 minutes. Then dissolve over hot water. Add to the chocolate mixture and stir until well blended.

THIRD When chocolate mixture has a mottled appearance, gently fold in 4 stiffly beaten egg whites.

FOURTH Beat 1 cup of heavy cream until stiff. Fold gently and evenly into the mixture. When thoroughly blended, add 1 tablespoon vanilla and combine. Place the pudding mixture in a cold, rinsed mold and set in the refrigerator. When ready to serve, unmold and decorate with one cup of heavy cream whipped until stiff, sweetened with ¼ cup sugar, and flavored with 1 tablespoon vanilla. Top the pudding with sparse scattering of shaved chocolate bits.

CHOCOLATE DATE CAKE WITH WHIPPED CREAM

[Pre-heat oven to 325°]

4 egg yolks
1 cup sugar
1 tablespoon orange juice
3 tablespoons flour
2 tablespoons grated *or* powdered chocolate

1 teaspoon baking powder
1 cup dates
1 cup walnuts
4 egg whites

GARNISH

1 cup heavy cream
¼ cup sugar

1 tablespoon vanilla
pitted dates

SERVES 6

FIRST Cream 4 egg yolks with 1 cup sugar until light. Stir in 1 tablespoon orange juice.

SECOND Sift 3 tablespoons flour with 2 tablespoons grated or powdered chocolate and 1 teaspoon baking powder. Sift second time into egg-yolk mixture. Cut up 1 cup dates into little pieces. Chop 1 cup walnuts. Dredge both with flour and fold into the batter.

THIRD Beat 4 egg whites until stiff and fold gently into the mixture. Bake in a 325° oven for 45 to 50 minutes.

FOURTH Whip 1 cup heavy cream until stiff. Sweeten with ¼ cup sugar and flavor with 1 tablespoon vanilla. Ice top and sides of cake with the cream and decorate top with pitted dates.

CHOCOLATE ICEBOX CAKE

½ pound butter
2 cups powdered sugar
4 egg yolks
4 squares cooking chocolate

1 tablespoon vanilla
4 egg whites
24 ladyfingers

GARNISH

¼ cup chopped nuts *or* chocolate decorettes
1 cup heavy cream
¼ cup sugar

1 tablespoon vanilla
additional chopped nuts *or* chocolate decorettes

SERVES 8

FIRST Cream ½ pound butter with 2 cups powdered sugar. Then beat in 4 thoroughly beaten egg yolks. Add 4 squares melted cooking chocolate and 1 tablespoon vanilla. Beat until well blended.

SECOND Beat 4 egg whites until stiff. Fold into the chocolate mixture and blend thoroughly but gently.

THIRD Lightly butter a spring form. Line with ladyfingers, split in half for the sides broken into pieces for the bottom, and reserving a few to crumble into bits over the top. (This will require approximately 24 ladyfingers.) Once the chocolate mixture is poured into the lined form, crumble the remaining ladyfingers over the top and sprinkle with ¼ cup of chopped nuts or chocolate decorettes. Place in the refrigerator for at least 24 hours.

FOURTH When ready to serve, unmold onto a round platter. Whip 1 cup heavy cream until stiff, sweeten with ¼ cup sugar, and flavor with 1 tablespoon vanilla. Arrange in mounds around the cake or serve separately in a bowl. If mounds are used, sprinkle each with additional chopped nuts or chocolate decorettes.

CHOCOLATE ROLL I *Marie's*

[Pre-heat oven to 350°]

1 cup powdered sugar	2 cups heavy cream
1 tablespoon flour	½ cup sugar
½ tablespoon baking powder	1 tablespoon vanilla extract
2 tablespoons powdered chocolate	Chocolate Sauce I (page 359) *or*
5 egg yolks	Chocolate Sauce II (page 360)
5 egg whites	

SERVES 6 TO 8

FIRST Sift together 1 cup powdered sugar, 1 tablespoon flour, ½ tablespoon baking powder, and 2 tablespoons powdered chocolate.

SECOND Beat 5 egg yolks until light. Sift in the dry ingredients and stir until completely blended.

THIRD Beat 5 egg whites until stiff but not dry. Fold the whites into the chocolate mixture with a gentle hand.

FOURTH Grease a cookie sheet and cover with a piece of greased waxed paper. Spread the batter on the greased paper evenly with a narrow spatula or knife. Bake in a 350° oven for approximately half an hour.

FIFTH Remove from oven and quickly invert the pan onto a clean, dry towel. Peel off the waxed paper, being extremely careful not to tear the cake. A sharp knife will be useful at this point. If the edges of the cake feel hard and brittle, cut them off and discard. Roll the cake in the towel and set aside until ready to use. When ready to serve, unroll and cover thickly with 2 cups heavy cream beaten until stiff, sweetened with ½ cup sugar, and flavored with 1 tablespoon vanilla extract. Roll up again. Serve with Chocolate Sauce I (page 359) or Chocolate Sauce II (page 360). If any whipped cream is left, it may be used to ice the top and sides of the roll.

CHOCOLATE ROLL II

[*Pre-heat oven to 350°*]

6 egg yolks
¾ cup sugar
4 tablespoons ground chocolate
6 egg whites

2 cups heavy cream
½ cup sugar
3 teaspoons vanilla
Chocolate Sauce II (page 360)

SERVES 6 TO 8

FIRST Beat 6 egg yolks. Measure out ¾ cup sugar. Stir half this amount into the yolks and work well. Stir in 4 tablespoons ground chocolate until well blended.

SECOND Whip 6 egg whites until almost stiff but not dry. Gradually beat in the remaining sugar. Fold gently into the chocolate mixture. Spread out on a buttered and floured sheet of wax paper placed on top of a cookie sheet. Bake approximately 30 minutes in a 350° oven.

THIRD When baked, remove from the oven, take the sheet off the tin, remove the wax paper, and roll it while warm in a slightly damp cloth. When ready to serve, remove the cloth. Unroll and fill with 2 cups heavy cream beaten until stiff, sweetened with ½ cup sugar, and flavored with 3 teaspoons vanilla. Reroll and place on a serving-platter.

FOURTH Pour half the amount of Chocolate Sauce II (page 360) over the roll. Serve the additional Chocolate Sauce slightly warm in a sauce boat.

NOTE If preferred, the roll may be filled with vanilla ice cream. If so, be certain the ice cream is not too hard when you fill the roll; otherwise it will be too difficult to spread, and pressure on the cake will be fatal to its texture. This Chocolate Roll is light as a feather.

COLD CHOCOLATE SOUFFLÉ

1 envelope gelatin
½ cup cold water
½ cup boiling water
5 squares cooking chocolate
1 cup milk

5 egg yolks
1 cup sugar
1 tablespoon vanilla
5 egg whites

GARNISH

1 cup heavy cream
¼ cup sugar
1 tablespoon vanilla

chopped nuts *or* maraschino cherries

SERVES 8

FIRST Stir 1 envelope gelatin in ½ cup water and let stand 5 minutes. Then dissolve by adding ½ cup boiling water.

SECOND Place 5 squares cooking chocolate and 1 cup milk in top of double boiler. Stir occasionally until the chocolate is completely dissolved. Cool slightly.

THIRD Beat 5 egg yolks with 1 cup sugar until smooth and creamy. Add to chocolate mixture and stir well. Add dissolved gelatin and 1 tablespoon vanilla. Stir again and cool thoroughly.

FOURTH Beat 5 egg whites until firm but not stiff. Gently fold into chocolate mixture. Pour into bowl or dish in which soufflé is to be served. Place in refrigerator all day. When ready to serve, decorate top with 1 cup heavy cream beaten until stiff, sweetened with ¼ cup sugar, and flavored with 1 tablespoon vanilla. Garnish with chopped nuts or maraschino cherries.

NOTE Only two things to remember. 1: Make this in the morning for the same evening. If you make it the day before, it will be too stiff, having stood too long in the refrigerator. 2. Do not beat the egg whites too stiff. If you do, the texture will be spongy instead of creamy.

HOT CHOCOLATE SOUFFLÉ Marie's

[Pre-heat oven to 350°]

4 ounces sweet *or* bittersweet chocolate
2 tablespoons warm water

generous ⅓ cup sugar
8 egg whites

GARNISH

1 cup heavy cream
¼ cup sugar

1 tablespoon vanilla

SERVES 6

FIRST Melt 4 ounces sweet or bittersweet chocolate in the oven in 2 tablespoons warm water. Remove from oven, stir briefly, and add generous ⅓ cup granulated sugar. Stir well.

SECOND Beat 8 egg whites until stiff. Stir about ⅛ amount beaten egg whites into chocolate mixture for about 10 minutes. (This long stirring makes the soufflé light.)

THIRD Then stir about ⅓ remaining beaten egg whites into chocolate mixture for about 10 minutes. At the end of this time fold in the remaining beaten egg whites and mix gently with a folding motion.

FOURTH Place in a buttered baking-dish and bake in a 350° degree oven for half an hour. Beat 1 cup heavy cream until stiff. Sweeten with ¼ cup sugar and flavor with 1 tablespoon vanilla. As soon as soufflé is ready, serve immediately. *It will not wait.*

NOTE This fluffy high soufflé was the delight of our childhood! It came to the table half again as high as the dish in which it had been baked, with a crusty top that had jagged cracks across the top. We called it, "Marie's earthquake." But, remember, serve it immediately it comes out of the oven. It positively WILL NOT WAIT!

DEVIL'S FOOD CAKE AS A BOX

4 layers Devil' Food Cake Maria (page 376)
1 pint vanilla ice cream *or*
1 pint heavy cream, ½ cup sugar, 1 tablespoon vanilla

1 recipe Seven-Minute Icing (page 426)
grated coconut

SERVES 6 TO 8

FIRST Bake 4 layers Devil's Food Cake Maria (page 376). Set 3 of the 4 layers, one on top of the other, and cut out the centers until only 1½-inch ring remains. Place these carefully on top of the bottom layer, which has been left intact.

SECOND Fill center with 1 pint vanilla ice cream or 1 pint heavy cream beaten until stiff, sweetened with ½ cup sugar, and flavored with 1 tablespoon vanilla.

THIRD Cover the entire cake with Seven-Minute Icing (page 426) and quickly sprinkle with grated coconut (fresh preferred). Of course, if the ice cream is used, it must be served immediately.

"KORSU CAKE"

[*Pre-heat oven to 375°*]

2 cups sugar
6 ounces butter
3 eggs
3 cups pastry flour
3 teaspoons baking powder
¼ teaspoon salt

1 cup milk
2 tablespoons vanilla
2 cups heavy cream
½ cup sugar
Chocolate Icing (page 422)
Chocolate Sauce I (page 359)

SERVES 8

FIRST Cream 2 cups sugar with 6 ounces butter. Add 3 eggs, beating them in one at a time.

SECOND Sift 3 cups pastry flour. Measure and resift 3 times with 3 teaspoons baking powder and ¼ teaspoon of salt.

THIRD Add the flour alternately to the batter with 1 cup of milk. Then stir in 1 tablespoon vanilla.

FOURTH Butter and flour a 2-quart melon mold. Pour the batter into the mold and bake in a 375° oven until a testing straw comes out clean and dry from the center of the cake. Unmold and cool on a cake rack.

FIFTH When cool, turn upside down and cut off about 1 inch from the bottom of the cake. Set the bottom aside very carefully. Scoop out the soft inside of the cake, leaving a shell all around about 1 inch thick. Fill this cavity with 2 cups heavy cream whipped stiff, sweetened with ½ cup sugar, and flavored with 1 tablespoon vanilla. Replace the bottom and stand the cake upright. Set in the refrigerator until ready to serve. Then ice with Chocolate Icing (page 422) and send to the table accompanied by a bowl of warm Chocolate Sauce (page 359).

NOTE This cake may be filled with vanilla ice cream instead of whipped cream, if preferred.

NOTE Alice was a wonderful little colored cook from Baltimore, Maryland. For years she regaled us with her "Korsu Cake." To repeated questionings as to the meaning of the delicious dessert's strange name, the only reply Alice ever gave was, "It's just Korsu Cake." And so it was, "just Korsu Cake" for twenty years. Recently a friend, well acquainted with Baltimore, wrote me: "I remember you were puzzled about Kossuth cakes. They were in honor of Louis Kossuth, the Hungarian patriot who lost out in his fight for independence, and came to America and Baltimore in the nineteenth century, and was more fêted than any man since Washington. The cakes are a regular Sunday dessert, sometimes individuals, sometimes one big one."

MOLDED CHOCOLATE HIDDEN AWAY

1 recipe white cake as in Old-Fashioned Coconut Cake (page 384)
Molded Chocolate Pudding (page 296)
2 cups heavy cream
½ cup sugar
2 tablespoons vanilla
shredded coconut
shreds of bittersweet chocolate

SERVES 8

FIRST Bake 1 white cake, as in Old-Fashioned Coconut Cake (page 384), in a deep cake tin. Cut out the center of the cake and remove all the insides, leaving a shell about 2 inches thick. Fill this shell with Molded Chocolate Pudding (page 296–7). Place in refrigerator until set (at least 6 hours).

SECOND When ready to serve, whip 2 cups heavy cream until stiff. Sweeten with ½ cup sugar and flavor with 2 tablespoons vanilla. Ice cake thickly with this cream. Sprinkle until well covered with freshly shredded coconut and decorate with fine shreds of bittersweet chocolate.

MOLDED CHOCOLATE PUDDING *Marie's*

1 cup milk	½ cup cold water
4 ounces sweet *or* bittersweet chocolate	4 egg yolks
⅓ cup sugar	⅓ cup sugar
¾ cup cold water	2 cups heavy cream
2 envelopes gelatin	½ cup sugar
	1 tablespoon vanilla

GARNISH

grated chocolate	¼ cup sugar
1 cup heavy cream	1 tablespoon vanilla

SERVES 8

FIRST Put 1 cup milk on stove to boil. Meanwhile take 4 ounces sweet or bittersweet chocolate and stir with ⅓ cup sugar and ¼ cup of cold water. Place on fire and stir constantly until well blended.

SECOND Soak 2 envelopes gelatin in ½ cup cold water 5 minutes. Dissolve over hot water. Add to chocolate mixture and blend. Pour into bowl, being certain to scrape in the entire amount.

THIRD Remove the boiled milk from the fire and stir in 4 beaten egg yolks and ⅓ cup sugar. Return to the fire and stir constantly until thick. Add to chocolate mixture, and stir well. Set in a cool place, stirring occasionally until cool, but do not allow to stiffen before folding in the whipped cream.

FOURTH Whip 2 cups heavy cream until stiff. Sweeten with ½ cup sugar and flavor with 1 tablespoon vanilla. Add slowly to the chocolate mixture, folding it gradually and very evenly until it is completely blended. Place in a cold, well-rinsed mold and set in the refrigerator.

FIFTH When ready to serve, unmold and garnish with grated chocolate and serve decorated with or accompanied by 1 cup of heavy cream beaten until stiff, sweetened with ¼ cup sugar, and flavored with 1 tablespoon vanilla.

NOTE For those who prefer a more bitter flavor in their puddings, use 3 squares of baking chocolate instead.

PETITS POTS AU CHOCOLAT
[6 *cups*]

1 cup light cream
½ pound bittersweet *or* **sweet chocolate**
4 egg yolks
salt

FIRST Boil 1 cup coffee cream. Finely grate ½ pound bittersweet or sweet chocolate into the cream. Stir, but do not allow the milk to come to a boil again. Remove from the fire.

SECOND Beat 4 egg yolks very thoroughly. Pour the chocolate mixture onto the eggs and stir well until slightly cooled. Sprinkle in a little salt and stir again.

THIRD Strain into ramekins or custard cups. Place the cups into the refrigerator for several hours, better still, all day or overnight.

NOTE You can make or break this marvelous recipe by the chocolate you use. As there is no sugar in the recipe you can very well see that an unsweetened baking chocolate will not do. Nor should it be too sweet. My choice is definitely bittersweet. In Paris and in the finer restaurants in the United States, these little chocolate pots are offered along with other delectable pastries and tarts. They never fail to be the first to disappear from the dessert wagons or trays!

TÊTES DE NÈGRES Marie's
[*Pre-heat oven to 325°*]

4 egg yolks	4 egg whites
4 heaping tablespoons vanilla sugar	1 cup heavy cream
	¼ cup sugar
salt	1 tablespoon vanilla
4 level tablespoons flour	Chocolate Icing (page 422)

SERVES 6

FIRST Beat 4 egg yolks with 4 heaping tablespoons vanilla sugar (see note) until smooth and light in color. Add a pinch of salt and continue to beat until bubbly.

SECOND Sprinkle in 4 level tablespoons of flour very slowly, folding in carefully after each addition.

THIRD Beat 4 egg whites until stiff and fold into the batter gently.

FOURTH Place brown paper on cookie sheets and sprinkle paper with flour. Take up large spoonfuls of the batter and drop onto the paper, spacing evenly, leaving room for the rounds to spread a little. Arrange them high in the center and as round in form as possible. If the rounds are from 2 to 3 inches across when first dropped onto the paper, they will be the correct size for use when baked.

FIFTH Bake in a 325° oven for 20 to 25 minutes. When done, remove from the paper with the back part of a knife while still warm. Turn the rounds upside down. Then with a small knife dig out some of the soft inside of the dough, leaving them slightly hollow. Cool. Ice with Chocolate Icing (page 422). This may be done an hour or two before serving.

SIXTH When ready to serve, fill rounds *generously* with whipped cream (1 cup heavy cream whipped until stiff, sweetened with ¼ cup sugar, and flavored with 1 tablespoon vanilla). Press each two gently together and serve at once.

NOTE Vanilla sugar, as suggested in Marie's original recipe, is made at home, by filling a quart jar with granulated sugar, plunging a split vanilla bean down into the sugar, and securing the jar with a lid to make it airtight.

CRÈME BRÛLÉE JUNE PLATT
[*Pre-heat oven to 325°*]

1 quart cream
2 tablespoons sugar
8 egg yolks

2 teaspoons vanilla
light brown sugar

SERVES 8

FIRST Heat 1 quart cream in a double boiler until hot but not scalding. Add 2 tablespoons sugar and stir until dissolved.

SECOND Beat 8 egg yolks until light. Add to the cream with 2 teaspoons vanilla. Mix well, strain, and pour into a shallow glass baking-dish of the right size so as to have the custard about 1½ inches deep. Place the dish in hot water and bake in a 325° oven until set.

THIRD Cool and place the dish in the refrigerator for several hours to chill thoroughly. Then remove from the refrigerator and cover the surface of the custard with ¼ inch, light brown sugar that is soft and completely free from lumps. Dark brown sugar will not do.

[*Pre-heat broiler*]

FOURTH Place the dish under red-hot broiler and watch very carefully—leave the broiler door open and *watch*. The top of the sugar should melt and run together, leaving a shiny caramel top. As I said before, watch very carefully or it will catch fire and burn. When the entire surface is glazed, remove and cool. Place in refrigerator to chill thoroughly. It must be served very cold. A light tap of the spoon breaks through the glaze.

NOTE I have used this superb recipe so often, I have come to feel that it is part of the family's gastronomic life. I am extremely grateful to my friend, that talented gourmet, June Platt, and to her publishers, Houghton, Mifflin and Company, for permission to use this recipe. It appears in two of Mrs. Platt's superlative cook books, in *June Platt's Dessert Cook Book* and in *June Platt's Party Cook Book*.

CUSTARD WHITE OR AMBER

[*Pre-heat oven to 350°*]

¾ cup sugar
½ cup water
6 eggs
¾ cup sugar

2 cups milk
2 cups light cream
⅛ teaspoon salt
1 tablespoon vanilla

SERVES 6

FIRST Dissolve ¾ cup sugar in ½ cup water and bring to a boil over a moderate flame. Continue to boil until it begins to turn light gold. If you wish the custard white, stop boiling the sugar at this point. If you wish the custard amber, continue boiling until it turns a rich golden brown in color. When the color you wish has been reached, pour half the liquid into a 2-quart glass casserole and tip the dish back and forth to coat the bottom and as much of the sides as possible. Set the casserole in the refrigerator.

SECOND Beat 6 eggs with ¾ cup sugar. Add 2 cups of milk and 2 cups of light cream. Add ⅛ teaspoon salt and 1 tablespoon vanilla. Blend well and pour in the remaining sugar syrup. As it hits the cold custard mixture, it will solidify. Place the entire mixture in a saucepan and stir constantly over a moderate flame until the syrup has melted into the custard and the custard has just begun to thicken. This should take about 5 minutes.

THIRD Remove the casserole from the refrigerator and *strain* the custard into it. Place the casserole in a pan containing lukewarm water (*not* hot) and set in a 350° oven. Just before closing the oven door, carefully pour enough additional lukewarm water into the pan in which the casserole is standing to reach almost the top of the casserole. (Half way up is not enough.) Bake for an hour and a half. Test with a knife. When it comes out clean, the custard is done. Cool and place in the refrigerator to chill completely.

FOURTH When ready to serve, this custard may be unmolded, if preferred, or served right from the dish itself. If you prefer unmolding it, be careful not to allow it to crack as it drops to the serving-platter. But remember, serve it very cold.

NOTE The darker your syrup, the darker your pudding and the more caramel in flavor. But for those who like it white, serve it with any chosen fruit sauce or just plain.

INDIAN PUDDING CUSTARD

AN EARLY AMERICAN RECIPE

[*Pre-heat oven to 300°*]

2 cups milk
2 cups light cream
6 tablespoons yellow corn meal
3 tablespoons butter
¾ cup molasses
1½ teaspoon salt
½ cup brown sugar
¾ teaspoon cinnamon

½ teaspoon ginger
¼ teaspoon nutmeg
½ teaspoon grated lemon rind
2 eggs
1 teaspoon vanilla
1 cup heavy cream
heavy cream (optional)

SERVES 6 to 8

FIRST Heat 2 cups milk and 2 cups light cream in top of large double boiler. Add 6 tablespoons yellow corn meal, bit by bit. Cook for 15 minutes, stirring constantly. This is important so that it will thicken evenly.

SECOND Stir in 3 tablespoons butter, ¾ cup molasses, 1½ teaspoons salt, ½ cup brown sugar, ¾ teaspoon cinnamon, ½ teaspoon ginger, ¼ teaspoon nutmeg, and ½ teaspoon grated lemon rind. Mix well.

THIRD Remove the mixture from the fire and beat in two eggs. Pour the mixture into a buttered casserole.

FOURTH Stir 1 teaspoon vanilla into 1 cup heavy cream and pour over the top of the mixture in the casserole. Set in a pan of lukewarm water and bake in a 300° oven without disturbing the cream. Bake until a knife comes out of the center of the custard clean. Cool to room temperature, then place in refrigerator until thoroughly chilled. Serve plain, or with a pitcher heavy cream.

COLD RICE PUDDING IN A MOLD *Marie's*

1 cup rice
½ cup milk
¾ cup water
1 envelope gelatin

½ cup sugar
1 teaspoon vanilla
scant 2 cups heavy cream

GARNISH

1 cup heavy cream
¼ cup sugar
1 tablespoon vanilla

Raspberry Sauce *or* Strawberry Sauce (page 450)

SERVES 8

FIRST Wash 1 cup rice in several waters. Then cook with ½ cup milk and ½ cup water in the top of double boiler for 1 hour or until soft.

SECOND Soak 1 envelope gelatin in ¼ cup cold water for 5 minutes. Stir carefully and thoroughly into rice. Then stir in ½ cup sugar and 1 tablespoon vanilla. Mix well but gently. *Cool.*

THIRD Whip a little less than 2 cups heavy cream until firm but not too dry and stiff. Fold into rice mixture. Pour into cold, rinsed mold and place in refrigerator to set at least 4 hours.

FOURTH When ready to serve, unmold and garnish with 1 cup heavy cream whipped until stiff, sweetened with ¼ cup sugar, and flavored with 1 tablespoon vanilla. Serve with a separate bowl of Raspberry Sauce or Strawberry Sauce (page 450).

NOTE The thrill and delight of childhood days with a dessert like this being served on a wintry day, with the memory of the fragrance that had drifted through the house in early summer while the berry sauce was being prepared!

ENGLISH GOOSEBERRY FOOL

1 cup hot water
2 cups sugar
½ teaspoon vanilla
1 pound fresh gooseberries

2 envelopes gelatin
½ cup cold water
1 cup powdered sugar
1 cup heavy cream

GARNISH

1 cup heavy cream
¼ cup sugar

1 tablespoon vanilla
sponge cake *or* ladyfingers

SERVES 6 TO 8

FIRST Make a syrup by bringing 1 cup hot water and 2 cups sugar to a boil. Add ½ teaspoon vanilla and 1 pound fresh gooseberries. Boil until soft, then rub gooseberries through a fine sieve.

SECOND Soak 2 envelopes gelatin in ½ cup cold water. Let stand 5 minutes, then dissolve over hot water. Stir into gooseberry purée and add 1 cup (more if desired) of powdered sugar. Blend very thoroughly and *cool*.

THIRD Whip 1 cup heavy cream stiff. Fold into gooseberry mixture very thoroughly and very carefully. Place in cold, rinsed mold and place in refrigerator several hours until set.

FOURTH When ready to serve, unmold and decorate with 1 cup heavy cream whipped until stiff, sweetened with ¼ cup sugar, and flavored with 1 tablespoon vanilla. Serve with sponge cake or ladyfingers.

NOTE This is an old English recipe. I have never tried to do it with any other berries, but I don't see why they would not do just as well. It is impossible to give you the exact amount of powdered sugar, as there is no way of knowing just how sweet the berries are going to be.

Use your palate and your judgment. I think you will like this recipe. It is strange, but Americans do not seem, generally speaking, to be well acquainted with gooseberry recipes. Gooseberries are very delicate in flavor.

FRUIT SALAD IN LAYER CAKE

2 envelopes gelatin
½ cup cold water
1 cup boiling water
1 cup sugar
2 cups sherry

2 cups cut-up fresh fruit
2 layers stale sponge cake
1 cup heavy cream
¼ cup sugar
1 teaspoon vanilla

SERVES 6

FIRST Soak 2 envelopes of gelatin in ½ cup cold water and let stand for 5 minutes. Dissolve in 1 cup boiling water.

SECOND Add 1 cup sugar and 2 cups sherry, stirring until the sugar is dissolved.

THIRD Cover the bottom of a 2-quart mold with 1 cup of cut-up fresh fruit (do not cut up too fine). Cover the fruit with cut pieces of one layer of stale sponge cake. Cover the cake with another cup of cut-up fresh fruit. Then cover the fruit with the cut pieces of the second layer of stale sponge cake.

FOURTH Add the gelatin mixture, allowing it to run down the sides of the fruit and the cake, submerging the entire thing. Place in the refrigerator until set.

FIFTH When ready to serve, unmold and serve with 1 cup heavy cream whipped until stiff, sweetened with ¼ cup sugar, and flavored with 1 teaspoon vanilla.

NOTE This dessert may be made with sugared, fresh berries or any single chosen fruit instead of the fruit salad, if preferred.

GINGER CREAM

2 beaten egg yolks	3 tablespoons Chinese ginger
1 cup milk	syrup
salt	1 teaspoon vanilla
¼ cup sugar	¼ cup ginger
1 tablespoon gelatin	2 cups heavy cream
¼ cup cold water	
	GARNISH
1 cup heavy cream	1 tablespoon vanilla
¼ cup sugar	ladyfingers

SERVES 6

FIRST Make a custard by stirring 2 beaten egg yolks with 1 cup milk, pinch of salt, and ¼ cup sugar over moderate fire. Stir constantly until mixture thickens. Remove from fire.

SECOND Soak 1 tablespoon gelatin in ¼ cup cold water for 5 minutes. Dissolve over boiling water. Add to hot custard and stir well. Add 3 tablespoons Chinese ginger syrup, 1 teaspoon vanilla, and ¼ cup ginger cut into tiny pieces. *Cool.*

THIRD When mixture starts to thicken, beat 2 cups heavy cream until stiff. Fold gently but thoroughly into ginger mixture and place in a cold, rinsed mold. Set mold in refrigerator until ready to serve.

FOURTH When ready to serve, unmold and decorate with 1 cup of heavy cream beaten until stiff, sweetened with ¼ cup sugar, and flavored with 1 tablespoon vanilla. Serve with ladyfingers.

WARNING Pay particular attention to the first direction. Have your flame moderate, and stir without stopping until it thickens; otherwise the mixture will be lumpy and may even curdle.

MACAROON FLUFF

¾ tablespoon gelatin	½ cup sherry
¼ cup cold water	4 egg whites
¾ cup boiling water	12 crumbled macaroons
½ cup sugar	Strawberry Sauce (page 450)
4 egg yolks	

SERVES 6

FIRST Soak ¾ tablespoon gelatin in ¼ cup cold water for 5 minutes. Fill the cup with ¾ cup boiling water and stir until the gelatin is dissolved.

SECOND Mix ½ cup sugar with 4 egg yolks until creamy and light. Add ½ cup sherry and stir in the top of the double boiler until thick. Remove from the stove.

THIRD Stir in the gelatin until thoroughly blended. *Cool.* When the mixture is cool, beat 4 egg whites until stiff and fold in gently. Add 12 crumbled macaroons and place in a cold, rinsed mold for 4 hours at least, or until firm.

FOURTH When ready to serve, unmold carefully and serve with Strawberry Sauce (page 450).

NOTE A most refreshing light, airy dessert. It is splendid for warm summer evenings. The amount given is a "family size." If a larger "party size" mold is required, double the recipe. But in that case, do not double the amount of boiling water.

MAPLE MOUSSE

4 egg yolks
1 cup maple syrup
2 envelopes gelatin
½ cup cold water

¼ pound maple sugar
4 egg whites
2 cups heavy cream

SERVES 8

FIRST Beat 4 egg yolks until light. Place on stove with 1 cup maple syrup. Bring to a gradual boil, stirring constantly. Remove from fire at once and strain.

SECOND Soak 2 envelopes of gelatin in ½ cup cold water for 5 minutes. Dissolve over hot water until the gelatin clarifies. Stir the gelatin into the egg mixture and *cool.*

THIRD Crumble ¼ pound of maple sugar and add to the mixture. Beat 4 egg whites until stiff. Beat 2 cups of whipping cream until stiff. Fold all this together. When well blended, add to the maple-syrup mixture. Pour into a cold, well-rinsed mold and place in the refrigerator to set for 4 hours or more.

NOTE   For the very best results use only pure maple syrup.

MOLDED EGGNOG PUDDING

[*An old-time holiday recipe*]

12 egg yolks
12 level tablespoons sugar
1 cup best rum
2½–3 envelopes gelatin
½ cup cold water

1 pint best bourbon
2 cups heavy cream
2 tablespoons vanilla
1 cup brandy-flavored mince meat

SERVES 12

FIRST   Beat 12 egg yolks until light and lemon-colored. Add 12 level tablespoons sugar and continue to beat until satiny smooth. The mixture *must* be very smooth and light in color. Hand beating will take about 20 minutes, an electric beater about 10. Add 1 cup best rum. Beat again until well blended and let stand for about 1 hour in a cool place.

SECOND   Soak 2½–3 (depending how firm you wish the pudding to be) envelopes gelatin in ½ cup cold water for 5 minutes. Dissolve over hot water and add to 1 pint best bourbon. Stir into egg mixture very thoroughly until well blended.

THIRD   Beat 2 cups heavy cream until stiff and add 2 tablespoons vanilla. Fold into mixture until completely combined. Pour into a large, cold, rinsed mold and place in the refrigerator until set—at least 5 or 6 hours.

FOURTH   When ready to serve, unmold and garnish with 1 cup of brandy-flavored mince meat that has been heated before using.

NOTE   This uses a large mold and is an excellent dessert to serve at Christmas time or on New Year's Eve. The last time we served this pudding, a well-known Hollywood wit stated emphatically that when the dessert came out of the refrigerator, it stood on its hind legs and announced: "I can lick any dessert in the house!"

ORANGE CREAM *Marie's*

skin of 2 small oranges
skin of ½ lemon
½ cup boiling water
4 egg yolks
1 cup sugar

4 oranges
2 lemons
1 envelope gelatin
¼ cup cold water
2 cups heavy cream

GARNISH

1 cup heavy cream
¼ cup sugar
1 tablespoon vanilla

skinned sections of 2 large oranges
or candied orange peel

SERVES 6 TO 8

FIRST Remove the outer skins from 2 small oranges and ½ lemon with a very sharp paring-knife being careful not to get any of the white pulp with the skins. Cut skins into little pieces and soak for ½ hour in ½ cup boiling water.

SECOND Beat 4 egg yolks with 1 cup sugar until light and smooth. Squeeze and strain the juice of 4 oranges and 2 lemons and add to the egg mixture, stirring until blended. Add the cut-up skins as well as the water in which they have been soaking. Stir again.

THIRD Pour everything into the top of double boiler and stir constantly over hot, but not boiling, water until thick. *Cool.*

FOURTH Soak 1 envelope of gelatin in ¼ cup cold water for 5 minutes. Dissolve over hot water. Cool somewhat, then add to the orange mixture. Stir well and strain through a fine strainer. When *completely* cool, whip 2 cups heavy cream until stiff. Fold gently and evenly into the orange mixture. Pour into a cool, rinsed mold and place in the refrigerator for several hours until set.

FIFTH Whip 1 cup of heavy cream until stiff, sweeten with ¼ cup sugar, and flavor with 1 tablespoon vanilla. When ready to serve, unmold and serve the pudding decorated with mounds of whipped cream, each mound topped with peeled wedges two large oranges or sprinkled with finely chopped candied orange peel.

PEACH CREAM

1 cup heavy cream
2 egg whites
1 heaping cup chopped ripe peaches
½ cup powdered sugar
1 tablespoon vanilla
1 envelope gelatin
¼ cup cold water
Peach Sauce (page 362)

SERVES 6

FIRST Whip 1 cup heavy cream until stiff. Whip 2 egg whites until stiff. Fold together gently.

SECOND Chop 1 heaping cup ripe, fresh peaches. Mix with ½ cup powdered sugar and 1 tablespoon vanilla.

THIRD Soak 1 envelope of gelatin in ¼ cup cold water for 5 minutes. Dissolve over hot water. Stir into the peaches.

FOURTH Fold the cream mixture in gently. Blend well and set in a cold, rinsed mold. Chill in the refrigerator until ready to serve. Serve with Peach Sauce (page 362).

PEPPERMINT-STICK CREAM

2 cups milk
½ pound peppermint sticks
2½ teaspoons gelatin
¼ cup cold water
1 cup heavy cream
1 tablespoon vanilla
Chocolate Icing (page 422)

SERVES 6 TO 8

FIRST Scald 2 cups milk and dissolve ½ pound peppermint sticks in it.

SECOND Soak 2½ teaspoons gelatin in ¼ cup cold water for 5 minutes. Add to the scalded milk and stir until dissolved. *Cool.*

THIRD When the mixture begins to set, whip it until it foams.

FOURTH Beat 1 cup heavy cream until stiff. Add 1 tablespoon vanilla extract and fold gently and thoroughly into the peppermint mixture. Pour into a cold, rinsed mold and place in the refrigerator until set (about 6 hours). Just before serving, cover with Chocolate Icing (page 422).

NOTE This delicate Peppermint Cream may be served without the Chocolate Icing, but most people prefer it.

PUNCH BAVARIAN

1½ teaspoons gelatin
¼ cup cold water
1½ ounces punch (Swedish punch preferred)
3 egg yolks
½ cup sugar

3 egg whites
1 cup heavy cream
strained raspberry sauce *or* commercially prepared sauce Melba

SERVES 6

FIRST Soak 1½ teaspoons gelatin in ¼ cup cold water. Dissolve over hot water. Add 1½ ounces punch (Swedish punch preferred).

SECOND Beat 3 egg yolks until light. Add ½ cup sugar and beat until light and smooth. Beat 3 egg whites until stiff. Beat 1 cup of heavy cream until stiff. Combine the three, folding, until evenly distributed.

THIRD Add this cream mixture to the gelatin, folding again until well blended. Place in a cold, well-rinsed mold and set in refrigerator for at least six hours.

FOURTH When ready to serve, unmold onto a platter and serve with a strained raspberry sauce or a commercially prepared sauce melba.

ROTE GREUTZE

2 cups fresh currants
4 cups raspberries
2 cups water
¾ cup sugar
⅔ cup cornstarch

Vanilla Sauce II (page 363) *or*
1 cup heavy cream
¼ cup sugar
1 tablespoon vanilla

SERVES 6

FIRST Combine 2 cups fresh currants with 4 cups raspberries and place in saucepan with 2 cups water. Boil until soft, then strain.

SECOND Measure the juice and add enough water to make 2 quarts. Add ¾ cup sugar to the liquid and stir until the sugar is dissolved. Remove 1 cup juice and rub into ⅔ cup cornstarch. Add cornstarch a little at a time, stirring well after each addition to be certain there are no lumps. Bring to boil and stir constantly until thick. Pour into mold and allow to cool.

THIRD When cool, place in refrigerator until cold and well set. When ready to serve, unmold and serve with Vanilla Sauce II (page 363), or with 1 cup heavy cream beaten until stiff, sweetened with ¼ cup sugar, and flavored with 1 tablespoon vanilla.

RUM BAVARIAN

1½ tablespoons gelatin
¼ cup cold water
¼ cup boiling water
½ cup sugar
⅓ cup rum

4 tablespoons rye *or* bourbon
   whisky
2 egg whites
2 cups heavy cream

GARNISH

1 cup heavy cream
¼ cup sugar
1 tablespoon vanilla

¼ cup rum
½ cup finely slivered almonds
grated nutmeg

SERVES 8

FIRST Soak 1½ tablespoons gelatin in ¼ cup cold water for 5 minutes. Dissolve in ¼ cup boiling water and stir until completely clear. Stir in ½ cup sugar, ⅓ cup rum, and 4 tablespoons rye or bourbon whisky. Continue to stir until sugar is dissolved. Strain and *cool*.

SECOND When mixture begins to thicken, beat with a wire whisk or rotaty beater until frothy. Beat 2 egg whites until stiff and gently fold into gelatin mixture.

THIRD Beat 2 cups of heavy cream until stiff. Add to the mixture, 2 tablespoons at a time. Blend each addition of cream thoroughly before proceeding. When all the cream has been added, beat gently for a minute or two until everything is completely blended and the mixture is airy and frothy. Pour into a rinsed, well-chilled mold. Place in the refrigerator to set for at least 4 hours.

FOURTH When ready to serve, unmold and decorate with 1 cup heavy cream beaten until stiff, sweetened with ¼ cup of sugar, and flavored with 1 tablespoon vanilla, and ¼ cup rum. Sprinkle entire pudding with ½ cup finely slivered almonds and dust lightly with grated nutmeg.

WINE JELLY *Marie's*

2 envelopes gelatin
½ cup cold water
1⅔ cups hot water
1 cup sugar
⅓ cup orange juice

3 tablespoons lemon juice
1 cup sherry
Vanilla Sauce II (page 363)
   (optional)

SERVES 6

FIRST Dissolve 2 envelopes gelatin in ½ cup cold water and soak for 5 minutes. Bring 1⅔ cups hot water and 1 cup of sugar to a boil and stir in the gelatin. Blend well. *Cool*.

SECOND Stir ⅓ cup fresh orange juice and 3 tablespoons fresh lemon juice into 1 cup sherry and add to the gelatin mixture. Stir again.

THIRD Place in individual glasses or in a shallow mold. Place in the refrigerator until set. If preferred, this jelly may be served plain, but Vanilla Sauce II (page 363) is an asset.

NOTE A choice of flavors is invited; muscatel wine, rum, brandy, kirsch, or orange curaçao. Marie used to unmold this delicious jelly and send it trembling and quivering to the table. As children we held our breaths for fear the dreadful moment would arrive when it would fall apart before reaching the table. I can't remember that it ever did, but I do remember that we used to nickname it: "Shaky Mary," the reason being self-evident.

APRICOT ICEBOX CAKE

⅔ cup butter
2 cups powdered sugar
4 egg yolks
1½ cups cooked, strained apricots
2 cups rolled vanilla wafers
1 teaspoon lemon extract

1 tablespoon vanilla
1 envelope gelatin
¼ cup cold water
2 cups heavy cream
soft butter
24 ladyfingers

GARNISH

½ cup broken pecan meats
1 cup heavy cream

¼ cup sugar
1 tablespoon vanilla

SERVES 12

FIRST Thoroughly cream ⅔ cup butter with 2 cups powdered sugar and 4 beaten egg yolks.

SECOND Stir in 1½ cups cooked, strained apricots, 2 cups rolled vanilla wafers, 1 teaspoon lemon extract, and 1 tablespoon vanilla. Cook this mixture until it thickens, stirring constantly until it is smooth. Soak 1 envelope gelatin in ¼ cup cold water for 5 minutes. Then dissolve over hot water until clarified. Stir into the mixture and *cool*.

THIRD When thoroughly cooled, beat 2 cups heavy cream until stiff. Fold into the apricot mixture until well blended.

FOURTH Grease a 10-inch spring form with soft butter. Line with approximately 24 split ladyfingers, standing them erect along the sides and breaking them to create a spaced design at the bottom.

FIFTH Pile in the apricot mixture. Cover the top with ½ cup broken pecan meats and set in the refrigerator for 24 hours. When ready to serve, run a knife around the edges of the spring form, release the clasp, and set the pudding on a platter. Serve with an accompanying bowl of 1 cup of heavy cream beaten until stiff, sweetened with ¼ cup sugar, and flavored with 1 tablespoon vanilla.

NOTE Fresh or dried apricots may be used. Dried apricots have a stronger flavor but require more sugar.

CORNUCOPIAS *Marie's*

[*Pre-heat oven to 350°*]

4 eggs	2 cups heavy cream
1¼ cups sugar	½ cup sugar
1 teaspoon vanilla	3 teaspoons vanilla
1½ cups flour	berries or sliced fruit

SERVES 12

FIRST Beat 4 eggs and 1¼ cups sugar until light and frothy. (The original recipe calls for 20 minutes by hand beating [an electric beater cuts this time in half]). Stir in 1 teaspoon vanilla.

SECOND Sift 1½ cups flour. Measure and resift into the batter, folding in carefully, a little at a time.

THIRD Butter a cookie sheet. Drop on 1 or 2 heaping tablespoons of batter and smooth into a thin round. Continue to fill the cookie sheets with rounds and bake in a 350° oven until light gold. As soon as baked, remove and quickly twist into the shape of a cornucopia. As soon as they cool it will be impossible to do this. If they should cool, return to the oven for a minute and continue to shape, one by one, then cool. As they cool, they will turn crisp. It is therefore very important to place them where they will not be broken.

FOURTH When ready to serve, whip 2 cups of heavy cream until stiff, sweeten with ½ cup sugar, and flavor with 3 teaspoons vanilla. Fold in any selected berries or cut-up fruits and fill the cornucopias *generously*, topping each with pieces of the fruits or the chosen berries.

NOTE Do not fill until just before serving; otherwise the pastry will lose its crispness.

CREAM PUFFS AND ÉCLAIRS *Marie's*
[*Pre-heat oven to 450°*]

scant 5 ounces butter
1½ cups water
2 cups flour
salt
6 eggs
1 cup heavy cream

¼ cup sugar
1 tablespoon vanilla *or*
Custard Cream (page 446),
Chocolate Sauce I (page 359), *or*
Chocolate Icing (page 422)

SERVES 12

FIRST Place scant 5 ounces butter (sweet preferred) in 1½ cups water and bring to a simmer.

SECOND Just before it begins to boil dump 2 cups flour and a pinch of salt into the liquid (and I mean *dump*). Stir vigorously until the mixture turns into a paste and forms a ball that comes away from the spoon (about 5 to 8 minutes). Remove from the fire and cool slightly.

THIRD When somewhat cool, beat in 6 eggs, one at a time. Beat after each egg has been added until paste is smooth again. After all the eggs have been added, beat again until the dough is of an even, well-blended texture.

FOURTH Warm cookie sheet slightly but do not overheat. Grease cookie sheet lightly, then place the dough in heaps (for cream puffs) about ⅔ inch apart, remembering that they will spread and swell in the cooking. For éclairs, éclair pans are available in some of the better hardware stores, but, failing these, place the dough in a pastry bag with a wide, open mouth and squeeze portions of the dough, 1 inch by 4½ inches, onto the cookie sheet. The spacing of these strips is also important, since they, like the puffs, swell in cooking.

FIFTH Bake in a 450° oven for approximately 25 minutes, or until gold in color. When they are done, turn off the oven, open the oven door, and allow the pastry to cool before removing.

SIXTH Just before serving, split and remove any of the soft insides. Fill with whipped cream (1 cup heavy cream beaten until stiff, sweetened with ¼ cup sugar, and flavored with 1 tablespoon vanilla). Or the cream puffs may be filled with vanilla ice cream, and the éclairs with Custard Cream (page 446). Serve iced with Chocolate Sauce I (page 359) or Chocolate Icing (page 422).

NOTE This is one of the most versatile recipes known to any gourmet! The basic recipe may be baked, as I have explained, into Cream Puffs or Éclairs; or into Profiterolles (page 315), a very elegant dessert served in many of the better restaurants; or as tiny puffs, filled with any number of hot fillings, such as melted cheese, sour cream with red or black caviar, lobster Newburg, creamed crab; or served cold with mashed sardines, or chicken salad, and so on. Any of these make very attractive appetizers. They require no especial skill, only a little patience and you are in a league with the best of chefs!

COCONUT CREAM TORTE LASHANSKA

3 nine-inch layers Sponge Cake (page 389)
¼ cup rum
Vanilla Cream Filling (page 341)

2 cups heavy cream
½ cup sugar
1 tablespoon vanilla
2 cups grated coconut

FIRST Bake 3 nine-inch layers Sponge Cake (page 389).

SECOND Sprinkle the 3 layers with ¼ cup rum and spread with Vanilla Cream Filling, the recipe for which may be found in Nut Torte (page 342).

THIRD Beat 2 cups heavy cream until stiff, sweeten with ½ cup sugar, and flavor with 1 tablespoon vanilla. Spread cream on top of

Vanilla Cream Filling, reserving some for the sides. Sprinkle the 3 layers generously with 2 cups grated coconut, reserving some for the sides.

FOURTH Place the layers together. Spread the remaining cream and sprinkle the remaining coconut on the sides of the Torte.

ICEBOX PUDDING PARFAIT

½ pound sweet butter
1½ cups sugar
6 beaten egg yolks
½ pound unpeeled almonds
3 teaspoons vanilla

6 egg whites
¾ pound macaroons
¼ cup sherry
soft butter
½ pound whole ladyfingers

1 cup heavy cream
¼ cup sugar
1 tablespoon vanilla

GARNISH

maraschino cherries
chopped pistachio nuts
green food coloring

SERVES 12

FIRST Cream ½ pound sweet butter with 1½ cups sugar until light and creamy. Add 6 beaten egg yolks, ½ pound ground unpeeled almonds, and 3 teaspoons vanilla.

SECOND Beat 6 egg whites until stiff. Fold in gently.

THIRD Place ¾ pound macaroons in a bowl and sprinkle with ¼ cup sherry. Toss in the bowl several times to distribute the sherry.

FOURTH Butter a 10-inch spring form with a little soft butter. Line the sides only with ½ pound *unsplit* ladyfingers. Cover the bottom of the form with a layer of macaroons. Then add half the egg mixture. Cover the egg mixture with a second layer of macaroons and cover with the second half of the egg mixture. Cover the top with a third layer of macaroons, top side up.

FIFTH Set in the refrigerator all day or for 24 hours. Just before serving, cover the top with 1 cup heavy cream whipped until stiff, sweetened with ¼ cup sugar, and flavored with 1 tablespoon vanilla.

Top off with maraschino cherries (arranging them along the edge, one per portion) and with a generous sprinkling of chopped pistachio nuts.

NOTE The pistachio nuts available are usually rather dry and therefore not as bright green in color as nature intended them to be. Blanch them in a little water and pop the skins off as you do with almonds. Chop them very fine and rub in *one drop* green food coloring mixed with 1 teaspoon water. Blot them with a paper towel and set them in the oven to dry.

MISHMASH MERINGUE *Marie's*

[*Pre-heat oven to 275°*]

8 egg whites
2 cups sugar
1 tablespoon vanilla
2 cups heavy cream

½ cup sugar
3 teaspoons vanilla
berries or fruit (optional)

SERVES 12

FIRST Beat 8 egg whites until stiff. While still beating, *gradually*, little by little, add 2 cups sugar. Then add 1 tablespoon vanilla, beating again until it holds its shape. Do not be afraid to beat too long. This is the meringue.

SECOND Place a 9-inch tin face down on a sheet of heavy paper. Draw a ring around it with a pencil. Repeat on a second piece of paper. Heap these 2 rings evenly with the meringue to make a 1-inch layer. Now place the remaining meringue in a pastry-decorator's bag or tube. Run an edging 1 inch high around the edge of the first layer and a lattice design on top of the second. Trim the edges of this ring with meringue kisses (small dabs with pointed tops). This is the "lid" of the cake. Bake both layers in a 275° oven for about an hour, or until the meringue is sandy-colored. Remove and allow to cool. When cool, carefully remove the papers. Gently sawing the meringue off the paper with a bread knife is an effective way to do this, but great care must be taken. If the papers stick, dampen them *very slightly*.

THIRD Whip 2 cups heavy cream until stiff. Sweeten with ½ cup sugar and flavor with 3 teaspoons vanilla.

FOURTH Place the first meringue layer on a serving-platter. Cover thickly with the whipped cream, adding berries or fruit if desired. Place second layer or "lid" on top and surround with a ring of small mounds of whipped cream, each topped with a berry or piece of fruit.

NOTE The meringue edge placed around layer number one is intended as a border to encompass the filling of cream, or of cream and fruit. The meringue lattice and kisses on the second layer or "lid" are for purposes of decoration.

WARNING This is a very festive cake and not too difficult to make successfully. It is advisable to use rounds of asbestos under the papers on which the meringue layers are to be baked. They prevent bottom of the meringue from scorching. If you don't use asbestos rounds, set the layers on cookie sheets with several extra folds of paper between the metal and the meringue.

ORANGE CREAM WITH CAKE *Marie's*

3 layers Sponge Cake (page 389)
1 recipe Marie's Orange Cream (page 308)
fresh orange wedges from 2 large oranges *or*
candied orange peel
2 tablespoons finely chopped pistachio nuts

SERVES 8

FIRST This festive, delicious cake is assembled by taking 3 layers Sponge Cake (page 389) and spreading the two bottom layers rather thickly with Marie's Orange Cream (page 308). Be sure Cream is almost set before spreading.

SECOND Top with the third layer Sponge Cake and ice the cake generously with the remaining pudding. Use a narrow spatula and smooth *all* surfaces as much as possible to give it a very trim appearance.

THIRD Garnish with fresh orange wedges from 2 large oranges, or with cut-up candied orange peel. In either case, sprinkle the cake evenly with 2 tablespoons finely chopped pistachio nuts.

NOTES 1. See directions regarding the use of pistachio nuts, in Icebox Pudding Parfait (page 317).
2. If you like, you may cover the top of the cake with whipped cream sweetened with sugar and flavored with vanilla. To cover the top of this cake ½ cup heavy cream beaten until stiff, sweetened with ⅛ cup sugar, and flavored with 1 teaspoon vanilla should be sufficient.

PROFITEROLLES *Marie's*

[*Pre-heat oven to 400°*]

half recipe basic Cream Puff
    dough (page 315)
vanilla ice cream *or*
1 cup heavy cream

¼ cup sugar
1 tablespoon vanilla
Chocolate Sauce I (page 359) *or*
Chocolate Sauce II (page 360)

SERVES 12

FIRST Using half the recipe, proceed exactly as for Cream Puffs (page 315).

SECOND Set the dough in mounds the size of a quarter on a slightly warmed and lightly greased cookie sheet. Place in a 400° oven and bake until golden brown. When done, turn off the heat, open the oven door, and allow to cool.

THIRD When ready to serve, split the puffs, removing all the soft insides, and fill quickly with vanilla ice cream or with 1 cup heavy cream beaten until stiff, sweetened with ¼ cup sugar and flavored with 1 tablespoon vanilla.

FOURTH Set a layer of the filled puffs on a serving-dish. Then heap the rest, pyramid fashion, on top of the bottom layer. Pour half a recipe Chocolate Sauce I (page 359) or Chocolate Sauce II (page 360) over the pyramid and serve the second half in an accompanying sauce boat.

DESSERTS

NOTE The Chocolate Sauce is best when very slightly warmed. If ice cream is used as a filling, half vanilla, half chocolate flavor adds to the festivity of this extremely popular dessert.

"RIEN DE TOUT"

[*Pre-heat oven to 300°*]

4 egg whites
½ teaspoon cream of tartar
1 cup sugar
4 egg yolks
½ cup sugar

3 tablespoons lemon juice
2 teaspoons grated lemon peel
1 cup heavy cream
¼ cup sugar
1 tablespoon vanilla

SERVES 8

FIRST Beat 4 egg whites until foamy. Add ½ teaspoon cream of tartar and beat until almost stiff. Add 1 cup sugar very gradually and beat until stiff enough to hold its shape. Spread on a lightly buttered 9-inch glass pie plate and bake in a 300° oven for 40 minutes.

SECOND Beat 4 egg yolks until thick and light in color. Beat in ½ cup sugar and work with the eggs until light and smooth. Add 3 tablespoons lemon juice and 2 teaspoons grated lemon peel.

THIRD Cook this lemon mixture in the top of a double boiler, stirring constantly until thick and smooth (about 15 minutes). Remember, it must be thick. *Cool completely.*

FOURTH Whip 1 cup of heavy cream until stiff, sweeten with ¼ cup sugar, and flavor with 1 tablespoon vanilla. Spread half this cream on top of the baked meringue. Spread the cooled lemon filling on top of the cream and cover the lemon filling with the remaining whipped cream. Assemble this dessert in the morning and chill in the refrigerator at least 8 hours before serving.

SPONGE-CAKE RING

1 sponge-cake ring
strained apricot jam
24 apricot halves
½ recipe Wine pudding (page 358)

1 quart ice cream
Grapenuts
Apricot Sauce (page 359)

SERVES 6

FIRST Use any good sponge-cake recipe and bake in a ring mold.

When cool, spread top and sides with strained apricot jam, using a pastry brush.

SECOND Take 24 apricot halves and place groups of apricots in the bottom of 6 teacups. Cover to the rim with ½ recipe Wine Pudding (page 358). Set these cups in the refrigerator for several hours, or until ready to serve.

THIRD When ready to serve, place the sponge-cake ring on a round serving-platter. Unmold the 6 cups around the ring in even design. Fill the center with 1 quart vanilla ice cream. Sprinkle top of ice cream with Grapenuts. Serve with a separate bowl of Apricot Sauce (page 359).

NOTE Strawberries, raspberries, or peaches (all sweetened, of course) will do just as well. Whatever berry or fruit you decide to use, be sure you use a corresponding sauce.

SPONGE-CAKE SURPRISE

3 layers Sponge Cake (page 389)
3 cups heavy cream
¾ cup sugar
3 teaspoons vanilla
5 bananas

SERVES 8

FIRST Whip 3 cups heavy cream until stiff. Sweeten with ¾ cup sugar and flavor with 3 teaspoons vanilla.

SECOND Cover first layer of sponge cake *thickly* with the whipped cream. Press 4 peeled, whole bananas, evenly spaced, down into the cream and cover with second layer of sponge cake. Repeat this process, topping with the third layer of sponge cake.

THIRD Ice the top layer of sponge cake and the sides of the cake thickly with whipped cream. Decorate the top with 1 sliced banana in a ring.

NOTE This dessert may be assembled with whole strawberries, the larger the better, instead of bananas. The surprise is in the cutting. This must be done with a sharp knife. The whole bananas or the whole strawberries will cut cleanly with a sharp knife and present a very pretty picture nestling in the cream as the slices are cut and served.

QUEEN'S DELIGHT

[*Pre-heat broiler*]

24 macaroons
24 ladyfingers
3 egg yolks
2 tablespoons sugar
1 teaspoon cornstarch

2 cups scalded milk
⅓ cup rum
3 egg whites
¼ cup sugar

GARNISH

1 cup heavy cream
¼ cup sugar

1 tablespoon vanilla
maraschino or candied cherries

SERVES 6 TO 8

FIRST Cover bottom of large round platter with 24 macaroons and top these with 24 ladyfingers.

SECOND Make a soft custard by beating 3 egg yolks with 2 tablespoons sugar and 1 teaspoon cornstarch. Add 2 cups scalded milk. Place in saucepan over a moderate flame, stirring constantly until the mixture thickens and coats the spoon. Then stir in ⅓ cup rum and pour the hot custard over the macaroons and ladyfingers.

THIRD Beat 3 egg whites until stiff. Add ¼ cup sugar, a little at a time, and continue to beat. Cover the custard with the beaten egg whites and place dish under hot, pre-heated broiler until the meringue is delicately browned. Remove from the broiler and place the dish in the refrigerator all day.

FOURTH When ready to serve whip 1 cup of heavy cream until stiff. Sweeten with ¼ cup sugar and flavor with 1 tablespoon vanilla. Decorate with mounds of whipped cream and top each mound with maraschino or candied cherries.

WARNING 1. This dessert must be made the morning before serving, so that it may set in the refrigerator all day.
2. When browning the meringue, leave the broiler door open and *watch it!*

APPLE CHARLOTTE Marie's

[*Pre-heat oven to 375°*]

CRUST

1 tablespoon butter
2 tablespoons vegetable shortening

1½ cups flour
10 thin slices stale white bread
melted butter

SERVES 6

FIRST Cut 1 tablespoon butter and 2 tablespoons vegetable shortening into 1½ cups flour until fine as meal. Then add sufficient water to allow dough to be handled, but no more.

SECOND Roll out dough on lightly floured board. Cut into strips and lay crosswise in a well-buttered baking-dish. Allow the ends to hang over edge of baking-dish.

THIRD Soak 10 thin slices stale white bread in melted butter. Place these slices over strips of pie crust, on the bottom and along the sides of the baking-dish. Reserve a few pieces to place on top. The Charlotte is now ready to be filled.

FILLING

6 sour green apples
¾ cup raisins
⅓ cup sliced almonds
2 ounces butter
3 tablespoons apricot preserves

1 teaspoon grated lemon peel
cinnamon, sugar
Hard Sauce (page 362) *or*
Vanilla Sauce I (page 363) *or*
heavy cream, brandy, sugar

FIRST Combine 6 sour green apples, ¾ cup raisins, ⅓ cup sliced almonds, 2 ounces butter, 3 tablespoons apricot preserves, 1 teaspoon grated lemon peel, and cinnamon and sugar to taste. Cook slowly over a low flame until slightly soft. Place in the baking-dish on top of the stale bread slices and cover with the remaining bread and the long ends of the pie crust draped on top of the top bread slices. Bake in a 375° oven until the crust is nicely browned. When ready to serve, turn out of baking-dish onto a serving-platter and serve with Hard Sauce (page 362), Vanilla Sauce I (page 363), or whipped cream flavored with brandy to taste and sweetened with sugar.

NOTE Always remember when you first set the pie-crust strips into the baking-dish that the care or carelessness you give this matter will reveal itself when the Charlotte is inverted onto your serving-platter. Allow the Charlotte to cool a little before serving.

BEIGNETS SOUFFLÉS

1 cup milk
¼ pound butter
½ teaspoon salt
4 tablespoons sugar
1¼ cups flour
6 whole eggs
1 teaspoon vanilla

oil
powdered sugar
Cold Vanilla Sauce I (page 363)
or
Strawberry Sauce (page 450) *or* strained apricot jam

SERVES 6

FIRST Boil 1 cup milk with ¼ pound butter, ½ teaspoon salt, and 4 tablespoons sugar. When the milk rises in the pan and comes to a hard boil, remove from the flame.

SECOND Dump in 1¼ cups flour and beat until all the flour is absorbed. Turn the flame down and return the pan to the fire. Beat until the mixture leaves the spoon and no longer sticks to the pan. Place in a bowl.

THIRD Beat in 2 eggs until blended. Add 2 more eggs and beat again until blended. Add 2 more eggs and beat until well blended. Beat in 1 teaspoon vanilla. *Beating throughout must be hard.*

FOURTH Divide the paste into individual pieces, each about the size of a fifty-cent piece. Place them in a frying-basket and plunge them into hot oil, frying them until they are light-brown. Serve them warm. Just before serving, sprinkle with powdered sugar. Serve with Vanilla Sauce I (page 363), Strawberry Sauce (page 450), or a strained apricot jam.

NOTE The fruit sauces are improved if they are stirred beforehand with ¼ cup any preferred liqueur, such as anisette, brandy, or rum. This delicious French dessert is only to be found properly prepared in a very few of America's finest restaurants. It is a dessert of which Parisians are duly proud.

BOOTHBAY-BLUEBERRY BETTY

[*Pre-heat oven to 350°*]

2½ cups small bread cubes	½ cup brown sugar
4 ounces melted butter	rum-flavored Hard Sauce (page 362) *or*
2 cups blueberries (fresh or canned)	1 cup heavy cream
2 tablespoons lemon juice	¼ cup sugar
¼ teaspoon salt	1 tablespoon vanilla

SERVES 6

FIRST Mix 1 cup small bread cubes with 2 ounces melted butter. Arrange in a layer in the bottom of a deep glass pie plate. Cover with 1 cup blueberries. Sprinkle with 1 tablespoon lemon juice, ⅛ teaspoon salt, and ¼ cup brown sugar.

SECOND Repeat the process for the second layer, using exactly the same ingredients and in exactly the same order. Having completed the second layer, sprinkle evenly with ½ cup fresh bread crumbs. Cover the dish and set in a 350° oven for about half an hour. Remove the cover for the last 15 minutes.

THIRD Cool slightly but serve warm with rum-flavored Hard Sauce (page 362) or with 1 cup of heavy cream beaten until stiff, sweetened with ¼ cup sugar, and flavored with 1 tablespoon of vanilla.

DESSERTS

NOTE Blueberries are blueberries, but there is something about them when you have picked them yourself, as we did at Boothbay in Maine. It made them seem very special too to have our friend Mrs. Stover share some of her precious Maine recipes with us. Mrs. Stover's family had lived in the same little white wooden house since the end of the eighteenth century. It sat in a meadow literally blue with blueberries. It is only fair to assume that the bushes that yielded us our berries were the same that had waved blue branches on sunny afternoons in 1776!

KAISERSCHMARREN *Marie's*

6 egg yolks
2 tablespoons sugar
1 cup milk
2 cups sifted flour
6 egg whites
salt
4 ounces of butter

½ cup raisins
2 tablespoons brandy
½ cup raisins
2 tablespoons brandy
powdered sugar
warm maple syrup or Strawberry Sauce (page 450)

SERVES 8

FIRST Beat 6 egg yolks with 2 tablespoons sugar until light. Add 1 cup milk, alternately with 2 cups sifted flour to the yolks.

SECOND Beat 6 egg whites with pinch salt until stiff. Fold gently into the yolk mixture.

THIRD Melt 2 ounces butter in a large skillet over a moderate flame. Put in *half* the batter. Brown slightly and turn. Turn once again and break up into fairly small pieces, using two forks.

FOURTH Add ½ cup raisins and 2 tablespoons brandy, turning the pieces of the pancake with a spatula over and over as they cook. Place on a serving-platter and keep warm in the oven.

FIFTH Repeat the entire process, using the second half of the batter, browning it, as before in 2 ounces butter, turning it, and breaking it into pieces. Again ½ cup raisins and 2 tablespoons brandy. Heap this second lot on top of the first and sprinkle with powdered sugar. Serve with warm maple syrup or Strawberry Sauce (page 450).

SABAYON

6 egg yolks
½ pound powdered sugar

2 cups best sherry wine
ladyfingers

SERVES 6

FIRST Beat 6 egg yolks with ½ pound powdered sugar until smooth and creamy white.

SECOND Add 2 cups of the best sherry wine, a little at a time. Continue to beat until well blended. Pour the entire mixture into the top of the largest double boiler and beat over boiling water.

THIRD Beat uninterruptedly with a wire hand whisk until the sauce is light, foamy, warm, and approximately 3 or 4 times the original amount. If it is sufficiently beaten, it will be firm and frothy enough to hold its shape. Serve warm in champagne glasses with an accompaniment of ladyfingers.

NOTE I have a particular fondness for this dessert sauce. The first time I enjoyed it was in Florence, in Italy. I thought I had never tasted anything so delicious as the warm, aromatic sauce with the soft, bland ladyfingers. Sponge cake of any sort makes an ideal accompaniment.

PUFF OMELETTE EDWIN

[*Pre-heat oven to 400°*]

5 egg yolks
2 tablespoons cream
1 heaping teaspoon flour
5 egg whites
1 heaping tablespoon butter

powdered sugar
strawberry jam *or*
crumbled maple sugar and maple syrup

SERVES 6

FIRST Beat 5 egg yolks until light. Beat again with 2 tablespoons cream and 1 heaping teaspoon flour.

SECOND Beat 5 egg whites until stiff. Gently fold into egg yolks.

THIRD Melt 1 heaping tablespoon butter in a large skillet. Pour in egg batter and cook over a low flame until fairly set. Place skillet in 400° oven until top of pancake is slightly browned. Slide (loosen with a flexible spatula) onto hot platter. Sprinkle powdered sugar on the top of the pancake and serve with strawberry jam, or sprinkle with crumbled maple sugar and serve with warm maple syrup. *Hurry to the table!*

NOTE Despite his prowess as an all around experimental chef, this is my husband's one and only dessert, and the pride with which he presents his *chef d'œuvre* is something to behold! Warning the guests to carry on conversationally while he prepares his beloved omelette, he rushes into the kitchen, hurries through the magical business, and rushes back again into the dining-room holding it proudly aloft! No one, who sat at our table one certain night during the war, will ever forget the expression of horror that flooded his face when just as he made his dramatic entrance with omelette held high the air-raid sirens blew, the lights were extinguished, and small boys in the neighborhood pounded on our front door to announce that they were rounding up the air raid wardens (he was one!). No air-raid practice could have taken place at a more inauspicious moment! Poor chef! Poor omelette! Poor disappointed guests! Another sacrificial offering to flag and country!

APPLESAUCE TORTE *Marie's*

[*Pre-heat oven to 400°*]

THE TART

¼ pound butter
⅓ cup sugar
1 egg
2 cups sifted flour

2 teaspoons baking powder
½ teaspoon salt
2 tablespoons milk

SERVES 6

FIRST Cream ¼ pound butter very thoroughly with ⅓ cup sugar. Beat in one egg and continue to beat until smooth.

SECOND Sift 2 cups flour. Measure and resift twice with 2 teaspoons baking powder and ½ teaspoon salt. Add alternately to the butter mixture with 2 tablespoons milk. Mix until smooth. Then place in a well-buttered spring form or press by hand into a deep glass pie plate. Bake until golden brown in a 400° oven.

THE FILLING

2 cups applesauce
1 cup heavy cream

¼ cup sugar
1 tablespoon vanilla

FIRST Fill baked and cooled shell with 2 cups applesauce.

SECOND Whip 1 cup of heavy cream until stiff. Sweeten with ¼ cup sugar and flavor with 1 tablespoon vanilla. Spread the beaten cream on top of the applesauce, concealing it entirely. If you have the ambition to create a festive atmosphere, reserve a third of the whipped cream, place it in a decorator's bag, and squeeze it around the rim of the tart to gain that professional look.

BLACK-BREAD CHERRY TORTE

[Pre-heat oven to 350°]

1⅓ cups powdered sugar
8 egg yolks
¼ pound ground unblanched almonds
1½ cups rye-bread crumbs
¼ cup red or sherry wine
1 ounce citron (optional)
grated rind 1 lemon

cinnamon
8 egg whites
3 #2½ cans black *pitted* Bing cherries
1 cup heavy cream
¼ cup sugar
1 tablespoon vanilla

SERVES 8

FIRST Beat 1⅓ cups powdered sugar with 8 egg yolks until satiny smooth. Stir in ¼ pound ground unblanched almonds and 1½ cups rye-bread crumbs (soft part of bread only) moistened in ¼ cup red or sherry wine.

SECOND Add grated rind 1 lemon, pinch of cinnamon, and 1 ounce of finely chopped citron (optional).

THIRD Beat 8 egg whites until stiff. Fold in carefully.

FOURTH Drain 2 #2½ cans black *pitted* Bing cherries. Squeeze cherries lightly in your hand to remove the last vestige of liquid. Add cherries to the mixture, folding gently. Butter and flour a 10-inch spring form. Pour in the batter and bake in a 350° oven until done. Cool on a cake rack until room temperature.

FIFTH When ready to serve, cover the Torte with 1 cup of heavy cream beaten until stiff, sweetened with ¼ cup sugar, and flavored with 1 tablespoon vanilla. Decorate the top of the Torte with a ring of black cherries. The contents of 2 cans of black pitted cherries weighs 1½ pounds. Use part of the third can for purposes of decoration; if you wish, the remainder of the third can may be added to the original amount in baking the Torte.

GRANDMOTHER'S THREE TORTES
THE CRUST

2 cups flour *or* 8 ounces cracker dust	2 heaping tablespoons sugar
	6 ounces butter
3 egg yolks	

EACH SERVES 6 TO 8

FIRST Place 2 cups sifted flour or 8 ounces cracker dust in a bowl. Form a hole in the center and drop in 3 egg yolks, 2 heaping tablespoons sugar, and 6 ounces butter. Work lightly into a smooth dough. Place in refrigerator for 24 hours before using.

SECOND When ready to use, press dough on bottom and sides of a 9-inch spring form. Place in refrigerator for 1 hour before baking.

[*Pre-heat oven to 375°*]

THIRD Bake in 375° oven until lightly golden. Cool. *Do not remove from spring form.*

THREE FILLINGS
LEMON FILLING

1 scant cup water	rind 1 lemon
1 scant cup sugar	5 egg whites
1 heaping teaspoon cornstarch	2 tablespoons powdered sugar
5 egg yolks	1 tablespoon lemon juice
juice 2 lemons	

FIRST Place 1 scant cup water and 1 scant cup sugar in the top of a double boiler and stir in 1 heaping teaspoon cornstarch softened in a little cold water. Beat 5 egg yolks with juice 2 lemons and grated rind 1 lemon. Add to the sugar and stir constantly until the mixture thickens. Remove from fire. Cool.

[*Pre-heat oven to 325°*]

SECOND Beat ½ the amount of 5 egg whites until stiff. When lemon mixture is thoroughly cool, gently fold in these beaten whites. Pour into baked crust. Bake in a 325° oven until a skin forms on top.

THIRD Beat the second half of the 5 whites until stiff. Add 2 tablespoons powdered sugar and 1 tablespoon lemon juice. Place on top filling and return to oven for a few minutes to lightly brown. Cool.

STRAWBERRY FILLING
FILLING

1 quart ripe strawberries	2 cups sugar
½ cup water	2¼ tablespoons cornstarch

FIRST Bring 1 quart ripe strawberries to a boil with ½ cup water and 2 cups sugar. Add 2¼ tablespoons cornstarch dissolved in a little cold water. Stir constantly and let it come to a boil again. Continue to stir until the mixture thickens. Remove from fire and cool.

SECOND When thoroughly cool, pour into baked pie crust. Cover with:

MY GRANDMOTHER'S CREAM SAUCE

1 cup milk or light cream	3 tablespoons sugar
2 egg yolks	1 cup heavy cream
1 teaspoon cornstarch	1 tablespoon vanilla

FIRST Place 1 cup milk or light cream in top of double boiler. Bring to a boil. Pour onto 2 beaten egg yolks in a bowl, stir until well blended. Add 1 teaspoon cornstarch dissolved in a little cold water and 3 tablespoons sugar. Return to double boiler and stir constantly until the mixture thickens. Cool.

DESSERTS 333

SECOND Beat 1 cup heavy cream until stiff. Flavor with 1 tablespoon vanilla. Then fold gently into the cooled custard until completely blended. Serve in a side bowl with the pie.

NOTE The original recipe calls for covering the top of the pie with the cream. I prefer the beautiful red glaze of the strawberry filling to gleam on its own as it comes to the table and to serve the cream separately.

HUCKLEBERRY FILLING

1 quart huckleberries (or blueberries)
2 teaspoons sugar
2 level teaspoons cornstarch

1 tablespoon lemon juice
1 cup heavy cream
¼ cup sugar
1 tablespoon vanilla

FIRST Wash 1 quart huckleberries (or blueberries). Place in a pot without adding any water. Bring to a gentle boil with 2 teaspoons sugar and 2 level teaspoons cornstarch dissolved in a little cold water. Stir continuously until the mixture thickens. Cool.

SECOND Put into baked pie crust. Cool completely and cover with 1 cup heavy cream beaten until stiff, sweetened with ¼ cup sugar, and flavored with 1 tablespoon vanilla.

CRANBERRY CREAM

1 can cranberry sauce
2 tablespoons lemon juice
¼ cup orange juice
2 teaspoons grated lemon rind

1 tablespoon grated orange rind
2 egg whites *or*
½ cup heavy cream

SERVES 6

FIRST Crush 1 can cranberry sauce with a fork. Blend with 2 tablespoons lemon juice, ¼ cup orange juice, 2 teaspoons grated lemon rind, and 1 tablespoon grated orange rind. Pour into the freezer tray of the refrigerator. Set the controls at the lowest.

SECOND When the sherbet is half frozen, beat 2 egg whites until stiff, remove the sherbet to a bowl, and fold in the stiffly beaten whites with a gentle hand. (½ cup whipping cream beaten until stiff may be used instead.) Return to the refrigerator and continue freezing until stiff. Serve in scoops, in saucers or glasses, as an accompaniment for poultry.

NOTE If you wish, this may be used as a dessert of course.

LEMON ICE CREAM IN LEMON SHELLS

1 cup milk	juice and rind 2 lemons
1 cup cream	6 largest lemons
1 cup sugar	

SERVES 6

FIRST Mix 1 cup milk, 1 cup cream, and 1 cup sugar. Stir until the sugar is completely dissolved. Place in the freezing-compartment of your refrigerator and turn controls to coldest.

SECOND At the end of 2 hours remove the partly frozen mixture, add the juice and grated rinds 2 lemons. Beat until smooth with a rotary egg-beater. Return to freezing-compartment.

THIRD At the end of 2 hours beat again and return to the refrigerator. Watch carefully and when entirely frozen turn controls back to normal.

FOURTH Cut the tops off and remove all the meat of 6 largest lemons with the help of a flexible grapefruit knife. Cut off the bottoms of the lemons to allow them to stand without toppling over. Fill the hollowed lemons with the Lemon Ice Cream and serve on individual plates, standing on a star of any fresh, pointed leaves.

NOTE A refreshing dessert for a warm summer evening. The flavor of this ice cream is particularly pleasant because of its citrus aroma.

MOUSSE AU CHOCOLAT, LASHANSKA

2 ounces Maillard's Double Vanilla Chocolate *or*	1 cup sugar
3 ounces bittersweet chocolate	6 egg yolks
cream	2 cups heavy cream

SERVES 8

FIRST Melt 2 ounces Maillard's Double Vanilla Chocolate or 3 ounces bittersweet chocolate in the top of a double boiler with a little cream. Add 1 cup sugar and 6 egg yolks. Stir until smooth and thick. Remove from the fire and cool completely.

SECOND Beat 2 cups of heavy cream until stiff. When the chocolate mixture is completely cold, fold in the cream evenly and gently until well blended.

THIRD Place in an icebox container and set in the freezing-compartment of the refrigerator for 6 hours. Once every 2 hours take it out and beat well. The third time leave it in the freezing-compartment overnight. Serve in glasses or in a mold, return the mold to the freezing-compartment or, better still, to deep freeze, if you have one. This mousse also makes an *excellent* filling for Profiterolles (page 320).

NOTES 1. The old-fashioned way of freezing a mousse in a mold is still effective. After the mold is filled, it is packed in a pail or bucket with about 15 pounds ice broken into small chunks mixed with about 2 quarts salt. Throw an old piece of carpet or heavy material on top of the bucket and allow the mousse to freeze from 5–6 hours. As the ice melts away add fresh ice and salt.

2. In the absence of any of the above-mentioned chocolate, I have used 3 ounces chocolate bits with great success. The mousse may also be varied by using $\frac{3}{4}$ cup Vermont maple sugar and $\frac{1}{4}$ cup granulated sugar instead of the prescribed 1 cup sugar.

RUMMY COFFEE ICE CREAM

2 cups milk
½ cup powdered sugar
1½ tablespoons flour
½ teaspoon salt
2 well-beaten eggs

1 teaspoon gelatin
1 tablespoon cold water
2 cups heavy cream
2 tablespoons rum
2 tablespoons coffee extract

SERVES 6 TO 8

FIRST Scald 2 cups milk. Stir ½ cup powdered sugar and 1½ tablespoons flour into ½ cup of the scalded milk. Rub smooth and stir into the remaining milk. Cook over a moderate flame, stirring constantly until thick. When thick, add ½ teaspoon salt and 2 well-beaten eggs, stirring again on a moderate flame until the mixture coats the spoon and has the consistency of a thin custard.

SECOND Soak 1 teaspoon gelatin in 1 tablespoon cold water and stir, until dissolved, into the custard mixture. *Cool.*

THIRD Beat 2 cups heavy cream until stiff. Stir in 2 tablespoons rum and 2 tablespoons coffee extract. Fold this flavored cream into the cooled custard. Freeze in ice-cream freezer or in a freezing-tray of refrigerator adjusted to coldest.

FOURTH Remove the ice cream to a bowl and beat thoroughly. Then return to the refrigerator freezing-compartment in same tray. Do this twice. Then turn the indicator down to normal and leave the cream at least overnight.

NEW YORK'S BEST VANILLA ICE CREAM

6 egg yolks
1½ cups sugar

4 cups heavy cream
2 tablespoons vanilla extract

SERVES 8

FIRST Beat 6 egg yolks until light. Add 1½ cups sugar and continue to beat until very smooth and very light in color.

SECOND Pour in 4 cups heavy cream. Add 2 tablespoons vanilla extract. Beat with a rotary beater until well blended.

THIRD Pour into electric freezer. Pack with alternate layers of broken ice and ice-cream salt. Freeze for about 20 minutes. Wipe the top of the freezer to be certain no salt water will creep into the ice cream. Remove the lid and examine the cream to see if it is well frozen. If so, remove the dasher, scrape it clean of ice cream, return the lid, repack with ice and salt, and cover with a cloth. This last rest period will mellow the ice cream until ready to serve.

DESSERTS

NOTE There is no better, richer ice cream than this! You will be delighted with its deliciousness! This recipe is a basic one. Any desired flavor may be added; melted sweet chocolate, sugared strawberry purée, or sugared fruit flavors of your individual preference. To be particularly inventive, try letting fudge drippings fall into the vanilla cream when it is half frozen. Delicious little streaks of chocolate will be found throughout the ice cream as it is eaten.

Variations of New York's Best Vanilla Ice Cream

Vanilla: add 3 teaspoons vanilla.

Coffee: add ½ cup very strong coffee.

Strawberry: Clean and crush 3 cups strawberries, add juice and pulp (more if you like; particularly if the berries are not thoroughly ripe and juicy). Sweeten strawberry purée to taste.

Chocolate: 4 ounces bittersweet chocolate, melted. Cool before adding.

OLD VIENNA VANILLA ICE CREAM *Marie's*

½ vanilla bean
½ cup milk
5 egg yolks

1½ cups sugar
1 quart heavy cream

SERVES 8

FIRST Cook ½ vanilla bean in ½ cup milk. When the vanilla bean has softened, split and carefully scrape all the insides of the pod into the milk. Return the hull and continue to simmer together for another few minutes.

SECOND Beat 5 egg yolks until light in color. Add 1½ cups sugar and continue to beat until smooth and very pale in color. Add 1 quart heavy cream to the egg mixture and beat together until well blended. Strain the vanilla bean out of the milk and stir into the egg mixture. Place on the fire over a moderate flame and gradually bring to a boil, stirring constantly until the mixture coats the spoon. Cool.

THIRD Freeze in a freezer, either hand crank or electric.

NOTE I gave this old recipe to a friend of mine who had nostalgic memories of the ice cream she had eaten as a child. She handed it to a very devoted cook who usually never disappointed her in following new recipes. Somehow this one was just too baffling for her. My friend returned home late in the afternoon to find the poor woman frantically picking out all the little black specks left by the vanilla bean!

VANILLA ICE CREAM WITH ANISETTE AND COCONUT, DAVE CHASEN

6 large scoops vanilla ice cream
¾ cup toasted coconut

anisette liqueur
Chocolate Sauce II (page 360)

SERVES 6

FIRST Place 6 large scoops vanilla ice cream into 6 champagne glasses. Cover each scoop of ice cream entirely with ⅛ cup of toasted coconut.

SECOND Serve the ice cream and pass a bottle of anisette liqueur, allowing each guest to sprinkle the liqueur on top of the individual scoops of ice cream. On no account must the liqueur be poured—only sprinkled.

THIRD Then serve Chocolate Sauce II, allowing each guest to cover each ball of ice cream with the sauce.

MARRONS PURÉE
CHESTNUT PURÉE

[*Pre-heat oven to 400°*]

2 pounds large chestnuts
1 cup sugar
¼ cup boiling water

1 tablespoon vanilla
¼ cup heavy cream

FIRST Slash 2 pounds large chestnuts with the sharp tip of a knife. Place them in a 400° oven for 10 to 15 minutes. Remove, peel, then boil in slightly salted boiling water until quite soft.

SECOND Mash the chestnuts to a paste. Add a sugar syrup made with 1 cup sugar and ¼ cup of boiling water. Stir until blended. Press through a ricer. Stir in 1 tablespoon vanilla extract and ¼ cup heavy cream. Chill.

NOTE This may be used in several ways. As a child in Paris, my greatest delight was to be taken to Rumpelmayer the unforgettable pastry tea shop on the Rue de Rivoli in Paris. Here on the long glass shelves were displayed the unsurpassed cakes and tartlets of the first decade of this century! Eyes glued to this absorbing array, fork poised in air (for you helped yourself), I struggled day after day between the elfin strawberry tarts, the creamy Napoleons, (sprinkled most elegantly with pistachio crumbs), and the chestnut purée nestling under chocolate icing, or between snow-white halves of powdery meringue! It is with nostalgic pleasure that I give you these recipes, remembered from my childhood, as well as an excellent chestnut purée dessert, discovered at a friend's house in later years.

MARRONS PURÉE EN MERINGUE
CHESTNUT PURÉE IN MERINGUE

Marrons Purée (page 338)
12 meringue halves
½ cup heavy cream

¼ cup sugar
1 teaspoon vanilla

SERVES 6

FIRST Hollow out 12 egg-shaped meringue halves on the under side to make room for the Marrons Purée (page 338). Fill both halves generously and press them gently together, leaving a rim of the purée showing.

SECOND Put ½ cup heavy cream (beaten until stiff, sweetened with ¼ cup sugar, and flavored with 1 teaspoon vanilla) into decorating-bag and run a broad line of the cream around the meringue halves where they touch the purée.

NOTE The recipe on page 318 for Mishmash Meringue is the correct one with which to make meringue halves. If, however, you are pressed for time, they may be ordered from your bakery.

MARRONS PURÉE SOUS CHOCOLAT
CHESTNUT PURÉE UNDER CHOCOLATE

1 layer sponge cake
raspberry jam
Chestnut Purée (page 338)

Chocolate Icing (page 422)
cream

SERVES 6

FIRST Split 1 layer sponge cake. Cut it into rounds the size of a silver dollar with a biscuit-cutter. Spread these rounds with raspberry jam and pile with Chestnut Purée, piling each with as much purée as it will support. Do not round top, but shape to a point, somewhat like a dunce cap.

SECOND Cover with a thin chocolate icing. Marie's Chocolate Icing (page 422), thinned with a little cream, will serve the purpose nicely. Never ice while the purée is warm, and never place the iced cakes in the refrigerator as the cold dulls the chocolate glaze.

MARRONS PURÉE WITH MARGUERITES

1 sponge-cake ring
strained apricot jam
rum
Chestnut Purée (page 338)
whole peeled almonds

green citron peel *or* angelica
1 cup heavy cream
¼ cup sugar
1 tablespoon vanilla

SERVES 6

FIRST Buy or bake a sponge-cake ring. Cover it with an apricot glaze made with strained apricot jam stirred with rum to taste.

SECOND Fill the center of the ring with Chestnut Purée (page 338).

THIRD Decorate the top of the sponge ring with whole skinned almonds and with green citron peel *or* angelica. Shape the almonds into the form of daisies or marguerites, joining them together with long, thin strips of green citron peel. Cut out some narrow leaves from the citron and place against the stems. The apricot glaze will help the almonds and the peel to adhere to the cake. The effect, if properly executed, is really charming. Serve with an accompaniment of 1 cup heavy cream whipped until stiff, sweetened with ¼ cup sugar, and flavored with 1 tablespoon vanilla.

DATE-AND-WALNUT TART

[*Pre-heat oven to 325°*]

4 egg yolks
¾ cup sugar
1 cup chopped dates
1 cup chopped walnuts
4 egg whites

1 cup heavy cream
¼ cup sugar
1 teaspoon vanilla
dates

SERVES 6

FIRST Cream 4 egg yolks with ¾ cup sugar. Roll 1 cup chopped dates in flour. Chop 1 cup walnuts, add to dates, and fold into the egg yolks.

SECOND Beat 4 egg whites until stiff. Gently fold into the batter Bake in a greased and floured tin for 20 minutes in a 325° oven. This recipe makes one good layer. If two are desired, double the recipe. When baked, remove from oven and cool.

THIRD When ready to serve, cover with 1 cup heavy cream beaten stiff, sweetened with ¼ cup sugar, and flavored with 1 teaspoon vanilla. Decorate with long, thin slices of dates.

NOTE In all date cakes, tarts, or recipes using this delectable desert fruit, the quality of your effort will stand or fall by the moist freshness of the dates.

NUT TORTE

[*Pre-heat oven to 325°*]

THE CAKE

¼ pound butter
2½ cups sugar
12 egg yolks

1 pound grated nuts (half walnut, half pecan)
12 egg whites

SERVES 8

FIRST Cream ¼ pound butter with 2½ cups sugar.

SECOND Beat 12 egg yolks until light. Add to the butter mixture and stir until foamy.

THIRD Grate 1 pound nuts (half walnuts and half pecans, or all walnuts, if preferred) by putting them through the finest knife on the grinder. Add them gradually to the mixture, stirring well after each addition.

FOURTH Beat 12 egg whites until stiff but not dry. Carefully and gently fold into the nut mixture. Do not handle any more than is absolutely necessary, as cake must remain exceedingly light. Bake 4 even layers in a 325° oven.

VANILLA CREAM FILLING

¼ cup milk
½ vanilla bean *or*
   1 tablespoon vanilla
4 egg yolks
1 cup heavy cream

1 rounded tablespoon cornstarch
½ pound soft butter
sugar
powdered sugar

FIRST Cook ¼ cup milk with ½ vanilla bean (or 1 tablespoon vanilla). While this is on the fire, stir 4 beaten egg yolks with 1 cup heavy cream and 1 rounded tablespoon cornstarch moistened in a little cream. Stir into the milk and continue to stir until the liquid thickens. Remove from fire and cool.

SECOND Work ½ pound butter until creamy. Add it, a spoon at a time, to the vanilla mixture. Add sugar to taste. Fill the layers and put together, but *not* long before serving. Sprinkle the top of the Torte with finely sifted powdered sugar.

NOTE If you have a hankering to gild the lily, cover the Torte with one cup heavy cream, beaten until stiff, flavored with 1 tablespoon of vanilla, and sweetened with ¼ cup sugar. Decorate with grated nuts, pistachio preferred.

PEANUT-BRITTLE DESSERT

1 pound peanut brittle
1 pint heavy cream
1 tablespoon vanilla

2 layers Sponge Cake (page 389)
small chunks peanut brittle

SERVES 6

FIRST Put 1 pound peanut brittle through the meat-chopper.

SECOND Whip 1 pint whipping cream until stiff. Add 1 tablespoon of vanilla and add the ground peanut brittle.

THIRD Spread this mixture between 2 layers Sponge Cake (page 389), over the top, and on the sides. Decorate with small chunks of peanut brittle.

APPLE PANCAKE

5 eggs
3 tablespoons flour
sugar
salt
1 cup milk
1 tablespoon melted butter

1 teaspoon vanilla
⅛ pound butter
4 cooking-apples
sugar, cinnamon
2 tablespoons butter
sugar, cinnamon

SERVES 1 TO 2

FIRST Beat 5 eggs with 3 tablespoons flour, pinch sugar, pinch salt, 1 cup milk, and 1 tablespoon melted butter. Beat well until smooth. Strain. Add 1 teaspoon vanilla.

SECOND Melt ⅛ pound butter in a skillet. Peel and slice 4 cooking-apples into the rendered butter. When apples are half cooked, chop the apples, but not too fine. Sprinkle generously with sugar and cinnamon and continue to cook until done.

THIRD Mix the apple mixture with the batter. Melt 2 tablespoons butter in the skillet and return the mixture to the skillet, frying the pancake lightly over a medium flame, until light brown. Fold as you would an omelet and slip out onto a hot platter. Sprinkle again with sugar and cinnamon and serve quickly.

NOTE This delicious, aromatic pancake will serve one (with a husky appetite) as a luncheon dish, and two as a dessert.

CRÊPES AU KIRSCH

3 egg yolks
2 tablespoons sugar
¼ teaspoon salt
2 tablespoons melted butter
1 cup milk

½ cup sifted flour
3 egg whites
½ cup powdered sugar
½ cup melted butter
½ cup kirsch

SERVES 8

FIRST Beat 3 egg yolks with 2 tablespoons sugar and ¼ teaspoon salt until light. Add 2 tablespoons melted butter and continue to beat until well blended.

SECOND Add 1 cup milk. Stir until well combined. Sift ½ cup flour. Measure and resift into the batter. Beat thoroughly until smooth.

THIRD Beat 3 egg whites until stiff. Gently fold into the batter.

FOURTH Fry small spoonfuls of the batter in a greased 6-inch frying-pan one at a time. Brown first on one side, then on the other. Remove from the skillet and roll. Keep warm by placing over heat in a chafing-dish. When 4 or 5 are made, sprinkle liberally with powdered sugar, melted butter, and kirsch. Half a cup of each should suffice for this operation.

NOTE If you have no chafing-dish, roll the crêpes, as they are fried, in a long glass baking-dish. Keep them warm in the oven until they are all fried. Then cover them with ½ cup powdered sugar, ½ cup melted butter, and ½ cup kirsch. Detailed directions for frying small crêpes or pancakes may be found by consulting the recipe for Rose's Crêpes Suzette (page 345).

CRÊPES SUZETTE
THE CRÊPES

2½ tablespoons sugar
4 tablespoons flour
3 eggs

½ cup milk
½ teaspoon salt
1 tablespoon vanilla

SERVES 4 TO 6

FIRST Mix 2½ tablespoons sugar with 4 tablespoons flour. Beat in 3 eggs. Add ½ cup milk, ½ teaspoon salt, and 1 tablespoon vanilla. Beat very well.

SECOND Heat a very small skillet and butter very sparsely. A pastry brush and some very soft butter make this operation quite simple. Pour in approximately 1½ tablespoons of the batter. (A large soup spoon is about the correct measure.) As soon as the batter hits the skillet, remove from fire and tip the skillet back and forth until the batter covers the bottom of the skillet completely. Then return to the fire. Under no circumstances pour any additional batter on top of the original amount, even if there are holes in the crêpe. It is of the greatest importance to have each crêpe as thin as possible. Work quickly and calmly. If you spoil the first one or two, just realize that experience is the best teacher. Pick up the edge of the Crêpe with a spatula and peek at the underside. When lightly browned, turn and fry on the other side.

THIRD Place a dinner plate on top of a pan of steaming water. This plate is to hold the Crêpes, one on top of the other, as they are fried. This process will keep them warm and moist. When all are fried, cover the plate with another, the same size or a little larger, and keep over the steaming water until ready to serve. These Crêpes will keep through dinner, but it is best not to keep them too long.

SAUCE

rind and juice 1 lemon
rind and juice 2 tangerines
rind and juice 1 orange
½ cup sugar

¼ pound sweet butter
1 wineglass curaçao (*or* any other preferred liqueur)

FIRST Stir ½ cup sugar into ¼ pound melted sweet butter until the sugar is dissolved. Add the grated rinds and juices of 1 lemon, 2 tangerines, and 1 orange. Then add 1 wineglass curaçao.

SECOND When ready to serve, bring the Crêpes on their hot plate to the table, also the sauce in a bowl or pitcher. Set a chafing-dish in front of you and pour in a little sauce. When the sauce bubbles, place 3 Crêpes into the sauce, folding each Crêpe in half and folding over again. Baste with the sauce and serve the Crêpes and the sauce on individual plates. Three Crêpes per person for first serving. Continue in this way until everyone is served. If you have no chafing-dish, this process may be attended to in the kitchen. But, of course, the glamour of performing this ritual at the table enhances the guests' enjoyment of this continental delight!

NOTE Ever since girlhood, I have been intrigued at watching a charming friend prepare these delicious Crêpes Suzette in her chafing dish, at her table. She bastes each Crêpe in turn and is careful not to appear hurried. Never fear that your guests will be impatient, since it is almost as satisfactory to watch this dish being prepared, as it is to enjoy the feathery lightness of the Crêpes brushing against your eager palate!

The greatest consternation I have ever witnessed in any restaurant, took place at Maxim's, one of Paris's most distinguished restaurants. Just before the last war, cold plates were served for Crêpes Suzette! When the Maître d'Hôtel discovered this blunder, he shouted in typical Gallic fashion at the head waiter: "Cold plates for Crêpes Suzette?" The head waiter turned hysterically to the waiter: "Cold plates for Crêpes Suzette?" he moaned! The befuddled waiter turned to the bus boy and with the greatest contempt, spat at him: "Cold plates for Crêpes Suzette?" The bus boy rushed off to the famed kitchens, to hurry back with hot plates. One wonders whether he may not have found some lowly dishwasher "backstage" to assail in turn, with: "Cold plates for Crêpes Suzette?" At all events, remember not to serve cold plates with Crêpes Suzette.

LITTLE JELLY PANCAKES

2 eggs
4 tablespoons sifted flour
¾ cup milk
butter

jelly *or* jam
1 tablespoon butter (optional)
¼ cup sugar (optional)

SERVES 6

FIRST Beat 2 whole eggs. Sift in 4 tablespoons flour and add ¾ cup milk, a little at a time. Stir well until quite smooth.

SECOND Heat a 6-inch frying-pan and grease lightly with butter. Place approximately 1 large soup spoon of the batter into frying-pan. Tilt the pan back and forth *off the flame* until the bottom of the pan is thinly covered. Return to flame and brown lightly, first on one side, then on the other. *Be sure you do not get too much batter in the pan. It is important to have the pancake very thin. The less batter put in the pan the better—barely enough to cover.* As you fry the pancakes, place them on a dish and keep them warm in a slow oven until they are all fried.
THIRD Spread them with any desired jam or jelly. Roll.

FOURTH If you feel that your pancakes have cooled while being rolled, it is possible to reheat them by making a syrup with 1 tablespoon butter and ¼ cup sugar, placing this syrup in a *larger* skillet and carefully warming the pancakes, 3 or 4 at a time. But as soon as this has been done, they must be served.

NOTE It is not unusual in Hungary and Austria to read in old cook books, the interesting suggestion that these pancakes be served with three or four different kinds of fillings at one time—one with jelly, one with apricot jam, one with chocolate sauce, one with soft cream cheese. The variety offers a decided novelty. Incidentally, these little pancakes make an excellent basic recipe for first courses on state occasions. Suggestions for fillings include: lobster Newburg creamed chicken, chopped mushrooms sautéed in butter with a dash of sherry, and so on.

MAPLE PANCAKE DESSERT ELIZABETH

8 eggs
4 cups milk
8 tablespoons sifted flour
¼ pound melted butter

grated rind 2 oranges
3 tablespoons sugar
9 ounces hard maple sugar
1½ tablespoons butter

SERVES 6

FIRST Beat 8 eggs until light. Add 4 cups milk and 8 tablespoons sifted flour. Beat well.

SECOND Fry the pancakes on a griddle or in a greased skillet, first on one side, then on the other. They should be large and very, very thin. Allow them to spread, as perfect shape is not important. As each pancake is fried, brush with butter (*using a pastry brush*), ¼ pound of which has been melted and set alongside your griddle in a small bowl.

THIRD As soon as each pancake is buttered, roll up and place in a large glass baking-plate. Continue placing one next to another until the first layer is complete. Sprinkle this layer with half the amount grated rind 2 oranges mixed with 3 tablespoons sugar. Set the dish in the oven to keep the pancakes warm while a second layer is being prepared.

FOURTH Repeat the process, and when the second layer is complete, sprinkle with the second half of the grated-orange-rind-and-sugar mixture. Melt 6 ounces hard maple sugar with 1½ tablespoons butter. Pour this syrup over the top of the pancakes and top off with the remaining 3 ounces hard maple sugar pounded into tiny bits. *Serve hot.*

NOTE Brown sugar might be used instead, in a pinch, but I do most seriously recommend the pure maple. If you have any difficulty finding it, it will be my pleasure to give you several addresses of those who tap their own trees in Vermont.

CAKE PUDDING *Marie's*

[Pre-heat oven to 300°]

2 layers stale *or* fresh sponge cake
thin apricot jam
light cream
soft butter

1 cup Chocolate Sauce (page 360)
2 egg whites
¼ cup sugar
1 teaspoon vanilla

SERVES 6

FIRST Cut up 2 layers stale or fresh sponge cake into oblong pieces. Spread on one side with thin apricot jam, on the other with light cream.

SECOND Pile layers of the prepared sponge cake into a buttered, deep glass baking dish until ⅔ full. Pour 1 cup Chocolate Sauce on top of the cake. Do not try to help the sauce mingle with the cake. It will gradually soak through.

THIRD Beat 2 egg whites until stiff and dry. Beat in ¼ cup sugar. Then stir in 1 teaspoon vanilla. Heap this meringue on top of the chocolate-covered cake and place in a 300° oven until the meringue is lightly browned, about 15 minutes. But watch it. Serve warm.

NOTE Can be made with left over layer cake too, but is not so light as when prepared with the sponge cake.

RICE PUDDING NORMA

½ cup rice
2 cups light cream
2 cups milk
¾ cup sugar
¼ teaspoon salt
4 eggs
2 cups heavy cream

½ cup soaked raisins
2 tablespoons vanilla
nutmeg
Strawberry Sauce (page 450),
  Raspberry Sauce, Apricot
  Sauce, *or* Chocolate Sauce
  (pages 359-60)

SERVES 6 TO 8

FIRST Mix ½ cup rice with 2 cups light cream and 2 cups milk. Stir in ¾ cup sugar and ¼ teaspoon salt. Put in top of the double boiler and cook slowly until the rice is tender, stirring occasionally.

SECOND Beat 4 whole eggs and add to the rice. Stir in carefully, being certain to blend throughout with mixture. Let cook once more in the top of the double boiler until it thickens, *but do not allow it to get too stiff*. Cool completely.

THIRD Beat 2 cups of heavy cream until firm. Fold gently into the cooled rice. Add ½ cup soaked raisins and 2 tablespoons vanilla extract. Then work up and over with a folding motion until everything is evenly distributed. Place in a deep serving-dish and sprinkle with nutmeg. Set in the refrigerator for several hours. Serve plain or with any preferred sauce: Strawberry, Raspberry, Apricot or Chocolate (pages 450, 359–60).

NOTE This is like no traditional rice pudding. It never fails to meet with enormous success, and if there is any left over, it is just as delicious the next day.

RICE PUDDING ROUND TABLE

¼ pound rice
1 cup light cream
3 cups milk
2 ounces butter
¼ teaspoon salt

4 egg yolks
1 cup sugar
1½ tablespoons vanilla
½ cup large, seeded raisins
grated nutmeg

SERVES 6

FIRST Mix ¼ pound rice with 1 cup light cream, 3 cups milk, 2 ounces butter, and ¼ teaspoon salt. Cook 1½ to 2 hours in the top of a double boiler until the rice is soft and the mixture thickens. Remove from the fire.

SECOND Beat 4 egg yolks and 1 cup sugar until light. Fold into rice until thoroughly blended. Stir in 1½ tablespoons vanilla and add ½ cup large, seeded raisins. Set into a serving-dish or, better still, into individual ramekins. If desired, sprinkle the tops with grated nutmeg. Serve at room temperature.

WARNINGS 1. During the long cooking time in the top of the double boiler, watch the water in the bottom of the double boiler, being certain to replace it with boiling water when it has cooked away.

2. The rice must cook until it is very soft and mushy. In this case, the rice kernels must lose their shapes and blend with the whole.

3. In folding the egg yolk-sugar mixture, blend well so that *all* the rice mixture benefits from this addition.

NOTE The leeway given in the cooking time for the rice is due to the fact that different brands of rice take more or less time in the cooking. For this pudding I prefer *not* to wash rice before cooking.

Ten Original Victorian Puddings

(SERVED IN A CUT-CRYSTAL BOWL)

CHOCOLATE CREAM PUDDING

2 cups light cream
⅓ cup cocoa
½ cup sugar
2 ounces grated sweet *or* bittersweet chocolate
1½ envelopes gelatin
¼ cup cold water

6 egg whites *or* 1 cup heavy cream
1 tablespoon vanilla
1 ounce grated chocolate
1 cup heavy cream (optional)
¼ cup sugar (optional)
1 teaspoon vanilla (optional)

SERVES 6

FIRST Bring 2 cups light cream to a boil. Stir in ⅓ cup cocoa, ½ cup sugar, and 2 ounces grated sweet or bittersweet chocolate.

SECOND Soak 1½ envelopes gelatin in ¼ cup cold water for 5 minutes, then dissolve over boiling water. Add to the hot chocolate mixture. Stir and pour into a mixing-bowl. Cool. Stir occasionally as it begins to thicken.

THIRD Beat 6 egg whites until stiff, or, if preferred, beat 1 cup heavy cream until stiff. Add one or the other to the chocolate mixture, folding until well blended. Stir in 1 tablespoon vanilla and pour into a cut-glass serving-bowl and place in refrigerator until set. Serve them thoroughly chilled. Just before serving, sprinkle the top of the pudding with one ounce grated chocolate.

NOTE This pudding may be served with 1 cup heavy cream beaten until stiff, sweetened with ¼ cup sugar, and flavored with 1 teaspoon vanilla.

COFFEE PUDDING

1 cup cream
scant ½ cup coarsely ground coffee
½ cup flour
4 egg yolks
1¼ cup heavy cream

½ cup sugar
4 egg whites
1 cup heavy cream
¼ cup sugar
1 tablespoon vanilla

SERVES 6

FIRST Bring 1 cup light cream to a boil with a scant ½ cup coarsely ground coffee. Strain through a fine sieve. Cool.

SECOND Sift ½ cup flour. Measure and stir to a *smooth* paste with the coffee-flavored cream. Beat 4 egg yolks and stir into the mixture.

THIRD Pour in 1¼ cup heavy cream and ½ cup sugar. Stir well and place on the fire. Stir constantly and bring to a boil. When thickened, pour into a mixing-bowl and allow to cool.

FOURTH When cool, beat 4 egg whites until stiff. Fold gently into the pudding until well blended. Pour into a cut-glass serving-bowl and place in refrigerator until set. Serve with 1 cup of heavy cream beaten until stiff, sweetened with ¼ cup sugar, and flavored with 1 tablespoon vanilla.

NOTE This pudding may be served without whipped cream, if preferred.

FRUIT-JUICE PUDDING

4 egg yolks
1 cup sugar
¾ cup orange juice
2 tablespoons lemon juice
½ cup white wine
¼ cup rum

2 envelopes gelatin
½ cup cold water
1 cup heavy cream
4 egg whites
orange segments (optional)

SERVES 6

FIRST Beat 4 egg yolks with 1 cup sugar until light and very smooth. Stir in ¾ cup orange juice, 2 tablespoons lemon juice,

½ cup white wine, and ¼ cup rum. Beat together until smooth. Place in the top of double boiler and stir constantly until thickened.

SECOND Soak 2 envelopes of gelatin in ½ cup of cold water for 5 minutes. Dissolve over boiling water. Add to the hot egg mixture and stir well. Then pour into a mixing-bowl to cool. Stir occasionally while cooling.

THIRD When thoroughly cool, *but not set*, whip 1 cup of heavy cream until stiff and gently fold into the mixture. Beat 4 egg whites until stiff and gently fold into the mixture. Continue to fold until everything is well blended. Pour into a cut-glass serving-bowl and place in the refrigerator until set. Serve plain, or with segments of oranges (with membranes removed) in a circular pattern around the top of the pudding.

HAZELNUT CREAM PUDDING

4 ounces hazelnuts
2½ light cups cream
½ cup sugar
3 egg yolks
1¼ envelopes gelatin
¼ cup cold water
salt

3 egg whites
1 tablespoon vanilla
1½ cups heavy cream (optional)
½ cup sugar
1 tablespoon vanilla
whole hazelnuts

SERVES 6

FIRST Blanch 4 ounces hazelnuts by scalding them and scraping the skins off. Pound or grate them thoroughly and set aside until ready.

SECOND Bring 1¼ light cream to a boil with ½ cup sugar, stirring until the sugar is dissolved. Beat 3 egg yolks with 1¼ cups additional cream and add slowly to the boiling cream. Bring to a boil again, stirring continuously until it thickens slightly.

THIRD Soak 1¼ envelopes gelatin in ¼ cup cold water for 5 minutes. Dissolve over boiling water until clear. Add to the hot cream, stir well, and add pinch salt. Pour into a mixing-bowl. Stir occasionally as it thickens.

FOURTH Beat 3 egg whites until stiff. When the pudding is *thoroughly cooled*, fold in the beaten whites until well blended. Now fold in the nuts and stir in 1 tablespoon vanilla. Pour into a cut-glass bowl and place in the refrigerator until set.

NOTE This pudding may be decorated with little mounds of whipped cream, an individual hazelnut imbedded in each mound. Serve with a bowl of whipped cream (1½ cups heavy cream in all, beaten until stiff, sweetened with ½ cup sugar, and flavored with 1 tablespoon vanilla).

LEMON PUDDING (OR ORANGE)

6 egg yolks
2 cups sugar
1 envelope gelatin
¼ cup cold water

6 tablespoons lemon juice
6 egg whites
grated rind of ½ lemon
1 teaspoon sugar

SERVES 6

FIRST Beat 6 egg yolks with 2 cups sugar until light and creamy.

SECOND Soak 1 envelope gelatin in ¼ cup of cold water for 5 minutes. Heat 6 tablespoons lemon juice and dissolve soaked gelatin in the hot lemon juice. Stir into the egg mixture.

THIRD Beat 6 egg whites until stiff. Fold into the mixture until thoroughly blended. Pour into a cut-glass bowl and place in the refrigerator until set. Mix grated rind ½ lemon with 1 teaspoon sugar and sprinkle on top of the pudding before serving.

NOTE Should you prefer to change this Lemon Pudding to Orange, use ½ cup orange juice and 2 tablespoons lemon juice instead of the 6 tablespoons lemon juice. Also substitute grated orange rind to sprinkle on top of the pudding.

PUNCH PUDDING

2 envelopes gelatin
½ cup cold water
1 cup white wine
4 egg yolks
1¼ cups sugar

½ cup rum
3 tablespoons lemon juice
4 egg whites
red jelly

SERVES 6

FIRST Soak 2 envelopes gelatin in ½ cup cold water for 5 minutes. Dissolve the soaked gelatin in 1 cup heated white wine. Cool slightly. Then place in refrigerator until partly set.

SECOND Beat 4 egg yolks with 1¼ cups sugar until light and creamy. Stir in ½ cup rum and 3 tablespoons lemon juice. Stir this carefully into the partly set wine jelly.

THIRD Beat 4 egg whites until stiff. Fold into the mixture with a gentle hand until thoroughly blended. Pour into cut-glass serving-bowl and place in refrigerator until set. When ready to serve, dot the top of the pudding with a circle of any preferred red jelly.

RUM PUDDING

3 cups light cream
½ cup sugar
1 cup milk
¼ cup sifted flour

1¼ envelopes gelatin
¼ cup cold water
½ cup rum
yellow vegetable coloring

SERVES 6

FIRST Bring 3 cups light cream to a boil with ½ cup sugar. Stir until the sugar is dissolved.

SECOND Take 1 cup cold milk. Pour a small amount into ¼ cup sifted flour, stirring until a smooth paste. Add to the rest of the milk. Add this paste to the boiling cream, and stir on the fire until smooth.

THIRD Soak 1¼ envelopes gelatin in ¼ cup cold water for 5 minutes. Dissolve until clear over hot water and add to the hot

TEN ORIGINAL VICTORIAN PUDDINGS 357

cream. Pour into a mixing-bowl and cool. Stir occasionally as it thickens.

FOURTH When the pudding begins to thicken, stir in ½ cup rum and a few drops of yellow vegetable coloring to give it a rich, creamy color. Pour into a cut-glass serving-bowl and place in refrigerator until set.

NOTE It is important not to serve this pudding until it is thoroughly chilled. I have found from experience, that it takes on a special flavor if it waits in the refrigerator for 48 hours. The pudding may be served with any desired sauce; Apricot, Peach, Raspberry, or Strawberry (pages 359, 362, 450).

VANILLA CREAM PUDDING

6 egg yolks
½ cup sugar
½ cup heavy cream
1 cup light cream
bicarbonate of soda
1¼ envelopes gelatin

¼ cup cold water
6 egg whites
1 tablespoon vanilla
red jelly
Strawberry, Raspberry, *or* Apricot Sauce (pages 450, 359)

SERVES 6

FIRST Beat 6 egg yolks with ½ cup sugar until light and very smooth. Add ½ cup heavy cream and beat together until well blended.

SECOND Bring 1 cup light cream to a boil with pinch bicarbonate of soda. Slowly add the egg mixture. Then slowly bring to a boil again, stirring constantly.

THIRD Soak 1¼ envelopes gelatin in ¼ cup cold water for 5 minutes. Dissolve over hot water and add to the hot custard. Stir well and pour into a mixing-bowl and cool. While cooling, stir occasionally.

FOURTH Beat 6 egg whites until stiff and fold gently into the cooled custard until the yellow and the white are completely blended. Pour into a cut-glass bowl and place in the refrigerator for several hours until set. When ready to serve, top with dabs of any preferred red jelly and serve with Strawberry, Raspberry, or Apricot Sauce (pages 450, 359).

WINE PUDDING

4 egg yolks
1 cup white wine
3 tablespoons lemon juice
½ cup sugar

½ envelope gelatin
¼ cup cold water
red jelly

SERVES 6

FIRST Beat 4 egg yolks with 1 cup white wine. Add 3 tablespoons lemon juice and ½ cup sugar. Beat thoroughly with a rotary beater. Place on fire and stir constantly until it thickens.

SECOND Soak ½ envelope gelatin in ¼ cup water for five minutes. Dissolve the gelatin in the hot wine mixture, stirring until thoroughly blended. Replace on the fire and bring to a boil, stirring constantly. Remove and cool. When cool, pour into a cut-glass serving-bowl and place in the refrigerator until set.

THIRD Just before serving, garnish the pudding with a circle of small dabs of any preferred red jelly.

Dessert Sauces

APRICOT SAUCE

1 cup heavy cream
¼ cup sugar
1 tablespoon vanilla

½ cup strained apricot jam
juice ½ lemon

FIRST Beat 1 cup heavy cream until stiff. Add ¼ cup sugar and flavor with 1 tablespoon of vanilla extract.

SECOND Stir in ½ cup strained apricot jam and the juice ½ lemon. Set in refrigerator until ready to serve. Serve very cold.

CARAMEL SAUCE

1¼ cups brown sugar
⅔ cup corn syrup

4 tablespoons boiling water
¾ cup half cream, half milk

FIRST Dissolve 1¼ cup brown sugar in ⅔ cup corn syrup and 4 tablespoons boiling water.

SECOND Add ¾ cup half milk, half cream and cook until thick and very smooth.

CHOCOLATE SAUCE I

4 squares cooking chocolate
1 tablespoon butter
1 cup sugar

½ cup half cream, half milk
1 tablespoon vanilla

FIRST Melt 4 squares cooking chocolate with 1 tablespoon butter in a double boiler. Mix 1 cup sugar with ½ cup half cream, half milk.

SECOND Remove the top of the double boiler and place directly on a slow fire. Stir constantly until the mixture comes to a boil.

Allow to boil for a few minutes until it thickens. Add 1 tablespoon vanilla. Then return to the double boiler until ready to serve.

CHOCOLATE SAUCE II

¼ pound sweet chocolate
¾ cup milk

1 egg
1½ cups sugar

FIRST   Place ¼ pound sweet chocolate in a double boiler with ¾ cup milk, 1 well-beaten egg, and 1½ cups sugar. Stir until well blended.

SECOND   Leave in double boiler over a moderate flame for 1 hour, stirring occasionally.

CRÈME D'ISIGNY

[*A shameless plagiarism of a magnificent French delicacy*]

3 packages cream cheese
1 cup heavy cream

2 tablespoons sugar
1 teaspoon vanilla (optional)

FIRST   Take 3 packages cream cheese out of the refrigerator and warm to room temperature. Crush in a mixing-bowl with a fork.

SECOND   Work in ½ cup heavy cream, a little at a time, beating with the fork. Pour in the second half of the cup of cream and beat uninterruptedly for about three minutes with a rotary beater.

THIRD   Add 2 tablespoons sugar and 1 teaspoon vanilla (optional). Beat once more with the rotary beater. Pour the sauce into a serving-bowl and set in the refrigerator until ready to serve. Just before serving, stir vigorously with a spoon, as the wait in the refrigerator has a tendency to thicken the sauce a little more than is desirable.

NOTE   In Paris, in the spring, world famous restaurants display little wild strawberries nestling in woven baskets lined with fresh, green strawberry leaves. With these fragrant, incomparably delicious berries, the Parisians serve a superb, thick cream which they ladle out of a small pottery jug. Nothing can compare to the diner's overwhelming anticipation, as the thick cream pours languidly over the ruby red "fraises des bois" or "strawberries of the woods." This recipe comes as close to the original as possible. Try it with all berries or over sliced peaches. The Hotel Meurice in Paris was never willing to stop there! They served it daily, over their fresh fruit strips and tarts. "Go thou, and do likewise!"

CUSTARD CREAM SAUCE

2 tablespoons sugar
1 egg yolk
⅓ cup milk

⅛ pound soft butter
¼ teaspoon almond essence *or*
½ teaspoon vanilla

FIRST Blend 2 tablespoons sugar with 1 egg yolk until smooth and velvety. Add ⅓ cup milk. Stir rapidly on a moderate fire, until thick and smooth. Bring to a boil, but *do not boil*. Cool.

SECOND Beat in ¼ cup soft butter until smooth. Then stir in ¼ teaspoon almond extract or ½ teaspoon vanilla extract, as preferred. Chill in refrigerator until ready to serve.

NOTE An excellent filling for éclairs or for use in the bottom of fruit tarts. The French use this a great deal. See Parisian Strawberry Tarts (page 445). This recipe is sufficient for 6 éclairs, for an 8-inch fruit tart, or 6 small tarts.

FOAMY SAUCE

1 egg yolk
¾ cup powdered sugar
1 egg white

½ teaspoon vanilla
½ cup heavy cream

FIRST Beat 1 egg yolk and stir in ¾ cup powdered sugar. Beat 1 egg white until stiff. Stir into the sugar mixture until smooth.

SECOND Add ½ teaspoon vanilla. Whip ½ cup heavy cream until stiff. Fold into sauce. Serve.

FRUIT CUSTARD SAUCE

4 egg yolks
1 tablespoon sugar
½ cup apricot juice

1 cup milk
1 tablespoon cornstarch

FIRST Beat 4 egg yolks with 1 tablespoon sugar until smooth and light.

SECOND Add ½ cup apricot juice, 1 cup milk, and 1 tablespoon cornstarch to the egg mixture. Boil until thick. Cool.

NOTE Try this with any other fruit or berry juice. This sauce is a splendid accompaniment with any light pudding, Bavarian cream, or custard.

HARD SAUCE

¼ pound butter
1 cup powdered sugar

3 tablespoons rum *or* brandy (*or* 1 tablespoon vanilla *or* lemon juice)
maraschino cherries

FIRST Cream ¼ pound butter until smooth and soft. Gradually beat in 1 cup powdered sugar and work together until absolutely smooth.

SECOND Flavor with 3 tablespoons rum or brandy (if you prefer, 1 tablespoon vanilla or lemon juice may be used instead). Heap the mixture into a glass or silver serving-bowl. Decorate with maraschino cherries and set in the refrigerator until ready to serve.

PEACH SAUCE

6 very ripe peaches
1 cup sugar

¼ teaspoon almond extract
lemon juice (optional)

FIRST Skin and mash 6 very ripe peaches, carefully removing any dark spots before mashing.

SECOND Quickly stir in 1 cup sugar and continue to stir until well blended. Stir in ¼ teaspoon almond extract. If too sweet for your taste, squeeze in a few drops lemon juice.

PINEAPPLE CREAM SAUCE

3 packages cream cheese   1 cup pineapple juice

FIRST Mash 3 packages cream cheese with a fork. Beat until as smooth as possible.

SECOND Work a little pineapple juice into the cheese, beating, at first with a fork, and later, as more juice is added, with a rotary beater, until 1 cup juice has been incorporated and the sauce is smooth and free of any lumps.

VANILLA SAUCE I

1 pint light cream   3 egg yolks
¼ cup sugar   1 tablespoon vanilla
salt

FIRST Bring 1 pint light cream to a slow boil with ¼ cup sugar and a pinch of salt.

SECOND Beat 3 egg yolks and add to hot cream. Remove from fire and stir until well blended. Then return to a low flame. Stir constantly until the mixture thickens. Add 1 tablespoon vanilla. Cool and serve when very cold.

WARNING Do not let sauce get too hot or the eggs will curdle. Under no circumstances allow sauce to boil.

VANILLA SAUCE II (WITH RUM) *Marie's*

6 egg yolks   1 tablespoon vanilla
1 cup light cream   2 tablespoons rum
sugar

FIRST Beat 6 egg yolks with 1 cup light cream. Add sugar to taste and set on a moderate flame, stirring constantly until it thickens.

SECOND Remove sauce from fire and stir in 1 tablespoon vanilla and 2 tablespoons good rum. Cool. Set in refrigerator and serve very cold.

NOTE This was my father's favorite, whether served over a pudding or however else. I can still see him with a twinkle in his eye, asking my mother, as she served the dessert to "drown it." I think that you will too.

WARM WINE SAUCE

6 egg yolks
2 cups white wine
1 small piece cinnamon stick (*or* ¼ teaspoon cinnamon)

¼ teaspoon grated lemon rind
¼ teaspoon lemon juice

FIRST Place 6 egg yolks and 2 cups of white wine in the top of a double boiler. Add 1 small piece of cinnamon stick (or ¼ teaspoon of cinnamon), ¼ teaspoon of grated lemon rind, and ¼ teaspoon of lemon juice.

SECOND Stir constantly until thick and somewhat foamy. Remove the cinnamon stick and serve while still quite warm.

NOTE Cider may be substituted for the wine. Be careful not to allow the mixture to become too hot, unless you wish to have wine-flavored scrambled eggs!

This sauce is perfect to serve with Marie's Apple Charlotte or any Brown Betty, and try it with apple pie.

WINE FROTH SAUCE *Marie's*

⅓ cup sugar
1 cup white wine *or* sherry
1 tablespoon lemon juice

3 egg yolks
2 egg whites

FIRST Dissolve ⅓ cup sugar in a double boiler with 1 cup white wine or sherry and 1 tablespoon lemon juice. Add 3 egg yolks. Beat with a wire whisk until smooth and thick.

SECOND   Beat 2 egg whites until stiff. Remove the top of the double boiler from the stove, fold in the whites, and continue to beat with the wire whisk until thick and very foamy.

NOTE   Marie liked to serve this wonderful light, winy sauce with:
         Christmas Plum Pudding
         Apple Charlotte
         Apple Dumplings

Chapter XIII: *"Baking and Caking"*

Her name was Anna and she applied to us for a position in 1926, when we were living in Rapallo on the Italian Riviera. She wrote: "I have cooking been in Chicago, and I make very good baking and caking." She had and she did. This chapter, over which I have lingered long and lovingly, is dedicated to Anna.

CAKES

Anna's 1-2-3-4 Cake
Banana Cake
Brown and White Cinnamon Cake
Bienenstich Cake
Butter Lemon Sponge
Chocolate Cake (Hungarian)
Chocolate Cake (Old Vienna)
Chocolate Cake, Helene (Rich)
Chocolate Linzer Torte
Devil's Food Cake Maria
Family Birthday Cake
Fruit Sponge Cake
Good Plain Cake
Lady Baltimore Cake
Lemon Curd Cake
Mocha Torte
Nut Cake with Coal Black Chocolate Icing
Old Fashioned Coconut Layer Cake
Orange Cake
Orange Nut Sponge Cake
Orange Puff Cake
Pound Cake, Chris
Sand Torte
Sponge Cake
Trieste Tart (Old Vienna)
Watermelon Cake

COOKIES

Apple Cookies
Christmas Cookies
Currant Cookies
Favorite Cookies, Miggie
Old Fashioned Cookies
Pretzel Cookies

SMALL PASTRIES

Apricot Turnovers
Butter Balls
Canadian Coconut Squares
Cherry Tartlets
Cup Cakes
Currant Jelly Squares
Fudge Squares
Lemon Curd Tartlets
Lemon Tartlets with Meringue
Macaroons with Almonds
Macaroons with Cornflakes
Madeleines, Sylvia
Marvelous Brownies, Wendy
Scotch Shortbread I
Scotchbread II
Spice Squares
Spoon Sponge Biscuits
Vanilla Crescents
Vienna Kipfel

PASTRY CRUSTS FOR TARTS AND PIES

Cream Cheese Crust
Marie's Tart Crust
Polish Tart Crust
Puff Paste
Swedish Tart Crust

PIES AND TARTS

Apple Graham Cracker Pie, Wendy
Apple Tart
Apricot Fluff Pie
Cherry Tart
Chess Pie
Citrus Grove Pie
Lemon Chiffon Pie
Lemon Fluff Pie
Plum Strip
Prune Tart
Pumpkin Pie, Ruth

ICINGS AND FROSTINGS

Black Chocolate Cup Cake Icing
Boiled Icing
Butter Cream Icing
Chocolate Filling

Chocolate Icing
Crumbly not Creamy Fudge
Emperor's Frosting
Glazed Nuts and Fruits

Old Time Decorator's Icing
Powdered Sugar Icing
Seven Minute Frosting
Thin Icing

ANNA'S 1-2-3-4 CAKE

[Pre-heat oven to 350°]

½ pound butter
2 cups sugar
4 egg yolks
3 cups flour
2 teaspoons baking powder

¼ teaspoon salt
1 cup milk
4 egg whites
1 tablespoon vanilla

FIRST Cream ½ pound butter with 2 cups sugar. Beat in 4 egg yolks, one at a time.

SECOND Sift 3 cups flour. Measure and resift 3 times with 2 teaspoons baking powder and ¼ teaspoon salt. Stir into the batter alternately with 1 cup milk.

THIRD Beat 4 egg whites until stiff. Fold into the batter gently. Fold in 1 tablespoon vanilla. Bake, in 3 layers or as a flat cake, in a 350° oven until a straw comes out of the center clean and dry.

NOTES 1. This makes an excellent basic cake for any preferred icing. Equally excellent as a flat cake cut into small diagonals to be used as little iced petits fours.

2. A simple method of resifting flour is to place a sheet of wax paper under sifter and another beside it. When flour is sifted through, set sifter on other sheet, lift the one with flour and pour into sifter.

BANANA CAKE

[Pre-heat oven to 350°]

¼ pound butter
1½ cups sugar
4 slightly beaten egg yolks
1 cup mashed banana pulp
1 cup chopped pecans
¼ cup buttermilk
1½ cups sifted pastry flour
½ teaspoon salt

1 teaspoon baking powder
4 egg whites
1 teaspoon baking soda
few tablespoons warm water
1 teaspoon vanilla
Pierre's Butter Cream Icing (page 422)
walnut *or* pecan halves

FIRST Cream ¼ pound butter with 1½ cups sugar. Add 4 slightly beaten egg yolks and beat until light.

SECOND Add 1 cup mashed banana pulp, 1 cup chopped pecans, and ¼ cup buttermilk. Beat well together until smooth.

THIRD Sift 1½ cups pastry flour. Measure and resift twice with ½ teaspoon salt and 1 teaspoon baking powder. Sift into butter mixture and beat well.

FOURTH Beat 4 egg whites until stiff. Fold into the mixture gently. Add 1 teaspoon baking soda dissolved in few tablespoons warm water. Stir in 1 teaspoon vanilla. Grease two 9-inch layer-cake pans with vegetable shortening, then flour the pans lightly. Place in a 350° oven and bake for 25 to 30 minutes.

FIFTH Remove the layers from the oven. Cool on wire racks. When entirely cool, fill and ice with Pierre's Butter Cream Icing (page 422) and decorate with walnut or pecan halves.

NOTE "Pierre" is not just any Frenchman named Pierre. He was my daughter's beloved French instructor. His friendship for his young pupils not only stimulated them to become real students of French, but earned him their undying affection. Scores of young people will go out into the world with nostalgic memories of the French language afternoons, spent in their teacher's little home, learning the wonderful, fluent language he taught as an accompaniment to afternoon tea and his incomparable (made by himself) banana cake!

BROWN-AND-WHITE CINNAMON CAKE

[*Pre-heat oven to 400°*]

THE CAKE

½ pound butter
1 cup sugar
2 whole eggs
2 cups pastry flour

1 teaspoon baking powder
1 cup milk
1 tablespoon vanilla

FIRST Cream ½ pound butter with 1 cup sugar until creamy. Stir in 2 eggs, one at a time, until each in turn is completely blended.

SECOND Sift 2 cups pastry flour. Measure and resift twice with 1 teaspoon baking powder. Add to the batter alternately with 1 cup of milk combined with 1 tablespoon vanilla. Pour into a shallow pan and bake in a 400° oven for 25 to 30 minutes. When the cake begins to set, and before a crust appears, ice with the following icing while cake is still in the oven.

THE ICING

1½ cups brown sugar
2 tablespoons butter

¼ cup water
1 tablespoon cinnamon

FIRST Combine 1½ cups brown sugar with 2 tablespoons butter, ¼ cup water, and 1 tablespoon cinnamon.

SECOND Combine and boil until it thickens. Pour over cake while still in the oven. Continue baking until straw comes out clean. If a little of icing runs into the batter, so much the better.

BIENENSTICH CAKE

[Pre-heat oven to 400°]

THE CAKE

¼ pound butter
⅓ cup sugar
1 egg
2 cups sifted flour

2 teaspoons baking powder
½ teaspoon salt
2 tablespoons milk

FIRST Cream ¼ pound butter very thoroughly with ⅓ cup sugar. Beat in one egg until smooth.

SECOND Sift 2 cups of flour. Measure and resift twice with 2 teaspoons baking powder and ½ teaspoon salt. Add alternately to the butter mixture with 2 tablespoons milk. Mix until smooth. Place in a well-buttered spring form.

THE TOPPING

¼ pound butter
½ cup sugar
4 ounces unblanched almonds, ground very fine

2 teaspoons vanilla
2 tablespoons milk

FIRST Melt ¼ pound butter in a small pot. Add ½ cup sugar, 4 ounces unblanched almonds ground very fine, 2 teaspoons vanilla, and 2 tablespoons milk.

SECOND Stir ingredients together and bring to a boil. Remove from fire and cool. When cool, pour over cake and spread evenly with a knife or narrow spatula. Place in a 400° oven and bake for half an hour.

THE FILLING

raspberry jam
sweet butter

sugar
powdered sugar

When the cake has cooled, cut through the middle and fill the center lightly with raspberry jam or any other preferred preserve. Butter cream used as a filling (sweet butter stirred for a long time with sugar) is the favorite filling of the original recipe. In any case, sprinkle a little sifted powdered sugar over the top of the cake before serving.

BUTTER-LEMON SPONGE

[Pre-heat oven to 375°]

½ pound butter
2 cups sugar
5 egg yolks
2 cups flour

5 egg whites
juice 1 lemon
grated rind 1 lemon
powdered sugar

FIRST Cream ½ pound butter with 2 cups sugar until light and satiny in texture. Stir in 5 egg yolks, one at a time.

SECOND Sift 2 cups flour. Measure and resift. Set aside. Beat 5 egg whites until stiff. Add alternately with the flour to the batter, blending thoroughly after each addition.

THIRD Add juice and grated rind 1 lemon to the batter. Bake in a buttered cake tin or spring form in a 375° oven until done (about an hour). Cool and serve plain, sprinkled with powdered sugar.

NOTE This is a "plain" cake, but extremely moist and very delicious by itself.

CHOCOLATE CAKE (HUNGARIAN) *Marie's*
[*Pre-heat oven to 375°*]

¼ pound butter
½ cup sugar
4 egg yolks
2 ounces ground unskinned almonds
4 ounces bittersweet chocolate
2 tablespoons water
4 tablespoons flour
1 tablespoon vanilla
8 egg whites

FIRST Cream ¼ pound butter with ½ cup sugar. Add 4 beaten egg yolks and beat all together until light and smooth.

SECOND Stir 2 ounces grated, unskinned almonds into the mixture for about 20 minutes.

THIRD Add 4 ounces bittersweet chocolate melted in 2 tablespoons water. Stir well. Add 4 tablespoons flour, folding in carefully so that every bit is absorbed. Stir in 1 tablespoon vanilla.

FOURTH Beat 4 egg whites until stiff. Work into the batter. This operation cannot be handled too delicately, as the batter is likely to be somewhat stiff. Beat 4 additional egg whites until stiff and fold in gently. Pour the mixture into a well-buttered and lightly floured cake tin or, better still, a spring form and bake in a 375° oven for about half an hour, or until a testing straw comes out of the center dry and clean.

NOTE If you have an electric beater, the stirring time may be cut in half. This is a very rich, "chocolaty" cake. The tart may, of course, be iced. It is, however, not necessary as it is moist and rich enough in itself. Cut your slices thin. This is one that will remind all those who have known the charm of Central European coffee houses, of the Chocolate tarts served them in the years gone by.

CHOCOLATE CAKE (OLD VIENNA) *Marie's*
[*Pre-heat oven to 375°*]

6 ounces butter
¾ cup sugar
6 egg yolks
4 squares bitter chocolate
2 ounces grated, unblanched almonds

½ cup flour
6 egg whites
Marie's Chocolate Icing (page 422)
blanched almonds

FIRST Cream 6 ounces butter with ¾ cup sugar until smooth. Beat 6 egg yolks and add to the butter. Melt 4 squares bitter chocolate and stir into the mixture for 20 minutes. Grate 2 ounces unblanched almonds and add.

SECOND Sift ½ cup flour. Measure and resift. Beat 6 egg whites until stiff. Add the flour alternately to the chocolate mixture with the beaten whites. Blend well after each addition. Place in a buttered flat tin. Bake in a 375° oven for half an hour. When ready to serve, cut into small squares. If preferred, ice with Marie's Chocolate Icing (page 422) before cutting, and ornament with blanched almonds, cut into strips.

NOTE If mixed in an electric beater, the stirring time may be cut in half.

CHOCOLATE CAKE HELENE (RICH)
[*Pre-heat oven to 375°*]

½ pound sweet butter
½ pound powdered sugar
8 egg yolks
½ pound bittersweet *or* sweet chocolate
¼ cup coffee
½ pound grated almonds

1 tablespoon bread crumbs
8 egg whites
Chocolate Icing (page 422) (optional)
peeled almonds, pistachio nuts, and candied cherries

FIRST Stir ½ pound sweet butter with ½ pound powdered sugar until creamy (about 20 minutes). Add 8 egg yolks, one at a time.

SECOND Melt ½ pound bittersweet or sweet chocolate in ¼ cup coffee or ¼ cup water. Add to the egg mixture.

THIRD Grate ½ pound almonds with their skins left on and add to the mixture with 1 tablespoon bread crumbs.

FOURTH Beat 8 egg whites until stiff and fold in gently. Bake *half* of this mass in 3 eight-inch layer-cake pans in a 375° oven for 10 minutes. Remove the layers from the oven and take out of the pans at once. When cool, fill with the second half of the mixture. Ice with the same, or fill the layers more generously and ice with Chocolate Icing (page 422). Decorate with evenly spaced peeled almonds, or with alternate pistachio nuts and candied cherries, if preferred.

CHOCOLATE LINZER TORTE *Marie's*

9½ ounces butter	1 tablespoon cinnamon
1¼ cups powdered sugar	¼ teaspoon salt
2 egg yolks	grated rind and juice 1 lemon
4 ounces melted cooking chocolate	raspberry jam
5 ounces grated, unblanched almonds	currant jelly (optional)
2 cups pastry flour	powdered sugar

FIRST Cream 9½ ounces butter with 1¼ cups powdered sugar. Beat in 2 egg yolks, one at a time. Add 4 ounces melted cooking chocolate and 5 ounces grated, unblanched almonds. Blend well.

SECOND Sift 2 cups pastry flour. Measure and resift with 1 tablespoon cinnamon and ¼ teaspoon salt. Add to the mixture and flavor with the grated rind and the juice 1 lemon. Place the batter in the refrigerator for several hours.

[*Pre-heat oven to 325°*]

THIRD Grease and flour a 9-inch spring form. Roll out the dough about ¼ inch thick and line the bottom of the spring form. Form an edging one inch high, then spread the bottom of the dough with a generous amount of raspberry jam. If you like things tart, make a mixture half of raspberry jam and half of currant jelly, for the filling.

FOURTH Cut strips of the dough and make a "grill" on top of the jam. Bake for about half an hour in a 325° oven. Just before serving, sprinkle with powdered sugar.

NOTE This cake improves with age. It also lends itself very well to being baked in a square tin and to being cut into small tea squares. Whichever way, cut your pieces small; it is very rich.

DEVIL'S FOOD CAKE MARIA

[*Pre-heat oven to 375°*]

¼ pound butter
1½ cups sugar
5 ounces cooking chocolate
3 tablespoons boiling water
5 tablespoons sugar
3 eggs
¾ cup flour

1 teaspoon cream of tartar
½ teaspoon soda
½ cup milk
3 drops red food coloring
1 tablespoon vanilla
Seven-Minute Frosting (page 426)

FIRST Cream ¼ pound butter until soft and smooth. Gradually work 1½ cups sugar into the butter until well blended. Continue to stir until the batter is very smooth and light in color.

SECOND Grate 5 ounces cooking chocolate. Add 3 tablespoons boiling water and 5 tablespoons sugar. Set on the fire and stir until smooth. Add to the butter-sugar mixture and stir until very well blended. Add 3 eggs, one at a time, beating well after each addition.

THIRD Sift ¾ cup flour. Measure and resift 3 times with 1 teaspoon cream of tartar and ½ teaspoon soda. Add to the batter alternately with ½ cup of milk. Beat well.

FOURTH Color with 3 drops red food coloring and flavor with 1 tablespoon vanilla. Put into 2 nine-inch layer-cake pans. Bake for 20 minutes in a 375° oven. Cool the layers on cake racks. Ice with Seven-Minute Frosting (page 426).

FAMILY BIRTHDAY CAKE *Marie's*

[*Pre-heat oven to 300°*]

16 egg yolks
1¼ cups sugar
16 egg whites
1½ cups pastry flour
3 drops red food coloring

3 tablespoons cocoa
apricot jam
rum, brandy, *or* punch
Seven-Minute Icing (page 426)

PREPARATION OF THE BATTER

FIRST Beat 16 egg yolks until light. Then beat in 1¼ cups sugar, a little at a time, until all the sugar is incorporated. Beat well. The original old recipe calls for 30 minutes "hand beating," but 30 minutes on the electric beater will do. In either case, the mixture must be pale yellow and smooth as satin.

SECOND Beat 16 whites until stiff but not dry. Fold gently into the yolk mixture and blend well.

THIRD Sift 1½ cups pastry flour. Measure and resift into the egg mixture a little at a time, folding gently after each addition.

FOURTH 1. Measure out 2 or 3 overflowing large stirring-spoons of batter. Place in a small mixing-bowl and stir in 3 drops red food coloring. Pour into buttered and floured small layer-cake tin.

2. Measure out two or three overflowing large kitchen stirring spoons of batter. Place in a small mixing-bowl and stir in 3 tablespoons cocoa. Pour into buttered and floured small layer-cake tin.

3. Pour the rest of the batter into an ungreased spring form or round baking-tin.

4. Bake all 3 tins in a 300° oven.

WARNING Watch the two little layers—they will be baked long before the large cake.

PREPARATION OF THE BAKED CAKE

FIRST When cool slice off about ¼ inch from the top of the large cake. Carefully scoop out the soft insides, leaving the bottom and the sides about ½ inch thick. Smear the insides of this "box" with apricot jam. Smear the underside of the "lid" with jam as well.

SECOND Cut pink layer, cocoa layer, and the scooped-out insides of the large cake into ½-inch cubes. Place the cubes in a large mixing-bowl and sprinkle with sufficient rum, brandy, or punch to moisten them lightly. Turn them so that they are evenly moistened, then pack tightly into the cake "box." Replace the "lid" and cover with a plate, weighted down (an electric iron makes an excellent weight). Let stand overnight. Next day, glaze top and sides with a very thin "runny" apricot jam. Cover with Seven-Minute Icing (page 426), and decorate to taste. This cake improves with age, and lasts at least a week.

NOTE This cake was the pride and joy of the family and was used only on special occasions. It was presented to each member of the family in turn on his or her birthday. It once went so far as to be used as a wedding cake. I was married in Biarritz, in France, near the Spanish border, and my sister crossed the ocean to be at the ceremony. She arrived carrying a small hat box containing a gift from Marie . . . this traditional family cake was done up *this* time as a wedding cake . . . with two tiny gold wedding rings suspended between the sugar beaks of two perfect little sugar doves! . . .

FRUIT SPONGE CAKE

[*Pre-heat oven to 325°*]

6 egg yolks
1 teaspoon lemon extract
¼ teaspoon salt
⅓ cup orange juice
grated rind 1 orange
1 cup sugar
1 cup sifted pastry flour

1¼ teaspoon baking powder
6 egg whites
fruit (optional)
1 cup heavy cream (optional)
¼ cup sugar (optional)
1 tablespoon vanilla (optional)

FIRST Beat 6 egg yolks until light. Add 1 teaspoon lemon extract, ¼ teaspoon salt, ⅓ cup orange juice, and grated rind 1 orange. Stir together for 2 minutes. Then gradually add 1 cup of sugar and beat thoroughly.

SECOND Sift 1 cup pastry flour. Measure and resift 3 times with 1¼ teaspoon baking powder. Fold in.

THIRD Beat 6 egg whites until stiff. Fold in. Pour the batter into an ungreased cake pan. Bake 45 minutes in a 325° oven. When baked, remove and cool.

FOURTH When ready to serve, serve plain or top with any favorite cut-up fruit and cover with 1 cup heavy cream whipped until stiff, sweetened with ¼ cup sugar, and flavored with 1 tablespoon vanilla extract.

GOOD PLAIN CAKE

[*Pre-heat oven to 375°*]

6 ounces butter
2 cups sugar
3 eggs
3 cups pastry flour
3 teaspoons baking powder

1 cup milk
1 tablespoon vanilla *or* 1 teaspoon lemon extract and grated rind 1 lemon

FIRST Cream 6 ounces of butter with 2 cups sugar until smooth. Beat in three eggs, one at a time, beating well after each addition until well blended.

SECOND Sift 3 cups pastry flour. Measure and resift 3 times with 3 teaspoons baking powder. Add flour to the batter alternately with 1 cup milk. Beat until smooth, then stir in 1 tablespoon vanilla or, if preferred, 1 teaspoon lemon extract and the grated rind of 1 lemon. Bake in buttered and floured layer-cake tins in a 375° oven until nicely browned.

NOTE This layer-cake recipe is an excellent basic recipe and may be used with any preferred filling or frosting.

LADY BALTIMORE CAKE

[*Pre-heat oven to 350°*]

THE CAKE

½ pound butter
2 cups sugar
1 cup milk
4 cups flour

10 egg whites
4 teaspoons baking powder
1 tablespoon almond extract

MAKES 2 CAKES

FIRST Cream ½ pound butter with 2 cups sugar until very light and smooth. Add 1 cup milk, a little at a time, and beat well.

SECOND Sift 4 cups flour. Measure and resift. Beat 10 egg whites until stiff. Add flour and egg whites alternately to the batter, *reserving the last cup of flour.*

THIRD Add 4 level teaspoons taking powder to the reserved cup of flour. Then add to batter, blending well with a gentle, folding motion. Fold in 1 tablespoon almond extract. Bake in a 350° oven until done (approximately 25 minutes). This makes 6 layers, enough for 2 cakes.

THE FILLING

4 cups sugar	1 cup chopped nuts
1 cup water	nuts
4 egg whites	maraschino cherries
1 cup chopped raisins	raisins

FIRST Cook 4 cups sugar with 1 cup water until it threads.

SECOND Beat 4 egg whites until stiff. Pour the syrup into the egg whites very slowly in a long, thin stream, beating all the while.

THIRD Place half of this mixture into another bowl. Add 1 cup chopped raisins and 1 cup chopped nuts. Put this mixture between the layers. Use the second half of the icing for the top and sides of the cake. Decorate with nuts, maraschino cherries, and raisins.

NOTE My friend in Richmond, Virginia, writes: "The Lady Baltimore cake is very old; mother got it from a friend in Charleston, S. C., and Helen copied it correctly. It was evolved in the days before baking powder was standardized. Ladies generally made their own with cream of tartar and soda. With this recipe we use 4 teaspoons of baking powder, levelled off sharply with the finger."

LEMON-CURD CAKE

[Pre-heat oven to 375°]

THE CAKE

¼ pound butter	2 teaspoons baking powder
2 cups sugar	¼ teaspoon salt
3 eggs	1 cup milk
3 cups pastry flour	1 teaspoon lemon extract

FIRST Cream ¼ pound butter with 2 cups sugar until fluffy. Add 3 eggs, beating them in one at a time.

SECOND Sift, measure, and resift 3 cups pastry flour with 2 teaspoons baking powder and ¼ teaspoon salt. Add to the batter alternately with 1 cup of milk. Stir in 1 teaspoon lemon extract and bake in four 8-inch layers in a 375° oven.

THE FILLING

grated rind 1 lemon
juice 2 lemons
1 cup sugar
1 egg

½ cup water
1 teaspoon butter
1 heaping tablespoon flour

FIRST Combine grated rind 1 lemon and juice 2 lemons with 1 cup sugar, 1 egg, ½ cup water, 1 teaspoon butter, and 1 heaping tablespoon flour. Place in the top of a double boiler and stir constantly until thick. Pour into a mixing-bowl and set aside until cool.

SECOND Spread the Lemon Curd thickly between the layers and over the top and on the side. Allow to set for several hours before serving.

MOCHA TORTE

[Pre-heat oven to 350°]

THE SPONGE CAKE

6 egg yolks
6 tablespoons powdered sugar
6 tablespoons flour
½ teaspoon baking powder

salt
6 egg whites
1 tablespoon vanilla

FIRST Stir 6 egg yolks with 6 tablespoons powdered sugar for 15 minutes—no less. (On an electric beater the time may be cut in half.)

SECOND Sift in 6 tablespoons flour, ½ teaspoon baking powder, and pinch salt. Blend well.

THIRD Beat 6 egg whites until stiff. Fold into mixture with a gentle hand. Add 1 tablespoon vanilla. Bake in 2 eight inch layer-cake tins in a 350° oven for approximately twenty minutes.

NOTE The pans in which sponge cakes are baked should *not* be buttered.

MOCHA FILLING

1⅓ cups sugar   ¾ pound sweet butter
1 cup strong coffee

FIRST Boil 1⅓ cups sugar with 1 cup strong coffee until syrupy. Cool to room temperature.

SECOND Cream ¾ pound sweet butter until very soft and pliable. Add a little of the syrup to the butter, working it in. Then continue to add the syrup, a little at a time, until all of it is well blended and completely smooth. Beat until it is the consistency of soft butter. Then spread between the layers, on the sides, and over the top of the Torte. If at any time you are having difficulty acquiring a satin-smooth consistency, use an electric or hand beater.

NOTE There are those who prefer a chocolate icing instead of the mocha. If you decide to use Chocolate to ice the cake, use only ⅔ cups sugar, ½ cup coffee, and 6 ounces butter. This will be sufficient to make a filling between the layers. Hopjes or coffee candies, crushed to a sprinkling powder, make a delightful decoration for the top of the Torte.

NUT CAKE WITH COAL-BLACK CHOCOLATE ICING

[*Pre-heat oven to 375°*]

CAKE

12 egg yolks
12 heaping tablespoons sugar
¾ pound walnuts *or* pecans (*or* both)
1 cup bread crumbs

grated rind 1 orange
grated rind 1 lemon
12 egg whites
rum (optional)

FIRST Beat 12 egg yolks with 12 heaping tablespoons sugar until light and smooth.

SECOND Grind ¾ pound walnuts or pecans (or a mixture of both) until very fine. Mix with 1 cup dry bread crumbs and the grated rinds 1 orange and 1 lemon. Add to the egg mixture. This will make a very heavy paste and will be difficult to work with a kitchen spoon. Therefore, wash hands thoroughly and work until well blended with your hands.

THIRD Beat 12 egg whites until stiff but not dry. Fold gently into the nut mixture, working carefully to break up all lumps and being sure that the egg whites have been thoroughly distributed. Butter three 8-inch layer-cake pans (be sure to use butter). Put in the batter and bake in a 375° oven for 30 minutes, until golden brown. Test with a straw and remove to cake-coolers. When cool, sprinkle rum on top of each layer if you like.

FILLING

¼ pound sweet butter
cocoa *or* powdered chocolate
sugar
4 tablespoons rum

FIRST Work ¼ pound sweet butter with cocoa or powdered chocolate until dark enough to suit you. Then work in sugar to taste—not too much sugar if you like a bitter-sweet flavor. Add 4 tablespoons rum and blend until smooth. Spread on the cooled layers.

ICING

6 ounces bitter chocolate
2 tablespoons water
sugar
light cream

FIRST Melt 6 ounces bitter chocolate over the fire with 2 tablespoons of water.

SECOND Add sugar to taste and enough light cream to form a spreading consistency. Cool and spread on top and sides of the cake. Place the cake overnight or all day in the icebox. Remove 1 hour before serving.

OLD-FASHIONED COCONUT LAYER CAKE
[*Pre-heat oven to 375°*]
CAKE

¼ pound butter
2 cups sugar
2¼ cups pastry flour
⅓ cup cornstarch

1 teaspoon baking powder
¾ cup milk
6 egg whites
1 tablespoon vanilla

FIRST Cream ¼ pound butter with 2 cups sugar until fluffy.

SECOND Sift 2¼ cups flour. Measure and resift 3 times with ⅓ cup cornstarch and 1 teaspoon baking powder. Add to butter mixture alternately with ¾ cup milk.

THIRD Beat 6 egg whites until stiff. Fold into the batter gently. Add 1 tablespoon vanilla. Bake in two 9-inch or three 8-inch layer tins in a 375° oven.

FILLING AND ICING

1 recipe Seven-Minute Icing (page 426)
1 cup heavy cream (optional)

1 tablespoon vanilla (optional)
2 cups moist coconut

FIRST Beat 1 cup heavy cream until stiff. Fold into 1 recipe Seven-Minute Icing (page 426) and stir in 1 tablespoon vanilla. Combine the whole with 1 cup moist grated coconut (fresh preferred). Fill between the layers and ice all over, sprinkling generously both top and sides with the second cup moist coconut.

NOTE This makes a very festive party dessert. The heavy cream may be omitted; in which case you will have a much simpler cake and one that will last outside the refrigerator. Because of the whipped cream this is not true of the original recipe.

ORANGE CAKE
[*Pre-heat oven to 350°*]

8 egg yolks
1 cup sugar
juice 2 oranges
grated rinds 2 oranges
½ pound almonds
2 tablespoons zweiback crumbs

8 egg whites
orange marmalade
Seven-Minute Icing (page 426) *or* any preferred white icing
fresh *or* glazed segments of oranges (page 425)

FIRST Beat 8 egg yolks with 1 cup sugar until velvety smooth. Stir in juice and grated rind 2 oranges.

SECOND Grate ½ pound almonds with their skins left on. Mix with 2 tablespoons zweiback crumbs.

THIRD Beat 8 egg whites until stiff and fold gently into mixture. Bake in 2 layers in a 350° oven until a testing straw comes out clean in the center. Remove at once—but carefully, as this cake is very delicate. Cool on cake racks.

FOURTH When cool, fill with orange marmalade and cover with Seven-Minute Icing or any preferred white icing. Decorate with fresh or with glazed segments of oranges (page 425).

ORANGE-NUT SPONGE CAKE

[Pre-heat oven to 325°]

6 egg yolks	1 cup orange juice
1¾ cups sugar	1 cup ground walnuts
½ teaspoon salt	grated rind 1 orange
2 cups matzo meal	6 egg whites

FIRST Cream 6 egg yolks with 1¾ cups sugar and ½ teaspoon salt until light.

SECOND Add 2 cups matzo meal alternately with 1 cup orange juice, combining well after each addition. Add 1 cup ground walnuts and the grated rind 1 orange.

THIRD Beat 6 egg whites until stiff. Fold gently into the mixture until thoroughly combined. Pour into tube pan or angel-food pan. Bake 1 hour in a 325° oven.

NOTE Matzo meal may be found in most delicatessen stores. It is also found in all Jewish markets.

ORANGE PUFF CAKE

[*Pre-heat oven to 325°*]

1 over-running cup egg whites (approximately 10 egg whites)
¼ teaspoon salt
1 teaspoon cream of tartar
1⅓ cups sugar
⅔ cup water
7 egg yolks
grated rind 1 large, deep-colored orange
4 tablespoons orange juice
1 cup pastry flour

FIRST Beat with a flat wire whip 1 over-running cup of egg whites (approximately 10 egg whites) with ¼ teaspoon salt on a large platter or in a large, wide bowl. When the whites are foamy, add 1 teaspoon cream of tartar, sifting into whites through a small strainer. Continue to beat until the mixture looks moist and shiny and forms peaks when the whip is lifted up.

SECOND Boil 1⅓ cups sugar and ⅔ cup water until it forms a thread when dropped from a *silver* fork.

THIRD Pour the cooked sugar over the egg whites in a thin stream, holding the pan high enough so as not to scald or curdle the egg whites. This will happen if the sugar syrup is added to the whites too rapidly. Pour with one hand and blend with the other, using silver fork, not the wire whip.

FOURTH After all the sugar syrup has been added, set the platter or bowl in a pan of cold water. Continue beating with the flat wire whip until cool, always using a high, lifting stroke to achieve a light texture.

FIFTH Beat 7 egg yolks until lemon-colored. Add grated rind 1 large, deep-colored orange and 4 tablespoons orange juice. Mix well and fold gently into the meringue.

SIXTH Sift 1 cup pastry flour. Measure and resift 4 times. Sift gently into mixture and fold in with a light, folding motion. Pour the mixture into an angel-food cake pan that has been rinsed in cold water, handling as little as possible. Use a spatula to scrape the bowl clean, then cut through the mixture in the pan with a knife to clear away the air pockets. Bake at 325° for 1 hour. Remove from oven and invert, allowing cake to "hang" until cool. Do not place by open window or in drafts, as this causes the cake to shrink.

NOTES 1. Most angel-food pans are equipped with small feet that allow the cake to "hang" (the pan is inverted but the cake does not touch the surface of the table). However, in case your pan is an ordinary tube pan and not a specially built angel-food pan, do not be discouraged. Insert a Coco-Cola bottle into the tube and allow the pan to "hang" supported by the bottle until cool.

2. At first glance, this cake may seem like a lot of trouble, but, believe me, this is the sort of adventure in baking that makes a cook's reputation. Just follow each direction separately, one at a time, and you will have it done before you know it. It is a superb achievement, and I heartily recommend it as one of the finest cakes in the entire collection.

POUND CAKE, CHRIS

[*Pre-heat oven to 325°*]

½ pound butter
2 cups confectioner's sugar
5 whole eggs
3½ cups pastry flour
3 teaspoons baking powder
1 cup milk

1 tablespoon vanilla extract
1 tablespoon brandy *or* Scotch whisky as preferred
rind of 2 lemons
juice of 1 lemon
confectioner's sugar

FIRST Cream ½ pound butter with 2 cups confectioner's sugar until very pale in color and smooth as satin. Add 5 whole eggs, one at a time, beating thoroughly after each addition. After all have been added beat for 20 minutes by hand or 10 minutes at beating speed on the electric mixer.

SECOND Sift 3½ cups pastry flour. Measure and resift three times with 3 teaspoons baking powder. Add flour alternately to the batter with 1 cup milk and beat until smooth. Then flavor with 1 tablespoon vanilla extract, 1 tablespoon brandy or Scotch whisky, the grated rind of 2 lemons, and the juice of 1 lemon. Bake in a buttered and floured loaf pan in a 325° oven for 1½ hours. Turn out to cool on a cake rack. Sprinkle lightly with confectioner's sugar before serving.

SAND TORTE

[Pre-heat oven to 400°]

½ pound sweet butter
1¼ cups sugar
4 eggs
1 cup cornstarch
1 cup flour

1 heaping teaspoon baking powder
1 tablespoon vanilla
sifted powdered sugar

FIRST Cream ½ pound of sweet butter with 1¼ cups sugar for about 20 minutes (or for half that time on an electric beater) until very light in color and satiny smooth in texture.

SECOND Beat in 1 egg and blend well. Add ½ cup sifted cornstarch and blend well.

THIRD Add 1 egg and blend well. Sift 1 cup of flour with 1 heaping teaspoon of baking powder. Sift *half* the amount into the mixture and blend well.

FOURTH Add 1 egg and blend well. Add ½ cup sifted cornstarch and blend well.

FIFTH Add 1 egg and blend well. Add the second ½ cup of flour and blend well. Add 1 tablespoon vanilla. Bake in a greased cake mold in a 400° oven. When the cake is cool, cover with sifted powdered sugar.

NOTE I am happy to share this delicious cake recipe with you and if you will follow the directions carefully, I believe that you will agree that it has a most extraordinary texture. I wish that I might share the warm nostalgia of adolescent afternoons spent in the public gardens of a then peaceful Europe listening with perfect leisure to Strauss waltzes while sipping raspberry lemonade along with ecstatic munchings of this fabulous Sand Torte. The texture of this cake will bring about an understanding of its title.

SPONGE CAKE

[*Pre-heat oven to 350°*]

6 egg yolks
6 tablespoons powdered sugar
6 tablespoons flour
½ teaspoon baking powder

pinch salt
6 egg whites
1 tablespoon vanilla

FIRST   Stir 6 egg yolks with 6 tablespoons powdered sugar for 15 minutes—no less. On an electric beater the time may be cut in half.

SECOND   Sift in 6 tablespoons flour, ½ teaspoon baking powder, and a pinch of salt. Blend well.

THIRD   Beat 6 egg whites until stiff. Fold into the mixture gently. Add 1 tablespoon vanilla. Bake in two 9-inch ungreased layer-cake tins in a 350° oven.

TRIESTE TART (OLD VIENNA)   *Marie's*

[*Pre-heat oven to 375°*]

½ pound butter
1 cup sugar
6 egg yolks
3 ounces grated almonds
4 ounces sweet *or* bittersweet chocolate

2 ounces dry bread crumbs
6 egg whites
Marie's Chocolate Icing (page 422)

FIRST   Cream ½ pound butter with 1 cup of sugar until light and creamy. Then add 6 well-beaten egg yolks.

SECOND   Grate 3 ounces of almonds (with their skins left on) and 4 ounces sweet or bittersweet chocolate. Add 2 ounces dry bread crumbs. Then add these 3 ingredients to the egg mixture.

THIRD   Beat 6 egg whites until stiff. Fold them gently into the batter.

FOURTH Butter and flour a spring form (approximately 8 inches). Pour in the mixture and bake in a 375° oven until the center is dry to a testing straw. Remove from the oven, take off the ring of the spring form, and allow to cool. Just before serving, cover with Marie's Chocolate Icing (page 422).

NOTE In the original recipe the chocolate was always grated or cut very fine with a sharp knife. It could be melted, however, if you preferred the cake to be chocolate throughout.

WATERMELON CAKE
[*Pre-heat oven to 350°*]

¼ pound butter
1 cup sugar
1 teaspoon lemon extract
2 cups pastry flour
3½ teaspoons baking powder
¼ teaspoon salt
1 cup milk
3 egg whites
½ teaspoon red vegetable coloring
½ cup raisins
Seven-Minute Icing (page 426)

FIRST Cream ¼ pound butter with 1 cup sugar until light. Stir in 1 teaspoon lemon extract.

SECOND Sift 2 cups pastry flour. Measure and resift twice with 3½ teaspoons baking powder and ¼ teaspoon salt. Add alternately to the butter mixture with 1 cup milk.

THIRD Beat 3 egg whites until stiff. Fold in gently. Place half the mixture in a well-buttered melon mold (preferred) or cake pan. Draw the batter up along the sides, leaving it somewhat hollow in the middle.

FOURTH Add ½ teaspoon red vegetable coloring and ½ cup well-floured raisins to the second half of the mixture and pour it in the direct center of the plain batter. Bake in a moderate oven for half an hour.

FIFTH Unmold and ice with any good icing, such as Seven-Minute Icing (page 426) colored bright green.

APPLE COOKIES

[*Pre-heat oven to 325°*]

1 cup sugar
1 tablespoon flour
1 teaspoon baking powder
¼ teaspoon salt

1 well-beaten egg
1 large apple
1 cup nut meats
1 teaspoon vanilla

FIRST Sift 1 cup sugar with 1 tablespoon flour, 1 teaspoon baking powder, and ¼ teaspoon salt. Add 1 well-beaten egg.

SECOND Grind 1 large apple (peeled and cored) and 1 cup nut meats through the grinder. Add to the batter. Stir in 1 teaspoon vanilla and flatten onto a buttered and floured baking-sheet. Bake in a 325° oven until the edges crisp. Before it cools,cut into diamond shapes or squares.

NOTE The choice of nuts is optional. A mixture of almonds, walnuts, and pecans is our favorite.

CHRISTMAS COOKIES

[*Pre-heat oven to 350°*]

1 cup molasses
1 cup dark corn syrup
1 cup sugar
2 eggs
½ pound butter *or* 1 cup vegetable shortening

1 teaspoon soda
½ tablespoon cinnamon
½ teaspoon allspice
½ teaspoon cloves
¼ teaspoon salt
5 cups pastry flour

FIRST Cook 1 cup molasses, 1 cup dark corn syrup, and 1 cup of sugar until the sugar is dissolved. Bring to a boil, remove from the fire and cool.

SECOND Beat 2 eggs until light. Beat with ½ pound butter or 1 cup vegetable shortening until well blended. Add 1 teaspoon soda dissolved in a little water and the following: ½ tablespoon cinnamon, ½ teaspoon allspice, ½ teaspoon cloves, and ¼ teaspoon salt.

THIRD Sift 5 cups pastry flour. Measure and resift into batter. It is best not to use too much flour. If the given measure does not permit the dough to be rolled out, place it in the refrigerator over night. This is best, however, if you are in a hurry: Add another cup of flour and roll at once to any preferred thickness on a lightly floured board and cut into any desired shapes. Bake on a greased and floured cookie sheet in a 350° oven.

NOTE These cookies are a Christmas tradition in our family. The children have always made it their business to invite in the entire juvenile neighborhood for an orgy of cooking-cutting, baking and decorating. Through the years, we have accumulated quite a collection of cookie-cutters, an array that is dear to our hearts. Because these cookies belong mostly to children (they ultimately find their place hanging from the Christmas tree), I have omitted some of the additional delicacies mentioned in the original recipe: cardamon seed and anise seed ground together, pecans, walnuts, or almonds chopped fine.

If you plan to use these (as we do) hanging from the branches of your Christmas tree, punch a hole in the top of each cookie before baking. When they are baked, put a string through each. They lend themselves beautifully to decoration. Colored sprinklets or colored icing mixed with imagination does the trick!

CURRANT COOKIES

[*Pre-heat oven to 400°*]

3 ounces butter
½ cup sugar
1 egg
grated rind of 1 lemon
1 cup pastry flour

1½ teaspoons baking powder
¼ teaspoon salt
2 tablespoons milk
½ cup soaked currants

FIRST Cream 3 ounces butter with ½ cup sugar until light. Add 1 beaten egg and the grated rind of 1 lemon.

SECOND Sift 1 cup pastry flour. Measure and resift 3 times with 1½ teaspoons baking powder and ¼ teaspoon salt. Add flour alternately to the batter with 2 tablespoons milk. When well blended fold in ½ cup soaked currants.

THIRD Spoon out batter with a teaspoon onto a greased and lightly floured baking-sheet. Bake in a 400° oven for 10 to 15 minutes.

FAVORITE COOKIES, MIGGIE

[*Pre-heat oven to 400°*]

¼ pound butter
½ cup sugar
1 egg yolk
1 cup pastry flour
1 egg white

¼ cup finely chopped blanched almonds *or* any other preferred nuts
2 tablespoons sugar
¼ teaspoon cinnamon

FIRST Cream ¼ pound butter with ½ cup sugar until light and smooth. Stir in 1 egg yolk and blend well.

SECOND Sift 1 cup of pastry flour. Measure and resift into the batter. Mix thoroughly.

THIRD Grease and flour a flat cake pan or cookie sheet. Spread the dough very thinly. If necessary use a wet knife. Beat 1 egg white until stiff. Sprinkle on top of the dough like snow and top with a mixture of ¼ cup finely chopped blanched almonds or any other preferred nuts, 2 tablespoons sugar, and ¼ teaspoon of cinnamon. Bake in a 400° oven until gold in color.

FOURTH When baked, cut quickly into diamond-shaped diagonals—and be certain to cut quickly before they start to cool and turn crisp. If you wait too long it will be difficult to cut and remove the cookies without breaking them.

NOTE These cookies are delicious! The thinner you spread them, the crisper the cookies will be. If you spread them on a cookie sheet, you will need only a portion of the tin. Spread evenly! Spread thinly!

OLD-FASHIONED COOKIES

½ pound butter
⅓ cup sugar
4 tablespoons light cream

3 cups pastry flour
sugar-cinnamon mixture
finely ground nuts

FIRST Cream ½ pound butter with ⅓ cup sugar. Add 4 tablespoons light cream.

SECOND Sift 3 cups pastry flour. Measure and resift twice. Gradually add to the butter mixture and beat until well blended. Place in the refrigerator.

[*Pre-heat oven to 400°*]

THIRD When cold enough to handle, roll out as thin as possible and quickly cut into various shapes with cookie-cutters. Place on a buttered and floured baking-sheet. Sprinkle each cookie with a mixture of sugar and cinnamon. Sprinkle with very finely ground nuts. Bake in a 400° oven.

NOTE I have found it useful to roll out half of the dough, leaving the other half in the refrigerator. Work quickly while the dough is still chilled—it is almost impossible to handle when it softens. These cookies are truly marvelous and are guaranteed not to last any time at all in anybody's house!

PRETZEL COOKIES

¼ pound butter
¼ cup sugar
2 eggs
2 tablespoons milk
1 cup flour

¼ teaspoon salt
½ cup white sugar
½ cup brown sugar
2 tablespoons cinnamon

FIRST Cream ¼ pound butter with ¼ cup sugar. Add 2 eggs and 2 tablespoons milk. Beat until smooth.

SECOND Sift 1 cup flour. Measure and resift with ¼ teaspoon salt. Add gradually to the dough until the whole is well blended. Set in refrigerator for several hours.

[*Pre-heat oven to 375°*]

THIRD Mix ½ cup white sugar with ½ cup brown sugar. Add 2 tablespoons cinnamon and stir well together. Sprinkle this mixture evenly on your pastry board.

FOURTH Roll out the dough onto the sugar mixture until about ¼ inch thick. Cut into strips about ½ inch wide. Shape these strips into pretzels. Sprinkle each in turn with the sugar mixture and place on a greased and floured cookie sheet. When all the pretzels are formed, bake in a 375° oven.

NOTE My brother-in-law ate these in his early youth. He had nostalgic memories of them. Nobody in his family, himself included, had the slightest idea how they were made. This recipe is a fifth attempt under his eager and nervous supervision. We hope you will understand why we labored so lovingly and so long.

APRICOT TURNOVERS

¼ pound cream cheese
4 tablespoons butter
¾ cup sifted flour

pinch of salt
1 can apricot halves
powdered sugar

FIRST Combine ¼ pound cream cheese and 4 tablespoons butter. Work in ¾ cup sifted flour measured and resifted with pinch of salt. Place the dough on a dish, cover with waxed paper, and leave in refrigerator for 24 hours.

[*Pre-heat oven to 400°*]

SECOND Roll the dough very thin and cut into squares. Place an apricot half in the center of each square. Fold the dough into a triangle so that the points meet, bringing the two touching points back toward the apricot half again. Use a small knife to trim the ends, then pink them with the prongs of a fork.

THIRD Grease and flour a cookie tin. Place the little turnovers on the sheet and bake in a 400° oven until golden brown. Cool on a cake rack and sprinkle freely with powdered sugar.

NOTE Roll the turnovers thin, but not so thin that the apricot halves are exposed in the baking. They must be completely concealed by the pastry.

BUTTER BALLS

[*Pre-heat oven to 325°*]

½ pound butter
⅔ cup sugar
2 egg yolks
2 cups flour

¼ teaspoon salt
1 tablespoon vanilla
tart jelly, preferably currant

FIRST Cream ½ pound butter with ⅔ cup sugar until smooth. Beat in 2 egg yolks, one at a time, until smooth.

SECOND Sift 2 cups flour. Measure and resift twice with ¼ teaspoon salt. Gradually add to the butter mixture. Beat again when all the flour has been added, and finally beat in 1 tablespoon vanilla.

THIRD Grease and flour a cookie sheet. Scoop out ½ teaspoon dough at a time. Roll between your palms into tiny "butter balls" about the size of a marble. Give them room to spread by placing them on the cookie sheet about 1 inch apart and 1 inch away from the edges. With the tip of a finger, form a depression on top of each "ball." Fill each depression with a small amount of tart jelly and bake in a 325° oven. Watch them carefully and bake them only until sandy-colored. They are done when slightly browned underneath. Approximately 12 to 13 minutes is the required time. This recipe makes about 75 "butter balls."

NOTE These cookies resemble a bowl of cherries in that it is almost impossible for the members of your family to leave them alone. Use the tip of a knife or the tip of a small spoon to insert the jelly (preferably currant) into the depressions on top of the cookies.

CANADIAN COCONUT SQUARES
[Pre-heat oven to 400°]

¼ pound butter
½ cup sugar
1 cup flour
1½ cups brown sugar
1 cup shredded coconut
1 cup chopped walnuts *or* almonds

pinch of salt
½ teaspoon baking powder
2 tablespoons flour
2 eggs
powdered sugar

FIRST Cream ¼ pound butter with ½ cup sugar.

SECOND Sift 1 cup flour. Measure and resift twice and add to the butter mixture. Grease a small square tin, 8" x 8", and force batter into it. It will be rather firm and will need to be pressed into the pan with your hand. Bake until light brown in a 400° oven.

THIRD Combine 1½ cups brown sugar, 1 cup shredded coconut, 1 cup chopped walnuts or almonds (skins left on), pinch of salt, ½ teaspoon baking powder, 2 tablespoons flour, and 2 beaten eggs. Spread evenly on the baked crust and return to the oven. Bake until the top is well browned. Cut while hot into squares and sprinkle with powdered sugar.

CHERRY TARTLETS

[*My grandmother's old recipe*]

3 ounces butter
¼ cup sugar
2 cups pastry flour
1 egg
2 tablespoons milk

1 can pitted red sour cherries
½ cup granulated sugar
dry grated bread crumbs
½ cup currant jelly

APPROXIMATELY 6

THE CRUST

FIRST Cream 3 ounces butter with ¼ cup sugar until light and creamy.

SECOND Sift 2 cups pastry flour. Measure and resift into the butter mixture. Beat 1 egg with 2 tablespoons milk until well blended. Combine with the dough. Set the dough in the refrigerator for several hours.

[*Pre-heat oven to 400°*]

THIRD Roll out the dough about ⅓ inch thick. Cut rounds with a biscuit-cutter about 2 to 3 inches in diameter. Form a little rim of dough standing up around each round. This can be done by rolling out long, pencil-like rolls with the flat of the palm and attaching by pinching to the rounds. Set on a cookie sheet and bake golden brown in a 400° oven.

THE FILLING

FIRST Drain 1 can pitted red sour cherries until completely free of liquid. Place them in a bowl and scatter them with ½ cup sugar, turning the cherries once so that all are evenly coated.

SECOND Sprinkle the bottom of each tart with dry grated bread crumbs and fill each heaping high with the pitted sour cherries.

THIRD Melt ½ cup currant jelly over a slow flame and spoon this glaze evenly over the cherries. Allow to cool and serve.

NOTE During the process of melting the jelly stir until smooth, avoiding any unmelted lumps.
This tart crust is rich and crumbling, but somewhat firm rather than flaky. Tarts, as described in this recipe, are the correct size for dinner, one per person, as they spread somewhat in the baking. If you wish to serve them for tea, cut them even smaller—they make a dainty, toothsome sight on the tea table.
And don't stop with using sour cherries. Apricots or peaches with an apricot glaze (thin apricot jam), strawberries with currant glaze, or apples with apricot glaze, make a charming addition to any table, whether dinner or tea. This dough keeps well in the refrigerator, if you do not wish to use it all at one time.

CUP CAKES *Marie's*
[*Pre-heat oven to 400°*]

2 ounces butter	¼ teaspoon salt
½ cup sugar	¼ cup milk
1 egg	1 teaspoon vanilla
1 cup pastry flour	Marie's Chocolate Icing (page
1 teaspoon baking powder	422)

FIRST Cream 2 ounces butter with ½ cup sugar until fluffy. Beat 1 egg to a froth. Add to butter mixture and beat until smooth.

SECOND Sift 1 cup pastry flour. Measure and resift twice with 1 teaspoon baking powder and ¼ teaspoon salt. Add alternately to the butter mixture with ¼ cup milk. Stir in 1 teaspoon vanilla and beat until smooth.

THIRD Fill greased and lightly floured muffin tins only *half full*. Bake in a 400° oven. When cool, ice with Marie's Chocolate Icing (page 422).

NOTE These delicious cup cakes defy the adage that one's palate becomes jaded through the years. Marie's cup cakes, with her incomparable Chocolate Icing, taste as good to me today as they ever did to the hungry child returning home from the snowbound streets of a wintry New York.

CURRANT-JELLY SQUARES

[*Pre-heat oven to 400°*]

5 ounces butter
1 cup sugar
2 egg yolks
5 ounces chopped almonds
¼ teaspoon orange juice
¼ teaspoon lemon juice
Grated rind ½ orange

grated rind ½ lemon
1½ cups flour
1 teaspoon cinnamon
1 teaspoon ground cloves
currant jelly
powdered sugar

FIRST Cream 5 ounces butter with 1 cup sugar. Beat in 2 egg yolks, one at a time. Add 5 ounces chopped almonds, ¼ teaspoon orange juice, ¼ teaspoon lemon juice, and the grated rind of ½ orange and ½ lemon.

SECOND Sift 1½ cups flour. Measure and resift three times with 1 teaspoon cinnamon and 1 teaspoon ground cloves. Fold into batter.

THIRD Pat or roll out on a cookie sheet about ¼ inch thick. Bake in a 400° oven for about 13 minutes. Cut immediately while hot. (When it cools it crumbles.) Cut first into long strips, then into even squares. Trim the edges and cool.

FOURTH When cool, cover half the squares with currant jelly, then top with the other squares. Sprinkle with powdered sugar and serve.

FUDGE SQUARES

[*Pre-heat oven to 375°*]

¼ pound butter
1 cup sugar
1 egg
3 squares bitter chocolate

1 scant cup flour
½ teaspoon baking powder
½ cup shelled walnuts (optional)
powdered sugar

FIRST Mix ¼ pound melted butter with 1 cup sugar.

SECOND Beat in 1 egg and 3 squares bitter chocolate melted over boiling water.

THIRD Sift 1 scant cup flour. Measure and resift twice with ½ teaspoon baking powder. Add the flour to the chocolate mixture and blend well. Fold in ½ cup shelled broken walnuts if desired. This batter is rather stiff and will have to be smoothed into a square "fudge pan" with a knife. Bake in a 375° oven.

FOURTH While still hot, cut into squares and cool. Sprinkle with powdered sugar before serving.

LEMON-CURD TARTLETS

2 cups sugar
¼ pound butter
juice and grated rind of 4 lemons
6 egg yolks

3 teaspoons arrowroot powder
2 tablespoons cold water
2 tablespoons flour
Marie's Tart Crust (page 408)

MAKES 6 TO 8

FIRST Place 2 cups sugar, ¼ pound butter, and the juice and grated rind of 4 lemons in a pan on the fire. Stir until dissolved. Remove from fire.

SECOND Beat 6 egg yolks and add to sugar mixture, stirring until blended. Replace on fire and stir constantly until mixture coats the spoon. Add 3 teaspoons arrowroot powder stirred smooth with 1 tablespoon cold water, and 2 tablespoons flour stirred smooth with 1 tablespoon cold water. Stir until mixture thickens. Let boil until it *really* thickens. Then remove from fire, pour into a bowl, and cool to room temperature, at which time it is ready to fill the tarts. (Marie's Tart Crust page 408.)

NOTE The number of lemons used is purely optional. There are those who like it tart enough to set their teeth on edge! Whatever you decide, 3 is minimum.

LEMON TARTLETS WITH MERINGUE

1 cup sugar
¼ pound butter
2 tablespoons flour
juice 2 lemons
grated rind 3 lemons
3 egg yolks

1 egg white
1 cup hot water
Polish Tart Crust (page 409)
4 egg whites
4 tablespoons sugar

FIRST Combine 1 cup sugar, ¼ pound butter, 2 tablespoons flour, juice of 2 lemons, grated rind of 3 lemons, 3 egg yolks, 1 egg white, and 1 cup hot water in the top of a double boiler. Stir constantly over hot water until the mixture thickens. Bring to a boil and continue to stir until it is as thick and smooth as possible. Remove from fire and cool. It will thicken further as it cools.

[*Pre-heat oven to 325°*]

SECOND Fill baked tart shells (Polish Tart Crust—page 409) with the lemon mixture. Heap high with a meringue made by beating 4 egg whites until stiff and combining gradually with 4 tablespoons sugar. Bake until lightly browned in a 325° oven.

MACAROONS WITH ALMONDS

[*Pre-heat oven to 250°*]

½ pound almonds
½ pound powdered sugar

4 egg whites
few drops lemon juice

FIRST Grind ½ pound almonds with their skins left on. Combine with ½ pound powdered sugar.

SECOND Beat 4 egg whites until stiff. Add to the sugar and almonds, folding in gently. Add a few drops lemon juice. Continue to blend the mixture by stirring gently for several minutes.

THIRD Place paper sheets on cookie tins and space the batter on the sheets in even mounds. Bake until light gold in a 250° oven. Cool somewhat, then remove carefully from the paper sheets with a spatula.

MACAROONS WITH CORNFLAKES

[*Pre-heat oven to 350°*]

3 cups cornflakes
1 cup sugar
1 cup coarsely chopped walnuts

2 egg yolks
2 egg whites

FIRST Combine 3 cups cornflakes with 1 cup sugar, 1 cup coarsely chopped walnuts, and 2 beaten egg yolks.

SECOND Beat 2 egg whites until stiff. Fold into the mixture.

THIRD Drop the mixture, a tablespoon at a time (2 or 3 inches apart), onto a well-buttered baking-tin and bake in a 350° oven until light brown. Allow the macaroons to cool somewhat before attempting to remove from the cookie sheet.

WARNING If you try to remove them while they are hot, they will break.

MADELEINES, SYLVIA

[*Pre-heat oven to 425°*]

½ pound sweet butter
½ pound powdered sugar
5 egg yolks
grated rind 1 lemon

½ teaspoon vanilla
2 cups sifted flour
5 egg whites
powdered sugar

FIRST Beat ½ pound sweet butter with ½ pound powdered sugar until light. Add 5 egg yolks and continue to beat. Add grated rind of 1 lemon and ½ teaspoon vanilla. Beat together until very, very light and smooth.

SECOND Sift 2 cups flour. Measure and resift. Add to the batter, a little at a time, beating well after each addition.

THIRD Beat 5 whites to a firm froth. Fold into the mixture gently. Pour into buttered and floured Madeleine tins. Bake in a 425° oven until delicate gold in color. Cool on a cake rack, then sprinkle generously with sifted powdered sugar.

NOTE These delectable little Madeleines are a great delicacy of the French and are to be found in most French homes and in all Parisian tea rooms during the tea hour. Nostalgic thoughts return at the memory of those typical egg-shaped portions of French vanilla ice cream with Madeleines at Rumpelmayer, at the Hotel Meurice (with the orchestra playing softly back of the palms), of the Pre-Catalan in spring, of the bois de Boulogne tea houses filled with gay people listening to violins playing the sentimental music of the day—the day—the early years of the century before 1914! (Madeleine tins may be bought in the better hardware stores of the bigger cities.)

MARVELOUS BROWNIES, WENDY

[*Pre-heat oven to 350°*]

2½ ounces bitter chocolate
6 ounces butter
3 eggs
1 cup sugar
⅓ cup flour
½ teaspoon baking powder
¾ teaspoon salt
1½ teaspoons vanilla
1 heaping cup coarsely chopped pecans
confectioner's sugar

FIRST Melt 2½ ounces bitter chocolate and 6 ounces butter together in the top of a double boiler and blend thoroughly. Remove from stove and cool.

SECOND Beat 3 eggs and cream them with 1 cup sugar until very light and almost like mayonnaise. Add the cooled chocolate to the egg-mixture.

THIRD Sift ⅓ cup flour. Measure and resift twice with ½ teaspoon baking powder and ¾ teaspoon salt. Sift the flour mixture into the chocolate mixture gradually—very gradually—mixing thoroughly after each addition. Add 1½ teaspoons vanilla.

FOURTH Add 1 heaping cup coarsely chopped pecans. Mix well and pour the batter into a buttered and floured square metal pan.

Bake in a 350° oven for 35 minutes. Cool in the baking pan for 10 minutes, then cut into squares. Cool again, then dust with confectioner's sugar sifted through a fine sieve.

NOTE The lightest! The most delicate! The most delicious! (The secret is—thorough blending and a light touch!)

SCOTCH SHORTBREAD I
[Pre-heat oven to 450°]

1 egg yolk
2 tablespoons sugar
2 tablespoons milk
6 ounces butter

2 cups pastry flour
1 tablespoon baking powder
¼ teaspoon salt

FIRST Beat 1 egg yolk with 2 tablespoons sugar. Add 2 tablespoons milk.

SECOND Cut 6 ounces butter, with two knives or a pastry-blender, into 2 cups pastry flour until the mixture resembles fine meal. Add 1 tablespoon baking powder. Stir into the egg mixture and blend well. Add ¼ teaspoon salt and blend again. Handle lightly and roll out only once (½" thick). Cut into small rounds with a biscuit-cutter. Prick tops with a fork, then bake until very pale gold in a 450° oven.

NOTE This dough will be very stiff, which is as it should be. When rolled thin, it is also an excellent crust for meat pies, in which case omit the sugar and use 1 teaspoon salt instead.

SCOTCH SHORTBREAD II
[Pre-heat oven to 350°]

1 cup sugar
2¾ cups flour

½ pound butter
¼ teaspoon salt (optional)

FIRST Mix 1 cup sugar with 2¾ cups flour.

SECOND Beat ½ pound butter until soft. Cut into dry mixture, with two knives or pastry-blender, until the whole resembles a fine meal.

THIRD Handle lightly. Roll out ½″ and cut into rounds with a small biscuit-cutter. Score the top of each round with the prongs of a fork and bake to a very light gold in a 350° oven. (Approximately 15 minutes.)

NOTE The addition of ¼ teaspoon salt is optional.

SPICE SQUARES

[*Pre-heat oven to 350°*]

5 eggs
1 pound brown sugar
2 cups flour
1 teaspoon cinnamon
1 teaspoon cloves
1 cup chopped unblanched almonds
¼ pound finely chopped citron and orange peel
grated rind 1 lemon
juice 1 lemon
1 tablespoon brandy
Boiled Icing (page 421)
peeled almonds
colored decorettes

FIRST Beat 5 eggs. Add 1 pound brown sugar and beat until well combined

SECOND Sift 2 cups of flour. Measure and resift twice with 1 teaspoon cinnamon and 1 teaspoon cloves. Add the flour mixture to the egg mixture and blend well. Add 1 cup chopped almonds (skins on), ¼ pound finely chopped citron and orange peel, the grated rind of 1 lemon, the juice of 1 lemon, and 1 tablespoon brandy. Stir well until thoroughly blended.

THIRD Butter a large cookie tin (the type that has edges all around). Pour the batter onto the tin and smooth it out evenly. Bake in a 350° oven until brown.

FOURTH When cool, ice with Boiled Icing (page 421) and decorate with peeled almonds and colored decorettes in design. Cut into small squares or into "sticks" 1″ x 4″.

SPOON SPONGE BISCUITS
[Pre-heat oven to 350°]

3 egg yolks	1 tablespoon vanilla
¾ cup sugar	pinch of salt
1 cup flour	powdered sugar
2 egg whites	pecans *or* walnuts

FIRST Beat 3 egg yolks with ¾ cup sugar until light and creamy.

SECOND Sift 1 cup flour. Measure and sift again. Set aside. Beat 2 egg whites until stiff. Fold beaten whites into egg yolks alternately with the sifted flour. Handle the mixture lightly. Stir in 1 tablespoon vanilla and a tiny pinch of salt.

THIRD Place a well-buttered white sheet of paper on a cookie sheet and drop the batter onto the paper, using a teaspoon for each Sponge Biscuit. Give them plenty of room as they have a tendency to spread. When they are all spaced, sprinkle with powdered sugar and center each with a pecan or walnut half. Bake until light gold in a 350° oven.

VANILLA CRESCENTS *Marie's*
[Pre-heat oven to 325°]

7 ounces butter	3 ounces finely chopped almonds
½ cup granulated sugar	1 teaspoon vanilla
2½ cups pastry flour	vanilla powdered sugar

FIRST Cream 7 ounces butter with ½ cup granulated sugar until fluffy.

SECOND Sift 2½ cups pastry flour. Measure and resift. Add to butter and mix well.

THIRD Peel 3 ounces almonds and chop until they are almost as fine as tiny grains of meal. Add to the dough and hand-knead well. Add 1 teaspoon vanilla. Roll out and cut into strips about ½ inch wide and 1½ inches long. Hand-roll each into a tiny crescent and bake on a cookie tin covered with a floured paper in a 325° oven until the crescents are barely gold or sandy in appearance. Remove and sprinkle generously with vanilla powdered sugar. Cool.

NOTE Vanilla powdered sugar, or vanilla granulated sugar, is achieved (and was constantly used by the great chefs of Vienna) by taking a quart jar, filling it with either sugar, sinking a split vanilla bean in the center of the jar, and then fastening the top of the jar tightly. The sugar becomes permeated with the enchanting aroma of the vanilla bean and adds a subtle flavor to the outside of the pastry achieved in no other way.

These little Crescents will literally melt in your mouth. Only one earnest entreaty: have your almonds fine, fine, fine!

VIENNA KIPFEL

[*Pre-heat oven to 300°*]

5 ounces butter
⅓ cup sugar
2 ounces sweet almonds

1½ cups flour
1 teaspoon vanilla

FIRST Cream 5 ounces butter with ⅓ cup sugar.

SECOND Grind 2 ounces unblanched sweet almonds on finest knife in the grinder. Mix with the butter until well blended.

THIRD Sift 1½ cups flour. Measure and resift. Add gradually to the butter mixture. When well blended, stir in 1 teaspoon vanilla, then knead with the hands for a few minutes until smooth. Shape into tiny rolls about 1½ inches long. Shape each roll in turn into the shape of a crescent and place on an unbuttered cookie sheet. Bake in a 300° oven until sandy colored, but never brown.

NOTE These crumbly little crescents melt in your mouth. Be sure to keep them small. Space them carefully—they spread somewhat in the baking.

CREAM-CHEESE CRUST

1 package cream cheese (3 ounces)   pastry flour
3 ounces soft butter

FIRST   Blend 1 package cream cheese and 3 ounces soft butter until thoroughly combined.

SECOND   Add enough sifted pastry flour to permit the dough to be handled. Knead thoroughly by hand. Place in refrigerator overnight.

THIRD   If you leave the dough in the refrigerator overnight, you will have no trouble rolling it out. If you cannot spare the time, you may find it somewhat difficult to handle, in which case pat the dough by hand into the pie plate you are going to use.

NOTE   I recommend this dough for all pies and tarts with only one word of caution. When using it with juicy fruits or berries, shake ½ cup sifted bread crumbs combined with ¼ cup granulated sugar over the dough before the berries are placed in the plate. The fine crumbs will absorb the juices that would otherwise make a soggy mess of the under crust.

MARIE'S TART CRUST

½ pound butter   3 cups flour
½ cup granulated sugar   ice water

FIRST   Cream ½ pound butter with ½ cup granulated sugar until light and fluffy.

SECOND   Sift 3 cups flour. Measure and resift twice, the second time into the butter.

THIRD   Add just enough ice water to make a smooth paste. Chill in refrigerator overnight.

POLISH TART CRUST

¼ pound butter salt
1 cup flour 1 egg
sugar

FIRST Work ¼ pound butter into 1 cup flour, cutting it in with two knives or with a pastry-blender (preferred) until the whole resembles a fine meal.

SECOND Sprinkle in sugar and salt to taste, and beat in 1 egg. Place in the refrigerator, overnight if possible—at least for an hour or two.

NOTE The secret of Mrs. Artur Rubinstein's incomparable tarts! This makes the flaky and delicious crusts she uses for her tarts, pies, and fruit strips at her inimitable parties, at family anniversaries, and at midnight buffets after Mr. Rubinstein's concerts!

PUFF PASTE

[Particularly Puff-Paste Patty Shells]

3 cups pastry flour juice 1 lemon
1 heaping tablespoon butter ½ pound butter
scant ¾ cup ice water

FIRST Sift 3 cups pastry flour into a mixing-bowl. Work in 1 heaping tablespoon butter with a pastry-blender or with two knives.

SECOND Make a well in the center of the flour and pour in a scant ¾ cup of ice water and the juice of 1 lemon. Work together, gradually incorporating the flour until a smooth paste is achieved. Knead until smooth and let stand five minutes.

THIRD Roll into a square about ½ inch thick. Have ½ pound of butter firm enough to allow you to roll it out approximately the same size as the paste. Place the butter on top of the paste and fold the four sides toward the center to completely envelop the butter.

FOURTH Roll out gently in one direction only and fold into three layers. Set in the refrigerator for 15 minutes. Repeat the rolling and folding process 4 more times, allowing a 15-minute wait between each rolling. After final rolling, chill in refrigerator overnight.

[*Pre-heat oven to 475°*]

FIFTH Next morning roll the paste ¼ inch thick. Cut out rounds with a ¾-inch biscuit-cutter. Have another, slightly smaller, cutter on hand. Use this second cutter to cut out the center of *half* the rounds.

SIXTH Moisten the edges of the whole rounds with a little cold water. Place the rings on these and press together lightly and brush with cold water. Bake in a 475° oven for 25 minutes. When sufficiently baked, remove from oven and cool on cake racks. When ready to serve, carefully remove the tops with a sharp knife and scrape the insides hollow, using extreme caution as the finished product should be very brittle. Warm the patties before filling. Fill and serve.

Clarified and Detailed Schedule for Puff Paste

1. Combine flour, butter, ice water, and lemon juice.
2. Roll out paste ½ inch thick into shape of square.
3. Roll out butter approximately same shape. Place on paste.
4. Fold 4 sides toward the center to envelop the butter.
5. Roll out paste, in one direction only.
6. Fold into 3 layers. Set in refrigerator for 15 minutes.
7. Roll out, fold into 3 layers, set in refrigerator for 15 minutes.
8. Roll out, fold into 3 layers, set in refrigerator for 15 minutes.
9. Roll out, fold into 3 layers, set in refrigerator for 15 minutes.
10. Roll out, fold into 3 layers, set in refrigerator overnight.
11. Roll out paste ¼ inch thick. Cut out rounds ¾ inch in diameter.
12. Cut out center of *half* the rounds with smaller cutter.
13. Arrange circles on whole rounds.
14. Bake as directed.
15. Prepare for filling as directed.

NOTE Puff Paste is the most elegant of all pastry doughs. Nothing can compare to it, and nothing can equal its feathery deliciousness!

Even in the best restaurants it is not always as delicate as it should be. It is not complicated to make—it is not even difficult. It requires only time and patience. If you avail yourself of the careful directions and the detailed schedule, you will find yourself in a position to emulate the kitchen kings. Incidentally, my Aunt Ida used to run an excellent kitchen. I still remember her saying that when she interviewed a new cook she never beat about the bush. Her first question (and perhaps her only) was invariably: "Can you make puff paste?" If the cook replied yes (with head held high), she had made the grade and, like as not, stayed for years rolling butter back and forth on my aunt's pastry board. At that, Aunt Ida probably had a marble slab for this exact purpose, and if she did, it only goes to show she gave her "puff paste" cook every possible break! Incidentally, do not think for a moment that I do not know that you can *buy* patty shells, but not *these* patty shells! Use this recipe too, for wonderful, marvelous tarts—strawberry, apricot, apple, plum— or for tiny shells filled with any number of things as appetizers.

SWEDISH TART CRUST

¼ pound butter　　　　　　　1 cup flour
1 tablespoon sugar

FIRST　Cream ¼ pound butter with 1 tablespoon sugar until smooth and fluffy.

SECOND　Sift 1 cup flour. Measure and resift into the butter mixture, working it in with your hands. Do this quickly and with a sure hand.

THIRD　Do not try to roll out this dough. Pat it into the pie plate with your hand and flute the edge for a trim. Place the plate in the refrigerator for at least a half an hour.

[*Pre-heat oven to 450°*]

FOURTH　Bake in a very hot oven (450°) to set it quickly. Once it has set, the heat may be reduced somewhat. At all events, watch it carefully so that it does not scorch.

WARNING　If using sugared strawberries or other juicy berries, do not fill until just before serving.

APPLE GRAHAM-CRACKER PIE WENDY

[Pre-heat oven to 300°]

6 large cooking-apples
1½ cups sugar
¼ cup water
1 tablespoon lemon juice
24 graham crackers

2 tablespoons sugar
¼ pound butter
1 cup heavy cream
¼ cup sugar
1 tablespoon vanilla

FIRST Cut 6 large cooking-apples into pieces, but not too small. Boil slowly with 1½ cups sugar and ¼ cup water over a low flame until the apples are soft. When soft, sprinkle with 1 tablespoon lemon juice.

SECOND Grind 24 graham crackers into crumbs. Mix with 2 tablespoons sugar and ¼ pound melted butter. Line the bottom and sides of a glass pie plate with this crumb mixture, retaining enough crumbs to scatter over the top.

THIRD Fill the cracker crust with the cooked apples and sprinkle lightly with the remaining crumbs. Bake in a 300° oven for 1 hour. Cool. Just before serving, cover the top of the pie with 1 cup of heavy cream, beaten until stiff, sweetened with ¼ cup sugar, and flavored with 1 tablespoon vanilla.

NOTE If preferred, the whipped cream may be served in a separate bowl. For those who prefer things very cold, the pie may be set in the refrigerator for some time before serving. Personally I find that room temperature is more satisfactory and much more complimentary to the flavor of the apples.

APPLE TART

[Pre-heat oven to 400°]

THE CRUST

6 ounces butter
1 egg
2 egg yolks

¼ cup sugar
1 tablespoon water
2½ cups flour

FIRST Beat together 6 ounces butter, 1 egg, 2 egg yolks, ¼ cup sugar, and 1 tablespoon water.

SECOND Sift 2½ cups of flour. Measure and resift into the mixture. Work until smooth. Roll out and line bottom and sides of a shallow baking-pan 12" x 18". Bake in a 400° oven until set but not browned. Remove from oven.

THE FILLING

2 ounces sweet almonds	1 cup sugar
2 tablespoons sour cream	2 cups sour cream
grated bread crumbs	4 egg yolks
7 large green apples	¼ cup sugar
grated rind and juice 1 lemon	cinnamon-sugar mixture
¼ cup currants *or* ½ cup raisins	

Grate 2 ounces sweet almonds and mix with 2 tablespoons sour cream. Spread on top of the pastry, then sprinkle fairly generously with grated bread crumbs.

SECOND Peel 7 large green apples and cut into thin slices. Mix the slices in a bowl with the grated rind and juice 1 lemon, ¼ cup currants (or ½ cup raisins) and 1 cup of sugar. Arrange the apple slices and the sugar mixture in even rows the length of the pan on top of the bread crumbs. Spread the apples evenly with 2 cups sour cream beaten very thoroughly with 4 egg yolks and ¼ cup sugar. Return to the oven and finish baking until the apples are soft. When baked, sprinkle generously with a mixture of cinnamon and sugar. Serve cold or slightly warm as preferred.

NOTE 1. When serving, bring the tin to the table and cut into even squares. This makes approximately 12 servings. This is equally delicious with fresh halved apricots or red plums. When plums are used, a ¼ cup more sugar mixed with the fruit is advisable.
2. If apples are slow in cooking, cover the pan.

APRICOT-FLUFF PIE

[*Pre-heat oven to 375°*]

1 baked 8-inch pie shell (page 408)
½ cup apricot pulp
½ cup sugar
⅛ teaspoon salt
3 egg yolks

1½ teaspoons lemon juice
3 egg whites
¼ cup powdered sugar
1 cup heavy cream
¼ cup sugar
1 teaspoon vanilla

FIRST Put enough apricots, fresh, canned, or dried, (in the case of the latter, soaked and cooked with sugar) through a coarse sieve to make ½ cup apricot pulp. Add ½ cup sugar and ⅛ teaspoon salt. Then add 3 slightly beaten egg yolks. Put in top of double boiler and cook until thick. Remove from fire and add 1½ teaspoons lemon juice.

SECOND Beat 3 egg whites until stiff. Add ¼ cup powdered sugar. Gently fold into apricot mixture. Pour into a 8-inch baked pie shell and bake for 15 minutes in a 375° oven. Cool.

THIRD When cool, cover top of pie with 1 cup of heavy cream, beaten until stiff, sweetened with ¼ cup sugar and flavored with 1 teaspoon vanilla.

CHERRY TART

[*Pre-heat oven to 375°*]

½ pound butter
1 cup sugar
6 eggs
grated peel 1 lemon
2 cups pastry flour
1 cup potato flour
2 teaspoons baking powder
3 tablespoons dry bread crumbs

2 large cans drained black Bing cherries
3 tablespoons dry bread crumbs
powdered sugar
1 cup heavy cream (optional)
¼ cup sugar (optional)
1 teaspoon vanilla (optional)

FIRST Cream ½ pound butter with 1 cup sugar until light and fluffy.

SECOND Beat 6 eggs until light in color. Add to the butter mixture. Beat well together and add the grated peel 1 lemon.

THIRD Sift 2 cups pastry flour and measure. Sift 1 cup potato flour and measure. Resift both flours together with 2 teaspoons baking powder and add to the egg mixture.

FOURTH Butter a 10-inch spring form and pour in *half* the batter. Cover the batter with 3 tablespoons of dry bread crumbs. Drain the contents of 2 large cans of pitted black Bing cherries. Place these *well-drained* cherries on the crumbs, sprinkle the top of the cherries with 3 more tablespoons of dry bread crumbs, and cover them with the *second half* of the batter.

FIFTH Place in a 375° oven and bake for 1 hour. Remove from spring form and sprinkle with sifted powdered sugar. Serve plain, or with 1 cup heavy cream beaten until stiff, sweetened with ¼ cup sugar, and flavored with 1 teaspoon vanilla.

NOTES 1. Pitted fresh cherries may be used instead of the canned, but in that case they must be generously sprinkled with sugar before using and then drained if any juice collects. Blueberries may be treated in the same way—or fresh plums, even more generously sprinkled with sugar.

2. The memories of the years of my childhood are punctuated by my mother's visits to a watering-spa in central Europe, where she rested in the "Sprudel baths." On our way from Paris, the train passed through a small town where my father's Aunt Rosa used to be found standing on the station platform, smiling a welcome, her famous Cherry Tart in her hand. The train had no sooner pulled out of the station than the Cherry Tart was in a fair state of being completely demolished!

CHESS PIE

[*Pre-heat oven to 350°*]

1 unbaked pastry shell
2 tablespoons butter
1 cup maple sugar *or* brown sugar
2 eggs
1 tablespoon flour
¼ teaspoon salt

1 cup maple syrup
1½ cups chopped pecans
1 cup heavy cream
¼ cup sugar
1 tablespoon vanilla

FIRST Cream 2 tablespoons butter with 1 cup maple sugar *or* brown sugar. Add 2 well-beaten eggs.

SECOND Stir in 1 tablespoon flour, ¼ teaspoon salt, and 1 cup maple syrup. Beat until smooth.

THIRD Fold 1½ cups chopped pecans into mixture and mix well. Pour into unbaked pie shell and bake for 35 minutes in a 350° oven. You can be sure the pie is done when the filling is firm except for a soft spot in the center. The pie may be served either hot or cold. Either way, serve with 1 cup heavy cream beaten stiff, sweetened with ¼ cup sugar, and flavored with 1 tablespoon vanilla.

CITRUS-GROVE PIE

8-inch baked pie shell
3 egg yolks
6 tablespoons sugar
¼ teaspoon salt
3 tablespoons unstrained orange juice
1 tablespoon lemon juice

1 teaspoon grated orange rind
juice 1 lemon, unstrained
juice ½ orange, unstrained
3 tablespoons orange Jello
3 egg whites
¼ teaspoon cream of tartar
6 tablespoons sugar

FIRST Place the following ingredients in the top of a double boiler and cook for about 5 minutes, or until the mixture coats the spoon and thickens considerably: 3 egg yolks, 6 tablespoons sugar, ¼ teaspoon salt, 3 tablespoons unstrained orange juice, 1 tablespoon lemon juice, and 1 teaspoon grated orange rind.

SECOND When the mixture is well thickened, heat the unstrained juice of 1 lemon and the unstrained juice of ½ an orange. Dissolve 3 tablespoons orange Jello in the hot juices and stir into the egg-yolk mixture. Stir until well combined. Cool.

THIRD Beat 3 egg whites, ¼ teaspoon cream of tartar, and 6 tablespoons sugar until stiff. Carefully fold this meringue into the cooled orange mixture and continue to fold until well blended. Pile into an 8-inch baked pie shell. Place in the refrigerator and chill for at least 2 hours before serving.

NOTE If a stronger lemon flavor is preferred instead of orange, direction number two may be changed as follows: Heat the juice of 1 lemon and the juice of ½ an orange. Dissolve 3 tablespoons of lemon Jello in the hot juices, etc. Tangerine juice in season makes a very interesting novelty substituting for orange juice.

LEMON CHIFFON PIE

9-inch baked pie shell (Polish Tart Crust—page 409)
10 egg yolks
1 cup sugar
1 cup lemon juice
¼ teaspoon salt
2 envelopes gelatin

½ cup cold water
1 tablespoon grated lemon rind
10 egg whites
1 cup sugar
1 cup heavy cream
¼ cup sugar
1 teaspoon vanilla

FIRST Beat 10 yolks until light. Add 1 cup sugar and beat until smooth and very light in color. Add 1 cup lemon juice and ¼ teaspoon salt, mixing thoroughly until well blended.

SECOND Place in the top of a double boiler and stir constantly until it thickens and is of custard consistency.

THIRD Soak 2 envelopes gelatin in ½ cup cold water. Stir into the hot custard until the gelatin is dissolved. Stir very thoroughly. Add 1 tablespoon grated lemon rind. Remove from fire and cool.

FOURTH When mixture begins to thicken, beat 10 egg whites until stiff, gradually adding 1 cup sugar, beating after each addition. Fold egg whites into the lemon mixture carefully and thoroughly until completely blended. Heap into a 9-inch baked pie shell (Polish Tart Crust—page 409) and place in refrigerator. Just before serving, spread the top with 1 cup heavy cream beaten until stiff, sweetened with ¼ cup sugar and flavored with 1 teaspoon vanilla.

LEMON FLUFF PIE

[*Pre-heat oven to 300°*]

1 large baked pie shell (Swedish Tart Crust—page 411)
1 cup sugar

8 egg yolks
juice and grated rind 2 lemons
8 egg whites

FIRST Beat 1 cup sugar and 8 egg yolks together until light in color and smooth as satin.

SECOND Add the juice and grated rind 2 lemons. Place in the top of a double boiler and stir constantly until it thickens considerably, approximately 12 to 15 minutes. Cool.

THIRD Beat 8 egg whites until stiff but not dry. Gently fold into the lemon mixture until well blended. Pile into a large baked shell of Swedish Tart Crust (page 411). Bake until nicely browned in a 300° oven. Excellent served while still warm.

PLUM STRIP
[*A nostalgic memory of a hotel in Paris*]

triple any preferred pie-crust recipe
3 pounds red and yellow plums
1 cup sugar
1 cup finely sifted bread crumbs
¼ cup sugar
4 shakes cinnamon
powdered sugar
Crème D'lsigny (page 360)

FIRST Triple any preferred pie-crust recipe. Place in refrigerator for at least an hour.

SECOND Cut 3 pounds red and yellow plums into quarters. Cover with 1 cup sugar and let stand.

[*Pre-heat oven to 375°*]

THIRD Take a baking tin 12" x 18" with an approximate ½-inch edge. Cover bottom and sides with the pie dough, fitting it in with your hands. Flute the sides of the dough to make a trim. Reserve some of the pie dough for a lattice of strips to be placed on top of the fruit.

FOURTH Mix 1 cup finely sifted bread crumbs with ¼ cup sugar and 4 shakes cinnamon. Sprinkle this evenly and thickly on top of the dough. Press the quartered plums into the dough in even straight up-and-down lines the whole length of the pan. Cover the strip with a criss-cross of twisted or straight strips of pastry dough.

FIFTH Place all the juice and sugar that has gathered in the bottom of the bowl in which the plums have been soaking in a small pot and cook over a slow fire. Drip this glaze between the lined pastry strips. Place the plum strip in a 375° oven and bake for about ½ hour. Watch carefully, and when it is pale gold, turn the oven to broil and brown for 10 minutes. Remove, cool, and sprinkle with sifted powdered sugar. Serve with Crème D'lsigny (page 360).

NOTE An excellent substitute sauce is the use of 1 package cream cheese beaten together with 4 tablespoons plum jam and ½ cup cream. Use a rotary beater, and when well blended, add ¼ cup sugar and place the sauce in the serving-bowl in the refrigerator.

This recipe may be used with equal success with apricots, peaches, or apples instead of the plums.

PRUNE TART

[*Pre-heat oven to 350°*]

1 double pie crust
2 pounds large cooked prunes
½ cup sugar
1 tablespoon cinnamon
juice and grated rind 1 lemon
1 tablespoon flour

2 ounces butter
few drops milk
1 cup heavy cream (optional)
¼ cup sugar (optional)
1 tablespoon vanilla (optional)

FIRST Prepare enough pie crust to make top and bottom. Place in refrigerator until ready to use.

SECOND Cut 2 pounds large cooked prunes into quarters. Arrange them evenly on top of the bottom pie crust. Sprinkle with ½ cup sugar, 1 tablespoon cinnamon, the juice and grated rind 1 lemon, and 1 tablespoon flour. Dot with 2 ounces of butter.

THIRD Place the second half of the crust on the floured pastry board and cut into strips. Interlace the strips on top of the pie plate. Press them into the rim of the undercrust and brush the "lacings" with a few drops of milk. Set in a 350° oven until crust is light golden brown.

NOTE This may be made ahead of time but is best if slightly warmed just before serving. Whipped cream, sweetened with ¼ cup sugar and flavored with 1 tablespoon vanilla, may be used in a side dish to serve with the tart, but is not required.

PUMPKIN PIE, RUTH

[*Pre-heat oven to 425°*]

1 unbaked 9-inch pie shell	2 cups strained pumpkin
1 cup sugar	1½ tablespoons molasses
1 tablespoon flour	1½ tablespoons melted butter
½ teaspoon salt	3 eggs
1 teaspoon ginger	1¾ cups milk
¾ teaspoon cinnamon	2 tablespoons brandy (optional)
⅛ teaspoon nutmeg	

FIRST Mix 1 cup sugar, 1 tablespoon flour, ½ teaspoon salt, 1 teaspoon ginger, ¾ teaspoon cinnamon, and ⅛ teaspoon nutmeg in a large mixing-bowl.

SECOND Add 2 cups strained pumpkin, 1½ tablespoons molasses, 1½ tablespoons melted butter and blend well.

THIRD Slightly beat 3 eggs. Add 1¾ cups milk to the eggs, pour into pumpkin mixture, and mix well. Pour the whole into an unbaked 9-inch pie shell and bake in a 425° oven for 40 minutes or until an inserted knife comes out clean.

NOTE If in a festive mood add 2 tablespoons brandy to the milk. This bakes a far better than usual pumpkin pie. Even without this added touch, it is the best pumpkin pie I have ever enjoyed. I thought at first it might have been the atmosphere of Ruth's garden in which it was eaten that made it seem so superior, but prepared by me in my own unglamorous kitchen, it made me realize that Ruth's pumpkin pie does not need a setting to be appreciated for what it is!

Icings and Frostings

BLACK CHOCOLATE CUP CAKE ICING

12 cup cakes
5 squares bitter cooking-chocolate
1 tablespoon water

pinch salt
1 can sweetened condensed milk

FIRST Melt 5 squares of bitter cooking-chocolate in the top of a double boiler. Smooth with 1 tablespoon of water and a pinch of salt.

SECOND Pour in 1 can sweetened condensed milk and stir until smooth.

THIRD Cook in the top of a double boiler for 7 or 8 minutes, stirring occasionally. Cool.

TO USE

FOURTH Split 12 cup cakes. Ice them inside and on the tops and sides. Spread thickly. For the icing to be of the right consistency it should spread like soft butter.

BOILED ICING

1 cup sugar
¼ cup boiling water
¼ teaspoon cream of tartar

1 egg white
1 teaspoon vanilla

FIRST Bring 1 cup of sugar to a boil with ¼ cup of boiling water and ¼ teaspoon cream of tartar. Boil for 6 minutes. Do not stir the sugar while it is being boiled.

SECOND Beat the white of 1 egg until stiff. Remove the sugar syrup from the stove. Wipe the sides and edges of the pan with a damp cloth to remove all granular bits. Pour the syrup into the egg white, beating constantly and pouring the sugar into the egg white in a fine, thin stream.

THIRD After the last of the syrup has been added, beat uninterruptedly for five minutes. Flavor with 1 teaspoon of vanilla and beat again.

BUTTER-CREAM ICING

2 cups powdered sugar
3 tablespoons soft butter
3 tablespoons cream

1 tablespoon vanilla *or* 1 tablespoon rum flavoring

FIRST Make a smooth icing by combining 2 cups of powdered sugar with 3 tablespoons of soft butter and 3 tablespoons cream. Work until of a spreading consistency.

SECOND Beat in 1 tablespoon vanilla or 1 tablespoon rum flavoring.

CHOCOLATE FILLING *Marie's*

4 ounces cooking-chocolate
½ cup sugar
4 tablespoons hot water
¾ cup boiling water

½ cup light cream
½ cup sugar
1 teaspoon vanilla
1 egg white

FIRST Scrape 4 ounces of cooking-chocolate and combine with ½ cup of sugar. Place in a small saucepan and stir in 4 tablespoons of hot water. Stir until the chocolate and the sugar dissolve and until the mixture is smooth and shiny.

SECOND Add ¾ cup of boiling water, ½ cup of light cream, and ½ cup of sugar. Stir until the sugar dissolves. Continue to stir over fire until the mixture comes to a boil.

THIRD When the mixture boils add 1 teaspoon of vanilla and the beaten white of 1 egg. Cook until it thickens. Pour into a small bowl and cool until ready to spread between the layers of a cake.

CHOCOLATE ICING *Marie's*

4 squares sweet chocolate
¼ cup water
½ cup sugar (scant)

3 tablespoons water
1 heaping teaspoon butter
2 tablespoons heavy cream

FIRST Place 4 squares of sweet chocolate in a pan with ¼ cup water. Melt slowly over a low flame.

SECOND Make a syrup of a scant ½ cup of sugar and 3 tablespoons water. Add the chocolate and stir until it boils. Add 1 heaping teaspoon butter and 2 tablespoons of heavy cream. Cook a little longer. Stir when it begins to thicken, then remove from fire. As soon as it cools, use as icing.

WARNING Once your cake or pastry is iced, never place it in the refrigerator as this icing has an unusually high glaze, which it loses when chilled.

CRUMBLY, NOT CREAMY, FUDGE

2 cups sugar
¾ cup light cream
salt
4 squares bitter baking-chocolate
2 tablespoons light corn syrup (see note)
1 ounce butter
1 tablespoon vanilla

FIRST Stir 2 cups of sugar with ¾ cup of light cream, a pinch of salt, 4 squares of bitter cooking-chocolate, and 2 tablespoons light corn syrup (see note). Continue to stir together over fire until the mixture starts to boil. Once it has started to boil, turn the flame down to very low to prevent scorching yet not to stop the boiling.

SECOND Boil until it reaches the hard boil stage. A candy thermometer makes this very simple as it indicates when that particular stage has been reached. However, failing this, after the mixture has been boiling for about thirty minutes, test by dropping a few drops off a spoon into a cup of very cold water. When the fudge solidifies it is ready to remove from the flame. If it becomes brittle in the water, then it has been cooked too long and a little cream must be added to save it. Try not to let this happen.

THIRD Beat in the pot away from the stove, beating in 1 ounce of butter until the texture of the whole is as smooth as velvet. Pour in 1 tablespoon vanilla and beat again. Pour quickly into a square pan (approximately 8″ square) that is well greased with butter. Place the pan near an open window or in a cool place until it hardens. Under no circumstances place the pan in the refrigerator, as this ruins the glaze.

FOURTH Cut the fudge into squares about one inch square as soon as it has solidified, but do not remove from the pan until the fudge is solid, otherwise it is apt to crumble. With a spatula remove to a serving-plate or to a small bowl. Never invert the pan, as this is too likely to break the pieces. Remember this is a crumbly fudge, not creamy.

NOTE The recipe above has been my favorite for years, ever since the chafing-dish days of my high-school years. My daughter believes her fudge far superior to my old version. Unobserved, she edited this recipe by scribbling across the bottom of the recipe the following observation: "The secret of this has been left out here! Light corn syrup! 2 tablespoons! Love, Wendy."

EMPEROR'S FROSTING
[*for fillings and for cakes*]

1 recipe for Seven-Minute Frosting (page 426)
1 cup heavy cream
1 tablespoon vanilla
½ cup slivered almonds

FIRST Prepare 1 recipe for Seven-Minute Frosting (page 426). Cool.

SECOND Beat 1 cup of heavy cream. Flavor with 1 tablespoon vanilla and continue to beat until quite stiff. Fold the cream into cooled Seven-Minute Frosting and blend thoroughly.

THIRD Spread this superb frosting between the layers of any favorite cake, over the top, and down on the sides. Cover the top and sides of the cake with ½ cup slivered almonds toasted until a very light brown.

NOTE This recipe makes a very delicious and rather elaborate frosting and turns an ordinary cake recipe into an extremely glamorous dessert. *If* there is any left over, the cake must be kept in the refrigerator, *not* in the cake box in the kitchen.

GLAZED NUTS AND FRUITS

[grapes, nuts, orange segments, cherries, etc.]

2 cups sugar
2 tablespoons vinegar
½ teaspoon vanilla

½ cup water
nuts or fruits (see above)

FIRST Boil 2 cups sugar with 2 tablespoons vinegar, ½ teaspoon vanilla, and ½ cup water. Place a candy thermometer in the syrup. When the thermometer indicates 300°, continue to boil without stirring.

SECOND Take a damp cloth and wipe the edges of the pot to remove all the grainy bits of sugar.

THIRD With a fork and a steady hand, dip the nuts or fruits into the syrup. Drop them lightly on a buttered pan (a marble slab is better) and leave them until they harden.

NOTE For the sake of convenience a pan is suggested on which to set the glazed fruits or nuts, but really a marble slab is much the best. Certain success is best assured if your kitchen is cool and the air clear without any steam in the room. A cool day is the best kind of a day in which to operate. These glazed fruits make an ideal and very elegant decoration for cakes.

OLD-TIME DECORATOR'S ICING

1 teaspoon lemon juice
2 tablespoons rum *or* white wine
few drops any preferred food
  coloring

¾ pound powdered sugar
4 to 6 tablespoons heavy cream

FIRST Mix 1 teaspoon of lemon juice, 2 tablespoons of rum or white wine, and a few drops of any preferred food coloring with

¾ pound of powdered sugar. Work until a moist mass has formed, adding 4 to 6 tablespoons heavy cream.

SECOND Place the icing in a decorating-bag, and form designs of your own choosing on top of a cake.

POWDERED-SUGAR ICING

1 egg white	1 teaspoon vanilla
2 tablespoons water	additional powdered sugar
½ cup powdered sugar	(optional)

FIRST Place 1 egg white, 2 tablespoons of water, and ½ cup of powdered sugar in a bowl. Beat together until smooth.

SECOND Flavor with 1 teaspoon of vanilla. If icing is too thin, add more powdered sugar and beat again until smooth.

NOTE This icing is perfect for use over coffee cakes and very plain tea cakes. It will spread well, but do not expect it to hold its shape.

SEVEN-MINUTE FROSTING

2 egg whites	½ teaspoon cream of tartar
¾ cup granulated sugar	pinch of salt
2½ tablespoons cold water	1 teaspoon vanilla extract

FIRST Place 2 egg whites, ¾ cup granulated sugar, 2½ tablespoons cold water, ½ teaspoon cream of tartar, and a pinch of salt in the top of a double boiler. Beat with a beater (preferably rotary) until well blended.

SECOND Place over hard-boiling water and beat continuously for seven minutes. The mixture should stand up in peaks and must be removed from the fire and cooled.

THIRD When sufficiently cool to use as a frosting, add 1 teaspoon vanilla. Spread on top of the cake with a narrow spatula or a broad-bladed knife.

NOTE This is a standard recipe. There are many delightful variations. Melted chocolate, crushed strawberries, or shredded coconut may be added. It may also be used for a filling between the layers of a cake as well as for frosting on top.

THIN ICING

1 egg white
1 cup granulated sugar

½ cup water
1 tablespoon rum, brandy, *or* lemon juice

FIRST Beat 1 egg white very stiff.

SECOND Boil 1 cup granulated sugar and ½ cup water until it spins a thread (about 20 minutes). Add very slowly to the beaten egg white, continuing to beat without interruption.

THIRD Add 1 tablespoon rum, brandy, or lemon juice as preferred. Continue to beat until smooth and slightly cooled. Smooth very thinly and very evenly on top of cakes and coffee cakes that call for thin icing.

Chapter XIV: *Strawberries*

Doubtless God could have made a better berry,

but doubtless God never did

Ascribed to WILLIAM BUTLET or BOTELEB in

IZAAK WALTON: *The Compleat Angler*

DESSERT AND CREAM RECIPES

Rhubarb Ring with Strawberries
Strawberry Baked Alaska
Strawberry Cream with Kirsch
Strawberries Curaçao
Strawberry Divine
Strawberry Ice Box Cake
Strawberry Mousse
Strawberries over Mock Cheesecake
Strawberry Parfait
Strawberry Pink Rice Pudding
Strawberries Romanoff
Strawberry Torte
Strawberries with Sherbert
Winter Strawberry Ice Cream
Glazed Strawberry Pie

PIES

Strawberry Chiffon Pie
Strawberry Pie with Wine
Winter Strawberry Pie

TARTS AND PASTRIES

Coconut Strawberry Cream Tarts
Parisian Strawberry Tarts
Strawberry Preserve Turnovers
Strawberry Tartlets
Strawberry Tarts without Filling

SAUCES AND PRESERVES

Strawberry Preserves
Strawberry Sauce for Ice Cream
Strawberry Sauce for Winter Use

RHUBARB RING WITH STRAWBERRIES

3 cups pink spring rhubarb
2 cups sugar
1 cup boiling water
2 envelopes gelatin
½ cup cold water
2 cups strawberries
¼ cup powdered sugar
Vanilla Sauce II with Rum (page 363)

SERVES 8

FIRST Cut 3 cups of pink spring rhubarb into 1-inch pieces—*do not peel*. It is the peelings that give the finished sauce its lovely color.

SECOND Place in a saucepan and cover with 2 cups sugar and 1 cup boiling water. Bring to a gentle boil and simmer until tender.

THIRD Soak 2 envelopes gelatin in ½ cup cold water for 5 minutes. Add to hot rhubarb and stir until the gelatin is dissolved. Pour the cooked sauce into a large-sized ring mold. Cool to room temperature and set in refrigerator.

FOURTH When ready to serve, unmold onto a round serving-platter. Fill the center with 2 cups hulled, washed, and drained strawberries. Cover the berries with ¼ cup powdered sugar and serve the ring with Vanilla Sauce II with Rum (page 363) or, if preferred, with 1 cup of whipped cream sweetened with ¼ cup sugar and flavored with 1 tablespoon vanilla extract.

NOTE If preferred, this ring may be served with whipped cream, as described above, heaped in the center of the ring and with a bowl of Strawberry Sauce (page 450) served as an accompaniment.

STRAWBERRY BAKED ALASKA

[*Pre-heat oven to 450°*]

1 Sponge Cake (page 389)
2 cups strawberries
½ cup sugar
6 egg whites
1 cup sugar
2 quarts strawberry ice cream
Strawberry Sauce (page 450)

SERVES 8

FIRST Place 1 Sponge Cake (page 389) baked oval or square, about two inches high, on a serving-platter.

SECOND Slice 2 cups of strawberries. Add ½ cup sugar and turn them several times in the bowl until thoroughly coated with the sugar. Spread them evenly on top of the sponge-cake platform.

THIRD Beat 6 egg whites until stiff. Add 1 cup of sugar, a little at a time, until the meringue is stiff and firm enough to hold its shape. Set aside for a moment.

FOURTH Heap 2 quarts strawberry ice cream on top of the sponge-cake platform. Then quickly mask with the meringue, covering both ice cream and sponge cake completely. Pop into a 450° oven briefly to allow the egg whites to brown very lightly. Watch this process carefully. It will take only a few minutes, and the ice cream will *not* melt if the oven has been properly pre-heated so that the Alaska need stay in the heat only very briefly. Serve immediately with a bowl of Strawberry Sauce (page 450).

NOTE This is one of the more festive and elaborate desserts, served with great pride and some important gestures, in the finest hotels and on some of the more luxurious ocean liners. If you will read the directions carefully, you will see that there is a great deal of unnecessary fuss made about assembling this dessert. Once your Sponge Platform is baked, you'll just sail along! Needless to say, this may be used in any other flavor combination—sliced peaches with peach ice cream and peach sauce, etc.

STRAWBERRY CREAM WITH KIRSCH

2 tablespoons gelatin
6 cups strawberries
1 cup sugar
2 tablespoons lemon juice
2 cups heavy cream

¼ cup kirsch
1 cup heavy cream
¼ cup sugar
1 tablespoon vanilla
Strawberry Sauce (page 450)

SERVES 8

FIRST Soak 2 tablespoons gelatin in ½ cup cold water for 5 minutes. Dissolve over hot water.

SECOND Wash, hull, and dry 6 cups of strawberries. Set aside one cup of the largest berries, to be used later as a decoration. Mash the rest of the strawberries and measure out 2 cups of juice and pulp. Add 1 cup of sugar and 2 tablespoons lemon juice. Set over a moderate flame and stir continually until thick and smooth. Remove from fire and stir in gelatin. Cool.

THIRD When the strawberry mixture begins to thicken, whip 2 cups of heavy cream until thick. Fold gently into the strawberry mixture, until completely blended. Stir in ¼ cup kirsch. Set in a cold, rinsed mold and place in refrigerator until set (from 4 to 6 hours).

FOURTH When ready to serve, unmold and decorate with 1 cup of heavy cream beaten until stiff, sweetened with ¼ cup sugar, and flavored with 1 tablespoon vanilla. Set one large sugared strawberry on top of each mound of whipped cream. Serve with an accompanying bowl of Strawberry Sauce (page 450).

NOTE Why not try this with raspberries, peaches, or fresh apricots? They are all equally delicious.

STRAWBERRIES CURAÇAO

3 packages cream cheese
¼ cup confectioner's sugar
1 cup cream

⅓ cup Curaçao
4 cups strawberries

SERVES 8

FIRST Mash three packages cream cheese with a fork. Add ¼ cup confectioner's sugar and 1 cup of cream, a little at a time. Blend together with a fork and beat with an egg-beater until smooth. Add ¼ cup Curaçao and beat again.

SECOND Wash, hull, and dry 4 cups strawberries. Fold the berries into the sauce with a gentle hand. Cover them completely with the sauce.

THIRD Place the whole in a serving-bowl. Place in refrigerator. Just before serving, sprinkle remaining Curaçao over the top.

STRAWBERRY DIVINE
[A very gala dessert]

2 envelopes gelatin
½ cup cold water
4 cups strawberries
½ cup sugar
4 cups heavy cream

¾ cup sugar
1 tablespoon vanilla extract
2 tablespoons red wine
Strawberry Sauce (page 450)

SERVES 12

FIRST Soak 2 envelopes gelatin for 5 minutes in ½ cup cold water. Dissolve over hot water. Cool.

SECOND Hull, wash, and drain 4 cups ripe strawberries, reserving the largest for purposes of decoration. Sugar the rest lightly in a mixing-bowl with ½ cup sugar.

THIRD Whip 4 cups heavy cream until stiff. Add ¾ cup of sugar, 1 tablespoon of vanilla extract, and 2 tablespoons of red wine. Continue to beat. Add the dissolved gelatin. Fold until well blended.

FOURTH Fill your largest mold with alternate layers of berries and cream. Set in refrigerator overnight and all the next day. When ready to serve, unmold and serve with a bowl of Strawberry Sauce (page 450).

NOTE This pudding may be served as an icebox pudding, with the mold lined with ladyfingers (approximately two dozen). If your mold does not hold the entire amount, mold the rest in individual custard cups. You will be surprised to see how quickly they disappear if left standing idly in the refrigerator. Because the strawberries are sugared, a little juice may gather at the bottom of the mold. For a tidier appearance this may be carefully poured away during the process of unmolding.

NOTE This is a very old recipe and came out of a ragged notebook compiled during the gay nineties. The original cook, whose name is now forgotten, left a footnote that reads: "For real swell parties, for peoples that know how to eat good, and eats only the best what is."

STRAWBERRY ICEBOX CAKE

2 envelopes gelatin
½ cup cold water
1 cup mashed strawberries
1 cup sugar

2 dozen ladyfingers
2 cups heavy cream
1 tablespoon vanilla
1 cup sliced strawberries

GARNISH

1 cup heavy cream
¼ cup sugar
1 teaspoon vanilla

1 cup whole strawberries
powdered sugar

SERVES 8

FIRST Soak 2 envelopes gelatin in ½ cup cold water for 5 minutes. Dissolve over boiling water.

SECOND Heat 1 cup mashed strawberries with 1 cup sugar until the sugar is dissolved. Add the gelatin to the warm strawberry mixture. Stir, then *cool*.

THIRD Split 2 dozen ladyfingers and line the bottom and sides of a lightly buttered 10″ spring form.

FOURTH Whip 2 cups of heavy cream until stiff. Flavor with 1 tablespoon vanilla. Fold gently into the gelatin mixture. Blend well. Fold in 1 cup sliced strawberries. Then pour the whole on top of the ladyfingers. Chill in refrigerator until firm. Unmold. When ready to serve, decorate with 1 cup heavy cream whipped until stiff, sweetened with ¼ cup sugar, and flavored with 1 teaspoon vanilla extract. The cream is best placed in small mounds around the Icebox Cake, each mound being decoratively topped with a large whole strawberry generously dipped into powdered sugar.

STRAWBERRY MOUSSE

1½ cups crushed strawberry pulp
1 cup sugar
1 teaspoon lemon juice

3 cups heavy cream
1 tablespoon vanilla

SERVES 6

FIRST Crush 1 or 2 boxes strawberries until you have 1½ cups crushed pulp. Stir in 1 cup sugar and 1 teaspoon lemon juice until well blended. Strain off the juice.

SECOND Whip 3 cups of heavy cream until stiff. Fold into the pulp and stir in 1 tablespoon vanilla. Place in a cold, rinsed mold and freeze for 3 hours in a pail packed with salt and ice. If preferred, the mixture may be placed in the refrigerator tray, in which case, of course, no mold is used. In this way, the mousse will freeze but the texture will not be so smooth.

NOTE In freezing the mousse in salt and ice, grease the edges of the mold with vegetable shortening to prevent any of the salt from seeping into the mixture. Then, before opening the mold wipe carefully with a clean cloth to remove any drops of salty water. Four cups of ice cream salt packed with the ice around a 1-quart mold will freeze this amount of mousse in the prescribed time. If the ice melts, additional ice and salt must be added. Place a heavy piece of burlap or old carpeting on top of the pail as a cover.

STRAWBERRIES OVER MOCK CHEESECAKE
[*Pre-heat oven to 350°*]

6 egg yolks
1 can condensed milk
juice of 2 lemons
grated rind of 2 lemons
6 egg whites

1 box vanilla cookies
½ cup melted butter
4 cups large ripe strawberries
1 cup currant jelly

SERVES 6

FIRST Beat 6 egg yolks until light. Stir in 1 can condensed milk, the juice of 2 lemons, and the grated rind of 2 lemons.

SECOND Beat 6 egg whites until stiff. Fold into the yolk mixture, using a gentle hand.

THIRD Roll 1 box vanilla cookies until thoroughly crushed. Mix with ½ cup melted butter. Line a buttered glass pie plate with this mixture. Reserve a few crumbs. Fill pie shell with egg mixture sprinkling top with reserved crumbs. Bake in a 350° oven for 20 or 30 minutes. Test center with a straw before removing. Cool.

FOURTH When cold, cover with large ripe strawberries (about 4 cups). Glaze the berries with 1 cup currant jelly (melted and cooled). It is best to do this at the last moment before serving.

NOTE This is equally attractive with pitted raw Bing cherries—the largest and best quality of course.

WARNING This dessert suffers as a left-over.

STRAWBERRY PARFAIT

2 cups strawberries
12 marshmallows
1 cup sugar
1 teaspoon lemon juice

2 cups heavy cream
1 tablespoon vanilla
1 cup sliced strawberries

SERVES 6

FIRST Hull, wash, and dry 2 cups strawberries. Place them in a pot with 12 marshmallows, ¾ cup sugar, and 1 teaspoon lemon juice. Simmer. Stir occasionally, always watching to see that it does not scorch.

SECOND Remove from stove. Mash through a sieve and cool.

THIRD Beat 2 cups of heavy cream until stiff. Stir in 1 tablespoon vanilla and blend completely with the strawberry mixture. Place in freezing-tray of refrigerator and stir twice while freezing. When ready to serve, place in glasses (tall, thin parfait glasses preferred) and top each glass with an even distribution of 1 cup sliced strawberries sweetened with ¼ cup sugar.

STRAWBERRY PINK RICE PUDDING

2 cups milk
2 cups light cream
½ cup white rice
¾ cup sugar
salt

4 eggs
1 cup strained strawberry juice
2 cups heavy cream
2 tablespoons vanilla

SERVES 8

FIRST Place 2 cups milk, 2 cups light cream, ½ cup white rice,

¾ cup sugar, and a pinch of salt in the top of a double boiler. Stir once in a while and let cook until rice is tender.

SECOND Beat 4 eggs. Add to rice and continue to cook until the mixture thickens, but not too much. Remove to a bowl and cool.

THIRD Stir in 1 cup of strained strawberry juice and blend thoroughly. Beat 2 cups of heavy cream until stiff. Fold into the rice mixture and add 2 tablespoons of vanilla. Place in a deep serving-bowl and set in the refrigerator for several hours before serving.

NOTE If you wish to serve this dish in the wintertime, the ideal thing, of course, is to have some Strawberry Sauce, for winter use (page 450) on hand. If not, a box of frozen strawberries may be thawed, mashed, and rubbed through a strainer.

STRAWBERRIES ROMANOFF

5 egg yolks
1 cup sugar
1 cup good sherry

3 pints strawberries
1 cup heavy cream
powdered sugar

SERVES 6

FIRST Break 5 egg yolks into the top of a double boiler and beat with egg-beater until lemon colored. Add 1 cup sugar and beat until velvety. Pour in 1 cup good sherry and replace the beater with a spoon. Stir until thick. Place in a bowl and cool.

SECOND Wash, hull, and dry 3 pints strawberries. Set aside the largest berries to use as decoration.

THIRD No longer than half an hour before serving time, beat 1 cup heavy cream until very stiff. Then fold into custard until completely blended. Add the strawberries, turning them carefully until completely covered by the custard cream. Place the whole on a round flat platter and decorate with the largest berries dipped in powdered sugar. Serve icy cold.

NOTE This is a magnificent dessert, not difficult to assemble, very gala, and quite novel to most tables. I have heard of its being made with a soft vanilla ice cream, but for my part there is a velvety texture to the sauce when the whipping cream is combined with the sherry custard that is never achieved by any other method. No use trying it with frozen strawberries. The results won't come anywhere near it. If you wish to deviate, try using fresh raspberries when they are in season.

WARNING This does not do well as a left-over.

STRAWBERRY TORTE

[*Pre-heat oven to 250°*]

½ cup butter
2 cups sugar
4 egg yolks
1⅓ cups pastry flour
1⅓ teaspoons baking powder
¼ teaspoon salt
5 tablespoons milk

½ tablespoons almond flavoring
4 egg whites
⅛ teaspoon cream of tartar
4 cups strawberries
2 cups heavy cream
1 tablespoon vanilla
powdered sugar

SERVES 6

THE CAKE

FIRST Cream ½ cup butter with ½ cup sugar until light and fluffy. Add 4 egg yolks, one at a time, beating well after each addition.

SECOND Sift 1⅓ cups pastry flour. Measure and resift three times with 1⅓ teaspoon baking powder and ¼ teaspoon salt. Add to butter mixture alternately with 5 tablespoons milk. Beat. When well blended, add ½ tablespoon almond flavoring. Line two 8-inch layer-cake tins with buttered paper. Divide batter evenly between the tins.

THE MERINGUE

THIRD Beat 4 egg whites until fluffy. Add ⅛ teaspoon cream of tartar and gradually beat in 1 cup sugar. Continue to beat until glossy and stiff. Spread the meringue evenly on top of the unbaked batter in the two tins. Bake in a 250° oven for 25 minutes Then increase the heat to 350° and continue to bake for 20 minutes longer. Remove from oven *but do not invert tins.* When somewhat cooled, carefully remove layers with a broad spatula.

THE FILLING AND ICING

FOURTH Wash, hull, and dry 4 cups strawberries. Set aside the largest berries and cut the rest into halves. Whip 2 cups of heavy cream until stiff. Sweeten with ½ cup sugar and flavor with 1 tablespoon vanilla. Fold the halved berries into the cream. Spread this combination between the layers and over the top and sides of the Torte. Decorate the top with the largest berries generously dipped in powdered sugar.

NOTE This dessert also lends itself to the use of raspberries, pitted Bing cherries, fresh peaches, or bananas. It is a beautiful and festive dessert. It is not widely known and never fails to delight.

STRAWBERRIES WITH SHERBET

4 cups strawberries
½ cup sugar
½ cup Curaçao
1 quart orange sherbet

grated rind of 1 orange
1 tablespoon brown sugar
shredded coconut

SERVES 6

FIRST Wash and hull 4 cups strawberries. Place in a bowl and cover with ½ cup sugar and ½ cup Curaçao, turning the strawberries over and over in the sugar and liqueur. Place in the coldest shelf of the refrigerator for an hour or more.

SECOND When ready to serve, pour the juice off the strawberries and stir it into a quart of orange sherbet. Spread the sherbet at the bottom of a glass serving-bowl and heap the strawberries on top.

THIRD At the last moment sprinkle the grated rind of 1 orange mixed with 1 tablespoon brown sugar on top of the strawberries. Serve with a side bowl of shredded coconut (moist preferred).

WINTER STRAWBERRY ICE CREAM

1 quart vanilla ice cream
1 quart frozen strawberries
1 cup heavy cream
1 teaspoon vanilla

2 egg yolks
½ cup sugar
red vegetable coloring (optional)

SERVES 6

FIRST Allow 1 quart vanilla ice cream to soften. Stir in 1 quart frozen strawberries that have thawed.

SECOND Whip 1 cup heavy cream until stiff. Stir in 1 teaspoon vanilla. Beat 2 egg yolks with ½ cup granulated sugar until light. Then stir into the strawberry mixture. If the color is not deep enough to satisfy, add a drop or two or red vegetable coloring.

THIRD Place in freezing-tray in refrigerator. Stir twice while freezing.

GLAZED STRAWBERRY PIE

1 baked pie shell—Polish Tart Crust (page 409)
4 cups strawberries
3 tablespoons cornstarch
½ cup sugar

1 tablespoon lemon juice
1 cup heavy cream
¼ cup sugar
1 tablespoon vanilla

SERVES 6

FIRST Bake 9-inch pie shell, using Polish Tart Crust (page 409) or any preferred pie-crust recipe. Cool.

SECOND Wash, hull, and dry 4 cups strawberries. Reserve 2 cups of the largest berries. Mash the other half. To the mashed half add 3 tablespoons cornstarch, ½ cup sugar, and 1 tablespoon lemon juice. Set on a moderate flame and stir constantly until thick and clear. Cool, then chill.

THIRD Fill bottom of the pie shell with the largest strawberries. Coat them completely with the chilled strawberry glaze. Place in refrigerator while preparing the cream.

FOURTH Whip 1 cup heavy cream until stiff. Sweeten with ¼ cup sugar and flavor with 1 tablespoon vanilla extract. Place the whipped cream around the edge of the tart, leaving the center exposed so that the red makes a bright contrast. Drippings of glaze may be used to decorate the cream just before serving. Once the cream is added serve the tart at once.

NOTE There are those who feel that a filling of soft custard (page 446) is traditional. If you prefer it this way, by all means have it. I feel that the bland texture of the custard interferes with the pleasure achieved by the tangy flavor of the berries and the glaze.

STRAWBERRY CHIFFON PIE

1 baked nine-inch pie shell
1 tablespoon gelatin
¼ cup cold water
3 egg yolks
¼ cup sugar
½ teaspoon salt
2 teaspoons lemon juice
2 cups crushed strawberries
3 egg whites
½ teaspoon cream of tartar
½ cup sugar

To decorate:

1 cup heavy cream
¼ cup sugar
1 tablespoon vanilla
large, ripe strawberries
powdered sugar

SERVES 6–8

FIRST Soak 1 tablespoon gelatin in ¼ cup cold water for 5 minutes. Dissolve over hot water.

SECOND Beat 3 egg yolks until light. Place in double boiler. Stir in ¼ cup sugar, ½ teaspoon salt, and 2 teaspoons lemon juice until well combined. Continue to cook over hot water, stirring constantly until smooth. Stir in the liquid gelatin and 2 cups crushed strawberries. Beat with a rotary beater for one minute, then remove from the fire. When sufficiently cool, place in refrigerator until thick. Then beat once again for one minute, or until very smooth.

THIRD Beat 3 egg whites with ½ teaspoon cream of tartar until stiff. Continue to beat, gradually adding ½ cup sugar. Beat until glossy, then fold into the strawberry mixture with a gentle hand. Blend thoroughly and pile into a cooled baked nine-inch shell. Chill in the refrigerator for at least an hour.

FOURTH Just before serving decorate with a wreath of whipped cream sweetened with ¼ cup sugar and flavored with 1 tablespoon vanilla. Top the cream with large, ripe strawberries dipped in powdered sugar.

STRAWBERRY PIE WITH WINE *Marie's*

THE CRUST

½ cup butter
¼ cup sugar
1 egg yolk

⅛ cup sherry
1½ cups flour
¼ teaspoon salt

SERVES 6

FIRST Cream ½ cup butter with ¼ cup sugar. Beat in 1 egg yolk and ⅛ cup sherry. Sift 1½ cups flour. Measure and resift with ¼ teaspoon salt. Work into the butter and chill overnight in the refrigerator.

[*Pre-heat oven to 425°*]

SECOND Roll out on lightly floured board or press with your hands into a 9-inch glass pie dish. Prick with a fork and bake in a 425° oven until *just set* but *not* browned. Remove from oven.

THE FILLING

¼ cup rolled zwieback crumbs
4 cups strawberries
1 tablespoon flour
½ cup sugar
2 eggs

6 tablespoons cream
⅛ cup sherry
1 tablespoon sugar
cinnamon

FIRST Sprinkle the baked crust with ⅛ cup rolled zwieback crumbs. Fill with 4 cups washed, hulled, and dried strawberries. Cover the berries with ⅛ cup rolled zwieback crumbs combined with ½ cup sugar and 1 tablespoon flour. Distribute this evenly over the strawberries. Place the pie in the oven and bake until the strawberries are somewhat soft but *not* mushy.

SECOND Beat 2 eggs with 6 tablespoons cream, $\frac{1}{8}$ cup sherry, 1 tablespoon sugar, and a pinch of cinnamon. Spread this mixture evenly over the pie and return the pie to the oven, turning down the heat to 350° until the custard sets. This may be determined by inserting a knife—if the custard feels firm to the tip of the knife, it is time to remove the pie from the oven.

NOTE It is at its best when not entirely cool. The aroma of the strawberry juice is most fragrant at that point. All of us have enjoyed strawberry pies in our times, but I think that you will agree that this one is completely unique. Incidentally, it is equally delicious with big black cherries. In this case it may be necessary to invert another pie plate over the cherries while they are baking. The tops of the cherries have a tendency to shrivel when exposed to the heat of the oven. Try to plan to eat this strawberry pie all at one sitting. It doesn't keep too well—has a tendency to get soggy. But when fresh, it is delicious!

WINTER STRAWBERRY PIE

9-inch baked pie shell—Polish Tart Crust (page 409)
Two 12-ounce packages frozen strawberries
2 tablespoons cornstarch
3 egg whites
6 tablespoons sugar

SERVES 6 TO 8

FIRST Bake a 9-inch pie shell of any preferred recipe—Polish Tart Crust (page 409) suggested.

SECOND Place two 12-ounce packages frozen sweetened strawberries on a moderate flame and bring to a gentle boil. Add 2 tablespoons cornstarch smoothed in a little water. Stir until smooth and thick. Pour in pie shell and *cool*.

[*Pre-heat oven to 325°*]

THIRD Beat 3 egg whites until stiff. Add 6 tablespoons sugar, 2 tablespoons at a time, beating thoroughly after each addition. Cover top of the pie with the meringue. Place in 325° oven just long enough to brown the meringue lightly.

COCONUT STRAWBERRY CREAM TARTS

1 cup heavy cream
¼ cup sugar
1 teaspoon vanilla
1 egg white
1 cup freshly grated coconut
1 cup sweetened, sliced strawberries

6 Strawberry Tartlets (page 448)
½ cup freshly grated coconut (preferred)
6 large strawberries (optional)
powdered sugar (optional)

SERVES 6

FIRST Beat one cup heavy cream until stiff. Sweeten with ¼ cup sugar and flavor with 1 teaspoon vanilla. Beat 1 egg white until stiff. Combine cream and egg white and fold in 1 cup freshly grated coconut.

SECOND Place 1 cup sweetened strawberries in the bottom of 6 baked Strawberry Tartlets (page 448). Cover the berries with the cream mixture and sprinkle the remaining ½ cup freshly grated coconut evenly on top of each tart. If in a festive mood, decorate each tart with 1 large strawberry dipped in powdered sugar. Serve as soon as assembled. If allowed to stand the tarts become somewhat soggy.

NOTE Coconut canned in its own milk or freshly grated is by far the best. However, since these particular ingredients may sometimes be difficult to get, just be sure that whatever you use is moist, *never* stale or dry.

PARISIAN STRAWBERRY TARTS

I
TARTS

¼ pound butter
¼ cup sugar

1 egg
1½ cups sifted flour

8 TARTS

FIRST Cream ¼ pound butter with ¼ cup sugar until light and fluffy. Add 1 beaten egg and blend thoroughly.

SECOND Sift 1½ cups flour. Measure and resift twice. Add to the butter mixture, a little at a time. Chill in refrigerator, preferably overnight.

[*Pre-heat oven to 375°*]

THIRD Roll out very thin, cut into circles large enough to cover the forms on inverted muffin pans, and bake in a 375° oven for 10 to 15 minutes. Cool before filling.

II
CUSTARD FILLING

2 tablespoons sugar
1 egg yolk
⅓ cup milk

⅛ pound soft butter
¼ teaspoon almond extract *or* ½ teaspoon vanilla extract

FIRST Blend 2 tablespoons sugar with 1 egg yolk until smooth and velvety. Add ⅓ cup milk. Stir rapidly on a moderate flame until thick and smooth. Bring to a boil, but do not boil. Cool.

SECOND Beat in ⅛ pound soft butter until smooth. Then stir in ¼ teaspoon almond extract or ½ teaspoon vanilla extract as preferred. Chill in refrigerator until ready to serve.

III
GLAZE

4 cups strawberries
grated rind of 1 orange
¾ cup water

2 tablespoons lemon juice
¾ cup sugar

FIRST Wash, hull, and dry 4 cups strawberries, setting the largest ones aside.

SECOND Grate the rind of 1 orange and add to the smaller strawberries. Add ¾ cup water. Crush the berries, put through a strainer, and measure them. There should be approximately ¾ cup of strawberry liquid.

THIRD To this liquid add 2 tablespoons lemon juice and ¾ cup sugar. Bring to a boil and boil 12 to 15 minutes until the jelly stage is reached. Cool.

IV
TO ASSEMBLE

FIRST Place two tablespoons custard in the bottom of each tart form. Top the custard with the largest strawberries, which have been reserved. Then with a spoon drip the glaze over each strawberry until all are thoroughly coated. Serve.

NOTE Not only are these strawberry tarts delicious, but extremely professional! If you will read the recipe for Chestnut Meringues, you will see that I have mentioned these completely Parisian, "tartes aux fraises," as having set my childish mind on the horns of a sad dilemma!

WARNING Do not assemble tarts until ready to serve—and above all, do not bake them too large.

STRAWBERRY-PRESERVE TURNOVERS

1 cup vegetable shortening	⅛ teaspoon salt
2 packages cream cheese	2 tablespoons sugar
1 beaten egg yolk	strawberry preserves
2 cups sifted flour	powdered vanilla sugar (see Note)

FIRST Cream 1 cup vegetable shortening with 2 packages of cream cheese. When well blended, add 1 beaten egg yolk.

SECOND Sift 2 cups flour. Measure and resift 3 times with ⅛ teaspoon salt and 2 tablespoons sugar. Add to the cream-cheese mixture, a little at a time, and mix until smooth. Shape into a roll (not too narrow), wrap in waxed paper, and place in refrigerator overnight.

[*Pre-heat oven to 400°*]

THIRD Cut the roll into ½-inch slices. Roll each slice thin on a slightly floured board. Fill each rolled slice with thick strawberry preserves and shape into turnovers (triangles). Press edges together with the prongs of a fork and gently prick each center. Bake in a 400° oven for about 20 minutes. Sprinkle with powdered vanilla sugar just before serving. Serve while still slightly warm. Apricot jam may be used as a substitute.

NOTE ONE To prepare powdered vanilla sugar, insert a cut vanilla bean down the center of a quart jar of powdered sugar. Cap jar tightly.

STRAWBERRY TARTLETS

[*Pre-heat oven to 425°*]

1½ cups flour	½ cup sugar
½ cup vegetable shortening	3 tablespoons condensed milk
3 tablespoons ice water	1 cup sour cream
2 cups large strawberries	powdered sugar

SERVES 6

FIRST Sift 1½ cups flour. Measure and resift into ½ cup vegetable shortening. Beat together until smooth. Add 3 tablespoons ice water and beat again. Roll pastry onto a lightly floured board. Then invert a muffin tin and cover the forms with the pastry. Bake in a 425° oven until very light brown. This recipe makes 6 tartlets.

SECOND Reserve 6 or 8 of the largest strawberries out of 2 cups large strawberries. Slice the remaining strawberries and cover with ½ cup granulated sugar. Set them in a refrigerator for 1 hour.

THIRD Stir 3 tablespoons condensed milk into 1 cup sour cream. Place one tablespoon cream in the bottom of each tartlet. Add the sugared strawberries. Then heap the rest of the sour cream evenly over the strawberries. Top each tartlet with 1 large strawberry dipped in powdered sugar.

NOTE When rolling the pastry (previous to covering the backs of the muffin tins) be sure to roll as thin as possible. This makes a very crisp shell that imparts a delicate quality to the whole.

STRAWBERRY TARTS WITHOUT FILLING

Parisian Strawberry Tarts (page 445)
4 cups strawberries
3 tablespoons cornstarch
1 cup sugar
1 teaspoon lemon juice
heavy cream (optional)
¼ cup sugar (optional)
1 tablespoon vanilla extract (optional)

SERVES 6 TO 8

FIRST Bake tart shells as for Parisian Strawberry Tarts (page 445). Hull, wash, and dry 4 cups strawberries, reserving largest, most perfect ones. When the tarts are cool, fill with the reserved strawberries.

SECOND Cover the berries with the following glaze:
Mash the remaining, smaller berries until you have 1 cup pulp. If the cup is not full, add a little water. Add 3 tablespoons cornstarch to 1 cup sugar and stir into the berry juice. When well blended, add 1 teaspoon lemon juice. Then place on the fire and stir until the mixture thickens. Cool.

THIRD Pour the prepared glaze over the strawberries in the tart shells until they are completely covered. Serve with or without whipped cream. If whipped cream is used, beat 1 cup of heavy cream until stiff, sweeten with ¼ cup sugar, and flavor with 1 tablespoon vanilla extract.

NOTE I prefer these tarts without whipped cream. The delicate flavor of the berries, blending with the pastry and the glaze is sufficient unto itself.

STRAWBERRY PRESERVES

5 cups strawberries
5 cups sugar
½ cup lemon juice

FIRST Examine the contents of approximately 5 cups strawberries discarding all the berries that are not perfectly ripe and in excellent condition. Hull, wash, and dry the remaining strawberries. Put them in the pan in which they are to be cooked. Cover with 5 cups sugar and allow to stand overnight or all day.

SECOND Bring to a rolling boil for *exactly* 8 minutes. *The timing is important.* At the end of eight minutes add ½ cup lemon juice. Bring to a boil again for *exactly* 3 minutes longer. *The timing is again important.* Remove from the fire and cool in the same pan.

THIRD When completely cool, pour into sterilized glasses or jars and seal with paraffin.

NOTE Whether you know it or not, this is what you have been asking for, when you have asked for strawberry jam! It has a brilliant, shining strawberry color and the flavor is as sharp and bright as newly picked strawberries in the early mornings! Only one word of warning, be certain that your berries are ripe and of the very best possible quality. Shabby ones, or half green ones are OUT!

STRAWBERRY SAUCE FOR ICE CREAM

¾ cup sugar
½ cup water

1½ cups strawberries

FIRST Boil ¾ cup granulated sugar and ½ cup water for ten minutes. Remove from fire, stir a little, then cool.

SECOND Wash, hull, and dry 1½ cups strawberries. Crush lightly with a fork. Add to the sugar syrup and stir until well combined. Serve, either at room temperature or very cold, as preferred.

STRAWBERRY SAUCE FOR WINTER USE *Marie's*

(These are very old recipes brought by Marie from the old country. I have eaten them many times, and although the method of preparation is a far cry from our methods of today, the results are superlative. I quote them verbatim, hoping that you will have the patience and the interest in the ways of other times to try them, if only to know the thrill we knew as children when tasting fresh, homemade strawberry sauce on our rice pudding while the snow was deep on the winter ground!)

Without Sugar

Use ripe berries. Put through a fine strainer. Put up in pint glasses, without any sugar at all. Seal well and cook in steam for ten to fifteen minutes. Sugar is used, according to taste, when the sauce is ready for use. Also, a very little lemon juice. If you want to make a mousse, add ½ pint of sauce to one pint of whipped cream.

With Sugar

Hull only the best and finest of strawberries. Put them through a fine strainer and mash with a new wooden potato masher. Weigh off same amount of berries and of sugar, and let stand together in ice box overnight. Next morning, stir for one hour with a new wooden spoon. The stirring is very important. Fill in pint glasses, but not too full. Seal well and cook in glasses in steam for ten or fifteen minutes, then store in a dark place.

NOTE As I think back it seems to me that everything stopped functioning while these sauces were being prepared. Everyone helped hull and hands were stained and perfumed for hours afterwards. After the long day, the family invariably went to a restaurant for dinner, leaving the heavenly aroma of strawberry in every crevice of our brownstone house. Nor was "the heavenly aroma" the only thing that was left behind—for there was Marie, with the enormous mixing bowl still held securely in her lap, continuing to stir and stir and stir. As she sat in her warm kitchen, with a look of trancelike dedication on her face, she actually stirred each batch for one hour.

NOTE II: Two Suggestions
These sauces are equally good with raspberry.

Your electric mixer might take the place of Marie's painstaking hand stirring. Perhaps half an hour might do the trick. This fine, old recipe probably will not suffer *too* much by making this concession to the machine age.

Chapter XV: *Fruits*

The ripened fruit is golden to the core.

STEPHEN VINCENT BENÉT

APPLES

Apples and Cheese, Albert
Apples Meringue in Casserole
Apples Under Blanket
Butterscotch Apples in Rum
Buttery Baked Apples
Snow Apples
Stewed Apples Dressed Up

BANANAS

Baked Bananas
Bananas from Brussels

CHERRIES

Black Cherries in Brandy Sauce
Cherries in Wine
Cherry Cocktail
Hot Rum Cherries

MELONS

Ice Honey Dew Melon with Lime
Watermelon Basket
Watermelon Surprise

PEACHES

Baked Peaches, Cornell
Peaches in Cups
Peach Surprise
Yellow Peaches with a Red Blanket

PEARS

Baked Pears
Blushing Pears

PINEAPPLE

Pineapple Quarters with Crème de Menthe
Meli Meko
Pineapple Boat

ASSORTED FRUITS

Apricots Joined Together
Citrus Fruit Ring
Figs in Crème de Cacao and Sour Cream
Frozen Fruit Salad
Fruit Salad
Fruit Salad Dressing
Nectarines Evangeline
Orange Slices in Chilled Red Wine
Three Hot Fruits

APPLES AND CHEESE ALBERT

4 apples ½ ripe Camembert cheese

SERVES 6

FIRST Pare and quarter 4 apples.

SECOND Spread each quarter apple with the softest parts of ½ ripe Camembert cheese.

APPLES MERINGUE IN CASSEROLE *Marie's*

6 medium cooking-apples
½ cup white wine
½ cup sugar
¼ teaspoon cinnamon
1 cup water

maraschino cherries (approximately 12)
Vanilla Sauce II (page 363)
3 egg whites
¼ cup sugar

SERVES 6

FIRST Peel and core 6 medium cooking-apples. Stew them in a pot with ½ cup white wine, ½ cup sugar, ¼ teaspoon cinnamon, and 1 cup water until they are soft, but not too soft. Cool.

SECOND Drain the apples and place carefully in a deep glass baking-dish. Insert a maraschino cherry inside each apple and fill each crevice between the apples with additional maraschino cherries. Completely cover the apples with Vanilla Sauce II (page 363).

[*Pre-heat oven to 400°*]

THIRD Beat the 3 egg whites until stiff. Slowly add ¼ cup sugar and continue to beat. Heap the meringue on top of the sauce over the apples and set the dish in a 400° oven only long enough to lightly brown the top of the whites. Cool. Place in refrigerator and serve very *cold*.

NOTE This is one of the most satisfactory simple desserts you can possibly serve.

APPLES UNDER BLANKET

[*Pre-heat oven to 350°*]

3 cups boiling water	5 eggs
1¼ cups sugar	½ teaspoon salt
6 cooking-apples	4 cups milk
nutmeg	tart jelly

SERVES 6

FIRST Bring 3 cups boiling water and ½ cup sugar to a rolling boil. Peel and core 6 cooking-apples and place them in a stew pot. Pour the boiling syrup over them and cook gently, without breaking the apples, for about 15 minutes. Drain the apples and place in a glass baking-dish. Sprinkle the apples with ¼ cup sugar and nutmeg to taste. Place the dish in a 350° oven for 10 minutes.

SECOND While the apples are in the oven prepare a custard by breaking 5 eggs into a mixing-bowl. Add ½ teaspoon salt and ½ cup sugar. Beat thoroughly until well blended. Then slowly add 4 cups of milk. Mix and stir. Then strain the mixture over the apples in the baking-dish. Set the baking-dish into a pan of warm water and return to oven for approximately half an hour longer. Cool. Set in refrigerator to chill. Scatter bits of tart jelly on top of the custard and inside the apples before bringing to the table.

BUTTERSCOTCH APPLES IN RUM

[*Pre-heat oven to 350°*]

6 baking apples	¼ cup rum
1½ cups brown sugar	1 cup heavy cream
6 tablespoons butter	¼ cup sugar
½ cup water	1 teaspoon vanilla

SERVES 6

FIRST Core 6 baking-apples without peeling. Fill each hole with 1 tablespoon brown sugar. Close each top with 1 tablespoon butter.

SECOND Simmer 1 cup brown sugar in ½ cup water and ¼ cup rum for 10 minutes.

THIRD Place the apples in a well-buttered shallow baking-dish. Pour the caramel around the apples and bake in a 350° oven for half an hour. Cool, then set in refrigerator to chill. Serve with 1 cup heavy cream whipped, sweetened with ¼ cup sugar, and flavored with 1 teaspoon vanilla. They may also be served plain.

NOTE The baking time varies according to the type and the age of the apples. It may be necessary to bake them only 20 minutes. Watch carefully.

BUTTERY BAKED APPLES
[*Pre-heat oven to 350°*]

12 baking-apples
12 teaspoons sugar
½ teaspoon cinnamon
6 tablespoons butter
½ cup water

12 maraschino cherries (optional)
1 cup heavy cream
¼ cup sugar
1 tablespoon vanilla

SERVES 12

FIRST Peel and core 12 baking-apples. Butter a shallow glass baking-dish, set the apples in the dish. Fill the cavity of each with a teaspoon sugar and sprinkle each with a pinch cinnamon (½ teaspoon in all).

SECOND Melt 6 tablespoons butter in ½ cup water and bring to a quick boil. Pour half this liquid over the apples and place in a 350° oven. Bake approximately half an hour, basting every 10 minutes with the remaining half of the syrup. Test to see whether the apples are sufficiently tender. This exact baking time will depend on the size and ripeness of the apples.

THIRD When done, remove the apples carefully to a glass serving-dish. Cover with the syrup. As the syrup cools, baste the apples with it several times. A maraschino cherry may be placed inside each apple before serving. Serve with a bowl of whipped cream (1 cup heavy cream whipped, sweetened with ¼ cup sugar, and flavored with 1 tablespoon vanilla), or a pitcher of heavy cream. In either case have the cream very cold.

SNOW APPLES

[*Pre-heat oven to 350°*]

9 baking-apples
1 cup sugar
1 cup water
juice of ½ lemon
3 egg whites

8 tablespoons powdered sugar
½ teaspoon vanilla
additional sugar (approximately ¼ cup)
red food coloring

SERVES 9

FIRST   Peel and core 9 baking-apples. Bring 1 cup sugar, 1 cup water, and the juice of ½ lemon to a rolling boil. Pour over apples in a deep stew pot. Cook until almost tender. Drain, then set in a 350° oven for about 15 minutes.

SECOND   Remove the apples from the oven and cover each with a meringue made by beating 3 egg whites until stiff, adding 8 tablespoons powdered sugar, and beating again with ½ teaspoon vanilla until the meringue is smooth and glossy. Sprinkle each meringue-covered apple with sugar and return to oven until lightly browned. Remove and cool.

THIRD   Boil down the remaining syrup until it has reduced itself to almost half. Color with a few drops of red food coloring, pour into pie plate, and place in refrigerator to set. When this apple jelly is set, cut into any desired shapes and decorate the serving-dish on which the apples are to be served.

NOTE   When the meringue-covered apples are put in the oven to lightly brown, do not make the mistake of closing the door and forgetting about them. Leave the oven door open, stand by, and watch closely.

STEWED APPLES DRESSED UP

1 scant cup sugar
1 cup water
juice of ½ lemon
nutmeg (optional)
6 tart cooking-apples

1 cup heavy cream
¼ cup sugar
1 tablespoon vanilla
2 tablespoons chopped pecans

SERVES 6

FIRST Bring 1 scant cup sugar and 1 cup water to a boil. Boil for 15 minutes. Add the juice of ½ lemon, nutmeg (optional) to taste, and 6 tart cooking-apples pared and cut into quarters. Cover the stew pan and set on a very low flame. Stew the apples for about half an hour. The stewing time will depend on the apples themselves. Watch them carefully.

SECOND Remove the apples carefully to a serving-dish. Do not break them, but remove them with a spoon or a spatula allowing the syrup to drain as the apples are lifted from the pan. Return the pan to the fire and reduce the remaining syrup by boiling it for 5 minutes more.

THIRD Pour the syrup over the apples on the serving-dish and cool to room temperature. Set in refrigerator. Beat 1 cup heavy cream until stiff. Sweeten with ¼ cup sugar and flavor with 1 tablespoon vanilla. Heap over apples. Sprinkle with 2 tablespoons chopped pecans. Serve very cold.

BAKED BANANAS

[*Pre-heat oven to 350°*]

3 tablespoons butter
6 tablespoons sugar
3 tablespoons lemon juice

6 bananas
3 tablespoons rum or sherry

SERVES 6

FIRST Render 3 tablespoons butter. Stir in 6 tablespoons sugar and 3 tablespoons lemon juice. Stir until well blended. Remove from fire.

SECOND Remove the skins of 6 bananas and place on a glass baking-plate slightly separated one from each other. Sprinkle with 3 tablespoons rum or sherry. Then pour on the butter sauce and place in a 350° oven for half an hour. During the baking, baste several times with the butter sauce. Serve from the baking-dish.

NOTE Try baking bananas in their skins and serving them hot and perfectly plain alongside a roast.

BANANAS FROM BRUSSELS

½ cup sugar
¼ pound melted butter
rind and juice of 1 lemon
rind and juice of 1 orange

rind and juice of 2 tangerines
½ cup Curaçao
6 bananas

SERVES 6

FIRST Stir ½ cup sugar into ¼ pound melted butter.

SECOND Add the rind and juice of 1 lemon, the rind and juice of 1 orange, and the rind and juice of 2 tangerines. Add ½ cup of Curaçao. Pour all these ingredients into a chafing-dish (this is traditional) or into a skillet and bring to a simmer.

THIRD Cut 6 bananas lengthwise in halves. Place them in the sauce in the chafing-dish or skillet and cook slowly until soft but not mushy. Baste with the sauce while cooking. Serve, two halves per person, distributing the sauce evenly over each portion.

BLACK CHERRIES IN BRANDY SAUCE

4 egg yolks
2 whole eggs
½ cup sugar
¼ teaspoon salt

½ cup best brandy
1 cup cherry juice
2 cans black cherries (*or* stewed fresh in season)

SERVES 6

FIRST Stir 4 egg yolks and 2 whole eggs with ½ cup sugar and ¼ teaspoon salt.

SECOND Combine ½ cup best brandy with 1 cup cherry juice and add little by little to egg mixture. Stir constantly over slow flame until thickened. Remove from fire and stir occasionally until cool. Pour sauce over 2 cans black cherries (or stewed fresh cherries in season) that have been thoroughly chilled in the refrigerator.

FRUITS

CHERRIES IN WINE

2 pounds fresh black Bing cherries
2 cups red wine (claret preferred)

¾ cup sugar
cinnamon (optional)
3 tablespoons currant jelly

SERVES 6

FIRST Stew 2 pounds fresh black Bing cherries in 2 cups red wine (claret preferred), ¾ cup sugar, and a pinch of cinnamon (optional).

SECOND When the cherries are soft, remove them to a servingbowl. Return juice to the stove and simmer to reduce by one-third.

THIRD Just before removing juice from stove, stir in 3 tablespoons currant jelly and pour the sauce over the cherries. Cool. Set in refrigerator and serve cold.

CHERRY COCKTAIL

2 pounds fresh black Bing cherries

½ cup kirsch
1 cup sugar

SERVES 6 TO 8

FIRST Select only the darkest, ripest black Bing cherries. Pit, place in glasses (champagne glasses are excellent for this purpose), and let stand in the refrigerator until just before serving.

SECOND Sprinkle the cherries with ½ cup kirsch. Then cover evenly with 1 cup of sugar. Serve quickly while the sugar still looks like a crystallized snow over the cherries.

HOT RUM CHERRIES

2 large cans black Bing cherries
4 teaspoons cornstarch

½ cup rum
1 pint heavy sour cream

SERVES 6

FIRST Heat the contents of 2 large cans of black Bing cherries in their own juice.

SECOND Remove a teacupful of the warm juice. With a spoon rub 4 teaspoons cornstarch into the juice in the cup until quite moist and smooth. Add this to the whole, a little at a time. Stir for a few minutes until the liquid thickens slightly. Allow to simmer gently on the stove for 20 minutes.

THIRD Just before serving, turn off the flame, add ½ cup rum to the cherries. Pour the contents of the pot into a good-sized serving-bowl that has been heated in the oven. Serve while still very warm with a side bowl containing 1 pint very cold heavy sour cream.

NOTE Brandy, sherry, or kirsch may be substituted for rum. The cherries may, of course, be served cold, but the novelty of this simple but delicious dessert is in having the cherries very hot and the sour cream very cold.

ICED HONEYDEW MELON WITH LIME

1 large ripe honeydew melon
3 limes
grated nutmeg

SERVES 6

FIRST Cut into 6 even slices 1 large ripe honeydew melon that has been thoroughly chilled.

SECOND Cut 3 limes into halves. Just before serving, squeeze the juice of half a lime over each melon slice and sprinkle with grated nutmeg.

WATERMELON BASKET

1 watermelon, high in the center
fresh fruits of all varieties
sugar to taste
1 cup white wine, sherry, *or* rum

SERVES 12

FIRST Cut a basket with a handle out of the top third of a watermelon that is shaped rather high in the center. Scoop out the pulp with care. Then cut "dragon's teeth" around the edge of the "basket." Great care must be taken in handling these operations, since the rind is extremely brittle and likely, at almost any time, to crack, thereby ruining the "basket."

SECOND Cut up all the fresh fruits available into your largest mixing-bowl. Add berries and sliced bananas last. Cover with plenty of sugar and turn the fruit over and over with a large kitchen spoon. Taste, and add more sugar if necessary. Then pour in 1 cup white wine, sherry, or rum. Turn again several times. Set bowl in icebox until ready to use as filling.

THIRD Shortly before serving, tie flowers and ribbon bow on the handle of the "basket." Pour the fruit in the "basket," set the whole on a serving-tray or platter, and serve.

NOTE Fruits that make an excellent combination for use in this dish are: peaches, apricots, plums, seedless grapes, nectarines, pineapple, melon balls from watermelon pulp and cantaloupe, oranges, grapefruit, sliced bananas, and any available berries.

Give yourself plenty of time to prepare the "basket" and fruit. This is an operation that permits no hurrying.

WATERMELON SURPRISE

1 long, rather flat watermelon
2 to 3 quarts raspberry sherbet
2 dozen small licorice lozenges

FIRST Lay one long, rather flat watermelon on its side. Cut in half Remove the pulp and score the edge of the rind with "dragon's teeth."

SECOND When ready to serve, fill flat and even to the brim with 2 to 3 quarts raspberry sherbet (the amount depends on the size of the melon). Decorate, to simulate watermelon seeds, with small licorice lozenges.

BAKED PEACHES, CORNELL
[Pre-heat oven to 350°]

6 ripe peaches	½ cup water
1 cup sugar	2 tablespoons butter
nutmeg	¼ teaspoon cinnamon

SERVES 6

FIRST Plunge 6 ripe peaches into boiling water. Slide off the skins. Set in a glass baking-dish that has a cover.

SECOND Caramelize 1 cup sugar and a pinch nutmeg with ½ cup water. Add 2 tablespoons butter and ¼ teaspoon cinnamon. Pour over peaches in baking-dish. Place cover on dish and set to bake in a 350° oven for about 20 minutes. Serve hot.

NOTE Serve them with a roast of beef.

PEACHES IN CUPS
[Pre-heat oven to 350°]

12 peach halves	2 egg whites
6 teaspoons sugar	6 tablespoons powdered sugar
6 teaspoons butter	½ teaspoon almond extract *or*
3 teaspoons lemon juice	vanilla
¾ cup port, tokay, or muscatel	

SERVES 6

FIRST Place half a stewed peach (fresh or canned) in each of 6 custard cups, cut side up. Fill each cavity with an equal share of a mixture of 6 teaspoons sugar, 6 teaspoons butter, and 3 teaspoons lemon juice. Pour ¾ cup port, tokay, or muscatel over the peaches.

SECOND Beat 2 egg whites until stiff, and add 6 tablespoons powdered sugar, little by little. Add ½ teaspoon almond extract or vanilla. Beat until glossy.

THIRD Top each peach with this meringue and heat in a 350° oven for 15 or 20 minutes until lightly browned.

PEACH SURPRISE

6 large ripe peaches
1½ cups sugar
1½ cups water
½ teaspoon vanilla

1 pint vanilla ice cream
apricot jam
1 cup slivered blanched almonds

SERVES 6

FIRST Cut 6 large ripe peaches into perfect halves. Remove pits. Stew the halved peaches in a syrup of 1½ cups granulated sugar, 1½ cups water, and ½ teaspoon vanilla until tender but not too soft. Cool.

SECOND When cold, put halves together with vanilla ice cream (1 pint in all). Then coat each "whole" peach with apricot jam. Roll each peach *quickly* and carefully in 1 cup slivered blanched almonds. This may also be done by placing the peaches on a bread board and tossing the almonds onto the peaches until all the almonds have adhered to the syrupy apricot jam.

YELLOW PEACHES WITH A RED BLANKET

2 pounds yellow peaches
3 cups sugar
3 cups water
1 tablespoon vanilla
¾ cup sugar

2 cups fresh raspberries
½ wine glass kirsch
½ cup thinly slivered blanched almonds

SERVES 6

FIRST Stew two pounds ripe yellow peaches in a syrup of 3 cups sugar, 2 cups water, and 1 tablespoon vanilla until soft. Cool. Drain peaches and place in a serving-bowl.

SECOND Cook ¾ cups sugar with 1 cup water to a fairly thick syrup. Pour it boiling hot over the contents of 2 cups of raspberries. Allow raspberries to stand for 20 minutes in the hot syrup, stirring occasionally.

THIRD Strain the raspberries and mash through a sieve into a bowl. Reduce the raspberry syrup by boiling it down to about half its original amount. Pour it over the strained pulp. Stir in ½ wineglass kirsch and cool. Pour over the peaches, covering them completely. Scatter the top of the "red blanket" with ½ cup thinly slivered blanched almonds. Chill. Serve very cold.

NOTE Shredded coconut may be used instead of the almonds if preferred.

BAKED PEARS

[*Pre-heat oven to 300°*]

12 baking pears	**½ teaspoon cinnamon *or* 1**
½ cup sugar	**tablespoon vanilla**
2 cups water	

SERVES 12

FIRST Stand 12 baking-pears upright in a buttered glass bakingglass dish.

SECOND Bring ½ cup sugar, 2 cups water, and ½ teaspoon cinnamon or 1 tablespoon vanilla to a quick boil. Pour over pears and set in a 300° oven. Cook until tender (about 2½ hours). The baking time will vary with the size and the ripeness of the fruit. Remove from oven and allow to cool in baking-dish.

BLUSHING PEARS

1 large can Bartlett pears	**angelica (optional)**
½ pound red cinnamon drops	**water cress**
2 packages cream cheese	**French Dressing (clear) (page 247)**
cream	

SERVES 4

FIRST Drain the juice from 1 large can Bartlett pears. Reserve the pear halves and bring the juice to a boil with ½ pound red cinnamon drops.

SECOND Pour the liquid over the pear halves and place in the refrigerator overnight.

FRUITS 467

THIRD Next day moisten 2 packages cream cheese with sufficient cream to make a smooth paste. Put the pear halves together with the cheese mixture. Insert "stems" of small sticks of angelica or watercress stems.

FOURTH Place the "Blushing Pears" on a bed of watercress or any other preferred salad green and sprinkle freely with a clear French Dressing (page 247).

PINEAPPLE QUARTERS WITH CRÈME DE MENTHE

1 large, fresh, ripe pineapple
freshly grated coconut

Crème de Menthe

FOR 4

FIRST Cut 1 large, fresh, ripe pineapple lengthwise in half, *leaving the plumes on*. Cut each half pineapple lengthwise in half again, always remembering to leave the plumes on.

SECOND With a flexible knife cut the meat of the pineapple loose from the rind in one slice, then set back on the rind. Now score each slice of pineapple into even pieces, ready to be served.

THIRD Sprinkle each ½ pineapple with freshly grated coconut. Pass a bottle of Crème de Menthe, permitting each guest to sprinkle his individual ¼ pineapple with the liqueur according to his own taste. This fruit should be served chilled.

MELI MELO

1 fresh, ripe pineapple
1 apple
1 large orange
2 bananas

½ cup white Queen Anne cherries
1 cup strawberries
¾ cup orange Curaçao
freshly grated coconut

SERVES 4–6

FIRST Pare and dice 1 fresh ripe pineapple and 1 apple. Peel 1 large orange and cut crosswise into thin slices. Cut each orange slice in half. Slice 2 bananas. Pit ½ cup white Queen Anne cherries. Wash and hull 1 cup strawberries.

SECOND Combine all the fruits and berries with ¾ cup orange Curaçao. Stir lightly, place in serving-bowl, and chill. Just before serving, sprinkle the top of the fruit with freshly grated coconut.

PINEAPPLE BOAT

1 very large ripe pineapple
sugar
¼ cup best brandy

12 maraschino *or* candied cherries
1 quart pineapple sherbet

SERVES 6

FIRST Lay 1 very large ripe pineapple on its side. Cut off the top carefully and not too deeply. With a sharp knife remove the inside of the pineapple, leaving a hollow box.

SECOND Remove the core of the pineapple, then crush and mix the fruit with sugar to taste and ¼ cup best brandy. Stir and set in refrigerator to marinate. Stir every now and then. This is the sauce.

THIRD Decorate the fronds of the pineapple with 12 maraschino or candied cherries. When ready to serve, fill "the Pineapple Boat" with 1 quart pineapple sherbet. Serve accompanied by the sauce in a bowl.

NOTE One quart should fill the "boat," but this is only an approximate measure. If you prefer, you may use half pineapple sherbet, and half orange sherbet. A sponge cake makes an excellent accompaniment.

APRICOTS JOINED TOGETHER

1 cup water
1½ cups sugar
½ teaspoon vanilla
12 whole apricots
1 pint vanilla ice cream
12 large macaroons

1 cup heavy cream
¼ cup sugar
1 tablespoon vanilla
freshly grated coconut *or* slivered blanched almonds

SERVES 12

FIRST Bring 1 cup of water, 1½ cups sugar, and ½ teaspoon vanilla to a boil. Drop 12 whole apricots into the boiling syrup and stew for ten minutes. Drain and cool.

SECOND When the apricots have cooled, skin and cut each in half. Fill the 24 halves with even amounts of one pint of vanilla ice cream. Press two halves together and set each "whole" apricot on an upturned large macaroon.

THIRD Conceal each macaroon and apricot with a thick layer of whipped cream (1 cup whipping cream beaten until stiff, sweetened with ¼ cup sugar, and flavored with 1 tablespoon vanilla). Sprinkle the whipped cream with freshly grated coconut or, if preferred, with slivered blanched almonds. Serve quickly, two per person.

CITRUS-FRUIT RING

2½ tablespoons gelatin
½ cup cold water
2 cups sugar
1 cup hot water
1 cup grapefruit juice
1 cup orange juice
¼ cup lemon juice

1 large grapefruit
2 large oranges
3 bananas
1½ cups grated pineapple
¼ cup rum
6 marshmallows (optional)

SERVES 6

FIRST Soak 2½ tablespoons gelatin in ½ cup cold water for 5 minutes. Boil 1½ cups sugar with 1 cup hot water until the sugar is melted. Stir the soaked gelatin in this until dissolved.

SECOND Add 1 cup grapefruit juice, 1 cup orange juice, and ¼ cup lemon juice. Blend and pour into a cold ring mold. Set in refrigerator.

THIRD When ready to serve, unmold and fill center with a mixture of cut-up fruits: the skinned sections of 1 large grapefruit, the skinned sections of 2 large oranges, 3 sliced bananas, and 1½ cups grated pineapple, all soaked for half an hour in ½ cup sugar and ¼ cup rum. When the fruit and the ring are combined, toss 6 chopped marshmallows on top (optional) and serve.

FIGS IN CRÈME DE CACAO AND SOUR CREAM

2 large cans drained Kadota figs
1 cup sour cream
Crème de Cacao
sugar

SERVES 6

FIRST Drain well 2 large cans Kadota figs. Chill.

SECOND To 1 cup sour cream add enough Crème de Cacao to suit your taste. (I use about 2 tablespoons, but you may prefer more or less.) Sweeten with a little sugar, depending on how much of the liqueur you use.

THIRD Place the chilled, well-drained figs in a serving-bowl and cover the top evenly with the sour-cream combination so that all the figs are concealed.

NOTE This may be done with greengages too.

FROZEN FRUIT SALAD

2 tablespoons flour
½ teaspoon dry mustard
½ teaspoon salt
1 teaspoon sugar
2 tablespoons oil
2 tablespoons vinegar
2 tablespoons lemon juice
4 egg yolks
1 cup boiling water
2 envelopes gelatin
½ cup cold water
1½ cups heavy cream
2 cups canned pears
2 cups canned pineapple
2 cups canned white cherries
Pineapple Cream Sauce (page 363)

SERVES 8

FIRST Mix 2 tablespoons flour with ½ teaspoon dry mustard, ½ teaspoon salt, and 1 teaspoon sugar. Stir in 2 tablespoons oil, 2 tablespoons vinegar, and 2 tablespoons lemon juice.

SECOND Beat in 4 egg yolks and add 1 cup of boiling water. Stir constantly in the top of a double boiler until thick. Remove from the fire and pour into a large mixing-bowl. Cool thoroughly.

THIRD Soak 2 envelopes gelatin in ½ cup cold water. Let stand for 5 minutes. Dissolve the gelatin over hot water. Then add to the mixture, stirring until blended.

FOURTH Whip 1½ cups of heavy cream until stiff and fold into the cooled mixture until thoroughly blended.

FIFTH Thoroughly drain 2 cups canned pears, 2 cups canned pineapple, and 2 cups canned white cherries. Drop the fruit into the cream. Fold in carefully in order to cover the fruit completely, but be careful in handling it to be certain that it does not break. Set in a cold, rinsed mold and place in the refrigerator for four or five hours until set.

SIXTH When ready to serve, unmold onto a serving-platter and serve with a Pineapple Cream Sauce (page 363).

NOTE This may be served as a dessert.

FRUIT SALAD

2 oranges
2 grapefruit
3 apples
1 small pineapple
1 box frozen raspberries
1 box frozen sliced peaches
2 cups strawberries *or* 1 box frozen strawberries

3 bananas
sugar to taste (at least 1 cup)
½ cup kirsch
grated Coconut
Fruit Salad Dressing (page 472) (optional)

SERVES 6

FIRST Cut 2 oranges, 2 grapefruit, 3 apples, and 1 small pineapple into a large mixing-bowl.

SECOND Add 1 box thawed frozen raspberries, 1 box thawed sliced frozen peaches, and 1 box thawed frozen strawberries (or 2 cups fresh strawberries), including juices. At the last (to prevent their discoloring) slice 3 bananas. Fold in 1 cup sugar. Turn the fruit in the sugar several times, then add ½ cup kirsch. Set the bowl in the refrigerator.

THIRD When ready to serve, turn the fruit into a serving-bowl and sprinkle grated coconut, like snow, over the top.

NOTE If preferred, Fruit Salad Dressing (page 472) may be used. This recipe makes an excellent fruit cup as a first course. Especially effective for the holidays.

FRUIT SALAD DRESSING

½ cup heavy cream
1 egg white
1 egg yolk

juice of 1 lemon
salt
1 teaspoon sugar

FIRST Beat ½ cup heavy cream until thick. Beat 1 egg white until stiff. Blend and beat together.

SECOND Beat 1 egg yolk until light and creamy. Then add the juice of 1 lemon, a pinch salt, and 1 teaspoon sugar. Beat together until well blended. Fold into the cream mixture. Serve with fresh fruits or fruit salad.

NOTE The juice of the lemon may be replaced by fresh strawberry or raspberry juice if preferred.

NECTARINES EVANGELINE

[Pre-heat oven to 400°]

6 squares thinly sliced Sponge Cake (page 389)
apricot jam
12 stewed *or* canned nectarine halves
brown sugar

unblanched almonds
6 tablespoons Jamaica rum
1 cup heavy cream
¼ cup sugar
1 tablespoon vanilla

SERVES 6

FIRST Place 6 squares thinly sliced Sponge Cake (page 389) in a shallow baking-dish. Spread each square with a thin layer of thin apricot jam. Arrange 2 stewed or canned nectarine halves on each slice of cake.

SECOND Sprinkle each nectarine half with brown sugar and unblanched almonds thinly sliced lengthwise. Pour 1 tablespoon Jamaica rum on each piece of cake.

THIRD Place in 400° oven and bake until the sugar melts. Serve hot, with 1 cup heavy cream whipped, sweetened with ¼ cup sugar, and flavored with 1 tablespoon vanilla. If preferred, serve with thick, plain cream instead.

ORANGE SLICES IN CHILLED RED WINE

¾ cup sugar
1 cup water
1 cup claret *or* Burgundy

small bag containing: 2 cloves, stick cinnamon, 2 slices tangerine, 2 slices lemon
6 large oranges
orange peel

SERVES 6

FIRST Dissolve ¾ cup sugar in 1 cup water and 1 cup claret or Burgundy. When the liquid comes to a boil, set a small bag in it containing 2 whole cloves, stick cinnamon, 2 slices tangerine, and 2 slices lemon.

SECOND Boil all these ingredients until syrupy. Then just before removing from the fire, take out the spice bag.

THIRD Remove the skins of 6 large oranges. Divide the segments into individual pieces, peel them carefully, removing all the membrane. Set them to soak in the syrup. Place the dish in the refrigerator until very, very cold.

FOURTH Serve with tiny, thin slivers of orange peel floating on top. Serve *cold!*

THREE HOT FRUITS

[*Pre-heat oven to 350°*]

1 large can Bartlett pears
1 large can peaches
1 large can black Bing cherries
1 tablespoon butter

¼ cup brown sugar
¼ cup brandy
¼ cup Cointreau

SERVES 6

FIRST Drain 1 large can each Bartlett pears, peaches, and black Bing cherries. Put all the fruit in a glass baking-dish.

SECOND Heat the juice from the 3 cans with 1 tablespoon butter and ¼ cup brown sugar. Pour over the fruit dish and set in a 350° oven for 20 minutes.

THIRD 5 minutes before serving, add ¼ cup brandy and ¼ cup Cointreau. Serve hot.

NOTE A plain sponge cake makes an excellent addition to this interesting fruit dessert.

Chapter XVI: *Coffee Cakes, Hot Breads, and Waffles*

Hot cross buns, hot cross buns

One a penny, two a penny,

Hot cross buns . . .

    Mother Goose

Apple Coffee Cake
Apple Muffins
Bacon Popovers
Blueberry Coffee or Tea Cake
Bran Muffins
Bundt Cake
Coffee Kringel
Corn Pouches
Cream Cheese Crescents
Dimpas Dampas, Grandmère
Garlic Loaf
Gesundheits Kuchen (Health Cake)
Ginger Coffee Cake
Hot Cross Buns
Lebkuchen for Christmas
Nut Cake
Pecan Bread

Sally Lund
Shortcake Smetana
Six Yeast Dough Coffee Cakes
   The Yeast Dough
   Bundt kuchen
   Cinnamon Coffee Cake
   Eisenkuchen
   Filled Coffee Cake
   Schnecken Noodle Strips
   Superlative Schnecken
Virginia Batter Bread
Virginia Batter Cakes
Virginia Corn Bread
Virginia Johnny Cake
Pat's Waffles
Wendy's Waffles

APPLE COFFEE CAKE

[*Pre-heat oven to 425°*]

2 eggs
1 cup milk
1 cup sifted flour
4 teaspoons baking powder
⅛ teaspoon salt
1 tablespoon sugar
2 cups diced green apples
4 tablespoons melted butter
sugar
cinnamon

FIRST Beat 2 eggs with 1 cup milk until blended.

SECOND Sift 1 cup flour. Measure and resift with 4 teaspoons baking powder and ⅛ teaspoon salt. Sift slowly into the milk and eggs. Beat until smooth. Add 1 tablespoon sugar and beat again.

THIRD Combine 2 cups diced green apples with 4 tablespoons melted butter. Stir into batter and fold in thoroughly. Pour into a glass pie plate and bake for 12 minutes in a 425° oven. Reduce heat to 350° and bake 15 to 20 minutes more. Turn out on serving-dish and sprinkle well with sugar and cinnamon.

NOTE I find it convenient to mix 1 tablespoon sugar with ½ teaspoon cinnamon before sprinkling. The coffee cake should be served slightly warm. Extra sugar and cinnamon may be served with it. It also makes a delicious dessert—in which case, serve with sour cream or with 1 cup of heavy cream, beaten stiff, sweetened with ¼ cup sugar, and flavored with 1 teaspoon vanilla.

APPLE MUFFINS

[*Pre-heat oven to 425°*]

½ cup sugar
4 tablespoons butter
1 beaten egg
2¼ cups pastry flour
3½ teaspoons baking powder
½ teaspoon salt
½ teaspoon nutmeg
½ teaspoon cinnamon
1 cup milk
1 cup chopped apples
2 tablespoons sugar

FIRST Cream ½ cup sugar with 4 tablespoons butter. Add 1 beaten egg and beat until smooth.

SECOND Sift 2¼ cups pastry flour. Measure and resift 3 times with 3½ teaspoons baking powder, ½ teaspoon salt, ¼ teaspoon nutmeg, and ¼ teaspoon cinnamon. Add alternately to the batter with 1 cup of milk. Beat after each addition until well blended.

THIRD Fold in 1 cup chopped, pared, and cored apples. Then fill greased muffin pans half full and sprinkle the top of each unbaked muffin with a combined mixture of: 2 tablespoons sugar, ¼ teaspoon cinnamon, and ¼ teaspoon nutmeg. Bake in a 425° oven for 25 minutes.

NOTE Try making these delicious muffins with a cup of pitted, fresh, sweet cherries or with the same amount of any other desired fruit. If you use any tart fruits or berries, such as plums or blackberries, the fruit must be allowed to stand in sugar beforehand.

Some years ago, my friend, June Platt asked me for my Apple Muffin recipe. It was with pride that I noted that she had used it in June Platt's "Plain and Fancy Cook Book," published by Houghton Mifflin Company.

BACON POPOVERS
[Pre-heat oven to 450°]

1 cup flour	1 cup milk
¼ teaspoon salt	¼ cup crisp, crushed bacon
2 eggs	

FIRST Sift and measure 1 cup flour. Resift with ¼ teaspoon salt.

SECOND Combine 2 well-beaten eggs with 1 cup milk and add to the dry ingredients. Beat with a rotary beater until light and foamy. Add ¼ cup of crisp, crushed bacon.

THIRD Grease muffin tins and heat in a 450° oven. Fill half full with the batter and bake in 450° oven for 20 minutes, then at 375° for 15 minutes longer. This recipe makes 12 popovers.

BLUEBERRY COFFEE OR TEA CAKE

AN OLD NEW ENGLAND RECIPE
[Pre-heat oven to 400°]

1 tablespoon soft butter
1½ cup sugar
1 egg
2½ cups sifted flour
3 teaspoons baking powder
¼ teaspoon salt
¼ teaspoon grated nutmeg
1½ cups milk
3 cups blueberries
sugar and cream *or*
Vanilla Sauce I (page 363)

FIRST Cream 1 tablespoon soft butter with 1 cup sugar. Beat in 1 whole egg.

SECOND Sift 2½ cups of flour. Measure and resift twice with 3 teaspoons baking powder, ¼ teaspoon salt, and ¼ teaspoon grated nutmeg. Add the flour alternately to the batter with 1½ cups milk. Blend well. This will make a fairly stiff dough.

THIRD Toss 3 cups of blueberries into a mixing-bowl and sprinkle them with ½ cup sugar. Shake the bowl to distribute the sugar evenly over the berries. Fold the berries into the batter, being careful not to crush them.

FOURTH Spread the mixture evenly on a buttered pan. Bake in a 400° oven for approximately 35 minutes. Remove from oven and cut immediately into squares, allowing it to cool in the pan. Sprinkle rather generously with sugar. Serve while slightly warm with thick cream or with Vanilla Sauce I (page 363).

NOTE The cake was originally served plain, with coffee or tea. The addition of either the thick cream or the Vanilla Sauce, however, makes a very successful dessert.

BRAN MUFFINS *Marie's*
[Pre-heat oven to 400°]

¼ cup sugar
¼ pound butter
½ cup vegetable shortening
1 teaspoon soda
1 cup buttermilk
½ cup flour
salt
2 cups bran
½ cup raisins
1 egg

FIRST Cream ¼ cup sugar with ¼ pound of butter and ½ cup vegetable shortening until light.

SECOND Stir 1 teaspoon soda into 1 cup buttermilk until dissolved. Add the liquid to the butter mixture.

THIRD Sift ½ cup flour. Measure and resift with a pinch of salt into the batter.

FOURTH Stir in 2 cups bran, ½ cup raisins, and 1 well-beaten egg. Spoon into hot greased muffin pans, filling them only ⅔ full. Bake in a 400° oven for approximately 20 minutes. Allow to stand 5 minutes in the pans. Remove carefully as these muffins are extremely delicate.

NOTE These bran muffins are delicious beyond words and never fail to create an enthusiastic stir at table. Butter may be served with them of course, but because of their rich resemblance to certain cupcakes, it is often found quite satisfactory to serve them plain.

BUNDT CAKE
[Pre-heat oven to 375°]

5 ounces butter
2 cups sifted sugar
5 egg yolks
2 cups sifted pastry flour
2 rounded teaspoons baking powder

¼ teaspoon salt
1 cup milk
2 teaspoons vanilla
2 teaspoons lemon extract
5 egg whites

FIRST Cream 5 ounces butter. Add 2 cups of sifted sugar, a little at a time. Beat until fluffy. Then add 5 egg yolks, one at a time, beating thoroughly after each addition.

SECOND Sift 2 cups pastry flour. Measure and resift 3 times with 2 rounded teaspoons baking powder and ¼ teaspoon salt. Add flour to butter mixture alternately with 1 cup milk, beating until smooth after each addition. Add 2 teaspoons vanilla and 2 teaspoons lemon extract, beating again.

THIRD Beat 5 egg whites until stiff. Fold them in with a gentle hand. Grease and lightly flour a cake mold or a fluted cake pan.

Pour in the batter and bake for 45 minutes in a 375° oven. Turn up the heat to 400° and bake for 15 minutes more.

FOURTH Cool the cake on a cake rack. Just before serving, sprinkle generously with sifted powdered sugar.

COFFEE KRINGEL

2 ounces butter
¼ cup sugar
2 eggs
1¼ cups sifted flour
½ teaspoon baking powder

1 teaspoon vanilla
strawberry jam
oil
additional sugar

FIRST Cream 2 ounces butter with ¼ cup sugar. Beat in 2 whole eggs and continue to beat until smooth.

SECOND Sift 1¼ cups flour. Measure and resift twice with ½ teaspoon baking powder. Sift into butter mixture. Beat in 1 teaspoon vanilla. Roll out on a lightly floured board.

THIRD Cut with a biscuit-cutter. Dab half the rounds with strawberry jam. Cover with the other halves. Press the edges together, then drop into steaming fat or oil (about 350° to 400°). Turn in the fat and brown lightly on both sides. Remove and drain on brown paper or paper towels. Just before serving roll freely in sugar.

NOTE Be careful not to fry too quickly or the Kringels will be dark brown on the outside and raw in the inside. These are delicious with coffee.

CORN POUCHES

[*Pre-heat oven to 450°*]

1½ cups flour
1 cup yellow corn meal
1 teaspoon salt
2 tablespoons baking powder
1 whole egg

1 egg yolk
1 scant cup milk
2 tablespoons melted butter
soft butter

FIRST Sift 1½ cups flour. Measure and resift 3 times with 1 cup yellow corn meal, 1 teaspoon salt, and 2 tablespoons baking powder.

SECOND Beat 1 whole egg with 1 egg yolk until blended. Add 1 scant cup milk and beat together. Pour in 2 tablespoons melted butter (somewhat cooled) and beat again. Pour into flour mixture and blend well.

THIRD Roll out about ¼ inch thick on a lightly floured board. Cut with a biscuit-cutter and smear with soft butter. Then fold in half to form little pouches. Place on a greased and floured baking-sheet and bake in a 450° oven for about 15 minutes.

WARNING Be certain that the melted butter is not *hot* when added to the eggs or they will curdle. Shape these pouches about the size you desire them. They do not change very greatly in size during baking.

CREAM-CHEESE CRESCENTS

1 tablespoon sugar
½ pound cream cheese
½ pound butter
2 beaten egg yolks
2 cups sifted pastry flour

apricot, strawberry, *or* raspberry jam *or*
chopped nuts and sugar
powdered sugar

FIRST Work 1 tablespoon sugar with ½ pound cream cheese, ½ pound butter, 2 beaten egg yolks, and 2 cups of sifted, measured, and resifted pastry flour. Place in refrigerator overnight or, better still, for 24 hours.

[*Pre-heat oven to 425°*]

SECOND Remove dough from refrigerator. Roll out thin and cut into squares. Cut each square into 2 triangles.

THIRD Fill each triangle with a choice of apricot, strawberry, or raspberry jam, or with chopped nuts mixed with a little sugar.

FOURTH Roll each triangle away from you, toward the point, into the shape of a crescent or horseshoe. Place on a greased and floured cookie tin and bake in a 425° oven until golden brown. Cool on a cake rack and sprinkle generously with powdered sugar.

DIMPAS DAMPAS GRANDMÈRE

[*Pre-heat oven to 375°*]

3 eggs
1 tablespoon sugar
2 heaping tablespoons flour
¼ teaspoon salt
¼ cup milk

4 green apples
2 tablespoons butter
sugar
cinnamon
1 tablespoon lemon juice

FIRST Beat 3 eggs until light. Then sprinkle in 1 tablespoon sugar and continue to beat well. Add 2 heaping tablespoons flour and ¼ teaspoon salt alternately with ¼ cup milk. Beat thoroughly until smooth.

SECOND Peel, core, and slice 4 green apples into thin slices. Fold into batter until well covered. Melt 1 tablespoon butter in a preheated glass pie plate. Pour in the batter and bake for 35 minutes in a 375° oven. After the first 20 minutes cover with an inverted pie plate and continue to bake for 15 minutes more, at which time the apples should be soft.

THIRD Remove from the oven and dot immediately with 1 tablespoon butter broken into bits. As soon as the butter has melted, sprinkle generously with a mixture of sugar and cinnamon to taste and 1 tablespoon of lemon juice. Allow to cool slightly, but be sure to serve while still warm.

NOTE This was my grandmother's idea of an ideal children's dessert. The fact that it was perfect for adults with a steaming cup of coffee, never seemed to have occurred to anyone in the family until later.

GARLIC LOAF
[*Pre-heat oven to 450°*]

1 loaf unsliced white sandwich bread
1 mashed clove garlic
½ pound butter

FIRST Cut the crusts off one loaf unsliced white sandwich bread. Cut loaf into ¼-inch slices. Tie slices together loosely with a piece of kitchen string.

SECOND Mash 1 clove of garlic in a bowl until almost a paste. Mix it with ½ pound soft butter. Thickly spread the butter on all sides of the tied loaf. Place in a covered baking-dish and bake 30 minutes at 450°. Serve hot.

GESUNDHEITS KUCHEN (*Health Cake*)   Marie's
[*Pre-heat oven to 325°*]

½ pound butter
1 cup sugar
8 egg yolks
2 cups pastry flour
2 teaspoons baking powder
¼ teaspoon salt
grated rind 1 lemon
juice ½ lemon
8 egg whites
powdered sugar

FIRST Cream ½ pound butter with 1 cup sugar until smooth and light in color. Add 8 egg yolks and stir very, very thoroughly.

SECOND Sift 2 cups pastry flour. Measure and resift 3 times with 2 teaspoons baking powder and ¼ teaspoon salt. Add to the batter. Stir in the grated rind 1 lemon and the juice ½ lemon.

THIRD Beat 8 egg whites until stiff. Fold into the batter with a gentle hand. Bake in a 325° oven for an hour, or until a straw comes out of the center clean. When ready to serve, sprinkle with powdered sugar.

NOTE This is strictly a "plain" cake. Perfectly delicious as a coffee cake, or cut thin and served with stewed fruit; or cut into portions and served with a covering of Marie's Vanilla Sauce (page 363).

GINGER COFFEE CAKE

[*Pre-heat oven to 350°*]

½ cup sugar
½ cup dark syrup
1 egg
¼ pound butter

½ cup warm water
1½ cups flour
1 teaspoon soda
2 tablespoons ginger

FIRST Mix ½ cup sugar with ½ cup dark syrup. Beat in 1 egg until well blended.

SECOND Melt ¼ pound butter in ½ cup warm water, but do not simmer—simply melt slowly. Add to the sugar and syrup and stir until well mixed.

THIRD Sift 1½ cups flour, 1 teaspoon soda, and 2 tablespoons ginger. Sift into the mixture and work until completely blended.

FOURTH Butter or grease a square pan or a single 9-inch layer-cake tin. Add batter and bake in a 350° oven until a straw comes out of the center clean and dry.

HOT CROSS BUNS

2 ounces butter
1 cup milk
1 cake yeast
2 eggs

4 cups flour
½ teaspoon salt
⅛ teaspoon grated nutmeg

FIRST Dissolve 2 ounces butter in 1 full cup warm milk. Add 1 cake crumbled yeast. Dissolve.

SECOND Beat 2 whole eggs separately and add to the milk. Then add to 4 cups flour sifted, measured, and resifted with ½ teaspoon of salt and ⅛ teaspoon of grated nutmeg. Knead well on a lightly floured bread board. The dough should be soft. Let it rise, covered with a cloth, overnight.

THIRD   Next morning shape the risen dough into buns. Work them into rather flat "cakes" and set them about 1 inch apart on buttered pans. Cover the pan and set in a warm place until double their original size. This process will take between 2 and 3½ hours depending on the temperature.

[*Pre-heat oven to 375°*]

FOURTH   Take a small, sharp knife and cut a cross in the center of the top of each bun. This cross is not to be cut so deep as to penetrate. Bake in a 375° oven for approximately half an hour. While still warm, spread the buns with Thin Icing (page 427) with a pastry brush.

LEBKUCHEN FOR CHRISTMAS

2½ ounces brandy
2 teaspoons ground cardamon seed
1 tablespoon cinnamon
1 tablespoon powdered cloves
1 level teaspoon mixture ginger, nutmeg, and white pepper
8⅔ cups flour
2 pounds 3 ounces strained honey
4⅓ cups sugar

4 eggs
12½ ounces ground unpeeled almonds
butter
rice paper *or* white of egg papers (optional)
Thin Icing (page 427)
colored decorettes
peeled whole almonds

TAKES TWO DAYS TO PREPARE

FIRST   Pour 2½ ounces brandy over 2 teaspoons ground cardamon seed, 1 tablespoon cinnamon, 1 tablespoon powdered cloves, and 1 level teaspoon mixture ginger, nutmeg, and white pepper. Let stand overnight.

SECOND   Place 8⅔ cups flour into a very large mixing-bowl. Make a hole in the center. Pour in 2 pounds 3 ounces of strained honey and 4⅓ cups sugar. Combine and let stand overnight.

THIRD   Next day knead well. Add 4 eggs, one at a time, beating until well blended. Knead for half an hour. Add 12½ ounces ground unpeeled almonds and knead again for half an hour.

[*Pre-heat oven to 450°*]

FOURTH Add the brandy and spices to the dough, a little at a time, until well blended.

FIFTH Butter generously two large cookie pans (with edges all around). If possible buy rice papers or white of egg papers to place underneath the batter. (This is traditional but not necessary.) Pour on dough and smooth evenly all around with a knife moistened in water after each stroke. Bake in a 450° oven for 8 minutes. Turn oven down to 400° and bake for 30 to 45 minutes. When cooled, ice with Thin Icing (page 427). Sprinkle with colored decorettes and set whole peeled almonds into the top. Cut into pieces 2 inches by 4 inches and wrap in cellophane or wax paper. These cakes keep well for 3 weeks, but are at their best 1 week after baking. However, if they must stand, keep in an airtight jar or tin with a fresh apple cut into quarters.

NOTE This ancient recipe originated at Nürnberg, Germany several centuries ago. It is not a difficult recipe to follow, but like so many old European recipes, requires lots of patience, and a helping hand from members of the family, especially when one finds an instruction such as: "Knead for half an hour." However, it is well worth the trouble; especially for those who have nostalgic memories of grandmothers who made these delicious Christmas cakes; or, who may only have heard of the famous Nürnberg Lebkuchen. Marie, as usual, kneaded without asking anybody's help!

NUT BREAD

[*Pre-heat oven to 350°*]

1½ cups whole-wheat flour
1½ cups white flour
4 tablespoons sugar
6 teaspoons baking powder
¾ teaspoon salt
1 teaspoon soda

4 tablespoons molasses or honey
2 cups milk
¼ cup coarsely chopped pecans
¼ cup coarsely chopped walnuts
¼ cup coarsely chopped almonds

FIRST Sift 1½ cups whole-wheat flour and measure. Sift 1½ cups white flour and measure. Resift both flours together 3 times with

4 tablespoons sugar, 6 teaspoons baking powder, ¾ teaspoon salt, and 1 teaspoon soda. Place in a large mixing-bowl. Make a well in the center and drop in 4 tablespoons molasses or honey and 2 cups of milk. Mix thoroughly so that the dry ingredients and the liquids are well blended.

SECOND Coarsely chop ¼ cup pecans, ¼ cup walnuts, and ¼ cup unpeeled almonds. Beat into the dough. Place in a greased bread pan and bake in a 350° oven for approximately 45 minutes, or until a straw comes out of the center clean.

NOTE Toast this. Try spreading it with butter and cream cheese.

PECAN BREAD
[*Pre-heat oven to 300°*]

6 egg yolks
1 cup sugar
1 teaspoon baking powder
1 cup bread crumbs

1 cup chopped pecans
juice 1 lemon
6 egg whites

FIRST Beat 6 egg yolks with 1 cup sugar until light.

SECOND Stir in 1 teaspoon baking powder mixed with 1 cup bread crumbs. Add 1 cup coarsely chopped pecans and the juice 1 lemon.

THIRD Beat 6 egg whites until stiff. Fold in gently. Bake in a buttered loaf pan in a 300° oven for about 35 minutes.

SALLY LUNN

6 ounces butter
1 cup sugar
1 cake yeast
4 eggs

2 cups milk
4 cups flour
¼ teaspoon salt

FIRST Beat 6 ounces butter with 1 cup sugar and 1 crumbled cake yeast until well combined. Add 4 whole eggs and beat again.

SECOND Beat in 1 cup milk and fold in 1 cup of sifted and measured flour. Beat until well blended. Add 1 cup milk and blend. Sift, measure, and resift 3 cups of flour and ¼ teaspoon of salt. Combine all ingredients until a smooth paste has been formed.

THIRD Cover the mixing-bowl with a clean cloth, place it in a warm place, and allow to rise until double in size (about 1½ hours). At the end of this time the batter should appear light and spongy.

[*Pre-heat oven to 425°*]

FOURTH Lightly grease and flour muffin tins. Fill half full with the batter. Set the tins back in the same warm place for the batter to rise again. Then bake in a 425° oven until golden. Allow to remain a few minutes in the muffin tins before removing.

NOTE This recipe is sufficient to make 12 muffins and 1 large loaf of Sally Lunn bread, the latter baked in a loaf pan.

SHORTCAKE SMETANA

[*Pre-heat oven to 425°*]

2 cups pastry flour
½ teaspoon salt
3½ teaspoons baking powder
2 tablespoons butter

½ teaspoon soda
1 cup sour cream
3 tablespoons milk

THE FILLING

soft butter
fruit *or* berries
2 cups heavy cream

½ cup sugar
3 teaspoons vanilla

FIRST Sift 2 cups pastry flour. Measure and resift 3 times with ½ teaspoon salt and 3½ teaspoons baking powder.

SECOND With 2 knives or a pastry cutter, cut 2 tablespoons cold butter into the dry ingredients. Stir ½ teaspoon soda into 1 cup sour cream and add to the flour. Mix with a fork instead of a spoon. Add 3 tablespoons milk, and continue to mix until well blended.

THIRD Toss onto a lightly floured board and roll out about 1 inch thick. This recipe makes about two 9-inch shortcakes or 12 individuals. Bake in a 425° oven.

FOURTH When baked, cut shortcake tops off in one piece, scoop out all the soft insides, leaving a shallow container. Butter these and fill thickly with 2 cups heavy cream beaten stiff, sweetened with ½ cup sugar, and flavored with 3 teaspoons vanilla extract and with any desired fruit or berries. Reserve some of this filling for the topping. Replace the shortcake tops and pile with the additional cream and fruit or berries.

NOTE This sour cream shortcake also makes excellent biscuits. When the dough has been rolled out, cut with a biscuit-cutter. Place the rounds close together and bake as above.

Six Yeast-Dough Coffee Cakes   MARIE'S

YEAST DOUGH   Marie's
[The basic dough]

1 cake yeast
⅓ cup water and milk combined
sugar
3 ounces butter
¼ cup sugar
1 whole egg

1 egg yolk
1 cup milk
salt
3 cups sifted flour
grated rind 1 lemon

FIRST   Crumble 1 cake yeast into a cup containing ⅓ cup water and milk combined and a pinch sugar. Let stand 20 minutes.

SECOND   Beat 3 ounces butter with ¼ cup sugar until smooth and light. Beat in 1 whole egg and an additional egg yolk and 1 cup of lukewarm milk until smooth—very smooth.

THIRD   Add pinch of salt to 3 cups flour and sift into batter, a little at a time, beating after each addition until smooth again. Beat in the grated rind 1 lemon and the dissolved yeast. Continue to beat until the dough leaves the spoon and no longer sticks to the bowl. At this point, cover with a clean cloth and let rise in a warm place for about 1 hour, or until double in size.

NOTE   Marie regaled us with six superlative coffee cakes. The sort of coffee cakes that were only to be found in the beginning of the century in the coffee houses of Vienna and Budapest, or possibly in a few rare kitchens in this country, where reigned cooks who had been born in Austria or Austria-Hungary. Such a one was Marie, and her six coffee cakes were of such a feathery, aromatic deliciousness, that their memory has kept me trotting through the years, from bakery shop to bakery shop, trying to discover one baker anywhere who could deliver their counterpart. There is no substitute for Marie's own incomparable recipes. I am resigned. I no longer trot from Yorkville in New York to Santa Monica in California. I bake myself, and if only temporarily, smell the smells and taste the tastes of my long-ago childhood again!

BUNDT KUCHEN Marie's
[Pre-heat oven to 350°]

1 recipe Yeast Dough (page 491)
2 eggs
¼ pound butter
½ cup sugar
grated rind 1 lemon
whole almonds

FIRST After Yeast Dough (page 491) has risen until double in size, add 2 beaten eggs, ¼ pound butter, ½ cup sugar, and the grated rind 1 lemon.

SECOND Put whole skinned almonds in the bottom of a well-buttered, deep baking-form. Pour in the mixture. Set in a warm place and let rise until double in size.

THIRD Bake in 350° oven until nicely browned, and a testing straw comes out of the center clean.

CINNAMON COFFEE CAKE Marie's

1 recipe Yeast Dough (page 491)
2 ounces melted butter
1 beaten egg
1 cup sugar
3 tablespoons cinnamon

FIRST Roll Yeast Dough (page 491) out very thin. Spread on a buttered tin and let rise in a warm place.

[Pre-heat oven to 350°]

SECOND When double in size, prick with a fork. Brush with 2 ounces melted butter and 1 beaten egg.

THIRD Mix 1 cup sugar with 3 tablespoons cinnamon. Cover dough with this mixture and bake in a 350° oven until nicely browned. Serve warm with coffee. If baked ahead of time, warm slightly before serving.

EISENKUCHEN Marie's

1 recipe Yeast Dough (page 491)
2 beaten eggs
¼ pound butter
½ cup sugar
grated rind 1 lemon
½ cup raisins
almonds

FIRST After Yeast Dough (page 491) has risen until double in size, add 2 beaten eggs, ¼ pound butter, ½ cup sugar, and the grated rind 1 lemon. Beat in ½ cup raisins.

SECOND Put whole almonds (skins removed) in the bottom of a well-buttered baking-form. Pour in the mixture.

THIRD Set in a warm place and let rise until double in size.

[*Pre-heat oven to 350°*]
FOURTH Bake in 350° oven until nicely browned or until a testing straw comes out of the center clean.

FILLED COFFEE CAKE *Marie's*

1 recipe Yeast Dough (page 491)	butter
¼ pound melted butter	1 beaten egg
2 cups cooked noodles	½ cup chopped almonds
½ cup brown sugar	Thin Icing (page 427)

FIRST After Yeast Dough (page 491) has risen until double in size, melt ¼ pound butter in a skillet. Warm 2 cups cooked noodles (boiled in salted water and drained thoroughly) in ¼ pound melted butter. Sprinkle noodles with ½ cup brown sugar.

SECOND Roll out the dough on a lightly floured board, dot with tiny bits of butter, then cover with the sugared noodles, arranging them evenly over the surface of the dough. Dot with butter again. Roll the dough and shape into a ring.

THIRD Brush top with 1 slightly beaten egg, and sprinkle all over with ½ cup chopped, skinned almonds. Allow to rise again in a warm place until double in size.

[*Pre-heat oven to 350°*]
FOURTH Bake in a 350° oven until golden brown. When cooled, cover top with Thin Icing (page 427).

SCHNECKEN NOODLE STRIPS *Marie's*

1 recipe Yeast Dough (page 491)
citron
raisins
grated rind 1 lemon

sugar
cinnamon
2 egg yolks
powdered sugar

FIRST Roll Yeast Dough (page 491) *thin*.

SECOND Generously cover the dough with chopped citron, raisins, grated rind 1 lemon, sugar, and cinnamon.

THIRD Cut the dough into 1-inch strips the width of the dough. Roll the strips individually. Set them in a well-buttered pan, brush the tops with the beaten yolk of 2 eggs, and let rise in a warm place.

[*Pre-heat oven to 350°*]

FOURTH Bake in a 350° oven until nicely browned. Sprinkle with powdered sugar.

SUPERLATIVE SCHNECKEN *Marie's*

1 recipe Yeast Dough (page 491)
¾ cup melted butter
½ cup sugar
1 tablespoon cinnamon

½ cup raisins
½ cup finely chopped nuts
soft butter
brown sugar

FIRST Roll out Yeast Dough (page 491) and brush with melted butter. Sprinkle with ½ cup brown sugar mixed with 1 tablespoon cinnamon, ½ cup raisins, ½ cup finely chopped nuts. Then roll tightly, like a jelly roll. Brush with melted butter.

SECOND Generously butter a round baking-form (such as a spring form). Sprinkle brown sugar all over bottom of the spring form or round cake tin until approximately ¼ inch thick. Cut the roll into 2-inch pieces and place one next to the other in the prepared form. Brush the pieces with additional melted butter and allow to rise again until double in size.

[*Pre-heat oven to 350°*]

THIRD Bake for 30–40 minutes in a 350° oven. Allow to cool for a few minutes in the pan. Then invert onto a platter. Serve slightly warm with tea or coffee.

NOTE All during those exciting years when Saturday nights were an adolescent adventure, I never came back home without the delicious odor of Marie's Schnecken floating through the house. The repeated assurance was always there that Marie had spent her usual Saturday night in the kitchen, laboring with love and with genius over her superlative Schnecken. Nostalgia presents one with the realization that it is of just such little things as these, of which an adolescent's sense of security is built. Home!

VIRGINIA BATTER BREAD

[*Pre-heat oven to 400°*]

A VERY OLD RECIPE

½ cup corn meal
½ teaspoon salt
2 cups boiling water
1½ teaspoons baking powder

2 eggs
1½ cups milk
1 tablespoon melted butter *or* bacon fat

SERVES 6

FIRST Sift ½ cup corn meal with ½ teaspoon salt into a mixing-bowl. Scald with 2 cups boiling water. To quote the original recipe: "Scalding meal, means to pour boiling water over it. There is no exact way to say how much water, for meal differs in thickening qualities. We use about 2 cups, stir briskly while pouring and use enough water to make a thick gluey paste like the kind a paper hanger uses to put up wall paper."

SECOND Add 1½ teaspoons baking powder, 2 beaten eggs, 1½ cups milk, and 1 tablespoon hot melted butter or bacon fat. Beat for a few minutes.

THIRD Pour the batter into a sizzling hot, greased baking-dish and set in a 400° oven until nicely browned. Serve very hot.

NOTE Shades of the wonderful Virginia breakfasts at Becky Yancey Williams' where her cook, Helen, reigns supreme. I am not a breakfast eater, but I did a complete right about face when visiting in Richmond. My habits were quickly changed by Helen's marvellous breakfasts! I shall never forget the platters of bacon, the baking dishes of Batter Bread or the platters of Batter Cakes! These, to a born Yankee, brought about an immediate conversion to the gastronomic banner of the south!

VIRGINIA BATTER CAKES

1 cup corn meal
½ teaspoon salt
2 cups boiling water
2 teaspoons baking powder

2 eggs
1 cup milk
maple syrup
crisp bacon

SERVES 6

FIRST Mix 1 cup corn meal with ½ teaspoon of salt and scald with 2 cups boiling water. (Page 495.)

SECOND Add 2 teaspoons baking powder and 2 well-beaten eggs. Stir in 1 cup of milk and beat for a few minutes.

THIRD Fry a few spoonfuls at a time on a hot, greased griddle or in a hot frying-pan. Serve quickly with warm maple syrup and a platter of warm, crisp bacon.

VIRGINIA CORN BREAD

1 cup yellow corn meal
1 tablespoon sugar
1 teaspoon salt
1 heaping tablespoon butter
1 cup boiling water

4 beaten egg yolks
1 cup milk
1 tablespoon flour
2 teaspoons baking powder
4 beaten egg whites

SERVES 6

FIRST Combine 1 cup yellow corn meal with 1 tablespoon sugar, 1 teaspoon salt, and 1 heaping tablespoon butter. Pour 1 cup boiling water over this and let stand overnight.

SECOND Beat 4 egg yolks with 1 cup milk. Add to corn-meal mixture. Add 1 tablespoon flour mixed with 2 teaspoons baking powder.

THIRD Beat 4 egg whites until stiff. Fold into the corn-meal mixture with a gentle hand. Turn into a flat, buttered baking-dish. Place in a 350° oven. Turn oven *off*. After 5 minutes turn oven to 350° again and bake for 20 minutes.

VIRGINIA JOHNNYCAKE

[*Pre-heat oven to 375°*]

3 eggs
1 pint buttermilk
2 cups sifted corn meal
1 teaspoon soda

2 tablespoons boiling water
2 tablespoons melted butter
1 teaspoon salt

SERVES 6

FIRST Beat 3 eggs until light. Add 1 pint of buttermilk and 2 cups sifted corn meal. Beat until well blended.

SECOND Dissolve 1 teaspoon soda in 2 tablespoons boiling water. Add 2 tablespoons melted butter and 1 teaspoon salt. Add this mixture to the batter. Stir well.

THIRD Pour batter in a well-buttered, rather shallow baking-pan and bake in a 375° oven for half an hour.

PAT'S WAFFLES

[*Pre-heat waffle iron*]

2 cups flour
4 teaspoons baking powder
2 teaspoons sugar
½ teaspoon salt
2 egg yolks
2 cups milk

¼ pound butter
2 egg whites
1 teaspoon vanilla
maple syrup *or* Strawberry Sauce
   (page 450)

FIRST Sift 2 cups flour. Measure and resift twice with 4 teaspoons baking powder, 2 teaspoons sugar, and ½ teaspoon salt.

SECOND Beat 2 egg yolks and add 2 cups milk. Beat together until well combined, then stir into the dry ingredients.

THIRD Melt ¼ pound butter and stir into batter. Beat for a few moments.

FOURTH Beat 2 egg whites until stiff but not dry. Fold them into the batter with a gentle hand. Fold in 1 teaspoon vanilla. Bake until waffles are brown and crisp. Serve with maple syrup or with Strawberry Sauce (page 450).

WENDY'S WAFFLES

[*Pre-heat waffle iron*]

1 cup pastry flour
2 teaspoons baking powder
1 teaspoon soda
⅛ teaspoon salt
2 tablespoons sugar
4 egg yolks
2 cups sour cream

scant 3 ounces melted butter
4 egg whites
maple syrup *or* Strawberry Preserves (page 449)
additional sugar (optional)
vanilla (optional)

FIRST Sift 1 cup of pastry flour. Measure and resift twice with 2 teaspoons of baking powder, 1 teaspoon soda, ⅛ teaspoon of salt, and 2 tablespoons sugar.

SECOND Beat 4 egg yolks until light. Blend well with 2 cups sour cream and add to dry ingredients, beating with a wire whisk until *very smooth*. Add scant 3 ounces melted butter and blend well.

THIRD Beat 4 egg whites until stiff but not dry. Fold into the mixture with a gentle hand. Fold until well blended.

FOURTH Pour onto a hot waffle iron. The waffles will be very light and fragile, so fill the iron fairly full. Serve with maple syrup or with Strawberry Preserves (page 449).

NOTE More sugar and a little vanilla may be added if these are to be served as dessert waffles. The thinness of the batter is important. Do not try to thicken the batter to make it appear like regular waffle batter. It should be thin and slightly bubbly.

This is what it weighs,

and this is what it measures

BUTTER
- 1 pound..16 ounces....2 cups...4 sticks
- ½ pound...8 ounces....1 cup....2 sticks
- ¼ pound...4 ounces...½ cup....1 stick
- ⅜ pound...6 ounces
- ⅛ pound...2 ounces
- 2 tablespoons...1 ounce

SPOONS
- 1 tablespoon.....3 teaspoons
- 4 tablespoons...¼ measuring cup
- standard measuring-spoon measures:
- 2 tablespoons sugar....1 ounce
- 2 tablespoons salt.....1 ounce
- 4 tablespoons flour....1 ounce
- 2 tablespoons liquid...1 ounce

- 1 tablespoon
- 1 teaspoon
- ½ teaspoon
- ¼ teaspoon

(All measurements level)

FLOUR AND SUGAR
- 1 pound flour.............4 cups
- 1 pound granulated sugar...2 cups
- 1 pound powdered sugar....2⅔ cups
- 1 pound brown sugar.......2⅔ cups

NUTS
- 1 cup walnut meats or shelled almonds...¼ pound
- 1 cup pecan meats..................⅓ pound
- 1 cup skinned (blanched) almonds.......3 ounces
- 1 pound walnuts or pecans in shells......¼ pound shelled

All human attests
That happiness for man . . . the hungry sinner!
Since Eve ate apples, much depends on dinner!
       LORD BYRON   (*1821*)

Index

A

Abalone Chowder, Monterey Peninsula, 37–8
Alaska, Strawberry Baked, 431–2
Albert, Apples and Cheese, 455
Allemande Sauce, 212
Almondine:
　Asparagus, 174–5
　Sauce, 201
Amsterdam, Romaine, 241
Anchovy:
　Eggs and Sour Cream, 51
　Spread, 9–10
Anna's 1–2–3–4 Cake, 369
Apple:
　and Banana Soup with Curry, 27
　Charlotte, 324–5
　Coffee Cake, 477
　Cookies, 391
　Graham-Cracker Pie Wendy, 412
　Muffins, 477–8
　Pancake, 343–4
　Tart, 412–13

Apples:
　and Cheese Albert, 455
　Butterscotch, in Rum, 456–7
　Buttery Baked, 457
　Meringue in Casserole, 455
　Snow, 458
　Stewed, Dressed Up, 458–9
　under Blanket, 456
Applesauce Torte, 329–30
Apricot:
　Fluff Pie, 414
　Icebox Cake, 313–14
　Sauce, 359
　Turnovers, 395
Apricots Joined Together, 468–9
Archiduc, Poulet à l', 104
Artichoke:
　Hearts, 173
　Hearts Parisian, 173–4
Artichokes:
　Filled with Mushrooms, 172–3
　preparation of, 169
Asparagus:
　Almondine, 174–5
　preparation of, 169
　Soufflé, 175

i

INDEX

Aspic:
  Eggs in, 51
  Gravy, Pheasant Knopf in, 112
  Pond, Brook Trout in an, 73–4
  Tarragon, Eggs in, 52

B

Bacon Popovers, 478
Bahama Sauce for Fish, 201
Baked:
  Alaska, Strawberry, 431–2
  Apples, Buttery, 457
  Bananas, 459
  Broilers in Cream, 88
  Corn, 178–9
  Creamed Spinach, 187
  Eggs in Spinach Boxes, 54
  Herb Potatoes, 190
  Lobster, 68
  Peaches Cornell, 464
  Pears, 466
  Scallops with Mushrooms in Cream, 63
  Virginia Ham, 134–5
Banana Cake, 369–70
Bananas:
  Baked, 459
  from Brussels, 460
Barnyard Soup with Matzo Balls, 34
Basket, Watermelon, 462–3
Basted Tuna Squares, 73
Batter:
  Bread, Virginia, 495–6
  Cakes, Virginia, 496
Bavarian:
  Cream, Chocolate, 287–8
  Punch, 310
  Rum, 311–12
Bean, String, Salad, 223–4
Beans:
  Black, in Rum, 175–6
  string, preparation of, 172
  String, Whole, 189
Beauzon, Salmon Mousse de, 82

Beef:
  Casserole, 121
  Chipped, Rolls, 12–13
  Fillets of, Rapallo, 127–8
  Grenadine of, 129
  Salad, 231
  Stew Bourguignonne, 122
  Stew in Six Minutes, 123
  Stew with Tomato Sauce, 122–3
  Tongue with Raisins, Prunes, and Almonds, 124
Beet Ring, 235
Beets:
  Harvard, 176
  Large, Sliced with Spring Onions, 222
  Polish, 176–7
  preparation of, 169
Beignets Soufflés, 325–6
Belgian or French Endive, 240
Bernese, Cauliflower, 265
Betty, Boothbay-Blueberry, 326–7
Beurre Noir, Calves' Brains au, 143–4
Bienenstich Cake, 371–2
Bird, A, in Tarragon Cream, 87
Bird's Nest, 191
Birthday, Family, Cake, 376–8
Biscuits:
  Cheese, 4
  Spoon Sponge, 406
Black:
  Beans in Rum, 175–6
  Bread Cherry Torte, 330–1
  Cherries in Brandy Sauce, 460
  Chocolate Cup Cake Icing, 421
  Chocolate Dessert Cake, 286–7
Blankets, 3
Blintzes:
  Cheese, 280–1
  Chicken, Sylvia, 92–3
Blueberry:
  Boothbay, Betty, 326–7
  Coffee or Tea Cake, 479
Blushing Pears, 466–7
Boat, Pineapple, 468

INDEX

Boats, Cucumber, 219–20
Bœuf à la Mode Margot, 125–6
Boiled:
    Icing, 421
    Salad-Dressing, 247
Bologna:
    Éclairs Jonathan, 269
    Pie with Chives, 10
Bonne Femme:
    Croutes, 257
    Salade, 267–8
Boothbay:
    Blueberry Betty, 326–7
    Broth, 35–6
Borsch:
    Jellied, 30
    Ring, 235
    Summer, 32
Bouchées (Golden Buck), 259
Bourguignonne, Beef Stew, 122
Brains, Calves', au Beurre Noir, 143–4
Bran Muffins, 479–80
Brazil Nuts Rolled in Bacon, 3
Bread:
    Batter, Virginia, 495–6
    Corn, Virginia, 496–7
    Nut, 487–8
    Pecan, 488
    Sauce with Poultry or Game, 201–2
Breast of Lamb or Veal, Stuffed, 145
Brizola, Steaks, 133
Broiled:
    Live Lobster with Pink Lobster Butter, 68–9
    Squab in Brandy, 114–15
    Steak with Roquefort Cheese, 126
Broilers, Baked, Cream, 88
Brook Trout in an Aspic Pond, 73–4
Broth:
    Boothbay, 35–6
    Mushroom, with White Wine, 43

Broth (*continued*)
    Turtle and Mushroom, 47–8
Brown-and-White Cinnamon Cake, 370–1
Brownies, Marvelous, Wendy, 403–4
Brûlée, Crème, June Platt, 299
Brussels, Bananas from, 460
Bruxelloise, Salade, 268
Bubbenspritze or Schupfnudeln, 166
Budapest Chicken Paprika ("Paprikas-Csirke"), 88–9
Buffet Table, Ham Decorated for a, 136
Bunches of Grapes, 234
Bundt:
    Cake, 480–1
    Kuchen, 492
Buns, Hot Cross, 485–6
Butter:
    Balls, 395–6
    Cream Icing, 422
    Lemon Sponge, 372–3
    Paprika, 210–11
    Pink Lobster, 211
    Steak, 214
Buttermilk Meat Balls, 129–30
Butterscotch Apples in Rum, 456–7
Buttery:
    Baked Apples, 457
    Chickens, 89

C

Cabbage:
    Red, 177
    red, preparation of, 171
Cake:
    Anna's 1–2–3–4, 369
    Apple Coffee, 477
    Apricot Icebox, 313–14
    Banana, 369–70
    Bienenstich, 371–2
    Black Chocolate Dessert, 286–7

INDEX

Cake *(continued)*
  Blueberry Coffee or Tea, 479
  Brown-and-White Cinnamon, 370–1
  Bundt, 480–1
  Cheese, Irene, 281–3
  Cheese, Refrigerator, 283–4
  Chocolate, Black, Dessert, 286–7
  Chocolate Date, with Whipped Cream, 288
  Chocolate, Helene (Rich), 374–5
  Chocolate (Hungarian), 373
  Chocolate Icebox, 289
  Chocolate (Old Vienna), 374
  Cinnamon Coffee, 492
  Devil's Food, as a Box, 294
  Devil's Food, Maria, 376
  Family Birthday, 376–8
  Filled Coffee, 493
  Fruit Sponge, 378–9
  Ginger Coffee, 485
  Good Plain, 379
  "Korsu," 294–5
  Lady Baltimore, 379–80
  Lemon-Curd, 380–1
  Nut, with Coal-Black Chocolate Icing, 382–3
  Old-Fashioned Coconut Layer, 384
  Orange, 384–5
  Orange-Nut Sponge, 385
  Orange Puff, 386–7
  Pound, Chris, 387–8
  Pudding, 349
  Sponge, 389
  Sponge, Ring, 321–2
  Sponge, Surprise, 322–3
  Strawberry Icebox, 435
  Watermelon, 390
Cakes:
  Batter, Virginia, 496
  Cup, 398–9
Calves':
  Brains au Beurre Noir, 143–4
  Liver in Sour Cream, 144

Camembert Cheese, Fried, 272
Canadian Coconut Squares, 396–7
Canoes, Zucchini, 226–7
Cantaloupe Balls in a Nest, 234–5
Capon par Excellence, 90–1
Caramel Sauce, 359
Carcass Soup, Fancy, 40
Carrot Soup, 28
Carrots:
  Glazed, 177–8
  preparation of, 169
Casserole:
  Beef, 121
  Cheese, with Hard-Boiled Eggs and Tomato Sauce, 270–1
  Economical Country, 127
  Frankfurters in, 128–9
  Veal, with Sour Cream, 146
Cauliflower:
  Bernese, 265
  Flowerlets, 10
  Ice-Cold, 221–2
Caviar:
  Cream, 11
  Red, Madrilène, 31
  Red, with Sour Cream on Rye, 20
Celery:
  Hearts in Tarragon Vinegar, 218
  in Consommé, 178
  preparation of, 169–70
  Root Sticks in Mustard Marinade, 218
  Roots with Pears, 219
Chaeswaehe, 260–1
Charlotte:
  Apple, 324–5
  Cheese, 261
  Potato, 195–6
Chasen, Dave:
  Spinach Salad, 223
  Vanilla Ice Cream with Anisette and Coconut, 338
Cheese:
  Balls, 270
  Biscuits, 4

Cheese (*continued*)
  Blintzes, 280–1
  Cake Irene, 281–3
  Cake, Refrigerator, 283–4
  Camembert, Fried, 272
  Casserole with Hard-Boiled Eggs and Tomato Sauce, 270–1
  Charlotte, 261
  Cream, Balls and Variations, 242–3
  Cream, Crescents, 482–3
  Cream, Crust, 408
  Cream, Porcupine, 14
  Cream, Warm, on Rounds, 9
  Fingers, Toasted, 8–9
  Melted, Neuchâtel Fashion, 257–8
  Melted, Valois Fashion, 258–9
  Puff, Cocktail, 5
  Rolls, 4–5
  Roquefort, Balls, 243
  Sauce, Rich, 204
  Soup of the Engadin, 46
  Spread Cornell, 11–12
  Spread, Delectable, 14
  Spreads (12 varieties), 12
  Sticks, 5
  Tartlets, Simple, 274
Cherries:
  Black, in Brandy Sauce, 461
  Hot Rum, 461–2
  in Wine, 461
Cherry:
  Cocktail, 461
  Tart, 414–15
  Tartlets, 397–8
  Torte, Black-Bread, 330–1
Chess Pie, 415–16
Chestnut Purée, 338–9
Chicken:
  à la King, Lily, 91–2
  Blintzes Sylvia, 92–3
  Breasts on the Wing, 93
  Croquettes, Parisian, 103
  Danish, 102

Chicken (*continued*)
  Fricasee of, Espagnole, 102–3
  Georgia, 96–7
  in Custard and Rice, 94
  in Garlic Cream, 95–6
  Liver Pâté, Paul, 106–7
  Liver Ring, 107–8
  Liver Soup, 36
  Livers and Mushroom Caps, 6
  Livers, chopped, 13
  Livers on Artichoke Hearts, 106
  Malibu, 97–8
  Mervyn, 98
  Normande, 99
  Paprika, Budapest, 88–9
  Romanoff, 99–100
  Salad Diddie, 232
  Timbale, 100–1
  Young, in Burgundy, 105–6
Chickens:
  Buttery, 89
  Two, in White Wine, 104–5
Chiffon Pie:
  Lemon, 417
  Strawberry, 442–3
Chiffonade Salad, 238–9
Chipped-Beef Rolls, 12–13
Chocolat:
  Mousse au, Lashanska, 334–5
  Petits Pots au, 297
Chocolate:
  Bavarian Cream, 287–8
  Black, Cup Cake Icing, 421
  Black, Dessert Cake, 286–7
  Cake Helene (Rich), 374–5
  Cake (Hungarian), 373
  Cake (Old Vienna), 374
  Cream Pudding, 352
  Date Cake with Whipped Cream, 288
  Filling, 422
  Hidden Away, Molded, 295–6
  Icebox Cake, 289
  Icing, 422–3
  Linzer Torte, 375–6
  Pudding, Molded, 296–7

Chocolate (*continued*)
  Roll I, 290
  Roll II, 291
  Sauce I, 359–60
  Sauce II, 360
  Soufflé, Cold, 292
  Soufflé, Hot, 293
Choldnik Soup, 27
Chop Suey, 141
Chopped Chicken Livers, 13
Chops:
  Lamb, Stuffed, 140
  Lamb, Wendy, 137–8
  Pork, in Gravy, 142–3
  Veal, in Tomato Sauce, 146–7
Chowder:
  Abalone, Monterey Peninsula, 37–8
  Clam, New England, 39
  Curry, 37
  Mussel, 38–9
Chris, Pound Cake, 387–8
Christmas:
  Cookies, 391–2
  Lebkuchen for, 486–7
Cinnamon:
  Cake, Brown-and-White, 370–1
  Coffee Cake, 492
Citrus:
  Fruit Ring, 469
  Grove Pie, 416–17
Clam Chowder, New England, 39
Clams, Deviled, Grandmère, 67
Cocktail:
  Cheese Puff, 5
  Cherry, 461
  Sandwich, Mosaic, 19
Coconut:
  Cream Torte Lashanska, 316–17
  Layer Cake, Old-Fashioned, 384
  Squares, Canadian, 396–7
  Strawberry Cream Tarts, 445
Cœur à la Crème, 283
Coffee:
  Ice Cream, Rummy, 335–6
  Kringel, 481

Coffee (*continued*)
  Pudding, 353
Coffee Cake:
  Apple, 477
  Blueberry, 479
  Cinnamon, 492
  Filled, 493
  Ginger, 485
Coffee Cakes, Six Yeast-Dough, 491–5
Cold:
  Chocolate Soufflé, 292
  Mustard Sauce, 202
  Rice Pudding in a Mold, 302–3
Cole Slaw, Double, 220–1
Company Salad Josephine, 239
Consommé:
  Garni, 36
  Sherried, 32
Cookies:
  Apple, 391
  Christmas, 391–2
  Currant, 392–3
  Favorite, Miggie, 393
  Old-Fashioned, 393–4
  Pretzel, 394–5
Corn:
  Baked, 178–9
  Bread, Virginia, 496–7
  Fritters, Virginia, 180–1
  on the Cob Country Style, 179
  Pouches, 481–2
  preparation of, 170
  Ring, 180
Cornell:
  Baked Peaches, 464
  Cheese Spread, 11–12
Cornucopias, 314–15
Country Casserole, Economical, 127
Cowl, Jane, Curried Eggs, 56
Crab:
  Lobster, or Shrimp Salad, 230–1
  Mayonnaise, 63–4
  Pie, 64
  Wendy, 64

INDEX

Cranberry Cream, 333–4
Crawfish, Shrimp, or Lobster Superb, 66–7
Cream:
  and-Cheese Dip, 13–14
  Caviar, 11
  Chocolate Bavarian, 287–8
  Cranberry, 333–4
  Ginger, 305
  Orange, 308–9
  Orange, with Cake, 319–20
  Peach, 309
  Peppermint-Stick, 309–10
  Puffs and Éclairs, 315–16
  Sauce, 203
  Sauce, Marie's, 203
  Sauce, Yellow, 204
  Smoked Salmon, 11
  Strawberry, with Kirsch, 432–3
Cream Cheese:
  Balls and Variations, 242–3
  Crescents, 482–3
  Crust, 408
  Porcupine, 14
  Warm, on Rounds, 9
Creamed:
  Mushrooms, 181
  Poached Eggs à la Hash, 55
  Potatoes, 191–2
  Spinach, 186–7
Crème:
  Brûlée June Platt, 299
  d'Isigny, 360–1
Crêpes:
  au Kirsch, 344
  Eighteen Small, Filled, 75
  Farcies, 271
  Suzette, 345–6
Crescents:
  Cream-Cheese, 482–3
  Vanilla, 406–7
Croquettes, Parisian Chicken, 103
Croutes (Crusts):
  Bonne Femme, 257
  Emmental (Emmental Fashion), 255

Croutes (Crusts) (*continued*)
  Oberland (Mountaineer Fashion), 256
  Vaudoises (Vaudois Fashion), 255–6
Crumbles, Potato, 196
Crumbly, Not Creamy, Fudge, 423–4
Crust:
  Cream-Cheese, 408
  Marie's Tart, 408
  Polish Tart, 409
  Swedish Tart, 411
Crusts, *see* Croutes
Cucumber:
  Boats, 219–20
  Ring, 236
  Sauce, 205
Cucumbers:
  in Sour Cream or French Dressing, 220
  Stuffed, 23
Cup Cake Icing, Black Chocolate, 421
Cup Cakes, 398–9
Curaçao, Strawberries, 433
Currant:
  Cookies, 392–3
  Jelly Squares, 399
Curried Eggs Jane Cowl, 56
Curry:
  Chowder, 37
  Sauce, 205–6
  Soup, 28–9
Custard:
  and Rice, Chicken in, 94
  Cream Sauce, 361
  Indian Pudding, 301
  White or Amber, 300–1
Cutlets:
  Kiev, 101
  Turkey, Nela, 117
  Veal, in Sherry, 147
  Veal, Stuffed, 264

Cutlets (*continued*)
  Veal, Vienna (Wiener Schnitzel), 148–9
  Veal, with Cheese, 264

D

Danish Chicken, 102
Date-and-Walnut Tart, 341
Decorator's Icing, Old-Time, 425–6
Delectable Cheese Spread, 14
Delight, Queen's, 323
Dellarobbia, Lamb Stew, 138–9
Dente, Spaghetti al, 158
Dessert:
  Maple Pancake, Elizabeth, 348
  Peanut-Brittle, 343
  Sauces, 359–65
Deviled:
  Clams Grandmère, 67
  Pecans, 6
Devil's Food Cake as a Box, 294
Devil's Food Cake Maria, 376
Diddie:
  Chicken Salad, 232
  Vegetable Salad, 226
Dill Pickle, Slices of, with Grated Cheese, 7
Dimpas Dampas Grandmère, 483
Dip, Cream-and-Cheese, 13–14
Divine, Strawberry, 434
Double Cole Slaw, 220–1
Dough, Yeast, 491
Dressing:
  Boiled Salad, 247
  French, 247
  French, George Fitzmaurice, 248
  Fruit Salad, 472
  Roquefort, I, 249
  Roquefort, II, 249–50
  Russian, 250
  Thousand Island, 250–1
Dried Pea Soup, 44

Duck:
  Fredericka, 108–9
  Pickings San Vicente, 109–10
  Superb, 110–11
Duckling with Sour Red Cherries, 108

E

Éclairs:
  and Cream Puffs, 315–16
  Bologna, Jonathan, 269
Economical Country Casserole, 127
Edwin:
  Mushroom Soup, 41–2
  Puff Omelette, 328–9
  Scrambled Eggs, 58
  Spaghetti Sauce, 159
Edwine, Mushrooms, 181–2
Edwin's Potatoes au Gratin, 192
Egg Ring, 52–3
Eggnog Pudding, Molded, 307–8
Eggplant au Gratin, 265
Eggs:
  Anchovy, and Sour Cream, 51
  Baked, in Spinach Boxes, 54
  Creamed Poached, à la Hash, 55
  Curried, Jane Cowl, 56
  in Aspic I, 51
  in Aspic Tarragon II, 52
  Scrambled, Edwin, 58
  Scrambled, Paysanne, 59
  Stuffed, Curried, 23
  Swiss, 59
  Swiss Scrambled, 60
  with Mushroom Stems, 56–7
Eighteen Small Crêpes Filled, 75
Eisenkuchen, 492–3
Elizabeth, Maple Pancake Dessert, 348
Emmental, Croutes, 255
Emperor's Frosting, 424–5
Endive:
  French or Belgian, 240
  French, Stuffed, 24
  with Breast of Turkey, 232–3
English Gooseberry Fool, 303–4

Espagnole, Fricassee of Chicken, 102–3
Evangeline, Nectarines, 472–3

F

Family Birthday Cake, 376–8
Fancy Carcass Soup, 40
Farcies, Crêpes, 271
Favorite Cookies Miggie, 393
Field Salad, 239–40
Figs in Crème de Cacao and Sour Cream, 470
Filled:
  Coffee Cake, 493
  Oranges Sweet Southern Style, 192–3
  Tiny Red Tomatoes, 15
  Yellow Tomatoes, 15
Fillets:
  in Parchment Paper Cases, 77
  of Beef Rapallo, 127–8
  of Sole Florentine, 75–6
  of Sole in Parmesan Cheese, 78
  of Sole Marguery, 76–7
  of Sole Queen Victoria, 78–9
  of Sole with Ham, 79–80
  of Sole with Rieseling, 80
  of Sole with White Wine, 80–1
Filling, Chocolate, 422–3
Filling, Vanilla, 342
Fingers, Toasted Cheese, 8–9
Fish-and-Tongue Spread, 15
Fish, Swedish, 83
Fitzmaurice, George, French Dressing, 248
Florentine, Fillets of Sole, 75–6
Flowerlets, Cauliflower, 10
Fluff, Macaroon, 305–6
Foamy Sauce, 361
Fondue:
  Neuchâteloise (Melted Cheese Neuchâtel Fashion), 257–8
  Old French, 259–60
Fontina (Melted Cheese Valois Fashion), 258–9
Frankfurters in Casserole, 128–9

Fredericka, Duck, 108–9
French:
  Dressing, 247
  Dressing George Fitzmaurice, 248
  Endive, Stuffed, 24
  Fried Onions, 183
  Old, Fondue, 259–60
  or Belgian Endive, 240
  Peas in a Lettuce Bowl, 184
  Rolls, Stuffed, 24
  Soufflé Omelette, 57–8
  Toast with French Bread, 164
Fresh Pea Soup, 45
Fribourgeoises, Tomates, 269
Fricassee of Chicken Espagnole, 102–3
Fried:
  Camembert Cheese, 272
  Philippine Rice, 163
  Shrimp, 70
  Whitebait, 83–4
Fritters, Corn, Virginia, 180–1
Frosting:
  Emperor's, 424–5
  Seven-Minute, 426
Frostings and Icings, 421–7
Frozen Fruit Salad, 470–1
Fruit:
  Custard Sauce, 362
  Frozen, Salad, 470–1
  Juice Pudding, 353–4
  Salad, 471–2
  Salad Dressing, 472
  Salad in Layer Cake, 304
  Sponge Cake, 378–9
Fruits:
  and Nuts, Glazed, 425
  Three Hot, 473–4
Fudge:
  Crumbly, Not Creamy, 423–4
  Squares, 399–400

G

Garden Salad with Sour Cream, 240–1

Garlic:
  Cream, Chicken in, 95–6
  Loaf, 484
Gay Nineties Rarebit, 272–3
Gelatin, instructions in use of, 280
Georgia, Chicken, 96–7
Gesundheits Kuchen, 484–5
Ginger:
  Coffee Cake, 485
  Cream, 305
Glaze for Meats and Fowl, 206–7
Glazed:
  Carrots, 177–8
  Nuts and Fruits, 425
  Strawberry Pie, 441–2
Gnocchi:
  Gruyère with Sour Cream, 153
  with Cream Sauce, 153–4
  with Parmesan Cheese, 154
Golden Buck, 259
Good Plain Cake, 379
Gooseberry Fool, English, 303–4
Goulash, Seafood, 71
Grandmère:
  Deviled Clams, 67
  Dimpas Dampas, 483
Grandmother's Three Tortes, 331–3
Grapes, Bunches of, 234
Gravy Aspic, Pheasant Knopf in, 112
Green Goddess Salad, 227
Green Spaghetti, 159–60
Greens, Salad, with Chicken Livers, 233
Grenadine of Beef, 129
Greutze, Rute, 311
Gruyère, Gnocchi, with Sour Cream, 153

H

Ham:
  Baked Virginia, 134–5
  Butt with Sauerkraut and Salami, 135–6

Ham (*continued*)
  Decorated for a Buffet Table, 136
  Roulades, 262–3
  Steak from Virginia, 136–7
  Tarts, Little, 18
  Tenderized, with Apricots, 137
  That Looks like Bacon, 16
Hamburgers, Tiny, 8
Hard Sauce, 362
Harvard Beets, 176
Hash, Creamed Poached Eggs à la, 55
Hawaiian Huacamole, 16–17
Hazelnut Cream Pudding, 354–5
Helene, Chocolate Cake (Rich), 374–5
Herring:
  Marinated, 20
  Salad, 228
  Salad with Fruits and Endive, 228–9
Hidden Away, Molded Chocolate, 295–6
Hollandaise:
  I, 207–8
  II, 208
Hominy, Tomato, and Cheese Soufflé, 164
Honeydew Melon, Iced, with Lime, 462
Horseradish Mold, 209
Hostess Tartlets, 273
Hot:
  Chocolate Soufflé, 293
  Cross Buns, 485–6
  Potato Salad, 221
  Rum Cherries, 461–2
Huacamole, Hawaiian, 16–17
Hungarian:
  Chocolate Cake, 373
  Stew, 144–5

I

Icebox:
  Cake, Apricot, 313–14
  Cake, Chocolate, 289

INDEX

Icebox (*continued*)
  Cake, Strawberry, 435
  Pudding Parfait, 317–18
Ice-Cold Cauliflower, 221–2
Ice Cream:
  Lemon, in Lemon Shells, 334
  New York's Best Vanilla, 336–7
  Old Vienna Vanilla, 337–8
  Rummy Coffee, 335–6
  Vanilla, with Anisette and Coconut Dave Chasen, 338
  Winter Strawberry, 441
Iced:
  Honeydew Melon with Lime, 462
  Pea Soup, 29
Icing:
  Black Chocolate Cup Cake, 421
  Boiled, 421
  Butter-Cream, 422
  Chocolate, 422–3
  Old-Time Decorator's, 425–6
  Powdered-Sugar, 426
  Thin, 427
Icings and Frostings, 421–7
Indian Pudding Custard, 301–2
Irene, Cheese Cake, 281–3
Isigny, Crème d', 360–1
Italian:
  Lasagne, 154–6
  Prosciutto, 17

J

Jambalaya, Shrimp, 70–1
Jellied Borsch, 30
Jelly:
  Pancakes, Little, 347
  Wine, 312–13
Johnnycake, Virginia, 497
Jonathan, Bologna Éclairs, 269
Josephine, Company Salad, 239
Jurassienne, Omelette, 58

K

Kaiserschmarren, 327
Kidneys, Veal:
  in Brandy Sauce, 149

Kidneys, Veal (*continued*)
  in White Wine with Mushrooms, 149–50
Kiev Cutlets, 101
Kipfel, Vienna, 407
Kirsch, Crêpes au, 344
Knopf:
  Pheasant, 111–12
  Pheasant, in Gravy Aspic, 113
  Seafood Salad, 229–30
"Korsu Cake," 294–5
Kringel, Coffee, 481
Kuchen:
  Bundt, 492
  Gesundheits, 484–5

L

Lady Baltimore Cake, 379–80
Lamb:
  Breast of, Stuffed, 145
  Chops, Stuffed, 140
  Chops Wendy, 137–8
  Rack of Spring, 139–40
  Stew Dellarobbia, 138–9
Large Beets Sliced with Spring Onions, 222
Lasagne, Italian, 154–6
Lashanska:
  Coconut Cream Torte, 316–17
  Mousse au Chocolat, 334–5
Lebkuchen for Christmas, 486–7
Lemon:
  Chiffon Pie, 417
  Curd Cake, 380–1
  Curd Tartlets, 400
  Fluff Pie, 417–18
  Ice Cream in Lemon Shells, 334
  Pudding (or Orange), 355
  Tartlets with Meringue, 401
Lilies of Salami, 17–18
Lily, Chicken à la King, 91–2
Lime Ring, 236–7
Little:
  Ham Tarts, 18
  Jelly Pancakes, 347
Liver, Calves', in Sour Cream, 144

Loaf, Garlic, 484
Lobster:
  Baked, 68
  Broiled Live, with Pink Lobster Butter, 68–9
  Butter, Pink, 211
  Crawfish, or Shrimp Superb, 66–7
  Rounds, 18–19
  Shrimp, or Crab Salad, 230–1
  Thermidor, 69
  Louis, Potage, 30–1

M

Macaroni Ring of Plenty, 165
Macaroon Fluff, 305–6
Macaroons:
  with Almonds, 401
  with Cornflakes, 402
Madeleines Sylvia, 402–3
Madrilène, Red Caviar, 31
Malibu, Chicken, 97–8
Maple:
  Mousse, 306–7
  Pancake Dessert Elizabeth, 348
Mardi, Potage de, 45–6
Margot, Bœuf à la Mode, 125–6
Marguery, Fillets of Sole, 76–7
Maria, Devil's Food Cake, 376
Marie, Mushrooms, 182
Marie's:
  Cream Sauce, 203
  Spätzle, 165–6
  Tart Crust, 408
Marinated Herring, 20
Marinière, Moules à la, 41
Mario's Risotto, 156–7
Marguerite, Mayonnaise, 248
Marrons Purée, 338–9
  en Meringue, 339
  sous Chocolat, 340
  with Marguerites, 340–1
Marvelous Brownies Wendy, 403–4
Matzo Balls for Soup, 35

Mayonnaise:
  Crab, 63–4
  Marguerite, 248
  with Horseradish, 249
Meat Balls:
  Buttermilk, 129–30
  in Mushroom-Stems Sauce, 130–1
  Swedish, 131
Meats, Sauce for, 212–13
Meli Melo, 467
Melon, Iced Honeydew, with Lime, 462
Meringue, Mishmash, 318–19
Mervyn, Chicken, 98
Midnight Sandwiches, 273–4
Miggie, Favorite Cookies, 393
Mishmash Meringue, 318–19
Mocha Torte, 381–2
Mold, Horseradish, 209
Molded:
  Chocolate Hidden Away, 295–6
  Chocolate Pudding, 296–7
  Eggnog Pudding, 307–8
Mongol Soup, 40–1
Monterey Peninsula Abalone Chowder, 37–8
Mornay Sauce, Swiss, 263
Mosaic Cocktail Sandwich, 19
Moules à la Marinière, 41
Mousse:
  au Chocolat Lashanska, 334–5
  Maple, 306–7
  Salmon, 81
  Salmon, de Beauzon, 82
  Strawberry, 435–6
Mousseline, Sauce, 213
Muffins:
  Apple, 477–8
  Bran, 479–80
Mushroom:
  Broth with White Wine, 43
  Soup Edwin, 41–2
  Soup Wendy, 42
  Stems and Tomato Sauce, 210
  Stems in Sherry Sauce, 209–10

INDEX xiii

Mushrooms:
  Creamed, 181
  Edwine, 181–2
  Marie, 182
  preparation of, 170
Mussel Chowder, 38–9
Mustard Sauce, Cold, 202

N

Nectarines Evangeline, 472–3
Nela, Turkey Cutlets, 117
Nests, Spaghetti, 160
Neuchâteloise, Fondue, 257–8
New England Clam Chowder, 39
New Orleans, Shrimp, 22
New York's Best Vanilla Ice Cream, 336–7
Noodle:
  Ring, 161
  Strips, Schnecken, 494
Noodleroom, 43–4
Noodles:
  Skillet, 162–3
  with Cottage Cheese, 161–2
Norma, Rice Pudding, 349–50
Normande, Chicken, 99
Nut:
  Bread, 487–8
  Cake with Coal-Black Chocolate Icing, 382–3
  Torte, 341–2
Nuts and Fruits, Glazed, 425

O

Oberland, Croutes, 256
Old-Fashioned:
  Coconut Layer Cake, 384
  Cookies, 393–4
Old French Fondue, 259–60
Old-Time Decorator's Icing, 425–6
Old Vienna:
  Chocolate Cake, 374
  Trieste Tart, 389–90
  Vanilla Ice Cream, 337–8

Omelette:
  French Soufflé, 57–8
  Jurassienne, 58
  Puff, Edwin, 328–9
Onions:
  French-Fried, 183
  preparation of, 170
Orange:
  Cake, 384–5
  Cream, 308–9
  Cream with Cake, 319–20
  Nut Sponge Cake, 385
  Pudding (or Lemon), 355
  Puff Cake, 386–7
  Slices in Chilled Red Wine, 473
Oranges, Filled, Sweet Southern Style, 192–3
Oyster Patties, 71–2
Oysters, Scalloped, Virginia, 72

P

Pancake:
  Apple, 343–4
  Dessert, Maple, Elizabeth, 384
Pancakes:
  Little Jelly, 347
  Potato, 197
Paprika Butter, 210–11
"Paprikas-Csirke," 88–9
Parfait:
  Icebox Pudding, 317
  Strawberry, 437
Parisian:
  Artichoke Hearts, 173–4
  Chicken Croquettes, 103
  Strawberry Tarts, 445–7
Parsnips:
  in Parmesan, 183
  preparation of, 170
Paste, Puff, 409–11
Pâté:
  Chicken-Liver, Paul, 106–7
  Polish, Rubinstein, 141–2
Pat's Waffles, 497–8
Patties, Oyster, 71–2
Paul, Chicken-Liver Pâté, 106–7

INDEX

Paysanne, Scrambled Eggs, 59
Pea:
  Dried, Soup, 44
  Fresh, Soup, 45
  Soup, Iced, 29
Peach:
  Cream, 309
  Sauce, 362–3
  Surprise, 465
Peaches:
  Baked, Cornell, 464
  in Cups, 464
  Yellow, with a Red Blanket, 465–6
Peanut-Brittle Dessert, 343
Pears:
  Baked, 466
  Blushing, 466–7
Peas:
  French, in a Lettuce Bowl, 184
  in Sour Cream, 184–5
  preparation of, 170–1
Pecan Bread, 488
Pecans, Deviled, 6
Peels, Potato, 6–7
Peppermint-Stick Cream, 309–10
Pernod, Salade au, 241–2
"Pertaters"! 195
Peter, Turkey Stuffing, 118
Petits Pots au Chocolat, 297
Pheasant:
  in Sour Cream, 112–13
  Knopf, 111–12
  Knopf in Gravy Aspic, 112
  Young, with Raisin Purée, 113–14
Philippine Rice, Fried, 163
Piccata (Veal Cutlets with Cheese), 264
Pickings, Duck, San Vicente, 109–10
Pickle, Dill, Slices of, with Grated Cheese, 7
Pie:
  Apple Graham-Cracker, Wendy, 412

Pie (*continued*)
  Apricot Fluff, 414
  Bologna, with Chives, 10
  Chess, 415–16
  Citrus-Grove, 416–17
  Crab, 64
  Glazed Strawberry, 441–2
  Lemon Chiffon, 417
  Lemon Fluff, 417–18
  Pumpkin, Ruth, 420
  Rum Cheese, 284–5
  Strawberry Chiffon, 442–3
  Strawberry, with Wine, 443–4
  Winter Strawberry, 444–5
Pineapple:
  Boat, 468
  Cream Sauce, 363
  Quarters with Crème de Menthe, 467
  Ring, 237
Pink Lobster Butter, 211
Plain, Good, Cake, 379
Platt, June, Crème Brûlée, 299
Plum Strip, 418–19
Poached Eggs, Creamed, à la Hash, 55
Polish:
  Beets, 176–7
  Pâté Rubinstein, 141–2
  Tart Crust, 409
Popovers, Bacon, 478
Porcupine, Cream-Cheese, 14
Pork Chops in Gravy, 142–3
Potage:
  de Mardi, 45–6
  Louis, 30–1
Potato:
  Charlotte, 195–6
  Crumbles, 196
  Pancakes, 197
  Peels, 6–7
  Salad, Hot, 221
Potatoes:
  Baked Herb, 190
  Creamed, 191–2
  Edwin's, au Gratin, 192

Potatoes (*continued*)
   four ways of preparing Spring, 193–3
   preparation of, 172
   Stuffed, 266
Pouches, Corn, 481–2
Poulet à l'Archiduc, 104
Pound Cake Chris, 387–8
Powdered-Sugar Icing, 426
Preparation of Vegetables, 169–72
Preserves, Strawberry, 449–50
Pretzel Cookies, 394–5
Profiterolles, 320–1
Prosciutto, Italian, 17
Prune Tart, 419–20
Pudding:
   Cake, 349
   Chocolate Cream, 352
   Coffee, 353
   Fruit-Juice, 353–4
   Hazelnut Cream, 354–5
   Indian, Custard, 301–2
   Lemon, 355
   Molded Chocolate, 296–7
   Molded Eggnog, 307–8
   Orange, 355
   Parfait, Icebox, 317–18
   Punch, 356
   Rice, Cold, in a Mold, 302–3
   Rice, Norma, 349–50
   Rice, Round Table, 350–1
   Rice, Strawberry Pink, 437–8
   Rum, 356–7
   Vanilla Cream, 357–8
   Wine, 358
Puddings, Ten Original Victorian, 352–8
Puff:
   Cocktail Cheese, 5
   Omelette Edwin, 328–9
   Paste, 409–11
Pufflets, Swiss, 7–8
Pumpkin Pie Ruth, 420
Punch:
   Bavarian, 310
   Pudding, 356

Purée:
   Marrons, 338–9
   Marrons, en Meringue, 339
   Marrons, sous Chocolat, 340
   Marrons, with Marguerites, 340–1
Squash, 187

Q

Queen's Delight, 323

R

Race-Horse Steaks, 131–2
Rack of Spring Lamb, 139–40
Raisin:
   Purée, Young Pheasant in, 113–14
   Sauce for Cold Fish, 211–12
Ramequin, 261–2
Rapallo, Fillets of Beef, 127–8
Rarebit, Gay Nineties, 272–3
Red:
   Cabbage, 177
   cabbage, preparation of, 171
   Caviar Madrilène, 31
   Caviar with Sour Cream on Rye, 20
Refrigerator Cheese Cake, 283–4
Relish Ring, 237–8
Rhubarb Ring with Strawberries, 431
Rice:
   Fried Philippine, 163
   Pudding, Cold, in a Mold, 302–3
   Pudding Norma, 349–50
   Pudding Round Table, 350–1
   Pudding, Strawberry Pink, 437–8
   Spanish, 163
   Wild, Stuffing, 116–17
Rich Cheese Sauce, 204
Rien de Tout, 321

Ring:
  Beet, 235
  Borsch, 235
  Chicken-Liver, 107-8
  Citrus-Fruit, 469
  Corn, 180
  Cucumber, 236
  Egg, 52-3
  Lime, 236-7
  Noodle, 161
  of Plenty, Macaroni, 165
  Pineapple, 237
  Relish, 237-8
  Rhubarb, with Strawberries, 431
  Shad-Roe, 82-3
  Sponge-Cake, 321-2
  Tomato-Aspic, 238
Risotto:
  Mario's, 156-7
  with Sausages, 157
Roll, Chocolate:
  I, 290
  II, 291
Rolls:
  Cheese, 4-5
  Chipped-Beef, 12-13
  French, Stuffed, 24
  Smoked Salmon, 22-3
Romaine Amsterdam, 241
Romanoff:
  Chicken, 99-100
  Strawberries, 438-9
Roquefort:
  Cheese Balls, 243
  Dressing I, 249
  Dressing II, 249-50
  Spread, 20-1
Rote Greutze, 311
Roulades, Ham, 262-3
Round Table, Rice Pudding, 350-1
Rounds, Lobster, 18-19
Rubinstein, Polish Pâté, 141-2
Rum:
  Bavarian, 311-12

Rum (*continued*)
  Cheese Pie, 284-5
  Pudding, 356-7
Rummy Coffee Ice Cream, 335-6
Russian:
  Dressing, 250
  Salad, 222-3
Ruth, Pumpkin Pie, 420

S

Sabayon, 328
Salad:
  Beef, 231
  Chicken, Diddie, 232
  Chiffonade, 238-9
  Company, Josephine, 239
  Dressing, Boiled, 247
  Field, 239-40
  Frozen Fruit, 470-1
  Fruit, 471-2
  Fruit, Dressing, 472
  Fruit, in Layer Cake, 304
  Garden, with Sour Cream, 240-1
  Green Goddess, 227
  Greens with Chicken Livers, 233
  Herring, 228
  Herring, with Fruits and Endive, 228-9
  Hot Potato, 221
  Making, Notes on, 217
  Russian, 222-3
  Sardine, 229
  Seafood, Knopf, 229-30
  Shrimp, Crab, or Lobster, 230-1
  Spinach, Dave Chasen, 223
  String-Bean, 223-4
  Sweetbread, 233-4
  Tossed, with Pecan Nut Balls, 242
  Vegetable, Diddie, 226
Salade:
  au Pernod, 241-2
  au Tomates, 268
  Bonne Femme, 267-8
  Bruxelloise, 268

INDEX   xvii

Salami, Lilies of, 17–18
Sally Lunn, 488–9
Salmon:
  Mousse, 81
  Mousse de Beauzon, 82
  Smoked, Cream, 11
  Smoked, Rolls, 22–3
San Vicente, Duck Pickings, 109–10
Sand Torte, 388
Sandwich, Mosaic Cocktail, 19
Sandwiches:
  Midnight, 273–4
  Waffle, 275–6
Sardine Salad, 229
Sardines on Fingers of Bread, 21
Sauce:
  Allemande, 212
  Almondine, 201
  Apricot, 359
  Bahama, for Fish, 201
  Bread, with Poultry or Game, 201–2
  Caramel, 359
  Cheese, Rich, 204
  Chocolate I, 359–60
  Chocolate II, 360
  Cream, 203
  Cream, Marie's, 203
  Cream, Yellow, 204
  Cucumber, 205
  Curry, 205–6
  Custard Cream, 361
  Foamy, 361
  for Meats, 212–13
  Fruit Custard, 362
  Hard, 362
  Hollandaise I, 207–8
  Hollandaise II, 208
  Mousseline, 213
  Mushroom Stems and Tomato, 209
  Mushroom Stems in Sherry, 209–10
  Mustard, Cold, 202
  Peach, 362–3

Sauce (continued)
  Pineapple Cream, 363
  Raisin, for Cold Fish, 211–12
  Spaghetti, Edwin, 159
  Strawberry, for Ice Cream, 450
  Strawberry, for Winter Use, 450–1
  Swiss Mornay, 263
  Tartar, 213–14
  Vanilla, I, 363
  Vanilla, II (with Rum), 363–4
  Warm Wine, 364
  Wine Froth, 364–5
Sauces, Dessert, 359–65
Sauerkraut:
  preparation of, 171
  Three, 185–6
Scalloped Oysters Virginia, 72
Scallops:
  around Tartar Sauce, 21
  Baked, with Mushrooms in Cream, 63
Schnecken:
  Noodle Strips, 494
  Superlative, 494–5
Schupfnudeln or Bubbenspritze, 166
Scotch Shortbread:
  I, 404
  II, 404–5
Scrambled Eggs:
  Edwin, 58
  Paysanne, 59
Seafood:
  Goulash, 71
  Salad Knopf, 229–30
Senegalese Soup, 31–2
Seven-Minute Frosting, 426–7
Shad-Roe Ring, 82–3
Sherried Consommé, 32
Shetgia, Supa (Cheese Soup of Engadin), 46
Shortbread, Scotch:
  I, 404
  II, 404–5
Shortcake Smetana, 489–90

INDEX

Shrimp:
  Crab, or Lobster Salad, 230–1
  Crawfish, or Lobster Superb, 66–7
  Fried, 70
  Jambalaya, 70–1
  New Orleans, 22
Simple Cheese Tartlets, 274
Sirloin Strip the Magnificent, 132–3
Skillet Noodles, 162–3
Slices of Dill Pickle with Grated Cheese, 7
Smetana, Shortcake, 489–90
Smoked Salmon:
  Cream, 11
  Rolls, 22–3
Snow Apples, 458
Sole, Fillets of:
  Florentine, 75–6
  in Parmesan Cheese, 78
  Marguery, 76–7
  Queen Victoria, 78–9
  with Ham, 79–80
  with Rieseling, 80
  with White Wine, 80–1
Soufflé:
  Asparagus, 175
  Chocolate, Cold, 292
  Chocolate, Hot, 293
  Hominy, Tomato, and Cheese, 164
  Omelette, French, 57–8
  Swiss, 262
Soufflés, Beignets, 325–6
Soup:
  Apple and Banana, with Curry, 27
  Barnyard, with Matzo Balls, 34
  Carcass, Fancy, 40
  Carrot, 28
  Chicken-Liver, 36
  Choldnik, 27
  Curry, 28–9
  Mongol, 40–1
  Mushroom, Edwin, 41–2

Soup (*continued*)
  Mushroom, Wendy, 42
  Pea, Dried, 44
  Pea, Fresh, 45
  Pea, Iced, 29
  Senegalese, 31–2
  Squash, 33
  Tomato, 33
  Tomato-Surprise, 47
  Tomato, with Cheese, 46–7
Spaghetti:
  al Dente, 158
  Green, 159–60
  Nests, 160
  Sauce Edwin, 159
Spanish Rice, 163
Spätzle, Marie's, 165–6
Spice Squares, 405
Spinach:
  Baked Creamed, 187
  Boxes, Baked Eggs in, 54
  Creamed, 186–7
  preparation of, 171
  Salad Dave Chasen, 223
Sponge, Butter-Lemon, 372–3
Sponge Cake, 389
  Fruit, 378–9
  Orange-Nut, 385
  Ring, 321–2
  Surprise, 332–3
Spoon Sponge Biscuits, 406
Spread:
  Anchovy, 9–10
  Cheese, Cornell, 11–12
  Cheese, Delectable, 14
  Fish-and-Tongue, 15
  Roquefort, 20–1
Spreads, Cheese, 12
Squab, Broiled, in Brandy, 114–15
Squabs:
  in Marjoram, 115–16
  Stuffed, 116
Squares:
  Basted Tuna, 73
  Canadian Coconut, 396–7
  Currant-Jelly, 399

INDEX

Squares (*continued*)
  Fudge, 399–400
  Spice, 405
Squash:
  preparation of, 171
  Purée, 187
  Soup, 33
  with Shredded Almonds, 188
Steak:
  Broiled, with Roquefort Cheese, 126
  Butter, 214
  Ham, from Virginia, 136–7
Steaks:
  Brizola, 133
  Race-Horse, 131–2
  Thin Tenderloin, 134
Stew:
  Beef, Bourguignonne, 122
  Beef, in Six Minutes, 123
  Beef, with Tomato Sauce, 122–3
  Hungarian, 144–5
  Lamb, Dellarobbia, 138–9
Stewed Apples Dressed Up, 458–9
Sticks, Cheese, 5
Strawberries:
  Curaçao, 433
  over Mock Cheesecake, 436–7
  Rhubarb Ring, with, 431
  Romanoff, 438–9
  with Sherbet, 440
Strawberry:
  Baked Alaska, 431–2
  Chiffon Pie, 442–3
  Cream Tarts, Coconut, 445
  Cream with Kirsch, 432–3
  Divine, 434
  Glazed, Pie, 441–2
  Icebox Cake, 435
  Ice Cream, Winter, 441
  Mousse, 435–6
  Parfait, 437
  Pie with Wine, 443–4
  Pie, Winter, 444–5
  Pink Rice Pudding, 437–8
  Preserve Turnovers, 447–8

Strawberry (*continued*)
  Preserves, 449–50
  Sauce for Ice Cream, 450
  Sauce for Winter Use, 450–1
  Tartlets, 449
  Tarts, Parisian, 445–7
  Tarts without Filling, 449
  Torte, 439–40
String-Bean Salad, 223–4
String Beans:
  preparation of, 172
  Whole, 189
Strip:
  Plum, 418–19
  Sirloin, the Magnificent, 132–3
Stuffed:
  Breast of Veal or Lamb, 145
  Cucumbers, 23
  Eggs Curried, 23
  French Endive, 23
  French Rolls, 23
  Lamb Chops, 140
  Potatoes, 266
  Squabs, 116
  Tomatoes, 266–7
  Tomatoes Fribourg Fashion, 269
  Tomatoes, with Smoked Salmon, 225–6
  Veal Cutlets, 264
Stuffing:
  Turkey, Peter, 118
  Wild-Rice, 116–17
Summer Borsch, 32
Supa Shetgia (Cheese Soup of Engadin), 46
Superb:
  Crawfish, Shrimp, or Lobster, 66–7
  Duck, 110–11
Superlative Schnecken, 494–5
Surprise:
  Peach, 465
  Sponge-Cake, 322–3
  Watermelon, 463
Suzette, Crêpes, 345–6
Swans on the Lake, 53–4

Swedish:
 Fish, 83
 Meat Balls, 131
 Tart Crust, 411
Sweetbread Salad, 233–4
Swiss-Chard Stalks, 267
Swiss:
 Eggs, 59
 Mornay Sauce, 263
 Pufflets, 7–8
 Scrambled Eggs, 60
 Soufflé, 262
 Tartlets, 274–5
Sylvia:
 Chicken Blintzes, 92–3
 Madeleines, 402–3

T

Tarragon Cream, A Bird in, 87
Tart:
 Apple, 412–13
 Cherry, 414–15
 Date-and-Walnut, 341
 Prune, 419–20
 Trieste (Old Vienna), 389–90
Tart Crust:
 Marie's, 408
 Polish, 409
 Swedish, 411
Tartar, Sauce, 213–14
Tartlets:
 Cherry, 397–8
 Hostess, 273
 Lemon-Curd, 400
 Lemon, with Meringue, 401
 Simple Cheese, 274
 Strawberry, 448
 Swiss, 274–5
Tarts:
 Coconut Strawberry Cream, 445
 Little Ham, 18
 Parisian Strawberry, 445–7
 Strawberry, without Filling, 449
Tea Cake, Blueberry, 479
Tenderized Ham with Apricots, 137

Tenderloin Steaks, Thin, 134
Têtes de Nègres, 298–9
Thermidor, Lobster, 69
Thin:
 Icing, 427
 Tenderloin Steaks, 134
Thousand Island Dressing, 250–1
Three:
 Hot Fruits, 473–4
 Sauerkrauts, 185–6
Timbale, Chicken, 100–1
Tiny Hamburgers, 8
Toast, French, with French Bread, 164
Toasted Cheese Fingers, 8–9
Tomates:
 Fribourgeoises (Stuffed Tomatoes Fribourg Fashion), 269
 Salade au, 268
Tomato:
 Aspic Ring, 238
 Soup, 33
 Soup with Cheese, 46–7
 Surprise Soup, 47
 Towers, 224–5
Tomatoes:
 en Marinade, 224
 Filled Tiny Red, 15
 Filled Yellow, 15
 Hot and Raw, 189
 preparation of, 172
 Stuffed, 266–7
 Stuffed, Fribourg Fashion, 269
 Stuffed with Smoked Salmon, 225–6
Tongue, Beef, with Raisins, Prunes, and Almonds, 124
Top Secret, 285–6
Torte:
 Applesauce, 329–30
 Black-Bread Cherry, 330–1
 Chocolate Linzer, 375–6
 Coconut Cream, Lashanska, 316–17
 Grandmother's Three, 331–3
 Mocha, 381–2

Torte (continued)
  Nut, 341–2
  Sand, 388
  Strawberry, 439–40
Tossed Salad with Pecan Nut Balls, 242
Towers, Tomato, 224–5
Trieste Tart (Old Vienna), 389–90
Trout, Brook, in an Aspic Pond, 73–4
Truffes Vertes, 275
Tuna Squares, Basted, 73
Turkey:
  Cutlets Nela, 117
  in Yellow Cream Sauce, 117–18
  Stuffing Peter, 118
Turnovers:
  Apricot, 395
  Strawberry-Preserve, 447–8
Turtle and Mushroom Broth, 47–8
Two Chickens in White Wine, 104–5

V

Vanilla:
  Cream Filling, 342
  Cream Pudding, 357–8
  Crescents, 406–7
  Ice Cream, New York's Best, 336–7
  Ice Cream, Old Vienna, 337–8
  Ice Cream with Anisette and Coconut Dave Chasen, 338
  Sauce I, 363
  Sauce II (with Rum), 363–4
Vaudoises, Croutes, 255–6
Veal:
  Breast of, Stuffed, 145
  Casserole with Sour Cream, 146
  Chops in Tomato Sauce, 146–7
  Cutlets in Sherry, 147
  Cutlets, Stuffed, 264
  Cutlets Vienna (*Wiener Schnitzel*), 148–9
  Cutlets with Cheese (Piccata), 264

Veal (continued)
  Kidneys in Brandy Sauce, 149
  Kidneys in White Wine with Mushrooms, 149–50
Vegetable Salad Diddie, 226
Vegetables, preparation of, 169–72
Vichyssoise, 34
Victoria, Queen, Fillets of Sole, 78–9
Vienna:
  Kipfel, 407
  Veal Cutlets (*Wiener Schnitzel*), 148–9
Vinaigrette, 251
Virginia:
  Batter Bread, 495–6
  Batter Cakes, 496
  Corn Bread, 496–7
  Corn Fritters, 180–1
  Ham, Baked, 134–5
  Ham Steak from, 136–7
  Johnnycake, 497
  Scalloped Oysters, 72

W

Waffle Sandwiches, 275–6
Waffles:
  Pat's, 497–8
  Wendy's, 498–9
Warm:
  Cream Cheese on Rounds, 9
  Wine Sauce, 364
Watermelon:
  Basket, 462–3
  Cake, 390
  Surprise, 463
Wendy:
  Apple Graham-Cracker Pie, 412
  Crab, 65
  Lamb Chops, 137–8
  Marvelous Brownies, 403–4
  Mushroom Soup, 42
Wendy's Waffles, 498–9
Whitebait Fried, 83–4
Whole String Beans, 189

Wiener Schnitzel, 148–9
Wild-Rice Stuffing, 116–17
Wine:
　Froth Sauce, 364–5
　Jelly, 312–13
　Pudding, 358
　Sauce, Warm, 364
Winter:
　Strawberry Ice Cream, 441
　Strawberry Pie, 444–5

Y

Yeast Dough, 491

Yellow:
　Cream Sauce, 204
　Peaches with a Red Blanket, 465–6
Young:
　Chicken in Burgundy, 105–6
　Pheasant with Raisin Purée, 113–14

Z

Zucchini:
　Canoes, 226–7
　Shredded with Sour Cream, 188